WINE BUYERS' GUIDE 2005

OVER 2,500 WORLD WINES
RATED BY QUALITY AND VALUE FOR MONEY

INTRODUCTION BY
ROBERT JOSEPH

MITCHELL BEAZLEY   *Wine* INTERNATIONAL

WINE BUYERS' GUIDE
by Robert Joseph

First published in Great Britain in 2004 by
Mitchell Beazley, an imprint of Octopus
Publishing Group Limited,
2–4 Heron Quays, London E14 4JP.

Copyright © Octopus Publishing
Group Ltd 2004
Text copyright © Robert Joseph 2004

All rights reserved. No part of this
work may be reproduced or utilized
in any form or by any means, electronic
or mechanical, including photocopying,
recording or by any information storage
and retrieval system, without the prior
written permission of the publishers.

A CIP catalogue record for this book
is available from the British Library.

ISBN: 1 84 533 090 0

The author and publishers will be grateful
for any information that will assist them
in keeping future editions up-to-date.
Although all reasonable care has been
taken in the preparation of this book,
neither the publishers, editors nor the
author can accept any liability for any
consequences arising from the use thereof,
or the information contained therein.

Commissioning Editor Hilary Lumsden
Executive Art Editor Yasia Williams
Design Tim Pattinson
Typesetting Michael Florence,
Mark Ginns
Production Julie Young

Typeset in The Sans, Gill Sans, Giovanni

Printed and bound by Rotolito Lombarda s.p.a.
Pioltello, Italy

HOW THE BOOK WORKS

You would easily be forgiven for imagining that you are surrounded by a jungle of confusing bottles and labels in your local off-licence or supermarket wine section. It is hardly surprising that some people react by choosing a wine they already know, or grab one that's covered with special offer stickers. But, that's no way to be sure of carrying home the most interesting, tasty, and great value bottles. This is where the *Wine Buyers' Guide* comes in. It is the next best thing to having a team of wine experts in your pocket or handbag every time you go shopping.

The book is split into three sections. The first section features an introduction by Robert Joseph that covers all of the basics – from the best temperatures for particular wine styles and the ideal dishes to drink them with to advice on storage, vintages, and investment.

Then comes the listing of the 2,500 medal winners and best-value wines from the 2004 International Wine Challenge, the world's biggest wine competition. The wines are listed by country (and region), award, and price. Also featured are descriptions culled from the tasting panels' notes, guide prices, and codes of the stockists. Finally, there is a crucially useful key to all those stockist codes and revealing where all of the wines can be bought.

KEY TO SYMBOLS USED

☆ particularly good value
★ truly great value
▲ 50CL bottle
■ 37.5CL bottle
● 10CL bottle

CONTENTS

- 03 How the Book Works
- 04 Introduction
- 05 Breaking News
- 06 Understanding the Taste
- 10 Storing
- 12 Serving
- 14 The Label
- 16 Grape Varieties
- 22 Wine Styles
- 26 A World of Wine
- 32 Buying
- 34 Vintages
- 37 Investment
- 38 Wine on the Web
- 40 Wine and Health
- 42 Wine and Food
- 44 The International Wine Challenge
- 46 Wines of the Year and Trophies
- 49 **ARGENTINA**
- 57 **AUSTRALIA**
- 119 **AUSTRIA**
- 124 **CHILE**
- 141 **EASTERN EUROPE** [BULGARIA, GEORGIA, HUNGARY, ROMANIA]
- 145 **FRANCE** ALSACE, BORDEAUX, BURGUNDY, CHAMPAGNE, LANGUEDOC-ROUSSILLON, LOIRE, RHÔNE, SOUTH WEST
- 207 **GERMANY**
- 213 **GREECE + CYPRUS**
- 215 **ITALY** PIEMONTE + NORTHWEST, NORTHEAST, TUSCANY + CENTRAL, SOUTH + THE ISLANDS
- 248 **NEW ZEALAND**
- 266 **NORTH AMERICA + CANADA** CALIFORNIA, PACIFIC NORTHWEST, EASTERN STATES, CANADA
- 279 **PORTUGAL** MADEIRA, PORT, TABLE WINES
- 300 **REST OF THE WORLD** [ENGLAND, LEBANON, MEXICO]
- 303 **SOUTH AFRICA**
- 325 **SPAIN** CATALONIA, RIOJA + NORTH-CENTRAL, RIBERA DEL DUERO + WEST, SOUTH + THE ISLANDS
- 355 List of Stockists

INTRODUCTION

Quickly, bring me a beaker of wine, so that I may wet my mind and say something clever.

Aristophanes

Winemaking may be the second oldest profession in the world. According to research by Patrick McGovern of the University of Pennsylvania, it looks as though primitive man was already crushing and fermenting grapes as long ago as 8,500BC. Even more fascinatingly for those who like to take the Bible literally, McGovern and his fellow researchers' discoveries in Turkey's Taurus Mountains seem to add credibility to the story that Noah planted the first wine grapes close to Mount Ararat almost as soon as he had landed the ark.

Whenever the tide of wine began to flow, until quite recently, the business of selecting the red or white you were going to drink was as simple as picking a draught beer in your local today. If there was any choice on offer, all you had to remember was the names of half a dozen – mostly French – regions and, if you wanted to appear really sophisticated, a few of the better recent vintages. Now, however, as a glance at the 8,700 different bottles that were lined up for tasting at the 2004 International Wine Challenge will tell you, the picture is very different.

Wine is now being produced almost everywhere from Dorking in Surrey to Dalat in Vietnam, and top-quality wines are increasingly being made in unfamiliar parts of traditional countries. Serious vintage charts now have to take as much account of the weather in Chile's Casablanca Valley and Sicily, as Chablis and St-Emilion.

Australia, which was once the subject of a Monty Python joke, now sells more wine in Britain, and at a higher price per bottle, than France. Twenty-five years ago, grape names rarely appeared on wine labels; now they not only feature on most of them, but also include a bewildering and ever-growing number of newcomers such as Tannat, Tarango, and Touriga Nacional, of which few non-wine-buffs will ever have heard. And if that were not confusing enough, the shelves are punctuated by bottles with names like Fat Bastard, Old Git, and Yellow Tail, which seem to have nothing to do with wine at all.

Some people, quite reasonably, turn their backs on the jungle of bottles and make straight for the same wine they bought last week, one whose name they know, or that's on offer at the biggest discount. But doing that can be rather like restricting your diet to a tiny repertoire of recipes, or your television viewing to a single channel.

This book is for everyone who enjoys wine and would like to get the best out of it. Within the main section, you will find details and descriptions of 2,500 of the best and best-value wines from the 2004 International Wine Challenge, the world's biggest and toughest wine competition. If you are looking for a great classic burgundy or Bordeaux, a top example from the New World, or a cheap, tasty red or white to serve at a party, this is the place to look.

In this first section I endeavour to provide a concise survival guide to wine drinking at the beginning of the twenty-first century. From advice on matching wine and food to tips on storing, serving, investing – and even information on wine and health…

Tis pity wine should be so deleterious,
For tea and coffee leave us much more serious.

Lord Byron

BREAKING NEWS

If there have been three main themes in the wine world over the past twelve months, they have involved corks and screwcaps; a revolution in the vineyards of France; and a conflict over the way wine should taste – and how much it should cost. All of these demonstrated the way in which wine has changed in recent years – and is continuing to change…

Screwing It Up

2004 was the year when screwcaps reached the tipping point between being thought of as a novelty popular with smaller innovators in the New World, and part of the mainstream. In March, André Lurton, one of the veteran château owners of Bordeaux, quietly took the historic step – for his region at least – of proposing top-class white wines in screwcaps. In the New World, producers like E&J Galllo, Villa Maria, and Penfolds had already taken the same step; and in Britain, Tesco – Britain's biggest wine retailer – announced that one bottle in every six that it sells has a screwcap – and that by 2005 that figure will have risen to one in two.

French Revolution

If screwcaps were once thought of as a fad that would never catch on for any but the cheapest wines, so, until not that long ago, were the fruits of vineyards in the New World. France, it was said, would inevitably regain its position at the front of the pack. Today, however, France's fall from vinous grace has been dramatic. In July, the region of Muscadet – historically the source of one of Britain's favourite whites – revealed that lack of demand had driven it to uproot one in five of its vines. Rene Renou, president of the all-powerful *Institut National des Appellations d'Origine*, predicted that "part of the French vineyard area will disappear" in the face of competition from the New World and surplus production at home. And, he wasn't just referring to Muscadet.

The same month, wine-growers took over the autoroute just outside Bordeaux in protest at the fact that the price they can get for a barrel of that region's wine today is less than half as much as it commanded in 1990. What they wanted was a guaranteed minimum price; what they got (after "crisis talks") was a relaxation of the rules that previously banned them from printing grape names on their labels. Few people believed that this would be enough to fight off competition from Jacob's Creek and E.&J. Gallo.

Price – and Style – Wars

While the producers of France's more modest wines were bewailing their fate, a small number of Gallic big names were doing very nicely thank you. A few dozen top Bordeaux châteaux sold their 2003 vintage for record prices *en primeur* – in barrel – and affronted British critics, both with the prices they were getting, and the rich, alcoholic style of some of their wines. Bordeaux, it was felt by traditionalists, was no longer the subtle, long-lived, extravagant-but-still-affordable stuff it used to be. On the other side of the Atlantic, and in Asia, however, the wines of the warmest summer in living history were much more warmly received. High marks from US critics like Robert Parker and plentiful dollars from the US economic revival ensured that the market price for wines like Château Montrose tripled within days. It is too early to say how long this boom will last, or whether the traditional style of wines that pleases those UK palates will supplant the current fashion for big, chocolatey, instantly delicious wines.

6 WINE BUYERS' GUIDE 2005

UNDERSTANDING THE TASTE

I rather like bad wine... one gets so bored with good wine.

Benjamin Disraeli

Buying wine today can often be like buying a gallon of paint. Just as the manufacturer's helpful chart can be daunting, with its endless shades of subtly different white, the number of bottles and the information available on the supermarket shelves can make you want to give up and reach for the one that is most familiar, or most favourably priced. If you're not a wine buff, why should you know the differences in flavour between wines made from the same grape in Meursault in France, Mendocino in California, and Maipo in Chile? Often, the retailer has provided descriptive terms to help you imagine the flavour of the stuff in the bottle. But, these too can just add to the confusion. Do you want the one that tastes of strawberries or raspberries, the "refreshingly dry", or the "crisp, lemony white"? I can't promise to clear a motorway through this jungle, but, with luck, I will give you a path to follow when you are choosing a wine, and one from which you can confidently stray. Stated simply, the flavour you get out of any wine is the result of a combination of twelve factors.

1. THE GRAPE VARIETY (or varieties) from which it is made. This is the DNA of the wine. If your parents are tall and fair haired, you will probably inherit these characteristics, just as wines made from Cabernet Sauvignon will tend to taste of blackcurrant and those produced from Gewurztraminer will remind people of lychees.

2. THE CLIMATE If your blonde parents brought you up on a farm in Australia you'll probably look and behave differently to someone with a similar-looking mother and father living in an apartment block in Liverpool. Wines made from grapes grown in warm countries – or in unusually warm years like 2003 in Europe – will taste richer and riper than ones from cooler places and vintages.

3. SOIL Merlot grapes, like roses, like to be grown in clay; Chardonnay, like clematis, prefers chalk. Whatever the climate, the character of the soil will have an influence on the flavour of the wine.

4. WINEMAKING The vine-grower and winemaker (sometimes one and the same person) are like a gardener and a chef. The way the vines are grown, the yield per plant, harvesting date, and method of picking (by hand or machine) will all have a role to play; as will the way the grapes are handled in the winery. Also crucial are the temperature of fermentation (cooler = fresher wine; warmer = richer), the use of oak barrels, the blending of different grapes, and the period in barrel or tank before bottling.

5. LAWS, CUSTOMS, AND LOCAL FASHION In Europe, strict laws control the way wines can be made. Chardonnay is illegal in Bordeaux, for example, and Spanish *gran reserva* wines have to be aged for longer than *reservas*. But in the New World, local fashion is important too. It's a rare Californian who doesn't age his Chardonnay in oak barrels.

6. AGE As humans age they become more or less attractive. Some grow wiser, others go senile. Some do both. As wine ages it also changes, losing its initial fruitiness and taking on other, "winier", characteristics. Grape varieties age differently (Chardonnay is generally better older than Sauvignon Blanc) but the climate, soil, and winemaking are important. Some wines – most inexpensive reds and whites of any price – are simply not built to last.

7. HEALTH Some wines are ill before they are bottled (because of faulty winemaking); some – around five per cent – are spoiled by mouldy corks that can make the wine taste musty or simply a little flat. Others that have escaped these fates can be spoiled by being stored in places that are too hot or dry. Corks can then leak and the wine will age prematurely and become like sherry or downright vinegary.

8. THE WAY IT IS SERVED If our first impressions of people are affected by the way they are dressed, our reaction to a wine is bound to reflect the smartness of the label, the use of a decanter, and shape and thinness of the glass. But temperature will be important too. Just compare warm and cool orange juice.

9. THE SETTING Meeting someone at a bus stop is very different from being interviewed by them or encountering them on a blind date. The same wine will taste quite different at a cocktail party, a barbecue, and a smart dinner.

10. FOOD Just try eating a Mars Bar with a glass of Coke. They don't go well together, but a cup of tea can go down a treat with fish and chips. A spicy dish can apparently strip all the flavour from a wine that was quite tasty with plainly roast chicken.

11. PRECONCEPTION If you have been told that the person you are about to meet is a supermodel or a convicted rapist, the information given to you will probably influence your reaction to them. It is hard to ignore the label on a bottle of Dom Pérignon Champagne or Château Latour – or a sticker saying "Bulgarian Bargain – Buy One Get Two Free".

12 PERSONAL TASTE If you don't have a sweet tooth, you probably won't enjoy a £200 bottle of Château Yquem any more than the best pudding Gordon Ramsay can invent. There's no law to say you have to like Champagne.

TASTING VS DRINKING

The English language offers some useful pairs of terms. You can simply see something happen, or you can watch it; you can hear a sound, or you can listen to it; you can drink a wine, or you can taste it. A recent survey revealed that over half the people questioned could not remember the nationality of the wine they last drank in a restaurant, its grape variety, or producer. Reading this, I wondered if they might have had stronger memories of the dishes they ate, or the waiter, or the decor. And I bet they would have had almost perfect recall of every goal and save in the most recent football match they watched. Our capacity to remember anything depends on how much attention we pay to it. And with even local bistros charging £75 for dinner with a bottle of house red, I reckon that, however delightful the company, it may be worth focusing a little more closely on the flavours in the glass.

Tasting

Wine tasting is surrounded by mystery and mystique. But it shouldn't be – because all it really consists of is asking yourself two questions: do you like the wine? And does it taste the way you expect it to? Champagne costs a lot more than basic Spanish *cava*, so it should taste recognizably different. Some do, some don't.

SEE The look of a wine can tell you a lot. Assuming it isn't cloudy (send it back if it is), it will reveal its age and hint at the grape and origin. Some grapes, like Burgundy's Pinot Noir, make naturally paler wines than, say, Bordeaux's Cabernet Sauvignon; wines from warmer regions will have deeper colours. Tilt the glass away from you over a piece of white paper and look at the rim of the liquid. The more watery and brown it is, the older the wine (Beaujolais Nouveau will be pure violet).

SWIRL Vigorously swirl the wine around the glass for a moment or so to release any reluctant and characteristic smells.

SNIFF You sniff a wine before tasting it for the same reason you sniff a carton of milk before drinking it. The smell can tell you more about a wine than anything else. If you don't believe me, try tasting anything while holding your nose. When sniffing, take one long sniff or a few brief ones. Concentrate on whether the wine seems fresh and clean, and on any smells that indicate how it is likely to taste.

What are your first impressions? Is the wine fruity, and, if so, which fruit does it remind you of? Does it have the vanilla smell of a wine that has been fermented or matured in new oak barrels? Is it spicy? Or herbaceous? Sweet or dry? Rich or lean?

SIP Take a small mouthful and (this takes practice) suck air between your teeth and through the liquid. Look in a mirror while you're doing this: if your mouth looks like a cat's bottom and sounds like a child trying to suck the last few drops of Coke through a straw, then you're doing it right. Hold the wine in your mouth for a little longer to release as much of its flavour as possible. Focus on the flavour. Ask yourself whether it tastes sweet, dry, fruity, spicy, herbaceous. Is there just one flavour, or do several contribute to a "complex" overall effect? Now concentrate on the texture of the wine. Some – like Chardonnay – are mouthcoatingly buttery, while others – like Gewurztraminer – are almost oily. Muscadet is a wine with a texture that is closer to that of water.

Reds, too, vary in texture; some seem tough and tannic enough to make the inside of one cheek want to kiss the inside of the other. Traditionalists rightly claim that tannin is necessary for a wine's longevity, but modern winemakers distinguish between the harsh tannin and the "fine" (non-aggressive) tannin to be found in wine carefully made from ripe grapes. A modern Bordeaux often has as much tannin as old-fashioned examples – but is far easier to taste and drink.

SPIT The only reason to spit a wine out – unless it is actively repellent – is simply to remain upright at the end of a lengthy tasting. I have notes I took during a banquet in Burgundy at which there were dozens of great wines and not even the remotest chance to do anything but swallow. The descriptions of the first few are perfectly legible; the thirtieth apparently tasted "very xgblorefjy". If all you are interested in is the taste, not spitting is an indulgence; you should have had ninety per cent of the flavour while the wine was in your mouth. Pause for a moment or two after spitting the wine out. Is the flavour still there? How does what you are experiencing now compare with the taste you had in your mouth? Some wines have an unpleasant aftertaste; others have flavours that linger deliciously in the mouth.

A Way with Words

Before going any further, I'm afraid there's no alternative but returning to the thorny question of the language you are going to use to describe your impressions.

When Washington Irving visited Bordeaux 170 years ago, he noted that Château Margaux was "a wine of fine flavour – but not of equal body". Lafite on the other hand had "less flavour than the former but more body – an equality of flavour and body". Latour, well, that had "more body than flavour". He may have been a great writer, but he was evidently not the ideal person to describe the individual flavours of great Bordeaux. Michelangelo was more poetic, writing that the wine of San Gimignano "kisses, licks, bites, thrusts, and stings…". Modern pundits say wines have "gobs of fruit" and taste of "kumquats and suede". Each country and generation comes up with its own vocabulary. Some descriptions, such as the likening to gooseberry of wines made from Sauvignon Blanc, can be justified by scientific analysis, which confirms

UNDERSTANDING THE TASTE

that the same aromatic chemical compound is found in the fruit and wine. Then there are straightforward descriptions. Wines can be fresh or stale, clean or dirty. If they are acidic, or overly full of tannin, they will be "hard"; a "soft" wine, by contrast, might be easier to drink, but boring. There are other less evocative terms. While a watery wine is "dilute" or "thin", a subtle one is "elegant". A red or white whose flavour is hard to discern is described as "dumb". Whatever the style of a wine, it should have "balance". A sweet white, for example, needs enough acidity to keep it from cloying. No one will enjoy a wine that is too fruity, too dry, too oaky, or too anything for long. The flavour that lingers in your mouth long after you have swallowed or spat it out is known as the "finish". Wines whose flavour – pleasant or unpleasant – hangs around, are described as "long"; those whose flavour disappears quickly are "short". Finally, there is "complex", the word that is used to justify why one wine costs ten times more than another. A complex wine is like a well-scored symphony, while a simpler one could be compared to a melody picked out on a single instrument.

Should I Send it Back?

Wines are subject to all kinds of faults, though far fewer than they were as recently as a decade ago.

ACID All wines, like all fruit and vegetables, contain a certain amount of acidity. Without it they would taste dull and go very stale very quickly. Wines made from unripe grapes will, however, taste like unripe apples or plums – or like chewing stalky leaves or grass.

BITTER Bitterness is quite different. On occasion, especially in Italy, a touch of bitterness may even be an integral part of a wine's character, as in the case of Amarone.

CLOUDY Wine should be transparent. The only excuse for cloudiness is in a wine like an old burgundy whose deposit has been shaken up.

CORKED Ignore any cork crumbs you may find floating on the surface of a wine. Genuinely corked wines have a musty smell and flavour that comes from mouldy corks. Some corks are mouldier, and wines mustier, than others, but all corked wines become nastier with exposure to air. Around five per cent of wines – irrespective of their price – are corked.

CRYSTALS Unless someone is trying to kill you with powdered glass, ignore fine white crystals at the bottom of the bottle. These are just tartrates that occur naturally.

FIZZY Don't.

MADERIZED/OXIDIZED Madeira is fortified wine that has been intentionally exposed to the air and heated in a special oven. Maderized wine is stale, unfortified stuff that has been accidentally subjected to warmth and air. Oxidized is a broader term, referring to wine that has been exposed to the air – or made from grapes that have cooked in the sun. The taste is reminiscent of poor sherry or vinegar – or both.

SULPHUR (SO_2/H_2S) Sulphur dioxide is routinely used as a protection against bacteria that would oxidize (*q.v.*) a wine. In excess, sulphur dioxide may make you cough or sneeze. Worse, though, is hydrogen sulphide and mercaptans, its associated sulphur compounds, which are created when sulphur dioxide combines with wine. Wines with hydrogen sulphide smell of rotten eggs, while mercaptans may reek of rancid garlic or burning rubber. Aeration or popping a copper coin in your glass may clean up these characteristics.

VINEGARY/VOLATILE Volatile acidity is present in all wines. In excess, however – usually the result of careless winemaking – what can be a pleasant component (like a touch of balsamic vinegar in a sauce) tastes downright vinegary.

STORING

> No man also having drunk old wine straightway desireth new: for he saith, The old is better.
>
> *Luke 5:39*

> Wine improves with age. The older I get, the better I like it.
>
> *Anon*

According to a widely touted statistic, the average bottle of wine is drunk within twelve hours of its purchase. This is, of course, nonsense; the correct figure is probably closer to a week. But in either case, most people have little need for anything more than a rack in the kitchen with sufficient space to accommodate the contents of your Teswaybury bag. But, sooner or later, most of us discover that it can be worthwhile buying in larger quantities – on a shopping trip to Calais, or by mail, or from a wine warehouse that only offers its wine by the dozen.

Keeping that wine for a while reveals another truth that is often forgotten nowadays: some wines do benefit from being left to themselves for a few years, and finding older wines on the high street isn't easy. Before you know it, you're well on your way to thinking about having a cellar – or at least some kind of storage area – where your bottles are not going to be spoiled by the central heating.

Perfect Conditions

> Wine is a living liquid containing no preservatives. Its life cycle comprises youth, maturity, old age, and death. When not treated with reasonable respect it will sicken and die.
>
> *Julia Child*

While many of us live in homes that are ill-suited for storing wine, one can often find an unused grate or a space beneath the stairs that offers wine what it wants: a constant temperature of around 7–10°C/45–50°F (never lower than 5°C/41°F nor more than 25°C/77°F), reasonable humidity (install a cheap humidifier or leave a sponge in a bowl of water), sufficient ventilation to avoid a musty atmosphere, and, ideally, an absence of vibration (wines stored beneath train tracks – or beds – age faster). Alternatively, invest in a fridge-like Eurocave that guarantees perfect conditions – or even adapt an old freezer. Beware of cellars that are too damp, however. The humidity in mine has been sufficient to destroy a fair few of my labels.

Racks and Cellar Books

Custom-built racks can be bought "by the hole" and cut to fit. Square chimney stacks can be used too. If you have plenty of space, simply allocate particular racks to specific styles of wine. Unfortunately, even the best-laid cellar plans tend to fall apart when two cases of Australian Shiraz have to be squeezed into a space big enough just for one.

If the size of the cellar warrants it, give each hole in the rack a cross-referenced identity, from A1 at the top left to, say, Z100 at the bottom right. As bottles arrive, they can then be put in any available hole and their address noted in a cellar book, in which you can record when and where you obtained it, what it cost, and how each bottle tasted (is it improving or drying out?). Some people, like me, prefer to use a computer program (a database or spreadsheet).

STORING 11

To Drink or Keep?

Bad news isn't wine. It doesn't improve with age.

Colin Powell

But it is not every wine that will repay you for tucking it away. There are plenty of wonderful examples that never improve beyond the first few years after the harvest, and are none the worse for that. There are plenty of actors and singers who never manage to match the successes of their youth. On the other hand, like children who turn out to be late developers in their last years at school, some wines take a very long time to live up to their potential.

What follows is a guide to which corks to pop soon and which bottles to treasure for a few years in the rack. But, before letting you loose on it, I must give you an essential couple of words of warning. The longevity of any wine – even from the best addresses – depends on the vintage. Château Margaux from the ordinary 1997 harvest, for example, will be dead and gone long before the far better 1996. On the other hand, the likely lifespan will also be influenced by the quality of the vineyard and the way the wine is made. So, that Château Margaux 1997 will enjoy a much longer life than most of the other Bordeaux produced in that year.

The following suggestions should help you to drink wines at their best. But, beware of the many bottles and vintages that defy the rules and behave unexpectedly – suddenly evolving into swans after appearing to be the most dowdy of ducklings, or reappearing after lengthy sulks. Wines like these take even the most experienced buffs by surprise – and often give the greatest, most serendipitous delight.

DRINK AS SOON AS POSSIBLE Most wine at under £7.50, particularly basic whites such as Chardonnay and Sauvignon Blanc, and reds such as Merlot, Cabernet, and Zinfandel. French *vins de pays* and all but the best white Bordeaux; cheap red Bordeaux and most Beaujolais Nouveau/*novello/joven* reds, Bardolino, Valpolicella, light Italian whites, almost all "blush" and rosé.

LESS THAN FIVE YEARS Most moderately priced (£5–10) California, Chilean, Argentine, South African, and Australian reds and whites. Petit-Château Bordeaux and *cru bourgeois*, and lesser *cru classé* reds from poorer vintages (such as 1997); basic Alsace, red and white burgundy, and better Beaujolais; Chianti, Barbera, basic Spanish reds; good mid-quality Germans. All but the very best Sauvignon from anywhere, Albariño from Spain, and Australian Verdelho.

FIVE TO TEN YEARS Most Cru Bourgeois Bordeaux from good years; better châteaux from lesser vintages; all but the finest red and white burgundy, and Pinot Noir and Chardonnay from elsewhere; middle-quality Rhônes; southern French higher flyers; good German, Alsace, dry Loire, Austrian Grüner Veltliner, and finer white Bordeaux; most mid-priced Italian and Portuguese reds; most Australian, California,and Washington State; South African, Chilean, and New Zealand Merlots and Cabernets on sale at under £15. Late-harvest wines from the New World and medium-quality Sauternes.

OVER TEN YEARS Top-class Bordeaux, Rhône, burgundy, and sweet Loire from ripe years; top-notch German and Bordeaux late-harvest, Italian IGT, Barolo, and the finest wines from Tuscany; top examples of Australian Shiraz, Cabernet Sauvignon, Riesling, and Semillon; and California Cabernet Sauvignon, and finest Merlot and Zinfandel.

SERVING

*The art in using wine is to produce the greatest possible
quantity of present gladness, without any future depression.*
                                  The Gentleman's Table Guide, 1873

The Romans used to add salt to their wine to preserve it, while the Greeks favoured pine resin. Burgundians often refer to Napoleon's taste for Chambertin, but rarely mention that he diluted his red wine with water. A century ago, the English used to add ice to claret – and in winter, skiers drink hot "mulled" wine, adding sugar, fruit, and spices. Today, snobs sneer at Chinese wine drinkers who apparently prefer their Mouton Cadet with a dash of Sprite, but they conveniently forget about the sangria they probably enjoyed drinking in Spain. It's well worth questioning accepted rules – especially when they vary between cultures. The following advice is based on common sense and experience – to help you to enjoy serving and drinking wine. Ultimately, the best way to serve a wine is the way you and your guests are going to enjoy it. If a dash of Sprite makes a meanly acidic red Bordeaux easier to swallow, it certainly gets my vote.

Some Like it Hot
Some styles of wine taste better at particular temperatures. White and sparkling wines are more often served too cold than too hot. Paradoxically, it is the reds that suffer most from being drunk too warm. Few who serve wines at "room temperature" recall that the term was coined long before the invention of central heating. Be ready to chill a fruity red in a bucket of ice and water for five to ten minutes before serving.

Red Wine
When serving red, focus on the wine's flavour. Tough wines are best slightly warmer. The temperatures given are a rule-of-thumb guide:

1. Beaujolais and other fruity reds: 10–13°C (50–55°F) – an hour in the fridge.
2. Younger red burgundy and Rhônes and older Bordeaux, Chianti, younger Rioja, New World Grenache, and Pinotage: 14–16°C (57–61°F).
3. Older burgundy, tannic young Bordeaux, Rhônes, Zinfandel, bigger Cabernet Sauvignon, Merlot, Shiraz, Barolo, and other bigger Italian and Spanish reds: 16–18°C (61–64°F).

Rosé
Rosé should be chilled at 10–15°C (50–59°F), or five to ten minutes in a bucket of ice and water.

White Wine
The cooler the wine, the less it will smell or taste. Subtler, richer wines deserve to be drunk a little warmer.

1. Lighter, sweeter wines and everyday sparklers: 4–8°C/39–46°F (two or three hours in the fridge or ten to fifteen minutes in ice and water).
2. Fuller-bodied, aromatic, drier, semi-dry, lusciously sweet whites; Champagne; simpler Sauvignons; and Chardonnays: 8–11°C (46–52°F).
3. Richer, dry wines – burgundy, California Chardonnay: 12–13°C (54–55°F).

The Perfect Outcome
The patented Screwpull is still the most reliable way to get a cork out of a bottle. The "waiter's friend" is the next best thing, especially the modern versions with a hinged section designed to prevent corks from breaking. Whatever corkscrew you choose, avoid the models that look like a large screw. These often simply pull through old corks. These fragile stoppers are often most easily removed using a two-pronged "Ah So" cork remover. But, these are tiresome for younger wines and useless for synthetic corks.

Which Glasses?
On occasions when no other glass was available I have enjoyed great wine from the glass in my hotel bathroom. I suspect, though, I'd have gotten more out of the experience if something a bit more stylish had come to hand. Glasses should be narrower across the rim than the bowl. Red ones should be bigger than white, because whites are best kept chilled in the bottle rather than warming in the glass. If you like bubbles in your sparkling wine, serve it in a flute rather than a saucer from which they will swiftly escape. Schott, Spiegelau, and Riedel are among a number of companies that now produce attractive glasses that are specially designed to bring out the best in particular styles of wine.

To Breathe or Not to Breathe?
After what may well have been a fairly lengthy period of imprisonment in its bottle, many a wine can be a bit sulky when it is first poured. Giving it a breath of air may help to banish the sulkiness and bring out the flavour and richness, which is why many people tend to remove the cork a few hours before the wine is to be served. This well-intentioned action, however, is almost a complete waste of time (the contact with oxygen offered by the neck of the bottle is far too limited). If you want to aerate a wine, you'd be far better off simply pouring it into a jug and back into the bottle just before you want to drink it. Broad-based, so-called "ship's decanters" not only look good, butalso facilitate airing wine as it flows down the inside of the glass in a fine film. Alternatively, small devices are now available that bubble air into wine to mimic the effect of decanting.

As a rule, young red and – surprisingly perhaps – white wines often benefit from exposure to air, especially when the flavour of a white has been temporarily flattened by a heavy dose of sulphur dioxide. Older red wines, however, may be tired out by the experience and may rapidly lose some of their immediate appeal. Mature red Bordeaux, Rhône, and port, for example, may need to be decanted in order to remove the unwelcome mudlike deposit that has dropped to the bottom of the bottle. This initially daunting task is far easier than it seems. Simply stand the bottle up for a day before decanting it. Pour it very slowly, in front of a flashlight or candle, watching for the first signs of the deposit. Coffee filters suit those with less steady hands.

Order of Service
The rules say that white wines and youth, respectively, precede red wines and age; dry goes before sweet (most of us prefer our main course before the dessert); the lighter the wine, the earlier. These rules are often impossible to follow. What are you to do, for example, if the red Loire is lighter-bodied than the white burgundy? Can the red Bordeaux follow the Sauternes that you are offering with the foie gras? Ignore the absolutes but bear in mind the common sense that lies behind them. Work gently up the scale of fullness, "flavoursomeness", and quality, rather than swinging wildly between styles.

THE LABEL

Labels are an essential part of the business of wine nowadays, but even a century ago they barely existed. Wine was sold by the barrel and served by the jug or decanter. Indeed, the original "labels" were silver tags that hung on a chain around the neck of a decanter and were engraved with the word "claret", "hock", "port" or whatever.

Today, printed labels are required to tell you the amount of liquid in the bottle, its strength, where it was made, and the name of the producer or importer. Confusingly, though, labelling rules vary between countries and between regions. Labels may also reveal a wine's style: the grape variety, oakiness, or sweetness, for example. And, lastly, they are part of the packaging that helps to persuade you to buy one wine rather than another. When buying, bear in mind the following:

1. Official terms such as "Appellation Contrôlée", "Grand or Premier Cru", "Qualitätswein", and "Reserva" are as reliable in quality terms as official statements by politicians.
2. Unofficial terms such as "Réserve Personnelle" and "Vintner's Selection" are either a genuine reflection of the winemaker's pride in the wine, or a device to increase sales.
3. Knowing where a wine comes from is often like knowing where a person was born; it provides no guarantee of how good the wine will be. Nor how it will have been made (though there are often local rules). There will be nothing to tell you, for instance, whether a Chablis is oaky, nor whether an Alsace or Vouvray is sweet.
4. But, do look out for terms like "Oak Aged" "Füt de Chêne", "Barrel Select" and "Show Reserve" which indicate woodiness and expressions, while Tradition" often refers to a less oaky French wine. "Moëlleux", "Doux", "Vendange Tardive", "Grains Nobles", "Amabile", "Late" or "Noble Harvest", all refer to sweetness.
5. "Old Vines" or "Vieilles Vignes" may indicate better wine.
6. "Big name" regions don't always make better wine than supposedly lesser ones. Cheap Bordeaux is far worse than similarly priced wine from Bulgaria.
7. Don't expect wines from the same grape variety to taste the same: a South African Chardonnay may taste drier than one from California. The flavour and style will depend on the climate, soil, and producer.
8. Just because a producer makes a good wine in one place, don't trust him, or her, to make other good wines, either there or elsewhere. The team at Lafite Rothschild produces less classy Los Vascos wines in Chile; Robert Mondavi's inexpensive Woodbridge wines bear no relation to the quality of his Reserve wines from Napa.
9. The fact that there is a château on a wine label has no bearing on the quality of the contents.
10. Nor does the boast that the wine is bottled at that château.
11. Nineteenth-century medals look pretty on a label; they say nothing about the quality of the twentieth- or twenty-first century stuff in the bottle.
12. Price provides some guidance to a wine's quality: a very expensive bottle may be appalling, but it's unlikely that a very cheap one will be better than basic.

THE LABEL 15

Germany

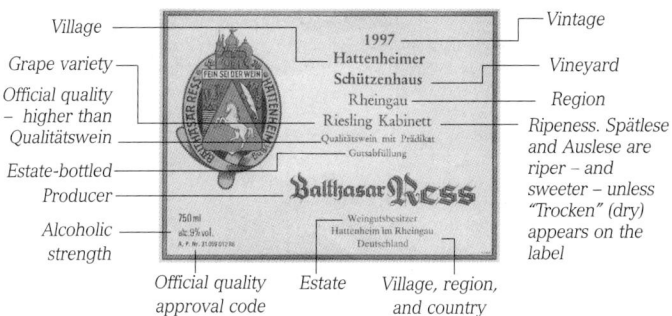

- Village
- Grape variety
- Official quality – higher than Qualitätswein
- Estate-bottled
- Producer
- Alcoholic strength
- Official quality approval code
- Estate
- Vintage
- Vineyard
- Region
- Ripeness. Spätlese and Auslese are riper – and sweeter – unless "Trocken" (dry) appears on the label
- Village, region, and country

Champagne

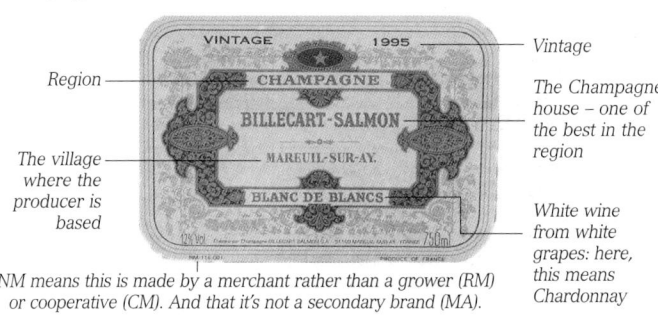

- Region
- The village where the producer is based
- The Champagne house – one of the best in the region
- Vintage
- White wine from white grapes: here, this means Chardonnay

NM means this is made by a merchant rather than a grower (RM) or cooperative (CM). And that it's not a secondary brand (MA).

Burgundy

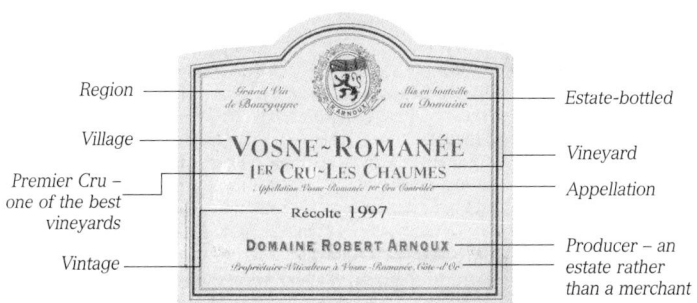

- Region
- Village
- Premier Cru – one of the best vineyards
- Vintage
- Estate-bottled
- Vineyard
- Appellation
- Producer – an estate rather than a merchant

GRAPE VARIETIES

Chardonnay, a character in the TV drama "Footballers' Wives", was the name given to 52 girls [in England] in 2002, with 14 others being called Chardonay. In 2003, the number of babies named Chardonnay rose to 91.
The Office for National Statistics

After tasting 120 bottles, Tim Atkin decides he'll drink "Anything But Chardonnay"
The Observer, Sunday May 30, 2004

Believe it or not, the first wines that described themselves as Chardonnay only began to arrive from Australia and California as recently as the beginning of the 1980s. Before that we drank plenty of Chardonnay, of course, but it came in bottles labelled as Chablis, white burgundy, or Mâcon Blanc. Merlot, once an unheralded ingredient in red Bordeaux, is now one of Britain's most popular styles, while in America, a wine called Marilyn Merlot (carrying a portrait of America's most famous actress and presidential mistress) enjoys cult status and sells for £50 per bottle. "Varietals" – made from single varieties of grape – are now officially the spice of wine.

Today, as the French authorities belatedly wrestle with the question of whether to allow regions like burgundy and Bordeaux to benefit from this trend, producers and wine drinkers are acknowledging that shelves full of subtly varying versions of the same grape are getting rather boring. So, there is a growing move towards "new" varieties, such as Pinot Grigio and Malbec, that are already well known in Europe, and more obscure efforts like Grüner Veltliner, Carmenère, and Tannat. If the broadening of the range on offer has to be welcome – Chile's Carmenère is a particularly exciting recent arrival – there is plenty of evidence of wines chosen for the sake of novelty rather than flavour. Watch out for watery, flavourless Pinot Grigio.

When choosing wines from the New or Old World, it is worth bearing in mind the following thoughts. Some wines are made from single grape varieties – e.g. red or white burgundy, Sancerre, German Riesling, most Alsace wines, and Barolo – while others, such as red or white Bordeaux, California "Meritage" wines, port, and Châteauneuf-du-Pape, are blends of two or more types of grape. Champagne can fall into either camp, as can New World "varietal" wines, which, though generally labelled as "Chardonnay", "Merlot", "Shiraz", etc., can often – depending on local laws – contain up to twenty-five per cent of other grape varieties. Blends are not, per se, superior to single varietals – or vice versa.

White Grapes

The quest for alternative white grapes is arguably more fierce than the hunt for reds to replace Merlot and Cabernet Sauvignon. Heavy bets are being placed on Pinot Grigio – especially in the USA – but Sauvignon Blanc is enjoying a wave of popularity, Riesling is enjoying a revival, and there is a buzz of excitement surrounding Austria's Grüner Veltliners.

ALBARIÑO/ALVARINHO A rapidly rising star, producing fresh, dry, floral wines, generally in cool Rias Baixas in the Northern Spanish region of Galicia close to Bilbao. Occasionally oaked, it is at its best within a couple of years of the harvest. Not unlike Australia's Verdelho. Also grown in Portugal, where it is called Alvarinho and used often in blends – for Vinho Verde.

GRAPE VARIETIES

CHARDONNAY The world's most popular and widely planted premium white grape variety, and the one whose name has become almost a synonym for dry white wine, is surprisingly hard to define. The flavour of any example will depend enormously on the climate, soil, and the particular type of clone. Burgundy, and the best California examples (Kistler, Peter Michael, Sonoma Cutrer), taste of butter and hazelnuts; lesser New World efforts are often sweet and simple, and often very melony (a flavour that comes from the clone). Australians range from subtle, buttery pineapple to oaky, tropical fruit juice. Petaluma, Giaconda, Coldstream Hills, and Leeuwin show how it can be done. New Zealand's efforts are tropical too, but lighter and fresher (Te Mata, Cloudy Bay). Elsewhere, Chile is beginning to hit the mark, as is South Africa (Jordan). In Europe, look around southern France (various *vins de pays*), Italy (Gaja), Spain, and Eastern Europe, but beware of watery cheaper versions..

CHENIN BLANC Loire variety with naturally high acidity that makes it ideal for fresh sparkling, dry, and luscious honeyed wines; also raw stuff like unripe apples and, when over-sulphured, old socks. Most California Chenins are semi-sweet and ordinary. South Africans once called it the Steen, and now use it for both dry and luscious sweet wines (the Forrester-Meinert is a great dry example). There are few good Australians (but try Moondah Brook) or New Zealanders (Millton).

GEWURZTRAMINER Outrageous, oily-textured stuff that smells of parma violets and tastes of lychee fruit. At its best in Alsace (Zind Humbrecht, Schlumberger, Faller), where identically labelled bottles can vary greatly in their level of sweetness. Wines that guarantee luscious sweetness will be labelled as either Vendange Tardive or – the intensely sweet – Sélection de Grains Nobles. Try examples from Germany (where the "ü" is used), Chile, New Zealand, and Italy, too.

MARSANNE A classic, flowery, lemony variety used in the Rhône in wines like Hermitage (from producers like Guigal); in Australia – especially in Goulburn in Victoria (Tahbilk and Mitchelton); in southern France (in blends from Mas de Daumas Gassac); in Switzerland (late-harvest efforts from Provins); and in innovative wines from California. At its best young or after five or six years.

MUSCAT The only variety whose wines actually taste as though they are made of grapes, rather than some other kind of fruit or vegetable. In Alsace, southern France, and northeast Italy it is used to make dry wines. Generally, though, it performs best as sparkling wine (Moscatos and Asti Spumantes from Italy, and Clairette de Die Tradition from France) and as sweet, fortified wine. Look out for Beaumes de Venise and Rivesaltes in southern France, Moscatel de Setúbal in Portugal, Moscatel de Valencia in Spain, and Liqueur Muscat in Australia (Morris, Chambers, Yalumba).

PINOT BLANC/PINOT BIANCO As rich as Chardonnay, but with less fruit, and far less often oaked. At its worst – when over-cropped – it makes neutral wine. At its best, however (usually in Alsace, where it is called Pinot Blanc), it can develop a lovely cashew-nut flavour. When well handled it can also do well in Italy, where it is known as Pinot Bianco (Jermann), and in Germany (especially in Baden), where it is called Weissburgunder.

PINOT GRIS/PINOT GRIGIO In 2003, Italy's winemakers shamelessly exported more Pinot Grigio to the USA (where it is now seen as a popular unoaked, easy-drinking alternative to woody, buttery Chardonnay) than they actually produced. Which was not bad going, when you consider just how many bottles bearing Pinot Grigio labels were still on offer in Italy and in pizza bars in the UK. The explanation for this particular loaves-and-fishes trick lies in the neutral flavour of most commercial Pinot Grigio; it was all too easy to use other grapes to produce wine that tasted just like it. Alsace variety also known as Tokay but unrelated to any other Tokay. Wines can be spicy, and sweet or dry. The perfumed, aromatic qualities are associated with later-harvest examples. In Germany it is called Rülander and Grauerburgunder. Look for examples from Oregon (Eyrie), California, and New Zealand.

RIESLING The king of white grapes. Misunderstood, mispronounced – as Rice-ling rather than Rees-ling – and mistaken – for cheap German wine made from quite different grapes. At its best, it makes dry and sweet, grapey, appley, limey wines, which develop a spicy, "petrolly" character with age. Quality and character depend on soil – ideally slate – more than climate, and while the best examples come from Germany, in the Mosel (Loosen, Maximin Grünhaus) and Rhine (Schloss Johannisberg), and Alsace (Zind-Humbrecht, Faller), this variety can perform well in such different environments as Washington State, Australia's Clare Valley (Grossett, Tim Adams) and Western Australia, and New Zealand (Villa Maria). Not to be confused with unrelated varieties such as Lazki, Lutomer, Welsch, Emerald or White Riesling. Particularly successful under screwcap.

SAUVIGNON BLANC The grape of Loire wines, such as Sancerre and Pouilly-Fumé, and white Bordeaux, where it is often blended with Sémillon. This gooseberryish variety performs wonderfully in Marlborough in New Zealand (where the flavours can include asparagus and pea-pods), in South Africa (Thelema), and in Australia (Shaw & Smith, Cullen). Chile has good examples (from Casablanca) and Washington State can get it right, as can California (Cakebread, Frog's Leap), but many examples are sweet or overburdened by oak. Oaked US versions, wherever they are produced, are usually labelled Fumé Blanc, a term first coined by Robert Mondavi. Only the best of these improve after the first couple of years.

SÉMILLON In Bordeaux – in blends with Sauvignon – this produces sublime dry Graves and sweet Sauternes. In Australia (with no é), there are great, long-lived dry, pure (often unoaked) Semillons from the Hunter Valley (especially from Tyrrels and McWilliams) and (more usually oaked) Barossa Valley. Good "noble" late-harvest examples have also been produced (by de Bortoli) in Riverina. Elsewhere in Australia the grape is sometimes blended with Chardonnay. Progress is being made in Washington State and South Africa (Boekenhoutskloof), but most examples from California, New Zealand, and Chile are disappointing.

VIOGNIER A cult grape, the Viognier was once only found in Condrieu and Château Grillet in the Rhône, where small numbers of good examples showed off its extraordinary perfumed, peach-blossomy, gingery character, albeit at a high price. Today, however, it has been widely introduced to the Ardèche, Languedoc-Roussillon, and California (where it is sometimes confused with the Roussanne), and made with loving care (though often over-oaked) in Eastern Europe, Argentina, and particularly Australia (especially Yalumba)

GRAPE VARIETIES 19

Red Grapes

The first red varietal to become a star was the Cabernet Sauvignon. Then the softer, Merlot claimed the spotlight, and now the featured artists range from Burgundy's Pinot Noir to Spain's Tempranillo, Italy's Sangiovese and Portugal's Touriga Nacional.

BARBERA A widely planted, wild-berryish Italian variety at its best in Piedmont, where it is increasingly successful in blends with Nebbiolo and Cabernet (look out for Elio Altare, Bava, and Roberto Voerzio). Good in Argentina; making inroads into California and Australia (Crittenden "I"; Brown Bros).

BONARDA A juicy, berryish Italian variety that is doing well in Argentina, both by itself and in blends with grapes like Malbec and Syrah (try Zuccardi).

CABERNET FRANC Cabernet Sauvignon's "kid brother", this grape is usually a supporting actor in Bordeaux (though taking the lead at Cheval Blanc). In the Loire, it is used neat to make wines like Chinon and Bourgueil, and in Italy it produces often quite ordinary stuff in the northeast. At its best, the wine should be brightly blackcurranty.

CABERNET SAUVIGNON Usually associated with the great reds of the Médoc and Graves (in blends with Merlot), and top New World reds, especially from California, Chile, and Australia. Bulgaria has good-value examples, as do southern France (*vin de pays*), Spain (in the Penedés, Navarra, and – though this is kept quiet – Rioja). The hallmark to look for is blackcurrant, though unripe versions taste like a blend of weeds and bell peppers. There are some great Cabernets in Italy, too. Good New World Cabernets can smell and taste of fresh mint, but, with time, like Bordeaux, they develop a rich "cigar box" character.

CARMENÈRE A recently rediscovered grape that was once widely grown in Bordeaux but is now only found in Chile (where it was mistaken for Merlot) and Italy (where the confusion is with Cabernet Franc). The flavour is like a cross between peppery Grenache and Merlot.

GAMAY The juicy, "boiled sweet" grape of Beaujolais and, to a lesser extent, the Loire and Gaillac. Needs the right soil and careful handling if it is not to make light, weedy wine.

GRENACHE/GARNACHA Freshly ground black pepper is the distinguishing flavour here, sometimes with the fruity tang of sweets. At home in Côtes du Rhône and Châteauneuf-du-Pape, it is also used in Spain (as the Garnacha) in blends with Tempranillo. There are good "bush vine" examples from Australia.

MALBEC Another refugee from Bordeaux, this lightly peppery variety is used in southwest France (for Cahors), the Loire, and Italy, where it generally produces dull stuff. It shines, however, in Argentina (Zuccardi, Catena), and is now also at home in both Chile and Australia.

MERLOT The most widely planted variety in Bordeaux and the subject of over-planting in California. In Bordeaux, where, in some vintages it performs better than Cabernet Sauvignon, it is at its best in Pomerol, where wines can taste of ripe plums and spice, and in St-Emilion, where the least successful wines show the Merlot's less lovable dull and earthy character. Wherever it is made, the naturally thin-skinned Merlot should produce softer, less tannic wines than Cabernet Sauvignon.

NEBBIOLO/SPANNA The red wine grape of Barolo and Barbaresco in Piedmont now, thanks to modern winemaking, increasingly reveals a lovely cherry and rose-petal character, often with the sweet vanilla of new oak casks. Lesser examples for earlier drinking tend to be labelled as Spanna.

PINOT NOIR The wild-raspberryish, plummy, and liquoricey grape of red burgundy is also a major component of white and pink Champagne. It makes red and pink Sancerre, as well as light reds in Alsace and Germany (where it is called Spätburgunder). Italy makes a few good examples, but for the best modern efforts look to California, Oregon, Australia, Chile, South Africa, and especially New Zealand (Martinborough, Felton Road).

PINOTAGE Almost restricted to South Africa, this cross between Pinot Noir and Cinsaut can, in the right hands, make berryish young wines that may develop rich, gamey-spicy flavours. Poorer examples can be dull and "muddy"-tasting. Try Beyerskloof, Kanonkop, Grangehurst, Spier, and Vriesenhof. Watch out also for "Cape Blends" made by adding Pinotage to other varieties such as Cabernet Sauvignon.

SANGIOVESE The grape of Chianti, Brunello di Montalcino, and a host of popular IGT wines in Italy, not to mention "new wave" Italian-style wines in California and Argentina.

SYRAH/SHIRAZ The spicy, brambly grape of the Northern Rhône (Hermitage, Cornas, etc.) and the best reds of Australia (Henschke Hill of Grace and Penfolds Grange), where it is also blended with Cabernet Sauvignon (just as it once was in Bordeaux). Marqués de Griñon has a great Spanish example, and Isole e Olena makes a fine one in Tuscany. Increasingly successful in California and Washington State and, finally, in South Africa. Surprisingly good, too, in both Switzerland and New Zealand.

TANNAT At home in Madiran in southwest France, this grape is now showing what it can do in Uruguay where its wines are less tough and more mulberryish than in Europe.

TEMPRANILLO Known under all kinds of names around Spain, including Cencibel (in Navarra), and Tinto del Pais (in Ribera del Duero) and Tinta Roriz in Portugal, the grape gives Spanish reds their recognizable strawberry character. Often blended with Garnacha, it works well with Cabernet Sauvignon. So far, little used in the New World, but watch out for examples from Argentina and Australia (Nepenthe).

ZINFANDEL/PRIMITIVO Until recently thought of as California's "own" variety, but now proved (by DNA tests) to be the same variety as the Primitivo in southern Italy. In California it makes rich, spicy, blueberryish reds (Turley and Ridge Vineyards), "ports", and (often with a little help from sweet Muscat) sweet pink "White Zinfandel". Outside California, Cape Mentelle makes a good example in Western Australia.

GRAPE VARIETIES 21

Other Varieties
Still members of the chorus rather than globally recognised stars in their own right, all of the following varieties can produce good wines when grown in the appropriate places and treated carefully. Watch out for them.

WHITE
Aligoté Lean Burgundy grape, well used by Leroy.
Arneis Perfumed variety in Piedmont.
Bouvier Dull variety, used for late-harvest wines in Austria.
Chasselas Usually bland variety that comes intro its own in Switzerland.
Colombard Appley, basic; grown in southwest France, USA, and Australia.
Furmint Limey variety, traditionally used for Tokaji.
Godello Ancient aromatic Spanish grape grown in the northwest.
Kerner Dull German grape. Can taste leafy.
Müller-Thurgau/Rivaner An occasionally impressive grape; grown both Germany and England.
Roussanne Fascinating Rhône variety that deserves more attention.
Scheurebe/Samling Grapefruity grape grown in Germany and Austria.
Silvaner/Sylvaner Often earthy variety of Alsace and Germany. Can shine in the Franken region of Germany.
Torrontés Grapey, Muscat-like variety of Argentina.
Ugni Blanc/Trebbiano Basic grape of southwest France and Italy.
Verdejo Lightly spicy Spanish grape that is not related to the Verdelho.
Verdelho Limey grape found in Madeira and Australian table wine.
Viura Widely planted, so-so Spanish variety.
Welschriesling Basic. Best in late-harvest Austrians. Like Lutomer and Laszki and Italico "Rieslings", not related to the genuine Riesling.

RED
Baga Portuguese variety used for Bairrada. Rhymes with Rugger.
Blaufrankisch Blueberryish variety used primarily in Austria.
Bonarda Light, juicy Italian variety that is now at home in Argentina.
Bracchetto Strawberryish Italian variety used to make off-dry sparkling red.
Cinsaut/Cinsault Spicy Rhône variety; best in blends.
Carignan Toffeeish, non-aromatic variety widely used in southern France.
Dolcetto Cherryish Piedmont grape, now being used in Australia. Drink young.
Dornfelder Successful, juicy variety grown in Germany.
Freisa Interesting, light, fruity Italian variety. Rare.
Gamay Beaujolais/Valdiguié Pinot Noir cousin, unrelated to Gamay.
Mourvèdre/Mataro Spicy Rhône grape; good in California and Australia, but can be hard and "metallic".
Petit Verdot Spicy ingredient of Bordeaux. It is now being used on its own in Spain and Australia.
Petite-Sirah Spicy; thrives in California and Mexico. Known as Durif in Australia.
Ruby Cabernet Basic Carignan/Cabernet Sauvignon cross.
St. Laurent Austrian variety that.is very similar to Pinot Noir.
Touriga Nacional Plummy variety used for port and Portuguese table wine, especially new wave efforts from the Douro.
Zweigelt Berryish variety used in Austria.

WINE STYLES

People who like this sort of thing will find this the sort of thing they like.
                                                                Abraham Lincoln

Earlier this year, the organizers of both of London's major antiques fairs, and the dealers who had taken stands on which to display their lovely old wares, had to confront an uncomfortable truth. Very few people had shown up to buy them. Given the choice, nowadays, most of us, it seems, would rather fill our homes with modern art and contemporary furniture than old oils and chairs and chests dating from the eighteenth or ninteenth centuries. If the exhibitors at those shows had been showing off bottles of delicate, subtly mature French, Italian, and Spanish wine, they might have had a similar experience. Except that, instead of sleek stainless-steel tables, they would have been vainly trying to compete with powerful young wine, most likely from Australia or California.

Fortunately, though, in wine, as in clothes nowadays, no single fashion is allowed to rule the roost completely, and there is a huge range of flavours out there for anyone who wants to look further than the "This Week's Special Offer" shelf. The key to getting the best out of wine lies in deciding on the styles you like – and learning where to go looking for them.

Any Colour But Black

Wine can be separated into easily recognizable styles: red, white, and pink; still and sparkling; sweet and dry; light and fortified. To say that a wine is red and dry says little, however, about the way it tastes. It could be a tough young Bordeaux, a mature Rioja, or a blueberryish Zinfandel.

Knowing the grape and origin of a wine can give a clearer idea of what it is like, but it won't tell you everything. The human touch is as important in wine as it is in the kitchen. Winemakers vary as much as chefs. Some focus on obvious fruit flavours, while others – in France, for example – go for the *goût de terroir* – the character of the vineyard. In a world that is increasingly given to instant sensations, it is perhaps unsurprising that it is the fruit-lovers rather than the friends of the earthy flavour who are currently in the ascendent.

New World/Old World

Until recently, these two philosophies broadly belonged to the New and Old Worlds. Places like California and Australia made wine that was approachably delicious when compared with the more serious wine being produced in Europe, which demanded time and food. Today, however, there are Bordeaux châteaux with a New World approach and South Africans who take a pride in making wine as resolutely tough and old-fashioned as a Bordeaux of 100 years ago.

Gurus, Flying Winemakers, and Consultants

These changes owe much to the influence of gurus like Robert Parker, the US critic whose word is nearly law on the other side of the Atlantic and among more impressionable wine buyers elsewhere. But supermarkets must take as much of the blame or credit. It is hard to say whether we buy balsamic vinegar and snow-peas nowaday because they are available on the high street, or if it's the other way round. But there is no question that the tradition of simply making wine the way one's father did and offering it for sale has been steadily replaced by a more tailored approach. And, if you can't ring the right bells with the critics, supermarkets, and their customers, you can simply call in a consultant – such as Michel Rolland – who helps to produce wine all over the world. Today, you can choose between a Chilean white made by a Frenchman – or a claret bearing the fruity fingerprint of a winemaker who learned his craft in the Barossa Valley.

Fruit of Knowledge

European old-timers like to claim that the Australians use alchemy to obtain those fruity flavours. In fact, their secret lies in the winemaking process. Picking the grapes when they are ripe (rather than too early); preventing them from cooking beneath the midday sun (as often happens in Europe while work stops for lunch); pumping the juice through pipes that have been cleaned daily rather than at the end of the harvest; fermenting at a cool temperature (overheated vats can cost a wine its freshness); and storing and bottling it carefully will all help a wine made from even the dullest grape variety to taste fruitier.

Come Hither

If the New Worlders want their wines to taste of fruit, they are – apart from some reactionary South Africans and Californians – just as eager to make wine that can be drunk young. They take care not to squeeze the red grapes too hard, so as not to extract bitter, hard tannins, and they try to avoid their white wines being too acidic.

Traditionalists claim these wines do not age well. It is too early to say whether this is true, but there is no question that the newer wave red Bordeaux of, say 1985, have given more people more pleasure since they were released than the supposedly greater 1970 vintage, whose wines often remained dauntingly hard throughout their lifetime. A wine does not have to be undrinkable in its youth to be good later on; indeed, wines that start out tasting unbalanced go on tasting that way.

Roll Out the Barrel

Another thing that sets many new wave wines apart has nothing to do with grapes. Wines have been matured in oak barrels since Roman times, but traditionally new barrels were only bought to replace ones that were worn out and were falling apart. Old casks have little flavour, but for the first two years or so of their lives, the way the staves are bent over flames gives new ones a recognizable vanilla and caramel character.

Winemakers once used to rinse out their new casks with dilute ammonia to remove this flavour. Today, however, they are more likely to devote almost as much effort to the choice of forest, cooper, and charring (light, medium, or heavy "toast") as to the quality of their grapes. Winemakers who want to impress their critics take pride in using 100 per cent – or more – new oak barrels to ferment and mature their wine. Some pricey, limited-production red Bordeaux actually goes through two sets of new oak barrels to ensure that it gets double helpings of rich vanilla flavour.

Oak-mania began when Bordeaux châteaux began to spend the income from the great vintages of the 1940s on replacements for their old barrels – and when New World winemakers noticed the contribution the oak was making to these wines. Ever since, producers internationally have introduced new barrels, while even the makers of cheaper wine have found that dunking giant "teabags" filled with small oak chips into wine vats could add some of that vanilla flavour too.

If you like oak, you'll find it in top-notch Bordeaux and burgundy (red and white), Spanish *crianza*, *reserva*, or *gran reserva*, and Italians whose labels use the French term "barrique". The words "Elévé en fût de Chêne" on a French wine could, confusingly, refer to new or old casks. Australian "Show Reserve" will be oaky, as will Fumé Blanc and "Barrel Select" wines.

Red Wines – Fruits, Spice, and Cold Tea

Red wines vary far more than many people suppose. Colours range from the dark pinky-violet of the Gamay to the near-black of some Zinfandel. Some grapes, such as the Pinot Noir are good at producing silky-soft wines, while others like the Nebbiolo and Cabernhet Sauvignon are far more macho in style.

SUMMER FRUITS If you enjoy your red wines soft and juicily fruity, the styles to look for are Beaujolais; burgundy and other youthful wines made from the Pinot Noir; Côtes du Rhône; Rioja and reds from Spain; inexpensive Australians; young St-Emilion and Merlots from almost anywhere. Look too for Barbera and Dolcetto from Italy, and *nouveau*, *novello*, and *joven* (young) wines.

THE BERRY BROTHERS Cabernet Sauvignon takes the prize for the most blackcurranty grape, but Pinot Noir is raspberryish, and the Tempranillo of Spain can taste of strawberries. Shiraz – when it is not strongly smoky and spicy – is blackberryish, while Merlot can be like mulberry.

THE KITCHEN CUPBOARD Italy's Sangiovese is not so much fruity as herby, while the Syrah/Shiraz of the Rhône and Australia, the peppery Grenache, and – sometimes – the Zinfandel and Pinotage can all be surprisingly spicy. Other peppery grapes include Malbec and Chile's greatest contribution to the wine world, the Carmenère.

SOME LIKE IT TOUGH Most basic Bordeaux and more traditional Bordeaux is fairly light and tannic, as are older-style wines from Piedmont and Portugal, and old-fashioned South African reds. Italy's Nebbiolo will almost always make tougher wines than, say, Merlot.

White Wines – Honey and Lemon

If dry wines with unashamedly fruity flavours are what you want, try the Muscat, the Torrontés in Argentina, Australian Riesling, and New World and Southern French Chardonnay and Sauvignon Blanc. Beware though the growing trend in the New World of leaving a bit of sweetness in examples of these grapes.

NON-FRUIT For more neutral styles, go for Italian Soave, Pinot Bianco, or Frascati; Grenache Blanc; Muscadet; German or Alsace Silvaner; and most traditional wines from Spain and southern France.

MINERAL WEALTH One of the characteristics treasured by European traditionalists – and rarely found in the New World – is a stony, "mineral" flavour that has nothing to do with tannin or acidity and is derived from the soil in which the grapes were grown. To taste this at its best in white wines, try top-class Chablis, Sancerre, or Pouilly-Fumé. Another Loire white – Savennières – can show off this character very well too, as will the best drier Rieslings from Germany.

RICHES GALORE The combination of richness and fruit is to be found in white burgundy; better dry white Bordeaux; and in Chardonnays, Semillons, and oaked Sauvignon (Fumé) wines from the New World.

AROMATHERAPY Some perfumed, spicy grapes, like the Gewurztraminer, are frankly aromatic. Also try late harvest Tokay-Pinot Gris – also from Alsace. Other aromatic varieties include Viognier, Arneis, Albariño, Scheurebe, and Grüner Veltliner.
MIDDLE OF THE ROAD Today, people want wine that is – or says it is – either dry or positively sweet. The Loire can get honeyed *demi-sec* – semi-sweet – wine right. Otherwise, head for Germany and Kabinett and Spätlese wines.

Sweet – Pure Hedonism

Sweet wine is making a comeback at last. The places to look for good examples are Bordeaux, the Loire (Moelleux), Alsace (Vendange Tardive or Sélection des Grains Nobles), Germany (Auslese, Beerenauslese, Trockenbeerenauslese), Austria (Ausbruch), the New World (late-harvest and noble late-harvest), and Hungary (Tokaji 6 Puttonyos). All of these wines should have enough fresh acidity to prevent them from being cloying. Also, they should have the characteristic dried-apricot flavour that comes from grapes that have been allowed to be affected by a benevolent fungus known as "botrytis" or "noble rot".

Other sweet wines such as Muscat de Beaumes de Venise are fortified with brandy to raise their strength to 15 degrees of alcohol or so. These wines can be luscious, too, but, like the sweet Muscats of Valencia in Spain and Samos in Greece, they never have the complex flavours of "noble rot".

Pink – The Perfect Compromise?

Pink is, or so we were told a few years ago, the "new black". Well, that may not have been true of the clothes being worn on the high street, but rosé wine is definitely making a comeback. But tread carefully when shopping. Provence and the Rhône should offer peppery-dry rosé, just as the Loire and Bordeaux should have wines that taste deliciously of blackcurrant. Sadly, many taste dull and stale. Still, they are a better bet than California's dire sweet "white" or "blush" rosé (Fetzer's sparkling Syrah and Bonny Doon's Cigare Volant are honorable exceptions). Australia and New Zealand have some good examples of Grenache and Cabernet. Whatever the origin, look for the most recent vintage and the most vibrant colour.

Sparkling – From Basic to Brilliant

If you find Champagne too dry, but don't want a frankly sweet grapey fizz like Asti, try a fruity New World sparkling wine from California or Australia, or a sparkling Riesling (but not a cheap Sekt) from Germany. If you don't like that fruitiness, try traditional Spanish Cava, Italian Prosecco, or French Blanquette de Limoux. Even within Champagne, styles vary widely. Some are always fuller in flavour than others (Bollinger is heftier than Pol Roger for example). Brut, is sweeter than Brut Sauvage (which can be downright acidic), but drier than Extra Dry. And to confuse matters further, one producer's Brut may be much sweeter than another's.

A WORLD OF WINE

Whatever the grape variety, climate, and traditions, and despite the popularity of "global brands" with flavours almost as "international" as that of Coca Cola, the local tastes of the place where a wine is made still largely dictate its style. Let's take a whirlwind tour of the most significant winemaking nations.

FRANCE

Still the benchmark, or set of benchmarks, against which winemakers in other countries test themselves. This is the place to find the Chardonnay in its finest oaked (white burgundy) and unoaked (traditional Chablis) styles; the Sauvignon (from Sancerre and Pouilly-Fumé in the Loire, and in blends with the Sémillon in Bordeaux); the Cabernet Sauvignon and Merlot (red Bordeaux); the Pinot Noir (red burgundy and Champagne); the Riesling, Gewurztraminer, and Pinots Blanc and Gris (Alsace). The Chenin Blanc still fares better in the Loire than anywhere else, and despite their successes in Australia, the Syrah (aka Shiraz) and Grenache are still at their finest in the Rhône.

France is handicapped by the unpredictability of the climate in most of its best regions; by the unreliability of winemakers, too many of whom are still happy to coast along on the reputation of their region; and by *appellation contrôlée* laws that allow them to get away with selling poor-quality wine and prevent them from innovating and blending across regions, as is commonplace in the New World.

Alsace

Often underrated, and confused with German wines from the other side of the Rhine, Alsace deserves to be more popular. Its odd assortment of grapes makes wonderfully rich, spicy, dry, off-dry, and late harvest styles. There is also sparkling wine and a little red Pinot Noir. One word of warning: while there are two categories for luscious late harvest wines – Vendange Tardive and Sélection de Grains Nobles – many wines you might expect to taste dry are actually quite sweet.

Bordeaux

For all but the most avid wine buff, Bordeaux is one big region (producing half as much wine as Australia) with a few dozen châteaux that have become internationally famous for their wine. Visit the region, or take a look at the map, however, and you will find that this is essentially a collection of quite diverse sub-regions, many of which are separated by farmland, forest, or water.

Heading north from the city of Bordeaux, the Médoc is the region that includes the great communes of St-Estèphe, Pauillac, St-Julien, and Margaux, where some of the finest red wines are made. The largely gravel soil suits the Cabernet Sauvignon, though lesser Médoc wines, of which there are more than enough, tend to have a higher proportion of the Merlot. For the best examples of wines made principally from this variety, though, you have to head eastward to St-Emilion and Pomerol, Fronsac and the Côtes de Castillon, and to the regions of Bourg and Blaye, where the Merlot is usually blended with the Cabernet Franc.

To the south of Bordeaux lie Pessac-Léognan and the Graves, which produce some of Bordeaux's lighter, more delicate reds. This is also dry white country, where the Sémillon and Sauvignon Blanc hold sway. A little farther to the southeast, the often misty climate provides the conditions required for the great sweet whites of Sauternes and Barsac.

Each of these regions produces its own individual style of wine. In some years, the climate suits one region and/or grape variety more than others. The year 2000, for example, was better for the Médoc than for St-Emilion. So beware of vintage charts that seek to define the quality of an entire vintage across the whole of Bordeaux. Beware too of cheap, basic Bordeaux of either colour, and of supposedly slightly better basic Médoc, St-Emilion, and Sauternes. As even the grandees of Bordelais are now admitting, these are rarely a good buy.

Burgundy

The heartland of the Pinot Noir and the Chardonnay and Chablis, Nuits-St-Georges, Gevrey-Chambertin, Beaune, Meursault, Puligny-Montrachet, Mâcon-Villages, Pouilly-Fuissé, and Beaujolais. The best wines theoretically come from the Grands Crus vineyards; next are the Premiers Crus, followed by plain village wines and, last of all, basic Bourgogne Rouge or Blanc. The region's individual producers make their wines with varying luck and expertise, often selling in bulk to merchants who are just as variable in their skills and honesty. So, one producer's supposedly humble wine can be finer than another's pricier *premier* or *grand cru*. The most important name on any label is that of the producer rather than the village or vineyard.

Champagne

Top-class Champagne has toasty richness and subtle fruit. Beware of cheap examples, though, and big-name producers who should know better. Among the big names, style is all: Pol Roger is light and crisp, while Bollinger and Krug are much richer and deeper in flavour. Choosing the brand of Champagne whose style you like, is a little like selecting a perfume (it is no accident that the many of the fizz and scent makers belong to the same companies).

The Loire Valley

The heartland of fresh, dry Sauvignons and honeyed, sweet Quarts de Chaume, Coteaux de Layon, and Bonnezeaux, and dry, sweet, and sparkling Vouvray, all of which, like dry Savennières, display the Chenin Blanc at its best. The Chinon and Bourgeuil reds do the same for the Cabernet Franc. As in Alsace, beware of Vouvrays that are sweeter than you expect.

The Rhône Valley

Every year, the popularity of this region continues to grow, helped in part by the success of the local Syrah grape in its incarnation as Shiraz in tthe New World. Today, the world wants the ripe, spicy flavours of this grape and of the Grenache and Viognier, the value for money of Côtes du Rhône, and the excitement of great good Condrieu. Bear in mind that this is a big region and years that are good in the north (Côte-Rôtie, St-Joseph, Cornas, Crozes-Hermitage, and Hermitage) are not always as fine in the south (Châteauneuf-du-Pape, Gigondas, etc.), and vice versa.

The South West

Despite their fame among French wine buffs, these were often pretty old-fashioned. Today, a new wave of winemakers is learning how to extract fruit flavours from grapes like the Gros and Petit Manseng, the Tannat, Mauzac, and Malbec. Wines like Cahors, Madiran, Gaillac, and Jurançon are worth the detour for anyone bored with the ubiquitous Cabernet and Chardonnay, and dissatisfied with poor claret.

Languedoc-Roussillon and Provence
Southern France in general, and Languedoc-Roussillon in particular, offers modern *vins de pays*, and improving Corbières, Fitou, Minervois, Coteaux de Languedoc (especially Pic St-Loup), and Limoux (where Mouton Rothschild has a venture). Increasingly dynamic winemaking is also raising the quality in Provence, where classics such as Cassis and Bandol now attract as much attention as rosé.

Eastern France
Savoie's zingy wines are often only thought of as skiing fare, but, like Arbois' nutty, sherry-style whites, they are characterfully different, and made from grape varieties that are grown nowhere else. Look out for rich Vin de Paille, made from grapes dried on mats.

GERMANY
Led by younger producers like Ernst Loosen, Rainer Lingenfelder, and Phillipp Wittmann, a quiet revolution is taking place. Expect to find rich, dry and fruitily off-dry whites (ideally, but not necessarily, made from Riesling), classic later harvest styles, and a growing number of good reds (especially Pinot Noir). The Pfalz, Mosel, and Baden are regions to watch.

ITALY
The most exciting and confusing wine country in the world. Bar none. While classics like Barolo and Chianti are still made the way they used to be, producers often do their own, frequently delicious, thing, using indigenous and imported grape varieties and designer bottles and labels in ways that leave legislators – and humble wine drinkers – exhilarated and exasperated in equal measure. The fast-improving south (especially Puglia) and Sicily are worth watching out for.

SPAIN
As elsewhere, the vinous revolution has been most fruitful in regions that were previously overlooked. So, while traditionalists focused their attention on regions like Rioja, Navarra, and Ribera del Duero, and early modernists such as Miguel Torres looked to the Penedés, some of the most exciting fireworks have been seen in Galicia (source of lovely, aromatic white Albariño) and Priorat, an area that used to make thick red wine in which a spoon could stand unaided. Now, producers like Alvaro Palacios are making deliciously stylish wines there that sell easily for $100 in New York (but are, perhaps for this very reason, rather harder to find in London).

Elsewhere, Rioja is improving fast (thanks often to the addition of a little Cabernet to the red blend) and increasingly good wines are coming out of Navarra, Somontano, Toro, and Rueda. Ribera del Duero offers some great reds (Vega Sicilia, Pesquera, and Pingus) but prices are high here too.

PORTUGAL
The sleeping beauty has awoken. In the year it hosted football's European Championship, Portuguese reds beat a range of big names from other countries in a blind tasting. The key to Portugal's growing success lies in grapes like the Touriga Nacional that are grown nowhere else, and innovative winemakers like Luis Pato, Jose Neiva, J Portugal Ramos, JM da Fonseca, and Sogrape, with a little help from Australians Peter Bright and David Baverstock, and the ubiquitous Michel Rolland.

Regions of interest are Douro Palmella, Estremadura, and Alentejo, as well as historically better-known Dão and Bairrada.

AUSTRIA
The source of wonderful late harvest wines from producers like Kracher and Opitz, dry whites (especially Grüner Veltliner) from Willi Brundlmayer, Rudi and FX Pichler, and Emmerich Knoll, as well as increasingly impressive reds (St-Laurent). The word Smaragd – which means emerald – on a label should be a mark of quality.

SWITZERLAND
Switzerland is the only place in the world where the Chasselas produces anything even remotely memorable – and the only one sensibly to use screwcaps for many of its wines. Other worthwhile grapes are the white (Petite) Arvigne and Amigne (de Vétroz), but Syrah can be good too and there are some curious white Merlots.

BULGARIA
The pioneer of good Iron Curtain reds, Bulgaria remains a source of inexpensive Cabernet Sauvignon and Merlot, as well as the earthy local Mavrud. Efforts to produce premium wines have yet to pay off.

HUNGARY
Hungary's strongest hand lies in the Tokajis, the best of which are being made by foreign investors. Reds are improving, as are affordable Sauvignons and Chardonnays.

ROMANIA, MOLDOVA, AND FORMER YUGOSLAVIA
Still struggling to make their mark beyond their own borders with better than basic fare. Romania has inexpensive Pinot Noir, Moldova produces aromatic white, and Croatia can offer interesting reds from local varieties.

ENGLAND AND WALES
Thanks to global warming, the vineyards of England and Wales are using recently developed German grape varieties to make Loire-style whites; high-quality late harvest wines; quirky reds produced under plastic polytunnels; and – particularly – sparkling wines that are now winning well-earned medals at the International Wine Challenge.

GREECE
In the year of the Olympics, outsiders are beginning to take some notice of Greece's new wave wines. The best producers use either "international" grapes or highly characterful indigenous varieties – or blends of both. Prices are high (so is demand in chic Athens restaurants), but worth it from producers like Tsantali, Château Lazaridi, Gentilini, Gaia, and Hatzimichali.

CYPRUS
Still associated with cheap sherry-substitute and dull wine, but things are changing. Look out for the traditional rich Commandaria.

TURKEY
Lurching out of the vinous dark ages, Turkey has yet to offer the world red or white wines that non-Turks are likely to relish.

LEBANON
Once the lone exemplar of Lebanese wines overseas, Château Musar is now joined by the similarly impressive Château Ksara, Château Kefraya, and Massaya (a joint venture with the co-owners of Le Vieux Telegraphe in Châteauneuf-du-Pape.

ISRAEL
Some of Israel's best Cabernet and Muscat are produced at the Yarden winery in the Golan Heights – which raises interesting questions as boundaries are drawn and redrawn in this region. Labels to look out for include Yarden, Askalon, and Mt. Tabor.

AUSTRALIA
The country whose wines were once the butt of a Monty Python joke astonishingly now not only outsells France in Britain, but commands higher prices per bottle. The combination of cooperation, competitiveness, and open-mindedness of its producers has been crucial. Where else would almost a complete region like the Clare Valley decide, for quality reasons, to switch from natural corks to screwcaps in a single vintage? Just as important has been the readiness to explore and exploit new regions – areas like the Barossa and Hunter valleys have now been joined by Orange, Robe, Mount Benson, Young, and Pemberton – and styles – such as Semillon-Chardonnay and Cabernet-Shiraz blends.

A more controversial factor has to be the dynamism and power of a quartet of giant companies – BRL Hardy, Mildara Blass, Orlando, and Southcorp – that collectively control over seventy-five per cent of the country's wines and approach winemaking in a way that is very reminiscent of the Japanese motor industry.

NEW ZEALAND
This New World country has one of the most unpredictable climates, but produces some of the most intensely flavoured wines. There are gooseberryish Sauvignon Blancs, Chardonnays, and innovative Rieslings and Gewürztraminers, and arguably even more impressive Pinot Noirs. Hawkes Bay seems to be the most consistent region for Cabernets and Merlots (and the occasional Shiraz), while Central Otago and Martinborough compete over Pinot Noir. Gisborne, Marlborough, Auckland, and Martinborough all share the honours for white wine.

NORTH AFRICA
Once the plentiful source of blending wine for French regions such as Burgundy, North Africa's vineyards have been hampered in recent years by Islamic fundamentalism. New investment is, however, now beginning to arrive from Italy and France (including a new venture in Morocco that is partly financed by French actor Gérard Départdieu).

SOUTH AFRICA
The fastest-improving country in the New World? No longer the source of "green" wines made from over-cropped and underripe grapes grown on virused vines, the Cape is now making terrific lean but ripe Rieslings and Sauvignons, and delicious reds made from Cabernet, Merlot, and the local Pinotage. Thelema, Boekenhoutskloof, Saxenburg, Plaisir de Merle, Rust en Vrede, Rustenberg, Naledi/Sejana, Zandvliet, Vergelegen, Fairview, Grangehurst, Kanonkop, and Vriesenhof are names to watch – as are the up-and-coming regions of Malmesbury and Robertson.

A WORLD OF WINE

THE USA
While California produces most of the wine in the USA, it would be a mistake to ignore the often impressive efforts of wineries in other states.

California
Despite a glut of grapes that led to the selling of a lot of wine at ludicrously low prices, the best-known winemaking state of the Union is still on a roll at the moment. The Napa Valley now faces serious competition from Sonoma (where the giant E&J Gallo is making some serious reds and whites), and southern regions such as Santa Cruz and Santa Barbara. The Merlot grape has now overtaken the Cabernet Sauvignon to become the most widely planted red wine grape, but there is a growing trend towards making wines from the Pinot Noir (especially in Carneros and Russian River) and from varieties more traditionally associated with the Rhône and Italy. Amid all this excitement, however, one problem remains. California may produce some of the very finest wines in the world, but its daily-drinking efforts still offer some remarkably poor value.

The Pacific Northwest
Outside California, head north to Oregon for some of the best Pinot Noirs in the USA (at a hefty price) and improving, but rarely earth-shattering, Chardonnays, Rieslings, and Pinot Gris. Washington State has some Pinot too, on the cooler, rainy, west side of the Cascade Mountains. While on the east, irrigated vineyards produce great Sauvignon and Riesling, as well as top-notch Chardonnay, Cabernet Sauvignon, and some impressive Syrah and Merlot.

New York and Other States
Once the source of dire "Chablis" and "Champagne", New York State is now producing worthwhile wines, particularly in the micro-climate of Long Island, where the Merlot thrives. The Finger Lakes are patchier but worth visiting, especially for the Rieslings and cool-climate Chardonnays. Elsewhere Virginia, Missouri, Texas, Maryland, and even Arizona are all producing wines to compete with California, and indeed some of the best that Europe can offer.

CANADA
Icewines, made from grapes picked when frozen on the vine, are the stars here, though Chardonnays and Cabernet Francs are improving fast. Okanagan in British Columbia seems to be the region to watch.

CHILE
One of the most exciting wine-producing countries in the world, thanks to ideal conditions, skilled local winemaking, and plentiful investment. The most successful grapes at present are the Cabernet, Merlot, and – especially – the local Carmenère, but the Chardonnay, Pinot Noir, Sauvignon, and Riesling can all display ripe fruit and subtlety often absent in the New World.

ARGENTINA
As it chases Chile, this is a country to watch. The wines to look for now are the peppery reds made from the Malbec, a variety once widely grown in Bordeaux and still used in the Loire. Cabernets can be good too, as can the juicy Bonarda and grapey but dry white Torrontés.

BUYING

I wonder what the vintners buy one half so precious as the stuff they sell?
Omar Khayyam

If a British Rip Van Winkle were to wake up after dozing for twenty-five years and pop down to the shops to buy a bottle of wine with which to celebrate, he'd be in for a shock. Most of the off-licence chains he'd have known – Peter Dominic, Fullers, Augustus Barnett et al. – have disappeared, and the Anjou Rosé, Bulls Blood, and Lutomer Riesling he'd have been used to drinking have been firmly elbowed into the shadows by Australian Chardonnay, Chilean Merlot, and California White Zinfandel. Prices have gone up of course, but less than Rip might have expected. Back in the 1970s, you'd have been lucky to be offered discounts of ten per cent; this year, buyers of Cordon Negro sparkling wine got two bottles for the price of one – £5.99. If "BOGOF's" are a novelty, so, of course, is the idea of doing your shopping over the Internet. But which of these options offers the best wines and the best value?

Supermarket/High Street

Over the past few years, supermarkets have performed the same magic trick on independent wine shops as they have on butchers, bakers, greengrocers, and fishmongers: they've made them disappear. Today, four out of five bottles of wine we buy pass through a checkout along with the soap powder and dog food. And, in the case of roughly one bottle in four, that checkout is in a Tesco store. Just as supermarkets have broadened the range of foods we eat, so they have introduced us to wines we might never otherwise have tried – and generally at prices we can afford. But there is a downside; while most of the better stores offer some fairly smart wines, the focus is increasingly on branded efforts and discounts.

Specialist Merchant

Buying from a specialist wine merchant is like going to an independent bookshop or boutique. The range on offer might not be bigger or better than in the high street, but it is likely to be more characterful and you are much more likely to deal with a person who actually knows something about the wines on offer. So you can, for example, ask about whether a particular wine is worth leaving to mature – and for how long. Some specialists, such as Berry Bros & Rudd and Lay & Wheeler offer hundreds of different wines from all over the world; others specialize in one country or area. Most sell by mail, but not all print lists. Go to **robertjoseph-onwine.com** for contact details.

By Mail/Internet

Apart from virginwines.com, there are few UK-based companies that only exist online (though the French-based wineandco.com and chateauonline are both geared up to supply UK customers). Some wine retailers, however, including Waitrose and Tesco, propose wines over the Net that are not available in their shops. The Net is also a worthwhile option when browsing traditional merchants' sales and *en primeur* offers.

Wine Clubs

If you are happy to leave other people to choose your wines for you, firms such as the Sunday Times Wine Club may suit you down to the ground. Another advantage of these monthly selections, of course, is that they may introduce you to styles of wine you might never otherwise have encountered. But, inevitably, for all the unexpected delights, there are bound to be occasional disappointments, and, once you have got beyond the ludicrously cheap case that attracted you to join the club in the first place, you may well find that the wine is costing rather more than it might elsewhere.

En Primeur

Once upon a time, the only wines that could be bought while still in the barrel were top clarets, but now producers everywhere have got in on the act. There are two reasons for buying in this way, usually through a traditional merchant. You should – though this is far from certain – save money. The price of top Bordeaux in a good vintage can shoot up after it is first released, but there are years when it is cheaper in bottle than in the cask. The second reason applies to wines such as burgundy that are produced in tiny quantities. If you don't buy a case now, you may never see it again.

Under the Hammer

Auctions offer two advantages to wine lovers. Now that traditional merchants rarely offer really old bottles, bidding against others may be your only option. But firms like Christie's and Sotheby's are also a good source of bargains. When restaurants and wine merchants go bust, their stock, whch may include the humblest house wine and cases of half-bottles of Champagne, is offered in the same sale rooms as the two-million-pound collections of wine buffs, although not usually on the same occasions. Bargain hunters make sure they are on the mailing lists of these auction houses, or follow the auction pages of magazines like *Wine International* and *Decanter*. As a rule, the humbler fare is to be found at sales not described as offering "fine wine". It is also worth looking out for auctions by regional houses such as Straker Chadwick (01873 852 624), Bigwood (bigwoodauctioneers.co.uk), and Lithgow (lithgows.auctions@onyxnet.com), and online sales by winebid.com and uvine.com. When bidding, remember other costs, such as VAT, the buyer's premium, and duty that would have to be paid on wine sold "in bond".

Cross Channel

Apparently, fifteen per cent of our wine now comes from the other side of the Channel. For anyone within easy driving distance of the south coast, there is every reason to save at least £20 per case when there are cheap crossings on offer. You can legally import as much as you like for your own and your guests' consumption, so this is an ideal way to buy the wine for a wedding. If you buy from a UK chain, such as Tesco's Calais store, you can save money on familiar wines, but there are more interesting French wines in locally owned shops. Beware of apparent bargains in French supermarkets – try one bottle before risking a dozen – but take advantage of their seasonal "Foires à Vins", when big-name Bordeaux are often sold at genuinely low prices.

From the Producer

Surprisingly perhaps, given all the wine we bring home from Calais, we have been very slow to catch on to the idea of buying directly from French producers. Drive through any village in France's major wine regions during the weekend and you are almost sure to see Belgians, Germans, and Swiss struggling to shoehorn an extra case or two into their already-overloaded cars. Seeing where a wine was born and brought up, and meeting the man or woman whose name appears on the label, can, at its best, be like spending a few moments with a favourite author. Prices are often lower than in French shops, and you might well find wines that would otherwise never reach these shores.

VINTAGES

> *On one occasion someone put a very little wine into a [glass], and said that it was sixteen years old. "It is very small for its age," said Gnathaena.*
> Athenaeus, "The Deipnosophists", XIII, 47 (c. AD200)

Thirty years or so ago, good wine was only produced when the climate was just right. Man had yet to develop ways – physical, chemical, and organic – of combating pests and diseases. Really disastrous years are a rarity now, however, but some places are naturally more prone to tricky vintages than others.

Northern Europe, for example, suffers more from unreliable sun and untimely rain than more southerly regions, let alone the warm, irrigated vineyards of Australia and the Americas. A dependable climate does not necessarily make for better wine; grapes develop more interesting flavours in what is known as a "marginal" climate – which is why New World producers are busily seeking out cooler, higher-altitude sites in which to plant their vines.

It's an Ill Wind

Some producers can buck the trend of a climatically poor year – by luckily picking before the rainstorms, carefully discarding rotten grapes, or even using equipment to concentrate the flavour of a rain-diluted crop. In years like these, well-situated areas within larger regions can, in any case, make better wines than their neighbours. France's top vineyards, for example, owe their prestige partly to the way their grapes ripen. The difference in quality between regions can, however, also be attributed to the types of grape that are grown. Bordeaux had a fair-to-good vintage for red wine in 1997, but a great one for Sauternes. Similarly, there are vintages where, for example, the St-Emilion and Pomerol châteaux have already picked their Merlot grapes in perfect conditions before rainstorms arrive to ruin the prospects of their counterparts' later-ripening Cabernet Sauvignon in the Médoc, only a few miles away.

The following pages suggest regions and wines for the most significant vintages of this and the past century.

> *I remember the taste of the vintage wine*
> *From '63 through to '69*
> *And I'm proud of the things we believed in then*
> *If I had the chance I'd go around again*
>
> The Moody Blues, Vintage Wine

2004 (SOUTHERN HEMISPHERE) Australia and New Zealand had their biggest-ever vintage and fine quality (though Central Otago was hit by frost). Chile made less wine, but quality, as in Argentina, was high. South Africa had a good, rather than great year.
2003 Extraordinarily hot year with very good, if atypical, Bordeaux (including Sauternes), Loire, and Germany. Champagne, Alsace, and burgundy did well, too, but the Northern Rhône was disappointing. South Africa was great, as was Marlborough Sauvignon Blanc.
2002 An underrated year in Bordeaux (though less good in St-Emilion/Pomerol). Great in red burgundy, Loire, Alsace, Champagne, Germany, and Austria. The New World did well, especially Australia and Argentina.

2001 Some surprisingly good red Bordeaux (especially in Pomerol and St-Emilion, where some wines equalled the more loudly lauded 2000s) and great sweet and dry whites. Whites are better than reds in Burgundy and the Northern Rhône and most good Loires were sweet. Piedmont and Tuscany produced great wines, as did Tokaji and the best sites in Germany. Spanish wines were not outstanding, but there will be some high-quality port. Chile, South Africa, and New Zealand did well, and there were signs of brilliance in California.

2000 Great Bordeaux (Médoc). Red burgundy, Sauternes, and most of Northern France fared less well. Spain saw one of its largest harvests ever; and Portugal produced fine table wines and vintage port. Italy saw its best results in the south and also in the whites of the northeast, while 2000 was not as spectacular as 1999 in Germany, but Tokaji was great. Australia's best wines were from Western Australia and the Hunter Valley.

1999 A patchy year, with great red and white burgundies and Sauternes, but variable red Bordeaux. Worthwhile Rhône, Loire, and Alsace. Look out for top Italian – especially Chianti – Tokaji, and German wines from the Mosel-Saar-Ruwer. Spain was good rather than great. Australia's stars were from Coonawarra and Victoria. New Zealand, Chile, and Argentina did well.

1998 Untimely rain made for a mixed vintage throughout the northern hemisphere. There were some great red Bordeaux (St-Emilion, Pomerol, and top Médoc and Graves), lovely Sauternes and Alsace, and fine white burgundies (especially Chablis) and ports. California reds were varied.

1997 Bordeaux produced light reds and brilliant sweet whites, and Burgundy had great whites and variable reds. Alsace, Germany, and Austria made terrific wines, as did the port houses of the Douro and producers in the USA, Australia, and New Zealand. Italy had a truly great year.

1996 Classic Bordeaux (especially Médoc, Graves, and Sauternes), white burgundy, and Loire. Patchy Alsace, Rhône, and Germany, and fair in Italy, Spain, and Portugal. California, New Zealand, and Australia produced top-class red and white wines.

1995 Classy red Bordeaux and white burgundy. Italian and Loire reds, Rhône, Alsace, German, Rioja and Ribera del Duero are all good, as are Australia, New Zealand, South Africa, and North and South America.

1994 Unripe red Bordeaux, fine northern Rhône reds, fading red burgundy, and great vintage port. Average-to-good Italian reds and German; California had a great vintage, and Australian were good to very good.

1993 Red Bordeaux is tiring now. There are excellent Tokaji, Alsace, and Loire (red and white), good red burgundy, and top-class whites. Wines were better in South Africa and New Zealand than in Australia.

1992 Poor Bordeaux but good white burgundy. Fading red burgundy. Taylor's and Fonseca produced great vintage port. Fine California Cabernet.

1991 Maturing Bordeaux and good Northern Rhône reds. Fine port and good wines from Spain, South Africa, California, New Zealand, and Australia.

1990 Great Bordeaux, Champagne, Germans, Alsace, Loire whites, red Rhône, burgundy, Australia, California, Barolo, and Spanish reds.

1985-9 1989 Great red and good white Bordeaux and Champagne. Stunning Germans and red Loire; excellent Alsace. Good red and superb white Rhône, good red burgundy. **1988** Evolving red Bordeaux and Italian reds, fine Sauternes and Champagne, Tokaji, German, Alsace, Loire reds and sweet whites, good Rhône, and red burgundy.

> *We may lay in a stock of pleasures, as we would lay in a stock of wine; but if we defer tasting them too long, we shall find that both are soured by age.*
> Charles Caleb Colton (1780–1832)

1987 Fading red Bordeaux and burgundy. **1986** Fine red and white Bordeaux, Australian reds, white burgundy. **1985** Reds from Bordeaux, Rhône, burgundy, Spain, Italy, Champagne; port, Champagne, Alsace, sweet Loire.

1980–4 1984 South African and Australian reds, Riesling. **1983** Red Bordeaux, red Rhône, Portuguese reds, Sauternes, madeira, vintage port, Tokaji, Alsace. **1982** Red Bordeaux, Australian, Portuguese and Spanish reds, Italian reds, burgundy, Rhône. **1981** Alsace. **1980** Madeira, port.

1970–9 1979 Sassicaia. **1978** Rhône, Portuguese reds, Bordeaux, burgundy, Barolo, Tuscan and Loire reds. **1977** Port, sweet Austrian. **1976** Champagne, Loire reds and sweet whites, sweet German, Alsace, Sauternes. **1975** Top red Bordeaux and port, Sauternes. **1974** California and Portuguese reds. **1973** Napa Cabernet, sweet Austrian. **1972** Tokaji. **1971** Bordeaux, burgundy, Champagne, Barolo, Tuscan reds, sweet Germans, red Rhône, Penfolds Grange. **1970** Port, Napa Cabernet, red Bordeaux, Rioja.

1960–9 1969 Red Rhône, burgundy. **1968** Madeira, Rioja, Tokaji. **1968** Sauternes, Châteauneuf-du-Pape, German TBA. **1966** Port, burgundy, red Bordeaux, Australian Shiraz. **1965** Barca Velha. **1964** Red Bordeaux, Tokaji, Vega Sicilia, Rioja, sweet Loire, red Rhône. **1963** Vintage port, Tokaji. **1962** Top Bordeaux and burgundy, Rioja, Australian Cabernet and Shiraz. **1961** Red Bordeaux, Sauternes, Champagne, Brunello, Barolo, Alsace, red Rhône. **1960** Port, top red Bordeaux.

1950–9 1959 Red Bordeaux, Sauternes, Tokaji, Germans, Loire, Alsace, Rhône, burgundy. **1958** Barolo. **1957** Madeira, Vega Sicilia, Tokaji. **1956** Yquem. **1955** Red Bordeaux, Sauternes, port, Champagne. **1954** Madeira. **1953** Red Bordeaux, Tokaji, Champagne, sweet German, Côte-Rôtie, burgundy. **1952** Red Bordeaux, madeira, Champagne, Barolo, Tokaji, Rhône, burgundy. **1951** Terrible. **1950** Madeira.

1940–9 1949 Bordeaux, Tokaji, sweet Germans, red Rhône, burgundy. **1948** Port, Vega Sicilia. **1947** Bordeaux, burgundy, port, Champagne, Tokaji, sweet Loire. **1946** Armagnac. **1945** Port, Bordeaux, Champagne, Chianti, sweet Germans, Alsace, red Rhône, burgundy. **1944** Madeira, port. **1943** Champagne, red burgundy. **1942** Port, Rioja, Vega Sicilia. **1941** Madeira, Sauternes. **1940** Madeira.

ANNIVERSARY WINES 1905 Madeira. 1915 red burgundy, Germany. 1925 Madeira. 1935 Port.

INVESTMENT

Wine can bring an annual return of fifteen per cent. But as with other investments, this depends on choosing well and following the market. Bear in mind, that the actual quality – drinkability – of the wine will rise and fall, often irrespective of its market value.

Youth Before Age

Once, the only wines worth investing in came from "blue chip" estates such as Châteaux Latour, Cheval Blanc, and Haut-Brion; top Burgundies and port. People always paid more for wines that would age and improve over 10–20 years – or that had already done so. Today, auctions are full of newcomers, both among the wines and the bidders. There are Bordeaux from small estates (e.g. Clinet) and recently launched "garage" wines produced in tiny quantities, such as Le Pin and Valandraud, and New World "cult" efforts from Napa and Barossa. The common quality of these wines is a rich, seductive, fruity, oaky character rarely encountered in traditional Bordeaux that required years to lose the tannic character of its youth. These immediately enjoyable young wines now often carry bigger price tags than earlier vintages. Their capacity to age – and retain their early value – is far less certain.

The Rules

1) Wines command different prices in different countries. 2) Wines don't last forever. 3) Be wary of wines with unproven potential. 4) Only buy *en primeur* from financially solid merchants. 5) Only buy wines that have been carefully cellared. 6) Store wines carefully – and insure them. 7) Follow their progress – read the critics and watch the auctions. 8) Beware of falling reputations for wines and vintages. 9) When bidding at auction, take note of possible extra costs. 10) It is easier to turn a gold ring into cash than a prize Bordeaux.

France

BORDEAUX Châteaux Angélus, Ausone, Cheval Blanc, Cos d'Estournel, Ducru-Beaucaillou, Eglise-Clinet, Figeac, Grand-Puy-Lacoste, Gruaud-Larose, Haut-Brion, Lafite, Lafleur, Latour, Léoville Barton, Léoville Las Cases, Lynch-Bages, Margaux, la Mission-Haut-Brion, Montrose, Mouton-Rothschild, Palmer, Pétrus, Pichon Lalande, Pichon Longueville, le Pin, Rauzan-Ségla, Valandraud. Vintages: 1982, 1983 (Margaux), 1988, 1989, 1990, 1995, 1996, 1998, 2000. 1999 and 2001 (top properties only).

BURGUNDY Drouhin Marquis de Laguiche, Gros Frères, Hospices de Beaune (from Drouhin, Jadot, etc.), Méo-Camuzet, Romanée-Conti (la Tâche, Romanée-Conti), Gouges, Lafon, Leflaive, Leroy, Denis Mortet, Roumier, de Vogüé.

RHONE Chapoutier, Chave, Guigal (top wines), Jaboulet Aîné "La Chapelle."

PORTUGAL (port) Cockburn's, Dow's, Fonseca, Graham's, Noval, Taylor's, Warre's.

CALIFORNIA Beaulieu Georges de Latour, Diamond Creek, Dominus, Duckhorn, Dunn, Harlan Estate, Howell Mountain, Grace Family, Matanzas Creek, Robert Mondavi Reserve, Opus One, Ridge, Spottswoode, Stag's Leap.

AUSTRALIA Armagh, Clarendon Hills, Tahbilk 1860 Vines Shiraz, Henschke Hill of Grace, Cyril Henschke, Mount Edelstone, Penfolds Grange and Bin 707, Petaluma Cabernet, "John Riddoch", Virgin Hills, Yarra Yering.

WINE ON THE WEB

I have a laptop which worke3 perfectl6 until I spille3 red wine 1 on the ke6boar3. I switched the power off and 1 moppe3 up what I coul3, then left it overnight. In the morning I foun3 that ever6thing worke3 fine but some ke6s 3on't work on the keyboard. Not onl6 that but the 1 computer sometimes thinks that the '1' ke6 is pressed down, so I get 1's t6pe3 ever6where! is there an6thing I can 3o to solve these problems?

Enquiry to an online forum

Somewhere lurking in the furthest reaches of the Net, there is probably a statistic revealing just how many people do irreparable damage to their computers every year while browsing for wine. When I typed "wine" "spill" and "keyboard" into Google, it came up with no fewer than 6,590 sites that might have offered the answer, but sadly I did not have time to stray beyond the first few pages.

Wine and the Web have been having a relationship for quite some time now. It began like love at first sight. Even when the expression "going online" was still the preserve of men with strange glasses who didn't get out very much, there were those who believed that the new medium and the wine industry were made for each other. Wine merchants and online publishers raised ludicrous sums and launched websites galore, filling their pages with informative words from writers who began to imagine that an electronic fortune was there for the taking.

Today, you don't have to surf for long before you discover that financial reality bit hard into those dreams. With the exception of Wine.com in the USA and Berry Bros & Rudd, which has one of the best online vinous news services, few of the pioneers have continued to offer much in the way of free wine information. But – and here's the good news – the maturing Web has found space for a wider range of wine-related material than most of us ever imagined.

News and Views

As flakier efforts have come and gone, it is interesting to see that the most informative sites have survived. The grandaddy of these is the US-based Robin Garr's Wine Lovers Page (www.wineloverspage.com) which combines first-class contributions from professional writers such as Sue Courtney and Natalie MacLean with quirky contributions from readers. There are wine recommendations and enough forums to keep the most eclectic wine lover engrossed.

On the other side of the Pacific, despite rumours of its demise, James Halliday's winepros.com is still very much alive. There are fewer bells and whistles than there were – this was once intended to be a global one-stop shop for wine information – but it remains essential reading for anyone wanting in-depth insight into the Antipodes.

Jamie Goode's wineanorak.com claims to be one of the most interesting and comprehensive wine resources on the Web, and it doesn't disappoint. Apart from reliable recommendations, book reviews, and thoughtful, well-researched features, it also offers a great little gallery of vinous photographs. Another similarly recommendable site with links to all the UK forums is Tom Cannavan's wine-pages.com, and winedine.com is worthwhile too.

Among the magazines that boast a good online presence, I'd particularly recommend the US-based *Wine Spectator* (winespectator.com) and *Decanter* (decanter.com) for their news coverage. The former magazine has a huge range of wine reviews, as does *Wine International* (wineint.com), which offers the results of the annual International Wine Challenge. Another US magazine whose online version is worth visiting for its archive of feaures is the *Wine Enthusiast* (winemag.com), while the site of the recently launched *World of Fine Wine* (finewinemag.com) also shows potential at the more intellectual end of the scale. All of these sites rely on advertising and sponsorship to survive. Subscription-based sites that stand apart from the herd include Jancis Robinson's first class Purple Pages (jancisrobinson.com), Steve Tanzer's International Wine Cellar (wineaccess.com) and Robert Parker's erobertparker.com, which is worth visiting, if only for the quality of its forum discussions. Also of note for anyone fascinated by Burgundy and interested in keeping track of what is happening there, is Allen Meadows' excellent Burghound.com.

Local Knowledge

One of the hazards of being a writer of any kind lies in the accumulation of books and other written material that one keeps because it may come in handy one day – despite the fact that the information is losing its accuracy by the week. Thanks to the Net, most of that material can be given away or shredded. If I want to know how many hectares of Pinot Noir there are in Sonoma, or the year that Arbois became an appellation, I can simply go onto Google and look it up. And so can you. Alternatively, you might speed up the search – or be happily distracted – by visiting a few sites that offer links to other sites. Try bestwinesites.com, wineinfonet.com (very US-focused), or winetitles.com (similarly Antipodean). My own robertjoseph-onwine.com also has a long list of links.

> *The Labtec spill-resistant keyboard is an excellent choice for those who require a simple, yet stylish product. This reliable keyboard will last for years thanks to its sturdiness and durability. Buy now for £5.80.*
>
> *Offer on www.comparestoreprices.co.uk*

Buying Online

While virginwine.com is the only survivor of the clutch of Net-only retailers in Britain, it is a rare and peculiarly Luddite terrestrial firm that has not yet set out its wares online. Among the recently arrived latecomers to the party are the Wine Society (www.thewinesociety.com), which can be joined at the click of a mouse, and Justerini & Brooks (www.justerinis.com), which only turned electronic after closing its earthly shops in London and Edinburgh. Both Berry Bros and Justerini's make no secret of the fact that their UK base is no hinderance to their ambitions as global traders. The first question you are asked on the latter's site refers to the country you are "currently in" (presumably this is targeted at wine-loving globetrotters), while the former firm offers the option of pages in Chinese and Japanese.

If these sites are looking for wine buyers beyond the shores of the UK, two firms based on the other side of the Channel are equally keen to sell wine here. Wineandco.com and chateauonline.com should both be of interest to anyone frustrated by the paucity of the Gallic range available here, though both performed surprisingly poorly when I went looking for wines from more obscure areas. Indeed I might have done as well or better at smaller UK-based companies like les Caves de Pyrène (www.lescaves.co.uk).

Finally, there is one site that all true wine lovers discover sooner or later. wine-searcher.com does what it says on the tin: it helps you find specific wines by browsing countless retailers' lists across the world. It is, in other words, a wine buyer's Google.

WINE AND HEALTH

It sloweth age, it strengtheneth youth, it helpeth digestion, it abandoneth melancholie, it relisheth the heart, it lighteneth the mind, it quickenth the spirits, it keepeth and preserveth the head from whirling, the eyes from dazzling, the tongue from lisping, the mouth from snaffling, the teeth from chattering and the throat from rattling; it keepeth the stomach from wambling, the heart from swelling, the hands from shivering, the sinews from shrinking, the veins from crumbling, the bones from aching,and the marrow from soaking.

Robert Noecker

This wonderful endorsement for wine which was written in the sixteenth century, copied by Joseph Lyons and published by Robin Garr on wineloverspage.com, is sadly incomplete. According to modern research, wine may, in moderation, also be effective against a range of other ailments – from Alzheimers to heart disease. Which is just as well, really, when one considers the damage alcohol of any kind can do when taken in excess.

For the sake of balance , let's look at the negative side first.

Why Wine is Bad for You

HANGOVERS All alcohol is hangover fare and port is worse than most. Try to drink plenty of water before going to bed. Take Vitamin B on the Morning After, or Marmite. Otherwise, go for protein and refreshing orange juice diluted with sparkling mineral water.

PREGNANCY Taken in excess, wine, like all alcohol, is dangerous for mothers-to-be. Less well-known is the fact that drinking soon after conception may actually impair the chances of becoming pregnant in the first place. Once the test proves positive, however, women who fancy the occasional glass of red or white will be pleased to hear that in 1997, the UK Royal College of Obstetricians and Gynaecologists reported that up to fifteen units per week should do no harm to a foetus.

CALORIES AND CARBS All wine is fattening. Muscadet and red Bordeaux with the same 12.5 degrees of alcohol strength, have the same number of calories (around 110 per glass). Stronger wines with, say, 14 have more, while sweeter, but less alcoholic German wines that weigh in at 9, have fewer than eighty calories.

A Stanford University survey suggests the action of the wine on the metabolism may make its calories less fattening. According to the US Department of Agriculture, a five-ounce glass of wine has about 0.8 to 1.8 grams of carbohydrates. A number of Californian Chardonnay however might have three carbs, because of their sweetness.

WINE, MIGRAINE, AND ALLERGIES Red wine, like chocolate, can inhibit a useful little enzyme called phenosulfotransferase-P, or PST-P, which detoxifies bacteria in the gut. An absence of PST-P is linked to migraine, which is why some people complain of headaches after drinking a glass or two of wine. Other people have found that red wine is also associated with episodic skin allergies.

Fortunately, some of these conditions can apparently come and go over time. Interestingly, there also seems to be differences in the effects of particular styles of wine. Chianti, for example, seems to have fewer histamines than red wines from other regions.

WINE AND HEALTH

WINE AND ASTHMA One side effect of wines that are heavily dosed with sulphur dioxide (used to combat bacteria in most dried, bottled, and canned foods) is an incidence of asthma attacks among those who are susceptible to this condition. Red wines in general, and New World and organic wines in particular, have lower sulphur levels. The highest levels of sulphur will be in sweet white wines and wines with low alcohol levels.

Why Wine Might be Good for You

Of all the alcoholic drinks we enjoy, red wine gets the strongest support from the medical researchers, but there are studies that suggest that white wine and beer (though rarely spirits) and even grape juice also may help to extend your life.

HEARTY GOOD WISHES For those following research into the relationship between wine and health, scarcely a month seems to pass without the publication of yet another report showing the beneficial properties of an anti-fungal compound called resveratrol that is found in high concentration in grape skins, as well as in peanuts, and some other foods. The magic property of the compound lies in helping blood to flow better. In other words a glass or three of red per day (Resveratrol is not as present in whites) seems, like aspirin, to prevent blood clots. Like that drug, it is now being prescribed to patients recovering from heart surgery.

PROTECTION AGAINST CANCER, STROKES, AND DEMENTIA? Fascinatingly, if one sets aside suggestions that wine might actually help to cause mouth and throat tumours (it may, but only in the case of heavy smokers), resveratrol may be similarly effective against various forms of cancer. These could, according to some researchers, include cancers of the bowel, breast and ovaries, as well as melanomas.. One theory is that the resveratrol inhibits the proliferation of human intestinal cancerous cells and the formation of tumours in mice predisposed to intestinal tumours. Prof. Djavad Mossalayi of the Victor Segalen University has proved that it is also toxic to cancerous cells in humans. Red wine is also rich in gallic acid, an acknowledged anticarcinogenic, and wine's role in reducing stress has also been associated with a lower incidence of certain forms of cancer.

Wine may also be effective against dementia and Alzheimers in the over-sixty-fives and there is some evidence that two to three glasses per day could reduce the risk of strokes by almost thirty per cent.

OTHER POSSIBLE BENEFITS Wine and beer both seem to combat a bacteria that causes peptic ulcers, and red wine in particular may be helpful against pneumonia and bronchitis. though the former drink is less likely to cause gout than the latter. Red wine may also be used to augment the treatment of Aids, according to Dr. Marvin Edeas of the Hôpital Antoine Béclère in Clamart in France, who is studying the way the polyphenols rejuvenate blood. It may also be effective against diseases such as sickle cell anaemia and thalassaemia. Another theory suggests that red wine may be beneficial in maintaining bone density in post-menopausal women, and this reducing the risk of fractures.

Young women who drink a glass or two of red per day may reduce the risk of getting Type 2 Diabetes, and Canadian studies suggest that the polyphenols in red wines may be effective against cold sores and even genital Herpes.

For more information, visit thewinedoctor.com/advisory/health1.shtml

WINE AND FOOD

What is the best wine with a Grilled Buffalo Burger with Blue Cheese?
Sent to the erobertparker.com online forum by Jason G,
Senior Executive Oenophile Member # 1765

Buffalo meat tastes like a cross between beef and ham. I'd try a German Spätlese.
Reply from Paul H, Executive Oenophile Member # 2694

It requires a certain type of mind to see beauty in a hamburger.
Ray Kroc, Chairman of McDonalds

Have no Fear

One of the most daunting aspects of wine has always been the traditional obsession with serving precisely the right wine with any particular dish – of only ever drinking red with meat and white with fish or shellfish. It may be reassuring to learn that some of these time-honoured rules are just plain wrong. In Portugal, for example, fishermen love to wash down their sardines and salt cod with a glass or two of harsh red wine. In Burgundy, they even poach fish in their local red.

On the other hand, the idea that a platter of cheese needs a bottle of red wine can be thrown away right now. Just take a mouthful of red Bordeaux immediately after eating a little goat's cheese or Brie. The wine will taste metallic and unpleasant because the creaminess of the cheese reacts badly with the tannin – the toughness – in the wine. A dry white would be far more successful (its acidity would cut through the fat), while the Bordeaux would be shown at its best alongside a harder, stronger cheese. If you don't want to offer a range of wines, try sticking to one or two cheeses that really will complement the stuff in the glass.

Don't take anything for granted. Rare beef and red Bordeaux surprisingly fails the test of an objective tasting. The protein of the meat somehow makes all but the fruitiest wines taste tougher. If you're looking for a perfect partner for beef, uncork a burgundy. However, if it's the Bordeaux that takes precedence, you'd be far better off with lamb.

The difference beteen an ideal and a passable food-and-wine combination can be very subtle. Most of us have, after all, happily quaffed red Bordeaux with our steak, but just as an avid cook will tinker with a recipe until it is just right, there's a lot to be said for making the occasional effort to find a pairing of dish and wine that really works. Like people who are happier as a couple than separately, some foods and wines simply seem to bring out the best in each other.

A Sense of Balance

There is no real mystery about the business of matching food and wine. Like classic food combinations, some flavours and textures are compatible, and some are not. Strawberry mousse is not really delicious with chicken casserole, but apple sauce can do wonders for roast pork.

The key to spotting which relationships are marriages made in heaven, andwhich have the fickleness of Hollywood romances, lies in identifying the dominant characteristics of the contents of both the plate and the glass. Then, learn by experience which are likely to complement each other, either through their similarities or through their differences.

Likely Combinations

Without question, the greatest invention in the history of mankind is wine. Oh, I grant you that the wheel was also a fine invention, but the wheel does not go nearly as well with pizza.

Dave Barry

Some foods and their characteristics, though, make life difficult for almost any drink. Sweetness, for example, in a fruity sauce served with a savoury dish seems to strip some of the fruitier flavours out of a wine. This may not matter if the stuff in your glass is a blackcurranty New World Cabernet Sauvignon, but it's bad news if it is a bone-dry white or a tough red with little fruit to spare. Try fresh strawberries with Champagne – delicious; now add a little whipped cream to the equation and you'll spoil the flavour. Creamy and buttery sauces can have the same effect on a wine and call for a similarly creamy white – or a fresh, zippy one to cut through the fattiness.

Spices are very problematic for wine – largely due to the physical sensation of eating them rather than any particular flavour. A wine may not seem nasty after a mouthful of chilli sauce, it will simply lose its fruity flavour and taste of nothing at all – which, in the case of a fine red, seems a pity. The way a tannic red dries out the mouth will also accentuate the heat of the spice. The ideal wine for most Westerners to drink with any spicy dish would be a light, possibly slightly sweet, white or a light, juicy red.

Always Worth a Try

Some condiments actually bring out the best in wines. A little freshly ground pepper on your meat or pasta can accentuate the flavour of a wine, just as it can with a sauce. Squeezing fresh lemon onto your fish will reduce the apparent acidity of a white wine – a useful tip if you have inadvertently bought a case of tooth-strippingly dry Muscadet. And, just as lemon can help to liven up a dull sauce, it will do the same for a dull white wine, such as a basic burgundy or a Soave, by neutralizing the acidity and allowing other flavours to make themselves apparent. Mustard performs a similar miracle when it is eaten with beef, somehow nullifying the effect of the meat protein on the wine.

Cooking with Wine

I cook with wine, sometimes I even add it to the food.

W.C. Fields

Finally, a word or two about how best to use wine in the kitchen (apart from its role as refreshment, and as a tranquilizer for the moments when sauces curdle). Wine that's not good enough to drink is probably not good enough to pour into the frying pan or casserole. On the other hand, despite the advice of classic French recipes, your "coq au vin" won't be spoiled by your unwillingness to make it with a pricey bottle of *grand cru* burgundy. A decent, humbler red will do perfectly well, though it is worth trying to use a similar style to the one suggested.

Second – and just as important – remember that, with the exception of a few dishes such as sherry trifle or zabaglione, in which wine is enjoyed in its natural state, wine used as an ingredient needs to be cooked in order to remove the alcohol. So, add it early enough for the necessary evaporation to take place.

THE INTERNATIONAL WINE CHALLENGE

From tiny acorns... Way back in 1984, wine writer and broadcaster Charles Metcalfe and I thought it might be interesting to compare a few English white wines with examples from other countries for a feature in a magazine we had launched a few months earlier that would later become *Wine International*. So, we set out a representative collection of some fifty carefully camouflaged bottles, in the basement of a London restaurant, and invited a group of experts to mark them out of twenty. We never imagined that the home team would surprise everyone by beating well-known bottles from Burgundy, the Loire, and Germany – or that the modest enterprise we had immodestly called "The International Wine Challenge" would develop into the world's biggest, most respected wine competition.

The following year's Challenge attracted around 200 entries, while the third and fourth competitions saw numbers rise to 500 and 1,000 respectively. This annual doubling thankfully slowed down eventually, but by the end of the century the competition was, by a substantial margin, the largest in the world, attracting entries from countries ranging from France and Australia to Thailand and Uruguay. In April 2004, there were over 9,000 wines.

Origins in London

It is no accident that the International Wine Challenge was born in London. For centuries, British wine drinkers have enjoyed the luxury of being able to enjoy wines from a wide variety of countries. Samuel Pepys may have been a fan of Château Haut-Brion from Bordeaux, but plenty of other eighteenth-century sophisticates in London (and elsewhere in Britain) were just as excited about the sweet, late-harvest whites that were being produced at that time by early settlers in South Africa.

More recently, as wine became steadily more popular, wines from California, Australia, New Zealand, and South America all found their way to these shores. Other arrivals were wines from regions, like the Languedoc-Roussillon in France and Southern Italy, that had often been overlooked. As the twenty-first century dawned, Britain's biggest supermarket chains boasted daunting ranges of 700 to 800 different wines. A well-run, truly impartial competition provided an invaluable means of sorting the best and most interesting of these bottles from the rest. Publishing their descriptions and information on where to buy them provided unequalled guidance for anyone wanting to broaden their drinking experience.

The Tasting Panels

If the diversity of the wines on offer in Britain created a need for the International Wine Challenge, the calibre of this country's wine experts provided the means with which to run the competition. The nation that spawned the Institute of Masters of Wine – the trade body whose members have to pass the world's toughest wine exam – is also home to some of the most respected wine critics and merchants on the planet.

These are the men and women – some 400 of them – who, along with winemakers and experts from overseas, make up the tasting panels for the Challenge. So, a set of wines might well have been judged by a group that included a traditional merchant, the buyer from a supermarket chain, an Australian winemaker, a French sommelier, and a Portuguese wine critic. Argument between these diverse palates is surprisingly rare; when agreement is impossible, one of my co-chairmen Charles Metcalfe and Derek Smedley MW, or myself, is called in to adjudicate.

THE INTERNATIONAL WINE CHALLENGE

Two-round Format
During the first of the two rounds of the competition, wines are assessed to decide whether or not they are worthy of an award – be it a medal or a seal of approval. At this stage, typicality is taken into account, and tasters are informed that they are dealing, for example, with Chablis, Chianti, or South African Chenin Blanc. Around thirty-six per cent of the wines will leave the competition with no award. A further thirty per cent will receive seals of approval; the remainder will be given gold, silver, or bronze medals. The entries that have been thought medal-worthy in the first round, and the "seeded" entries that won recognition in the previous year's competition, then pass directly to the second round. Now, the judges face the task of deciding on the specific award each wine should receive – if any (they can still demote or throw wines out completely). At this stage, the wines are still grouped by grape and region, but a team of tasters might be confronted with sets of similar wines from, say, Chile, Australia, and California.

Super-jurors
As a final check, after it has been open for a while, every wine goes before a team of "super-jurors". These are mostly Masters of Wine, winemakers, and professional buyers from leading merchants and retailers whose daily work involves the accurate assessment of hundreds of wines. The vital role of the super-jurors is both to ensure that tasters have not been overly harsh on wines that were reticent when first poured, or on ones with subtle cork taint that was initially unnoticed – and to watch out for entries that may have been over-estimated because of the immediate attraction of oakiness, for example. If two super-jurors agree, they can jointly up- or down-grade a wine.

Trophies and Great Value Awards
The super-jurors also decide which gold medal winners deserve the additional recognition of a trophy. These supreme awards can be given for any style, region, or nationality of wine. The judges are free to withhold trophies or to create them as they see appropriate (this year's several German trophies are a good example). The trophies, like all of the wines in the competition are judged irrespective of their price. Wines that are particularly fairly priced for their award get Good Value Awards and a set of widely available, most highly marked wines are named Great Value Wines of the Year after a tasting by the super-jurors. The International Wine Challenge 2004 Trophy winners are listed on pages 46–8.

In this book you will find the medal winners and seals of approval that represent particularly good value.

Grading of Awards and Key to Symbols Used in the Book
Gold medals have scored the equivalent of at least 18.5/20 (or 95/100) and are exceptional. Silver has scored over 17/20 (or 90/100), bronze over 15.5/20 (or 85/100), and seals of approval over 14/20 (or 80/100).

✰ particularly good value
★ truly great value
▲ 50CL bottle
■ 37.5CL bottle
● 10CL bottle

WINES OF THE YEAR AND TROPHIES

Winemaker of the Year

Sparkling	*Charles Heidsieck*
White	*Weingut Horst Sauer*
Red	*Maison Albert Bichot*
Fortified	*Taylors*

Great Value Award

Fortified	*Graham's LBV Port 1999*
	Waitrose Solera Jerezana Dry Oloroso Sherry NV
Sparkling	*Champagne Drappier, Millésime Exception 1999*
	Tesco Premier Cru Champagne Brut NV
	Tosti Sparkling Pinot Grigio NV
Red	*Penfolds Bin 28 Kalimna Shiraz 2001*
	Wakefield Promised Land Shiraz Cabernet 2002
	Bodegas Muriel, Barón de Barbón 2003
	Virginie de France Syrah 2003
	The Boulders Petite Sirah 2002
White	*Tesco Denman Vineyard Hunter Estate Reserve Semillon 2002*
	Nepenthe Sauvignon Blanc 2003
	L'Ecluse Chardonnay 2002
	D'Istinto Catarratto-Chardonnay 2002

Supreme Trophies

Daniel Thibault Trophy (for the best sparkling wine)
Charles Heidsieck Champagne Brut 1989
The Fortified Trophy *Taylors 40 Year Old Tawny Port*
The Red Trophy *Scirus 2001 Fattoria Le Sorgenti*
The Sweet Wine Trophy *Inniskillin Oak Aged Vidal Ice Wine 2002*
The White Wine Trophy *J.J. Prum Graacher Himmelreich Riesling Spätlese 1994*
James Rogers Trophy (for the best wine in its first year of production)
Quinta do Portal Auru 2001
Len Evans Trophy (for the most consistently successful IWC entrant over five years) *d'Arenberg Wines*

WINES OF THE YEAR AND TROPHIES

International Trophies

RED

Cabernet-Merlot Trophy	*Fattoria Le Sorgenti, Scirus 2001*
Pinot Noir Trophy	*Albert Bichot, Grands Echezeaux Grand Cru 2002*
Sangiovese Trophy	*Poggio San Polo, Brunello di Montalcino 1999*
Shiraz Trophy	*Jim Barry, The Lodge Hill Shiraz 2002*
Tannat Trophy	*Dom. Berthomieu, Madiran Cuvée Charles de Batz 2001*
Tempranillo Trophy	*Campillo, Reserva Especial 1995*

WHITE AND FORTIFIED

Chenin Blanc Trophy	*Domaine du Closel, La Jalousie 2002*
Dry Riesling Trophy	*Loimer, Steinmassl Riesling 2002*
Off-Dry Riesling Trophy	*J.J. Prum, Graacher Himmelreich Riesling Spätlese 1994*
Late-Harvest Trophy	*Kranz-Junk, Brauneberger Juffer-Sonnenuhr Riesling Auslese 2002.*
Botrytis Trophy	*Horst Sauer Escherndorfer Lump Riesling Trockenbeerenauslese 2002*
Silvaner Trophy	*Bocksbeutel-Hof Winzergenossenschaft, Escherndorfer Silvaner Auslese 2002*
Gewurztraminer Trophy	*Cave de Turckheim, Gewurztraminer Brand 2000*
Oaked Chardonnay Trophy	*Jean-Claude Boisset, St-Aubin "Sur Gamay" 2002*
Unoaked Chardonnay Trophy	*Jean-Marc Brocard, Chablis 1er Cru 2002*
Sauvignon Blanc Trophy	*Saint Clair, Wairau Reserve Sauvignon Blanc 2003*
Fortified Muscat	*Stanton and Killeen, Classic Rutherglen International*

Regional Trophies

RED

Argentinian Cabernet Sauvignon Trophy
Bodegas Trapiche, Broquel Cabernet Sauvignon 2002

Edmund Penning-Rowsell Trophy (for the finest Bordeaux)
Château Pape-Clement 2001

French Red Trophy	*Château Pape-Clement 2001*
Italian Red Trophy	*Fattoria Le Sorgenti, Scirus 2001*
Piedmont Trophy	*Paolo Scavino, Cannubi Barolo 1999*
Portuguese Trophy	*Quinta do Portal Auru 2001*
Burgundy Trophy	*Albert Bichot, Grands Echezeaux Grand Cru 2002*
Argentine Trophy	*Bodegas O Fournier, A Crux 2001*
Australian Red Trophy	*Bleasdale Frank Potts 2002*
Rhône Trophy	*Alain Graillot, Crozes-Hermitage 2000*

South African Syrah Trophy
Stellenzicht Syrah 2001

South American Syrah Trophy
Casa Lapostolle Cuvée Alexandre Syrah 2002

Southern French Trophy	*Virginie de France Syrah 2003*
Southern Italian Trophy	*Tenuta Le Querce, Aglianico del Vulture "Rosso di Costanza" 2001*
Spanish Trophy	*Finca Luzon, Altos 2002*
USA Red Trophy	*Beaulieu Vineyard Georges de Latour Private Reserve Cabernet Sauvignon 2000*
Victorian Shiraz Trophy	*Tyrrell's Rufus Stone Heathcote Shiraz 2002*

WHITE AND SPARKLING

Australian White Trophy	*Brookland Valley Reserve Chardonnay 2002*
Franken Riesling Trophy	*Horst Sauer Escherndorfer Lump Riesling Spätlese Trocken 2003*
French White Trophy	*Cave de Turckheim Gewurztraminer Grand Cru Brand 2000*
Italian White Trophy	*Cristina Ascheri, Roero Arneis 2003*
USA White Trophy	*Geyser Peak Winery Reserve Chardonnay 2002*
Veneto Trophy	*Gino Fasoli, Pieve Vecchia 2001*
Champagne Trophy	*Champagne Gremillet Brut Cuvée des Dames*
Vintage Champagne Trophy	*Charles Heidsieck Brut 1989*

SWEET AND FORTIFIED

Canadian Icewine Trophy	*Inniskillin Oak Aged Vidal Ice Wine 2002*
German Eiswein Trophy	*Horst Sauer Escherndorfer Lump Riesling Eiswein 2002*
German Trophy	*JJ Prum Graacher Himmelreich Riesling Spätlese 1994*
Rheingau Riesling Trophy	*Künstler, Hochheimer Kirchenstück Riesling Spätlese 2003*
Madeira Trophy	*Barbeito, 10 Year Old Reserve Sercial.*
Montilla Trophy	*Virgilio, Pedro Ximenez Virgilio 1925.*
Port Trophy	*Taylors 40 Year Old Tawny Port*
Sherry Trophy	*Lustau Don Nuno Dry Oloroso*
Vintage Port Trophy	*Smith Woodhouse Vintage Port 2000*

ARGENTINA

Definitely a New World country to watch for the range of wines it can produce. Among the white stars this year were examples of Pinot Grigio and Viognier and the unusual local Torrontés – a Muscat-like variety whose wines smell sweet but taste grapey and dry. The red wine grape usually asociated with Argentina is Malbec, and there were certainly plenty of award winners made from this peppery variety. There were also great blends (with Tempranillo and Merlot as in the case of the trophy-winning "A Crux") and a good range of other varieties, ranging from Cabernet Sauvignon and Syrah to Sangiovese and the local, berryish Bonarda.

GOLD
ARGENTINIAN WHITE

☆ **TUPUNGATO CHARDONNAY 2002, BODEGA CATENA ZAPATA** MENDOZA – *Tropical, pear and apple fruit, and floral aromatics over ripe, toasty oak. It has a bright acidity.*	£6.00 M&S

SILVER
ARGENTINIAN WHITE

☆ **INTI PINOT GRIGIO 2004, LA RIOJANA** LA RIOJA – *A heady blend of freshly picked wildflowers, burning leaves and vibrant citrus fruit. A rich wine.*	£5.00 JSM
LA CELIA RESERVA CHARDONNAY 2002, FINCA LA CELIA MENDOZA – *Powerful and spicy with citrus and toast aromas. The rich fruit palate is balanced by fresh acidity.*	£8.00 BUC

BRONZE
ARGENTINIAN WHITE

SANTA JULIA VIOGNIER 2004, FAMILIA ZUCCARDI **MENDOZA** – *A perfumed nose of passionfruit and roses. Soft and gentle with flowery notes and a well-structured palate.*	£5.30 TOS
TERRAZAS DE LOS ANDES ALTO CHARDONNAY 2003, TERRAZAS **MENDOZA** – *Golden-yellow-green. Fresh satsuma and delicate vanilla aromas. Soft butterscotch elements accentuate citrus flavours.*	£6.30 BNK/FEN FLA/OWC
DON DAVID TORRONTÉS 2003, MICHEL TORINO **CAFAYETE** – *Heavily perfumed with rose petal and lychee scents. Textured and warming palate with plenty of cinnamon spice.*	£7.70 BNK/FFW VGN/NFW NYW/CVE
Q CHARDONNAY 2003, FAMILIA ZUCCARDI **MENDOZA** – *Spice and creamy oak on the nose. The palate is ripe with citrus and melon notes. Mineral finish.*	£10.00 BOO
TERRAZAS DE LOS ANDES RESERVA CHARDONNAY 2003, TERRAZAS **MENDOZA** – *Bright lemon and lime flavours, hints of nutmeg, guava nuances, and a touch of cream.*	£10.00 BNK/FLA

SEAL OF APPROVAL
ARGENTINIAN WHITE

☆ **ESPERANZA SAUVIGNON BLANC 2002, WINERY EXCHANGE** **MENDOZA** – *Intensely herbaceous, with bright kiwi and lime flavours.*	£4.00 WXC MWW
☆ **TANGUERO CHARDONNAY 2003, FINCA FLICHMAN** **MENDOZA** – *Lemons, grapefuit, Conference pears, and white hedgerow flowers galore.*	£4.00 UNS/SGL

TROPHY
ARGENTINIAN RED

☆ **BROQUEL CABERNET SAUVIGNON 2002, BODEGAS TRAPICHE** MENDOZA – *Rich and weighty, with a smoky, tarry spiciness. Sleek and ripe, with classic Cabernet aromatic complexity.*	£7.00 HBJ
A CRUX 2001, BODEGAS O FOURNIER MENDOZA – *A wealth of fruit on the nose and endless layers of concentrated plum and blackberry on the palate.*	£16.20 SOM/FLA CCS/MOV NYW

GOLD
ARGENTINIAN RED

☆ **TRAPICHE OAK AGED SYRAH 2002, BODEGAS TRAPICHE** MENDOZA – *Creamy palate with sweet oak and ripe fruit. Loads of red berry and cassis. Deep, black, and solid.*	£7.00 HBJ
☆ **PAISAJE DE BARRANCAS 2001, FINCA FLICHMAN** MENDOZA – *Concentrated, deep, rich, and mature with lots of plum jam and spice. Long, intense finish.*	£10.60 FLY/SGL

SILVER
ARGENTINIAN RED

☆ **TRIVENTO SHIRAZ MALBEC 2003, CONCHA Y TORO** MENDOZA – *A deep pillow of damson and redcurrant fruit. A fresh, bright, and thirst-quenching wine from Argentina.*	£4.00 HOU/RAV RNS/GHL WRW
☆ **ELEMENTOS SHIRAZ MALBEC 2002, PEÑAFLOR** SAN JUAN – *A ripe, spicy nose, with ripe, but elegant, dark-cherry, and damson fruit on a big, chewy palate.*	£5.00 JSM
☆ **ETCHART PRIVADO SYRAH 2002, BODEGAS ETCHART** SALTA – *Rich chocolate and coffee bean aromas on the nose. Soft, sweet, and ripe with an elegant balance.*	£5.00 CAX

52 ARGENTINIAN RED SILVER

☆ **SANTA JULIA SHIRAZ 2003, FAMILIA ZUCCARDI** **MENDOZA** – *This vibrant wine has rich flavours of raspberries and strawberries and tones of smoke and leather.*	£5.00 SAF
☆ **PASCUAL TOSO MALBEC 2002, PASCUAL TOSO** **MENDOZA** – *Deep, with sweet mulberry and fruitcake aromas. Structured palate with fruit intensity and integrated tannins. Good length.*	£5.40 G&M/SWS WRW
☆ **RESERVA MERLOT 2002, NIETO SENETINER** **MENDOZA** – *Full and structured, with woody tannins, vegetal notes, and savoury currant and loganberry fruit on the medium-bodied palate.*	£6.30 FFW/HAX TRO/CPR INS
☆ **FINCA MONTE LINDO MALBEC 2002, LA CASA DEL REY** **MENDOZA** – *Mulberry scented with floral and spice notes. The palate is rich and moist with supple mouthfeel. Concentrated finish.*	£7.50 GSL
PASCUAL TOSO MALBEC RESERVA 2002, PASCUAL TOSO **MENDOZA** – *Perfumed violet, mulberry, and smoke notes. The palate is intense with rich fruit married to plump tannins.*	£9.00 SWS
NORTON MALBEC RESERVE 2002, BODEGAS NORTON **MENDOZA** – *Scented mulberry and violet nose, plus a lush and harmonious palate with soft blueberry fruit and velvety tannins.*	£9.30 CEB/VGN VIT/WSO WTS
PASSO DOBLE 2003, MASI **MENDOZA** – *A sweetly spiced oak basketful of juicy black-cherries. Hints of tar and mocha. Long and weighty.*	£9.30 VIT/CCS BWC
CATENA MALBEC 2002, BODEGA CATENA ZAPATA **MENDOZA** – *Great toastiness rises from the nose. Spicy, complex, and intense, with ripe boysenberry flavours and a tannic finish.*	£10.60 NYW/FLY BWL
PAISAJE DE TUPUNGATO 2001, FINCA FLICHMAN **MENDOZA** – *Deeply concentrated, with hedgerow fruit and powerful textured tree bark tannins. Full-bodied.*	£10.60 FLY/SGL
ISCAY 2001, BODEGAS TRAPICHE **MENDOZA** – *A bright vermilion colour. Rich, complex, intense smoky, berried fruit and grippy tannins underpin the soft, velvety fruit.*	£20.00 HBJ

ARGENTINIAN RED SILVER / BRONZE

MORA NEGRA FINCA MALBEC BONARDA 2002, FINCA LAS MORAS SAN JUAN – *Worn, sun-warmed saddle-leather and pepper feature on the nose. Fruit and wood tannins support its cherry fleshiness.*	£20.00 CRI
MALBEC 2001, BODEGA NOEMIA DE PATAGONIA PATAGONIA – *Wild briar, boysenberry, and violet aromas. Deep, inky palate with rich fruit intensity, silky tannins, and creamy oak.*	£57.30 NYW/LIB FLY

BRONZE
ARGENTINIAN RED

☆ **TRIVENTO CABERNET SAUVIGNON 2003, CONCHA Y TORO** MENDOZA – *The saturated purple colour complements the leafy nose of undergrowth, ink, and sweet fruit.*	£4.00 CYT
☆ **LA CONSULTA CABERNET SAUVIGNON 2002, FINCA LA CELIA** MENDOZA – *Mulberry scented wine with a lush fruit palate. The warming finish is balanced and clean.*	£4.50 RWM/BUC
☆ **LAVAQUE CABERNET SAUVIGNON 2003, BODEGAS FELIX LAVAQUE** SALTA – *This Cabernet Sauvignon's handsome brick-red colour is coupled with scents of olives and cherry fruit flavours.*	£5.00 VNO
☆ **PRIVADO MERLOT 2002, BODEGAS ETCHART** MENDOZA – *Clear, bright, garnet-red colour. Stewed plums, walnuts, and cherries line this Merlot's medium-bodied palate.*	£5.00 CAX
HIGH ALTITUDE MALBEC CABERNET 2003, BODEGAS ESCORIHUELA GASCON MENDOZA – *Tarry fruit on the nose. Firm and rich, with plenty of blueberries and a touch of toast.*	£5.40 ESL
NORTON BARBERA 2003, BODEGAS NORTON MENDOZA – *Summer pudding in a glass, with fresh, clean fruit balanced by hints of spice and a good length.*	£5.50 VIT/BWC
LA CONSULTA MALBEC 2002, LA REMONTA MENDOZA – *Dark, with raised blackberry and clove aromas. The palate is balanced with ample fruit, and soft tannic structure.*	£5.80 V&C/WOI CCS/RWM LIB/FLY

ARGENTINIAN RED BRONZE

SAN FELIPE ROBLE SANGIOVESE 2002, FAMILIA RUTINI Mendoza – Dark-prune flesh leads a velvet-smooth attack. Vanilla touches keep the fruit soft, sensual, and toothsome.	£6.00 C&D
ALTO CABERNET SAUVIGNON 2003, TERRAZAS DE LOS ANDES Mendoza – Juicy raspberries, strawberries, and blackcurrants spill from this Cabernet Sauvignon's fresh, vivacious, bright palate.	£6.20 BNK/FEN OWC
MENDOZA MALBEC 2003, ANUBIS Mendoza – Ripe with plum and damson aromas. The palate is thickly fruited and warmly spiced. Balanced finish.	£6.30 WIDELY AVAILABLE
TERRAZAS ALTO MALBEC 2003, TERRAZAS Mendoza – Flavours of blackcurrants, strawberries, and cherries. The wood is well-integrated into the vibrant fruit.	£6.30 BNK/FEN FLA/WES OWC WRW
TORINO COLECCIÓN MERLOT 2003, MICHEL TORINO Salta – The big, ripe, sweet nose is enhanced by a palate of spiced plum fruit. Smoky notes.	£6.70 FFW/NFW NYW/CVE HOH
ALTOS LAS HORMIGAS MALBEC 2002, ALTOS LAS HORMIGAS Mendoza – Sweet bilberry and tar aromas. The palate is lush with ripe fruit and velvety mouthfeel.	£6.80 NYW/LIB FLY
FINCA EL RETIRO SYRAH 2002, TITTARELLI Mendoza – Deep tar and berry nose. The palate is balanced and harmonious with fine tannins. Pure fruit finish.	£7.00 ENO
MALBEC RESERVA 2002, FINCA LAS MORAS San Juan – The palate is full-bodied and muscular, its ripe fruit displaying chocolatey notes.	£7.00 GOL
OAK CASK MALBEC 2002, BODEGAS TRAPICHE Mendoza – Nose has toast and spiced plum aromas. Palate shows ripe fruit with supple tannins. A clean, harmonious finish.	£7.00 HBJ
PREMIUM MALBEC 2002, BODEGA ALTA VISTA Mendoza – Dense, with perfumed mulberry and spice notes. The palate has layers of sweet fruit and supple tannins.	£7.50 L&W

ARGENTINIAN RED BRONZE 55

Wine	Price
VALENTIN BIANCHI FAMIGLIA 2002, VALENTIN BIANCHI Mendoza – *Perfumed with violet and mulberries. The palate is dense with blackberry richness. Supple finish.*	£8.00 CHN
FINCA EL RETIRO MALBEC RESERVA ESPECIAL 2002, TITTARELLI Mendoza – *Balanced, with overt berries and spice on the nose. Rich mouthfeel and warming finish.*	£9.00 ENO
Q CABERNET SAUVIGNON 2002, FAMILIA ZUCCARDI Mendoza – *Elegant with mint and cassis notes on the nose. Good fruit depth and a lick of spicy oak.*	£9.00 THI
SYRAH G 2001, BODEGAS GRAFFIGNA San Juan – *Big, chewy, balanced palate, with plenty of oak and a lingering finish. A rich chocolate, spicy fruit nose.*	£9.30 HAX
RESERVA CABERNET SAUVIGNON 2002, TERRAZAS DE LOS ANDES Mendoza – *Rich cassis fruit on nose and palate swathed in sultry coconut and caramel notes.*	£10.00 BNK/FLA
Q MALBEC 2001, FAMILIA ZUCCARDI Mendoza – *Plump, intense mulberry and tar perfume. The palate is packed with fruit and the tannins are well-integrated.*	£11.00 BOO
CLOS DE LOS SIETE 2002, DOURTHE KRESSMANN Mendoza – *Sweet, juicy mulberry fruit. Dense and dark, with intense tannins and inviting earthiness.*	£12.00 ODD
SUSANA BALBO MALBEC 2002, DOMINIO DEL PLATA Mendoza – *Leathery and elegant, the intense palate possesses a soy sauce savouriness.*	£13.00 WSO
GRAN CABERNET SAUVIGNON 1999, TERRAZAS DE LOS ANDES Mendoza – *Spicy, with a ripe nose. Chocolate and sweet brambles interwoven with creamy oak on the palate.*	£20.60 SEL/GGR P&R

SEAL OF APPROVAL
ARGENTINIAN RED

☆ **ASDA ARGENTINIAN MALBEC 2002, LA RIOJANA** FAMATINA VALLEY – *Strawberry and damson flavours with hints of tar, tree bark, liquorice, and leather.*	£3.50 ASD
☆ **CO-OP ARGENTINE MALBEC 2003, LA RIOJANA** LA RIOJA – *Deeply coloured and warming, with ripe leathery strawberry fruit.*	£4.00 CWS
☆ **ORIGIN MALBEC MERLOT 2003, TRIVENTO** MENDOZA – *Blackberries, prunes and mulberries spill from this robust, structured offering.*	£4.00 THS
☆ **SOMERFIELD ARGENTINE SANGIOVESE 2003, LA AGRICOLA** MENDOZA – *Bright, red-cherry fruit ensconced in melted chocolate and tea leaves.*	£4.00 SMF
☆ **TRIVENTO CABERNET SAUVIGNON MERLOT 2003, CONCHA Y TORO** MENDOZA – *Firm cassis, bright damsons and generous undergrowth notes.*	£4.00 CYT
☆ **TRIVENTO MALBEC 2003, CONCHA Y TORO** MENDOZA – *Hints of coal, tar, and earth add to the intense palate of damson fruit.*	£4.00 FOL /MNH FUL/SHJ THS
☆ **TRIVENTO MERLOT 2003, CONCHA Y TORO** MENDOZA – *A powerful attack of freshly picked little black plums and blueberry fruit.*	£4.00 CYT

FOR STOCKIST CODES turn to page 355. For regularly updated information about stockists and the International Wine Challenge, visit wineint.com. For a full glossary of wine terms and a complete free wine course, visit robertjoseph-onwine.com

AUSTRALIA

Not so long ago, Australia was often convincingly portrayed as the source of rich reds from the Barossa Valley, oaky Chardonnays, and reliable multi-regional blends – and not much else. This continent has undeniably grown-up into a true winemaking country with a wide variety of characterful regional styles. Western Australia and Tasmania, for example, are both playing a huge role in the broadening of the Australian range, but so is the greater availability of wines made from grapes like Riesling (often in screwcaps), Verdelho, and Durif; and innovative blends like d'Arenberg's Tempranillo-Grenache which expand the theme laid down by the traditional Cabernet-Shirazes.

TROPHY
AUSTRALIAN WHITE

Wine	Price
BROOKLAND VALLEY RESERVE CHARDONNAY 2002, BROOKLAND VALLEY VINEYARD WESTERN AUSTRALIA – *Green pepper and apple notes. This wine is crammed to the hilt with citrus fruit. Knife-edge acidity on the finish.*	£20.00 ODD

GOLD
AUSTRALIAN WHITE

Wine	Price
☆ **TESCO FINEST GREAT SOUTHERN RIESLING 2002, HOWARD PARK** WESTERN AUSTRALIA – *Honeyed lemon flavours and developing kerosene aromas. Crunchy acidity lends purity and bite.*	£5.50 TOS
☆ **BROWN BROTHERS LIMITED RELEASE RIESLING 1999, BROWN BROTHERS MILAWA** VICTORIA – *Kerosene notes and droplets of honey on the nose. Depth and complexity. Very fine, and bristling with laser-like acidity.*	£6.30 EVI/NRW
☆ **WILLOW BRIDGE SAUVIGNON BLANC SEMILLON 2003, WILLOW BRIDGE ESTATE** WESTERN AUSTRALIA – *This classic white displays broad waxy width and crisply acidic, zippy, grassy lemons.*	£7.20 FLY/WRW SGL

58 AUSTRALIAN WHITE GOLD

★ **TESCO DENMAN VINEYARD HUNTER ESTATE RESERVE SEMILLON 2002, SIMEON WINES** NEW SOUTH WALES – *Notes of lime cordial impart a sweetish breadth to the palate. Smooth, with many layers of citrus fruit and minerals.*	£8.00 TOS
☆ **VINEYARD SELECT CLARE VALLEY RIESLING 2003, ANGOVE'S** SOUTH AUSTRALIA – *Lemon meringue pie and l ime peel flavours are clean, bright, and fresh, and emphasized by zippy acidity.*	£8.00 D&D
★ **NEPENTHE SAUVIGNON BLANC 2003, NEPENTHE WINES** SOUTH AUSTRALIA – *This wine has notes of apple, gooseberry, asparagus, capsicum, and nettles in a wondrous multiplicity of layering.*	£8.30 WIDELY AVAILABLE
☆ **MOUNT BARKER RIESLING 2003, PLANTAGENET** WESTERN AUSTRALIA – *Floral overtones and passion-fruit flavours. This palate is scored with minerals and acidity.*	£8.40 WIDELY AVAILABLE
☆ **STARVEDOG LANE NO OAK CHARDONNAY 2003, RAVENSWOOD LANE** SOUTH AUSTRALIA – *From the cool Adelaide Hills. Creamy, with lifted grassy notes. Elegant and pure, with steely varietal expression.*	£10.10 EDC/FFW NRW/NFW CPR/NYW
☆ **VASSE FELIX CHARDONNAY 2003, VASSE FELIX** WESTERN AUSTRALIA – *There's a mineral freshness to the juicy fruit bursting with peach and apple character. Zippy acidity. Modern and beautifully made.*	£10.20 HAX/NFW TWM/NY W MWW
ART SERIES RIESLING 2003, LEEUWIN ESTATE WESTERN AUSTRALIA – *Lime blossoms, gooseberries, and apples. Elegant restraint, bright acidity, and a long finish.*	£12.70 SOM/RWM WTS
DEVILS LAIR MARGARET RIVER CHARDONNAY 2002, SOUTHCORP WESTERN AUSTRALIA – *Creamy richness with buttery texture and rich, rounded oak. Tropical fruit character with melon character. Well-integrated, toasty oak.*	£14.40 SOM/NYW
LEO BURING CLARE VALLEY RIESLING 2003, SOUTHCORP SOUTH AUSTRALIA – *Fine, racy, long, and elegant. The lime and lemon zest charm and the purity of fruit stand out.*	£15.00 TOS
PENFOLDS BIN 00A RESERVE CHARDONNAY 2000, SOUTHCORP SOUTH AUSTRALIA – *Laden with fresh white-peach fruit and lemony notes. A rich, buttery attack is lifted with lively acidity.*	£18.00 PEF

AUSTRALIAN WHITE GOLD / SILVER

THE VIRGILIUS EDEN VALLEY VIOGNIER 2002, YALUMBA South Australia – *Softly textured, concentrated apricot fruit. A subtle hint of violets coyly beckons. Great wine; both individual and typical.*	£19.30 WIDELY AVAILABLE
ART SERIES CHARDONNAY 2000, LEEUWIN ESTATE Western Australia – *A rich, spicy style with aromas of cloves and a yeasty creaminess. The leesy complexity is enhanced by understated oak.*	£36.70 SOM/RWM WTS

SILVER
AUSTRALIAN WHITE

☆ **BETHANY BAROSSA SEMILLON 2002, BETHANY WINES** South Australia – *Perfumed, weighty, and tropical. Lively, this Semillon's waxy palate possesses plenty of ripe-green fruit.*	£7.00 PON
☆ **MAGNUS RIESLING 2003, LEASINGHAM WINES** South Australia – *Rich, with loads of lemon curd and lime marmalade fruit flavour. Lavish sweet sherbet on the finish.*	£7.00 JSM
☆ **KNAPPSTEIN RIESLING 2003, KNAPPSTEIN WINES** South Australia – *Vigorous, with a zesty palate of grapefruit, limes and lemons. A haunting hint of sweetness on the nose.*	£7.30 NFW/ODD MWW
☆ **TRYST SAUVIGNON BLANC SEMILLON 2003, NEPENTHE WINES** South Australia – *The talented team at Nepenthe craft a winner. Earthy hints underscore weighty cut grass and candied lemon fruit.*	£7.30 EDC/NFW OZW/SWS ODD/JSM
☆ **VICTORIA RIESLING 2003, BEST'S WINES** Victoria – *Packed with honeyed passion-fruit, lime, pineapple, and spice. The take-home message: depth and great clarity.*	£7.30 JNW/HOT
EDEN VALLEY RIESLING 2003, ELDERTON WINES South Australia – *Crisp, with zesty lime and lemon sherbet flavours and a resonant kerosene note.*	£7.70 FLY/ODD
WINDY PEAK RIESLING 2003, DE BORTOLI WINES Victoria – *Excellent weight and layers of flavour, with spicy pear, apricot, lime, and peach. Complex, with a stealthy length.*	£7.70 UNS/GHL NFW/FLY WRW

AUSTRALIAN WHITE SILVER

BANWELL FARM RIESLING 2003, ST HALLETT WINES SOUTH AUSTRALIA – *Steely, with minerality supporting the fleshy lemon and apple fruit. Honeyed. Lime juice flavours.*	£8.00 M&S
NINTH ISLAND SAUVIGNON BLANC 2003, PIPERS BROOK VINEYARD TASMANIA – *Leafy, youthful, taut whitecurrant aromas. A hint of sweetness, discreet peach flavours, tropical notes, and zippy acidity. Very attractive.*	£8.10 WIDELY AVAILABLE
CLARE VALLEY RIESLING 2003, TIM ADAMS WINES SOUTH AUSTRALIA – *Perfumed with minerals, lemons, and orange flowers. Acacia honey flavours and laser-focused lime-juice acidity. Deeply elegant.*	£8.90 AUC/NFW TOS/OZW
MARGARET RIVER CHARDONNAY 2002, EVANS & TATE WESTERN AUSTRALIA – *Delicate apple blossom scents and clean, freshly sliced white apple and juicy peach flesh on the palate.*	£9.00 BNK/HPW SMF
PEWSEY VALE VINEYARD EDEN VALLEY RIESLING 2003, YALUMBA SOUTH AUSTRALIA – *Young and racy. Still a little restrained, manifested as elegance rather than insolence. It will blossom into something remarkable.*	£9.10 BEN/NFW NYW/ODD
UNWOODED CHARDONNAY 2003, CAPE JAFFA WINES SOUTH AUSTRALIA – *Elegant peach and citrus fruit; crushed almonds, cashews, powdery, and meadow-sweet flowers.*	£9.90 HAX/VDV
COLDSTREAM HILLS CHARDONNAY 2003, SOUTHCORP VICTORIA – *Warm notes of vanilla and coconut, walnuts, and butter. Approachable, open, and dripping with tropical fruit.*	£10.00 NYW
TAMAR RIDGE RIESLING 2003, TAMAR RIDGE WINES TASMANIA – *Key lime pie notes on the nose. A palate of crisp apples. Lively, tangy, sophisticated, and bright.*	£10.00 OZW/NYW
THE LUCKY LIZARD CHARDONNAY 2003, D'ARENBERG SOUTH AUSTRALIA – *Vivid buttered toast aromas are more than matched by powerful pineapple, kiwi, and white guava flavours.*	£10.00 ODD
EDEN VALLEY VIOGNIER 2003, YALUMBA SOUTH AUSTRALIA – *Warm alcohol weight and charry oak notes over apricot and rose-scented fruit. A very long flavour profile.*	£10.30 WIDELY AVAILABLE

AUSTRALIAN WHITE SILVER

PEWSEY VALE THE CONTOURS MUSEUM RESERVE EDEN VALLEY RIESLING 1999, YALUMBA **SOUTH AUSTRALIA** – Full-on, dry, ripe style with lemon pie, lime fruit, and layers of evolved kerosene notes adding depth.	£10.80 WIDELY AVAILABLE
THE TUARTS CHARDONNAY 2003, PAUL CONTI WINES **WESTERN AUSTRALIA** – Citrus and tropical fruit nose. A balanced palate of rich fruit, elegant mineral acidity, and toasty vanilla oak.	£11.50 ARM/ELV
CRAWFORD RIVER RIESLING 2001, CRAWFORD RIVER **VICTORIA** – Spiced, lifted lemon-lime fruit with a hint of petrol on the nose.	£11.90 VDV/J&B
VOYAGER CHARDONNAY 2001, VOYAGER ESTATE **WESTERN AUSTRALIA** – Spiced and tightly knit, with plenty of coconut, butter, ripe melon, and grapefruit aromas and flavours. Mouthfilling and long.	£12.50 NYW/J&B ODD
HEATHVALE CHARDONNAY 2002, HEATHVALE VINEYARD **SOUTH AUSTRALIA** – Tinged with green and lifted by mineral tones, its crisp citrus fruit broadening out on the finish.	£13.00 ORB
CAPE MENTELLE CHARDONNAY 2002, CAPE MENTELLE **WESTERN AUSTRALIA** – Rich and buttery, with toast and biscuit aromas. The palate displays concentrated fruit and mouthwatering acidity. Elegant.	£13.80 WIDELY AVAILABLE
HOWARD PARK CHARDONNAY 2002, HOWARD PARK WINES **WESTERN AUSTRALIA** – Opulent nose of rich buttery fruit. The palate has ripe citrus fruit and good acidity. Concentrated finish.	£13.80 JNW/WRK SOM/NYW FLY/BWL
LEO BURING EDEN VALLEY RIESLING 2003, SOUTHCORP **SOUTH AUSTRALIA** – Restrained and elegant, with lemon drop and lime fruit. Intense fruit offers a long finish.	£15.00 TOS
PENFOLDS AGED RESERVE CLARE RIESLING 1998, SOUTHCORP **SOUTH AUSTRALIA** – The nose is replete with honeysuckle and quince blossom. The palate has sharp yet honeyed citrus fruit. Balanced.	£15.00 PEF
M3 VINEYARD CHARDONNAY 2002, SHAW & SMITH **SOUTH AUSTRALIA** – Buttery and mouthfilling, with vivid peach flavours, hints of star anise and cleansing green crabapple acidity.	£15.80 WIDELY AVAILABLE

AUSTRALIAN WHITE SILVER / BRONZE

STONIER RESERVE CHARDONNAY 2002, STONIER WINES VICTORIA – *Splendid vibrancy, depth, fullness, and complexity. Serious, with a wide spectrum of citrus, oak, and minerals.*	£17.40 V&C/NYW
PENFOLDS YATTARNA CHARDONNAY 2000, SOUTHCORP SOUTH AUSTRALIA – *Nuances of oregano and thyme on the nose. The creamy lemon palate is rich, spiced, balanced, and lengthy.*	£37.60 SOM/NYW WTS

BRONZE
AUSTRALIAN WHITE

☆ **BILLYGOAT CHARDONNAY 2003, CHIVERTON ESTATE** NEW SOUTH WALES – *This placid wine possesses overtones of butterscotch, vanilla, and bags of citrus fruit. Long, saturated palate.*	£4.00 NFW
☆ **MHV SCENIC RIDGE SEMILLON, REDELLO WINES** SOUTH AUSTRALIA – *Waxy and lemony, with a slight spritzy lift. Lively, yet with enough weight to impart great balance.*	£4.20 BNK/MHV
☆ **CO-OP AUSTRALIAN LIME TREE CHARDONNAY 2003, ANGOVE'S** SOUTH AUSTRALIA – *Light grassy notes rise from the nose. Vibrant and deep, its apple flavours are dusted with vanilla.*	£4.30 CWS
☆ **TORTOISESHELL BAY SEMILLON SAUVIGNON 2003, CASELLA ESTATE** SOUTH AUSTRALIA – *Developed yet restrained. The lemon and lime palate has good richness and zingy acidity.*	£4.40 RAV/SMF NYW/SWS
☆ **DB BIG RIVERS VERDELHO 2003, DE BORTOLI WINES** NEW SOUTH WALES – *Pear-drops scent the nose. The palate is clean and light-bodied, with a pleasing texture.*	£5.00 BOR/SAF
☆ **KANGAS LEAP CHARDONNAY 2003, RIVERINA ESTATES** NEW SOUTH WALES – *The palate is harmonious and balanced, its range of citrus, oatmeal, and honey flavours beguiling indeed.*	£5.00 VER
☆ **NUDE UNOAKED CHARDONNAY 2002, CHIVERTON ESTATE** NEW SOUTH WALES – *Pineapple and green apple flavours spill from this clean wine. Refined and fresh, with a dry lemony finish.*	£5.00 PLB

AUSTRALIAN WHITE BRONZE 63

☆ **VARIETAL RANGE CHARDONNAY 2003, BRL HARDY** **SOUTH AUSTRALIA** – *Spicy, elegant, youthful and crisp, with floral tones and juicy pineapple fruit.*	£5.00 SMF/TOS JSM
FIRST STEP CHARDONNAY 2003, STEP WINES AUSTRALIA **SOUTH AUSTRALIA** – *Pineapple and guava flavours. Scents of rosehip, ruby grapefruit, and new-mown hay.*	£5.20 WRK/NFW NYW/WTS SWS
BROWN BROTHERS DRY MUSCAT 2003, BROWN BROTHERS MILAWA **VICTORIA** – *Candied lemon nose. Fresh acidity and light perfume. A mint twist on the finish.*	£5.30 WIDELY AVAILABLE
OXFORD LANDING CHARDONNAY 2003, YALUMBA **SOUTH AUSTRALIA** – *Pure fruit nose showing melon and apple notes. The palate is clean and linear. Fresh acid streak on the finish.*	£5.40 WIDELY AVAILABLE
HARDY'S STAMP OF AUSTRALIA SEMILLON CHARDONNAY 2003, BRL HARDY **SOUTH AUSTRALIA** – *Buttery, waxy texture and seductive baked apple flavours. A whisper of oak and pretty honeyed scents.*	£5.60 UNS/SMF FEN/TOS JSM
LINDEMANS BIN 65 CHARDONNAY 2003, SOUTHCORP **SOUTH AUSTRALIA** – *Notes of vanilla and caramel waft from the toasty nose. Ripe honeydew melon flavours sing on the palate.*	£5.80 WIDELY AVAILABLE
BEELGARA UNOAKED CHARDONNAY 2003, BEELGARA ESTATE **NEW SOUTH WALES** – *Pale starry-gold colour. Pure, clean, and balanced, with an attractive, unfettered peach nose and palate.*	£5.90 FFW/WPR NFW/CVE
BETHANY BAROSSA RIESLING 2003, BETHANY WINES **SOUTH AUSTRALIA** – *Delicate sweet flowers appear on the nose. The palate sings with refreshing lime fruit flavours. Lengthy finish.*	£6.00 PON/CRS MWW
HOUGHTON HWB 2003, HOUGHTON **WESTERN AUSTRALIA** – *Pale straw green hints. Deep peach and greengage fruit with delicious hints of marshmallow and fresh lime juice acidity.*	£6.00 BNK/FEN WSO
KINGSTON SELECTION CHARDONNAY 2002, KINGSTON ESTATE WINES **SOUTH AUSTRALIA** – *Concentration of soft, juicy pear fruit in the mouth. Hints of butterscotch. Tropical notes.*	£6.00 RVA

64 AUSTRALIAN WHITE BRONZE

ROCK CHARDONNAY 2003, HANGING ROCK WINERY **VICTORIA** – *The nose has a grassy aroma. Crisp, juicy green apples have a touch of minerality in the mouth.*	£6.00 THI
UNWOODED CHARDONNAY 2003, SERAFINO WINES **SOUTH AUSTRALIA** – *Vivid lime cordial and white peach scents and flavours radiate from the ripe palate.*	£6.00 NFW
WILLANDRA GENTLE PRESS CHARDONNAY 2003, TRENTHAM ESTATE **SOUTH AUSTRALIA** – *Vibrant and aromatic, this is an assemblage of peaches and apricots and pear-drop essence. Just off-dry.*	£6.00 SOM/CCS
POACHER'S BLEND 2003, ST HALLETT WINES **SOUTH AUSTRALIA** – *A powerful, focused, and vivid wine, with racy acidity and a lively rhubarb character. Long.*	£6.10 WIDELY AVAILABLE
EDWARD'S LAKE UNWOODED CHARDONNAY 2003, RIVERINA WINES **NEW SOUTH WALES** – *Intense, deep tropical lime and lemon flavours. An open-knit, round, approachable wine with an ochre colour.*	£6.20 LAI
NOTTAGE HILL CHARDONNAY 2003, BRL HARDY **SOUTH AUSTRALIA** – *Kiwi, satsuma, and grapefruit palate with a touch of banoffee sweetness. Flavoursome, mouthwatering, and big.*	£6.30 UNS/SMF FEN/TOS JSM
CV UNWOODED CHARDONNAY 2003, CAPEL VALE WINES **WESTERN AUSTRALIA** – *Crunchy green fruit bursts on the palate. Juicy, mouthwatering, and attractive.*	£6.50 D&D
DEEP RIVER OAKED CHARDONNAY 2003, RIVERINA WINES **NEW SOUTH WALES** – *The restrained nose is somewhat green. The palate is full, lush and warming, with a lifted, pretty finish.*	£6.50 LAI
ELEMENT CLASSIC WHITE 2003, SANDALFORD **WESTERN AUSTRALIA** – *Granny Smith apples and zesty lemons. Freshly cut grass and spice.*	£6.50 HAX
FAIRLEIGH ESTATE SINGLE VINEYARD CHARDONNAY 2002, WITHER HILLS **SOUTH AUSTRALIA** – *Abundant lemon and mandarin fruit is scored by a firm jolt of acidity. Very ripe, with honeyed notes.*	£6.50 MWW

AUSTRALIAN WHITE BRONZE 65

WOLF BLASS SOUTH AUSTRALIA RIESLING 2003, BERINGER BLASS SOUTH AUSTRALIA – *Golden green. Some evolution is apparent. Concentrated soft lime fruit flavours and toasty oak.*	£6.50 SMF/ODD
DEEN VAT 6 VERDELHO 2003, DE BORTOLI WINES NEW SOUTH WALES – *Pure quince fruit on the nose. The palate has a basketful of ripe green citrus fruit. Balanced.*	£6.70 BNK/GHL NFW/FLY INS/WRW
PENFOLDS KOONUNGA HILL CHARDONNAY 2003, SOUTHCORP SOUTH AUSTRALIA – *Buttery and broad, with a soft texture, hints of white pepper, and ripe tropical mangosteen and melon flavours.*	£6.70 WIDELY AVAILABLE
ANNIE'S LANE SEMILLON 2003, BERINGER BLASS SOUTH AUSTRALIA – *Fresh, attractive, and impressively tight-knit, with musky hints and ripe citrus fruit fatness all the way through.*	£7.00 ODD
DEAKIN SELECT CHARDONNAY 2002, WINGARA WINE GROUP VICTORIA – *Bready-yeast, cream, and tropical fruit characteristics shine on the nose and palate of this Chardonnay.*	£7.00 FXT/BWL
HOUGHTON VERDELHO 2003, HOUGHTON WESTERN AUSTRALIA – *Alluring tropical tones and notes of cream. Rich ripe citrus and green melon flavours.*	£7.00 BNK
RUTHERGLEN ESTATES MARSANNE 2003, RUTHERGLEN ESTATES VICTORIA – *Freshly mown hay scents. An appealing mouthcoating waxy texture. Grippy white fruit flavours.*	£7.00 NTD
SKUTTLEBUTT SAUVIGNON SEMILLON CHARDONNAY 2003, STELLA BELLA WINES WESTERN AUSTRALIA – *The nose is packed with pink blossom, peaches, and starfruit. Ripe, with good intensity and a hint of sweetness.*	£7.00 JSM
THE MILL VERDELHO 2003, WINDOWRIE ESTATE NEW SOUTH WALES – *Green, herbaceous, and minerally, with apple and citrus and a sprinking of pepper on the oily palate.*	£7.00 NRW/CPR INS
YALUMBA Y VIOGNIER 2003, YALUMBA SOUTH AUSTRALIA – *Pale-straw yellow. A fresh, ripe nose of sherbetty citrus fruit. Tangy and crisp, with good varietal definition.*	£7.10 WIDELY AVAILABLE

66 AUSTRALIAN WHITE BRONZE

Wine	Price / Stockist
AMBERLEY ESTATE SAUVIGNON BLANC 2003, AMBERLEY ESTATE WESTERN AUSTRALIA – *Very ripe tropical kiwi, passion-fruit, and guava elements. Herbal overtones. Full-bodied.*	£7.20 VDV/MWW
OLD WELL SEMILLON SAUVIGNON BLANC 2003, HILLSTOWE WINES SOUTH AUSTRALIA – *Green fruit melts into lanolin on the palate. Elegant and off-dry, with a long finish.*	£7.20 LAI
TAHBILK MARSANNE 2002, TAHBILK WINES VICTORIA – *Notes of grass, sweet orange melon, and honey lace the nose. The mouth fills with flavours of passion-fruit and rambutan.*	£7.20 VDV/WRK FLA
UNWOODED CHARDONNAY 2002, CHAPEL HILL WINERY SOUTH AUSTRALIA – *Lemon yellow. Pronounced tropical lime and grapefruit character. Elegant crisp finish.*	£7.30 TAU/AUC NFW/TOS FLA/OZW
CARLYLE MARSANNE 2002, CARLYLE WINES VICTORIA – *Pungent guava and sweet stone fruit elements. Sweet oak lends flavours of cashews to the long, weighty palate.*	£7.50 BON
CARLYLE RIESLING 2003, CARLYLE WINES VICTORIA – *Spicy apple and melon fruit on the nose and a rather crisp, fresh, approachable palate. User-friendly.*	£7.50 BON
SEXTONS ACRE UNWOODED CHARDONNAY 2003, WIRRA WIRRA VINEYARDS SOUTH AUSTRALIA – *Pure citrus and crabapple nose leads to an uncluttered palate of ripe fruit streaked with mouthwatering acidity.*	£7.50 VIT
ANNIE'S LANE RIESLING 2003, BERINGER BLASS SOUTH AUSTRALIA – *Elegant greengage and lime fruit. Bright and pure and perfectly balanced.*	£7.70 NYW/ODD
RIDDOCH CHARDONNAY 2002, WINGARA WINE GROUP SOUTH AUSTRALIA – *Butterscotch aromas and lemon flavours. Enticing velvety mouthfeel braced by brisk oak tannins.*	£7.70 NFW/FLY
MADFISH CHARDONNAY 2003, HOWARD PARK WINES WESTERN AUSTRALIA – *Rich Russet apple and melon nose. A glycerine texture, zippy acidity, and powerful citrus flavours.*	£7.80 WIDELY AVAILABLE

AUSTRALIAN WHITE BRONZE 67

MADFISH SEMILLON SAUVIGNON BLANC 2003, HOWARD PARK WINES WESTERN AUSTRALIA – *Passion-fruit and lychee aromas dance on the nose. Rich deep lemon and orange flavours fill the mouth.*	£7.80 JNW/RNS SOM/FLY BWL
MCLAREN VALE VERDELHO 2003, CHAPEL HILL WINERY SOUTH AUSTRALIA – *Rich tropical fruit with a glaze of caramel on the nose. Full and buttery, with melon and grapefruit flavours.*	£7.90 AUC/NFW FLA/OZW
ANNIE'S LANE CHARDONNAY 2003, BERINGER BLASS SOUTH AUSTRALIA – *Pineapple and vanilla pod nose. Sweet subtle oak wends its way through the ruby grapefruit palate. A class act.*	£8.00 ODD
BAROSSA VALLEY ESTATE CHARDONNAY 2002, BAROSSA VALLEY ESTATE SOUTH AUSTRALIA – *Soft stone fruit with buttery tones on the nose. Ripe melon and nectarine palate with a spicy finish.*	£8.00 CNT
EDEN VALLEY CHARDONNAY 2003, YALUMBA SOUTH AUSTRALIA – *Leesy, toasty aromas dance over the glass. Crisp, spicy, and balanced, with a vivid honey and lemon palate.*	£8.00 HOU/VIT NFW/NYW
JAMIESONS RUN CHARDONNAY 2003, BERINGER BLASS SOUTH AUSTRALIA – *A fragrant, richly textured, and focused wine, with warmth and good balance. Zippy and long.*	£8.00 MRN
SALTRAM BAROSSA CHARDONNAY 2003, BERINGER BLASS SOUTH AUSTRALIA – *Fresh lemons and notes of resin. Subtle aromatic oak, juicy fruit and excellent integration.*	£8.00 WFB
☆ **TESCO DENMAN VINEYARD HUNTER CHARDONNAY 2002, SIMEON WINES** NEW SOUTH WALES – *The restrained buttery nose complements a palate of vanilla pods, tangy starfruit, and Conference pear flavours.*	£8.00 TOS
WAKEFIELD ESTATE CHARDONNAY 2003, WAKEFIELD ESTATE SOUTH AUSTRALIA – *Young, fresh, weighty nectarine and melon fruit on the nose. The palate is laden with peaches and roast nuts.*	£8.00 EDC/WPR NFW/OZW SWS/WRW
WIRRA WIRRA WATERVALE RIESLING 2003, WIRRA WIRRA VINEYARDS SOUTH AUSTRALIA – *A lift of lemon and new mown hay on the nose. Zippy, with plenty of fresh acidity.*	£8.00 ODD

AUSTRALIAN WHITE BRONZE

ALKOOMI RIESLING 2003, ALKOOMI WINES **WESTERN AUSTRALIA** – *Zippy and fresh with restrained lime fruit character, a touch of apple peel and a sherbet finish.*	£8.30 BNK/JOB LAY
FAMILY RESERVE CHARDONNAY 2003, DE BORTOLI WINES **NEW SOUTH WALES** – *Honey and citrus peel notes hover over the nose. The weighty palate is loaded with ripe, sweet fruit.*	£8.30 LAI
UNWOODED CHARDONNAY 2003, NEPENTHE WINES **SOUTH AUSTRALIA** – *Good intensity and weight. Persistent crunchy green berries and white-fleshed peach fruit.*	£8.40 EDC/NFW SWS/ODD
BIN 7 RIESLING 2003, LEASINGHAM WINES **SOUTH AUSTRALIA** – *Greengages and peaches, with a light touch of lime and citrus. Lively and bright, with delicate elderflower touches.*	£8.50 NFW/WTS
BREMERTON VERDELHO 2003, BREMERTON **SOUTH AUSTRALIA** – *Pears and pineapples appear on the nose and palate. Round and flavoursome, with a mouthwatering quality.*	£8.50 WIDELY AVAILABLE
PETER LEHMANN RIESLING 2003, PETER LEHMANN WINES **SOUTH AUSTRALIA** – *Lime zest spritz and aromas of kerosene on the nose. Saturated with fruit. Very good balance and warmth.*	£8.50 EDC/G&M
STELLA BELLA SEMILLON SAUVIGNON 2003, STELLA BELLA WINES **WESTERN AUSTRALIA** – *Hints of sweetness grace the very soft lemon and gooseberry fruit. Touches of chalky minerality.*	£8.50 NFW/CCS ALL
STRATHBOGIE RANGES CHARDONNAY 2002, HANGING ROCK WINERY **VICTORIA** – *The creamy nose sports roast nut and peach aromas. The palate is a sultry array of apricots, honey, and flowers.*	£8.50 THI
TREVELEN FARM RIESLING 2001, TREVELEN FARM **WESTERN AUSTRALIA** – *Pungent aromas abound: elderflower, lemon custard, lime, and some classic petrolly notes. Spritzy and lean.*	£8.50 ROG
CLARE VALLEY SEMILLON 2002, TIM ADAMS WINES **SOUTH AUSTRALIA** – *A bit of sherbet on the nose, and a vivid citrus palate with creamy, toasty oak.*	£8.70 AUC/WSO NFW/TOS OZW MWW

AUSTRALIAN WHITE BRONZE 69

HUNTER VALLEY CHARDONNAY 2002, ALLANDALE WINES New South Wales – *Bright gold, with delicate honeyed peach flavours and a nose of flowers and cashew nuts.*	£8.70 AUC/OZW MOV
STELLA BELLA SAUVIGNON BLANC 2003, STELLA BELLA WINES Western Australia – *The cool Margaret River climate encourages the very pure, herby peachy fruit character and freshness.*	£8.70 NFW/ALL
CAPEL VALE VERDELHO 2003, CAPEL VALE WINES Western Australia – *Freshly sliced pineapple aromas and flavours ooze from this mouthwatering wine.*	£8.80 WRW
GREAT WESTERN RIESLING 2003, BEST'S WINES Victoria – *Lime and spicy baked apple aromas on the nose. A rich, spicy palate with depth and zesty style.*	£8.90 JNW/VDV FLA/CCS HOT
CAPE JAFFA CARDONNAY 2002, CAPE JAFFA WINES South Australia – *Smooth and fresh, with good complexity and loads of sweetly ripe fruit. Textured lemon pith structure.*	£9.00 VDV
CAPE JAFFA SAUVIGNON BLANC 2003, CAPE JAFFA WINES South Australia – *Pale gold, with a nose of asparagus and red bell peppers. Warming, with taut herbaceous notes.*	£9.00 HAX/VDV
CAPEL VALE RIESLING 2003, CAPEL VALE WINES Western Australia – *Lemon meringue pie notes and a developing petrolly nose. Complex, stylish, and approachable.*	£9.00 D&D
CAPEL VALE SAUVIGNON BLANC SEMILLON 2003, CAPEL CALE WINES Western Australia – *Highly herbal, with green fruit and capsicum notes. Bracing acidity balances and supports the rich flesh.*	£9.00 D&D
GULF STATION SEMILLON SAUVIGNON BLANC 2003, DE BORTOLI WINES Victoria – *Liquorice, spice, and pears appear on the nose; the tight, bright, elegant fruit flavours last and last.*	£9.00 NFW
HUNTER VALLEY SEMILLON 2003, BROKENWOOD New South Wales – *Very pale, with a pronounced lemon and lime character which criss-crosses the palate and lasts for the duration.*	£9.10 VDV/TAU MOV/NYW LIB/FLY

AUSTRALIAN WHITE BRONZE

Wine	Price / Availability
ZERK SEMILLON 2002, GRANT BURGE WINES SOUTH AUSTRALIA – *Lemon sherbet assails the nose. The palate has lots of lime zest and hints of toast.*	£9.10 NFW/RWM FLY/WRW
CAPE JAFFA CHARDONNAY 2003, CAPE JAFFA WINES SOUTH AUSTRALIA – *Complex, lifted, and mineral, with a firm, spicy crushed sultana character. Powerful and warm.*	£9.20 HAX/VDV
PREMIUM VERDELHO 2003, SANDALFORD WESTERN AUSTRALIA – *Mineral touches grace the green fruit nose. The palate has some complexity, zippy acidity, and a lasting finish.*	£9.20 HAX/NYW
PALANDRI CHARDONNAY 2001, PALANDRI WINES WESTERN AUSTRALIA – *Toasty oak laces this lemony wine. Intense concentration, hints of shredded coconut and a long juicy finish.*	£9.40 EDC/VIT
FONTY'S POOL CHARDONNAY 2001, FONTY'S POOL VINEYARDS WESTERN AUSTRALIA – *Hints of peat, herbs, and spices. Citrus-infused flavours. Concentrated, integrated, and long.*	£9.60 EDC/FFW NRW/CPR BOO
NEPENTHE RIESLING 2003, NEPENTHE WINES SOUTH AUSTRALIA – *Round and citrussy, with a burst of apple fruit flavour. Lime zest overtones lift the fruit.*	£9.60 EDC/NFW OZW/WTS SWS/ODD
UNWOODED CHARDONNAY 2003, SCARPANTONI ESTATE SOUTH AUSTRALIA – *Ripe melon, apricot, and peach flavours. Fine lime-zest acidity adds to the tropical richness.*	£9.60 LAI
UNOAKED CHARDONNAY 2003, SHAW & SMITH SOUTH AUSTRALIA – *Intense tropical passion-fruit aromas on the nose. Apples, almonds, and bananas flavour the zesty palate. The finish is long.*	£9.90 WIDELY AVAILABLE
ANNIE'S LANE COPPERTRAIL RIESLING 2003, BERINGER BLASS SOUTH AUSTRALIA – *Fresh and lively. Sicilian lemons and flowers grace the nose and palate of this lengthy wine.*	£10.00 ODD
EDEN VALLEY VIOGNIER SPECIAL RELEASE 2002, YALUMBA SOUTH AUSTRALIA – *A profusion of varietal flavours: stone fruit and apricot notes, flowers, and spice. Warming finish.*	£10.00 WTS

AUSTRALIAN WHITE BRONZE

GREEN POINT CHARDONNAY 2002, GREEN POINT **VICTORIA** – *Inviting pineapple and banana scents rise from the clean, clear nose. Very tropical, with a fresh youthful character. Light toast.*	£10.00 BNK/TAU
SHAW & SMITH SAUVIGNON BLANC 2003, SHAW & SMITH **SOUTH AUSTRALIA** – *Herbaceous: gooseberries and nettles on nose and palate. Good balance, hints of sweetness and crisp acidity.*	£10.00 WIDELY AVAILABLE
WAVECREST RIESLING 2003, NORFOLK RISE VINEYARD **TASMANIA** – *Spicy lime flavours and apricot fruit. The Wavecrest displays a fine cool-climate freshness together with good ripeness.*	£10.00 VGN
WOLF BLASS PRESIDENTS SELECTION CHARDONNAY 2003, BERINGER BLASS **SOUTH AUSTRALIA** – *Substantially weighty citrus fruit wrestles with powerful oak on this warm, brisk, intoxicating wine.*	£10.00 SMF/FEN WTS/ODD
ROSEMOUNT ESTATE SHOW RESERVE HUNTER VALLEY CHARDONNAY 2002, SOUTHCORP **NEW SOUTH WALES** – *Apples and sweet oak array the nose and palate. This is a seductive, full, ripe wine.*	£10.10 UNS/WTS
ESTATE GEWÜRZTRAMINER 2003, PIPERS BROOK VINEYARD **TASMANIA** – *The pleasant nose has peaches, mangoes, melons, and guava. Ripe, with soft acidity and a weighty structure.*	£10.30 FFW/HOU WRK/SOM CPR/NYW
HOWARD PARK RIESLING 2003, HOWARD PARK WINES **WESTERN AUSTRALIA** – *Floral and citric, with limes, starfruit, pear, and blossom characteristics.*	£10.40 JNW/NYW FLY/BWL
TINTARA CHARDONNAY 2001, BRL HARDY **SOUTH AUSTRALIA** – *Yeasty elements on the nose. Banana, lemon, and pineapple fruit flavours are shrouded in buttery oak.*	£10.50 CNT
PETALUMA HANLIN HILL RIESLING 2003, PETALUMA AUSTRALIA **SOUTH AUSTRALIA** – *Absolutely classic. Very racy, with clear lime and lemon fruit and the merest hint of petrol.*	£10.70 NYW/FLY
WOLF BLASS GOLD LABEL RIESLING 2003, BERINGER BLASS **SOUTH AUSTRALIA** – *Well-defined fruity nose, with peach aromas and a lemon zing. Pure and fresh, with solid weight. Very good balance.*	£11.00 LAI/NYW

AUSTRALIAN WHITE BRONZE

SHADOWFAX CHARDONNAY 2002, SHADOWFAX **VICTORIA** – *Slightly nutty, smoky nose. The mouth fills with zesty grapefruit, limes, and lemons.*	**£11.60** EVI/CCS FLY/WRW
PENFOLDS EDEN VALLEY RESERVE RIESLING 2003, SOUTHCORP **SOUTH AUSTRALIA** – *Spiced and apple-crisp, with a lemon zip, a touch of lime zest, and leafy herby fruit.*	**£12.00** TOS
YARRA VALLEY CHARDONNAY 2002, DE BORTOLI WINES **VICTORIA** – *Big and round. Smooth, ripe guava flavours integrate well with oak on the silky palate.*	**£12.00** BNK/NFW FLY
CLARE VALLEY RIESLING 2003, MOUNT HORROCKS **SOUTH AUSTRALIA** – *Good floral intensity provides the base for top notes of apricot and lime fruit. Balanced.*	**£12.10** WIDELY AVAILABLE
MITCHELTON AIRSTRIP 2002, MITCHELTON WINES **VICTORIA** – *Clear, deep straw yellow, with aromatic oak overlaying peach fruit on the warm aromatic palate.*	**£12.50** FLY
FOREST EDGE VINEYARD CHARDONNAY 2002, BROKENWOOD **NEW SOUTH WALES** – *Pineapples and sweet spices; puffs of smoke; bright Sicilian lemon flavours, and a rich, warming finish.*	**£13.30** BEN/V&C MOV/NYW LIB/FLY
HEGGIES EDEN VALLEY CHARDONNAY 2003, YALUMBA **SOUTH AUSTRALIA** – *Heavy, concentrated, and overlaid with vanilla, this creamy beauty has mineral and smoke scents.*	**£13.50** NFW/NYW RWM
JACOB'S CREEK LIMITED RELEASE CHARDONNAY 2002, JACOB'S CREEK **SOUTH AUSTRALIA** – *A long, restrained, and balanced Chardonnay, with soft, sultry yellow-apple flavours and herb hints.*	**£15.00** CAX
PETALUMA CHARDONNAY 2001, PETALUMA **SOUTH AUSTRALIA** – *Intense and nutty, with delicious, smooth-as-silk oak on the full-bodied, developing palate.*	**£15.00** WIDELY AVAILABLE
SUCKFIZZLE SAUVIGNON SEMILLON 2002, STELLA BELLA WINES **WESTERN AUSTRALIA** – *Zesty limes and lychee fruit flavours. A weighty, refreshing tipple with a long finish.*	**£15.10** SOM/NFW CCS/ALL

AUSTRALIAN WHITE BRONZE / SEAL

ST ANDREWS CHARDONNAY 2000, WAKEFIELD ESTATE SOUTH AUSTRALIA – *Big, clean, and buttery, with clove and nutmeg characters. Deep, with a firm cedary backbone.*	**£16.30** LAI/RAV WPR/NFW RWM/SWS
VAT 47 HUNTER CHARDONNAY 2001, TYRRELL'S VINEYARDS NEW SOUTH WALES – *Round and buttery, with natural refreshing acidity cutting through the attractive savoury yellow-fruit palate.*	**£20.90** WRW
REDBROOK CHARDONNAY 2001, EVANS & TATE WESTERN AUSTRALIA – *Smoky oak and nutmeg spice tinges, peaches and green peas. The finish is toasty, nutty, and very long.*	**£27.00** P&S
PENFOLDS YATTARNA CHARDONNAY 2001, SOUTHCORP SOUTH AUSTRALIA – *The citrus fruit nose has a steely quality. Tropical, with lemons and grapefruit and delicate floral hints.*	**£37.60** LAI/SOM NYW
TIERS CHARDONNAY 2001, PETALUMA AUSTRALIA SOUTH AUSTRALIA – *The wine's nutty elements forge a path through unctuously ripe quince and fig fruit flesh.*	**£42.60** NFW/NYW RWM/FLY BWL/ODD

SEAL OF APPROVAL
AUSTRALIAN WHITE

☆ **SI JOLI PETIT AUSTRALIAN SEMILLON CHARDONNAY NV, PAUL SAPIN,** SOUTH AUSTRALIA – *Lemons, musk, and lanolin flavour this balanced, refreshing wine.*	**•£1.00** ROG
☆ **BADGERS CREEK WHITE 2003, LES GRANDS CHAIS DE FRANCE** SOUTH AUSTRALIA – *White peaches, limes, hedgerow flowers, and ripe pears.*	**£3.00** ALD
☆ **FIRST FLIGHT COLOMBARD CHARDONNAY 2002, JINDALEE** SOUTH AUSTRALIA – *Floral tones grace the ripe tropical fruit salad flavours.*	**£3.50** SMF
☆ **COLDRIDGE ESTATE CHARDONNAY 2002, SIMEON** SOUTH AUSTRALIA – *Bright ripe Sicilian lemon and green apple flavours. Fruit-driven and intense.*	**£3.80** IWS/MWW

74 AUSTRALIAN WHITE SEAL **/ RED** TROPHY / GOLD

☆ **MASTERPEACE SEMILLON COLOMBARD CHARDONNAY 2003, ANDREW PEACE WINES** SOUTH AUSTRALIA – *Melange of grapefuit and lemons. Elderflower hints.*	£4.00 NTD/SAF THS

TROPHY
AUSTRALIAN RED

☆ **THE LODGE HILL SHIRAZ 2002, JIM BARRY WINES** SOUTH AUSTRALIA – *Cool, with distinct eucalyptus and buttermint nose. Black cassis fruit with hints of plum and sultanas.*	£9.30 WIDELY AVAILABLE
☆ **BLEASDALE FRANK POTTS 2002, BLEASDALE** SOUTH AUSTRALIA – *Deep and very concentrated. Pronounced ripe minty, berry, and plum fruit gives a wonderfully rich perfumed nose.*	£10.60 VDV/FEN NFW/NYW FLY/ODD
☆ **RUFUS STONE HEATHCOTE SHIRAZ 2002, TYRRELL'S VINEYARDS** VICTORIA – *Unctuous and hyper-ripe. Violets, blackberries and mint aromas; developed savoury elements. It's not just big... it's also clever.*	£12.00 ODD

GOLD
AUSTRALIAN RED

☆ **BERESFORD CABERNET SAUVIGNON 2001, STEP ROAD WINERY** SOUTH AUSTRALIA – *Super-ripe fruit, high alcohol and masses of currant and peppery flavour. Dense colour hints at the ripe structure.*	£8.00 NFW
☆ **SALTRAM MAMRE BROOK SHIRAZ 2001, BERINGER BLASS** SOUTH AUSTRALIA – *Lush and intensely rich, with a ripe concentration of tangy briar fruit and black spicy, chocolatey complexity.*	£9.00 NYW
☆ **CLAIRAULT CABERNET SAUVIGNON 2001, CLAIRAULT WINES** WESTERN AUSTRALIA – *Warm currant and black-fruited berry flavours mitigated by cooling cigar box and tobacco notes. An intense, elegant palate.*	£9.30 MOV/NYW SWS
☆ **CLARE VALLEY SHIRAZ 2002, TIM ADAMS WINES** SOUTH AUSTRALIA – *Lots of red brambly berry fruit and a hint of spice. Subtle oak adds complexity and depth.*	£9.70 AUC/TOS OZW

AUSTRALIAN RED GOLD 75

☆ **SCHOOL BLOCK 2002, SCARPANTONI ESTATE** **SOUTH AUSTRALIA** – *Black- and purple-berry flavours tinged with violets. Big weight and solid chewy new oak. Bang!*	**£10.00** LAI
★ **PENFOLDS BIN 28 KALIMNA SHIRAZ 2001, SOUTHCORP** **SOUTH AUSTRALIA** – *Essence of blackberry, plum, and vanilla oak. Immensely concentrated in a ripe, forward style, this has great weight.*	**£10.10** WIDELY AVAILABLE
☆ **PREMIUM SHIRAZ 2002, SANDALFORD** **WESTERN AUSTRALIA** – *Brambly, spicy, ripe and oaky, with user-friendly tannins. A splendid iron fist in a velvet glove.*	**£10.50** NYW
☆ **THE GALVO GARAGE CABERNET MERLOT PETIT VERDOT CABERNET FRANC 2002, D'ARENBERG** **SOUTH AUSTRALIA** – *Deep cassis, coffee, and chocolate oak of finesse and complexity. Big, spicy, and mouthfilling.*	**£12.10** NRW/NFW NYW/FLY ODD
☆ **ELDERTON ESTATE BAROSSA CABERNET SAUVIGNON 2001, ELDERTON WINES** **SOUTH AUSTRALIA** – *Supple tannins and refreshing acidity balance the vanilla scented oak, mocha, leather, flowers and bright berry elements.*	**£12.50** FLY
TAMAR RIDGE PINOT NOIR 2002, TAMAR RIDGE WINES **TASMANIA** – *Raspberry and cranberry fruit flavours. Developed farmy hints haunt the nose. Focused palate with firm structure and length.*	**£13.20** OZW/NYW
VOYAGER CABERNET MERLOT 1998, VOYAGER ESTATE **WESTERN AUSTRALIA** – *Menthol, buttermints, blackcurrant and a hint of green pepper, along with beautifully integrated oak.*	**£14.20** NYW/J&B ODD
DEVILS LAIR MARGARET RIVER CABERNET MERLOT 2001, SOUTHCORP **WESTERN AUSTRALIA** – *Concentrated, elegant velvet. Sublime minty capsicum, cassis Cabernet and a balanced structure backed up by stylish new oak.*	**£14.40** SOM/NYW
HEATHVALE SHIRAZ 2002, HEATHVALE VINEYARD **SOUTH AUSTRALIA** – *The nose is rich, with vanilla and toasted coconut. The palate sports spice and leather, blackberries, and cassis.*	**£15.00** ORB
PICTURE SERIES BRAVE FACES SHIRAZ 2002, TWO HANDS WINES **SOUTH AUSTRALIA** – *Deep and powerful, with developed meaty notes. Notes of spice, pepper, loam, and tarragon envelop the palate.*	**£15.70** VDV/SOM NFW/CCS JSM/ALL

AUSTRALIAN RED GOLD

ADAMS BROTHERS SHIRAZ 2001, TIM ADAMS WINES South Australia – Clean minty aroma. Cassis and blackcurrant flavours and soft round coffee and chocolate oak tannins.	£17.00 AUC
CLAIRAULT CABERNET MERLOT 1998, CLAIRAULT WINES Western Australia – Earthy blackcurrant fruit and mint with developed savoury, meaty elements. Also possesses subtle oak and fine grippy tannins.	£18.00 MOV/NYW SWS
TATACHILLA FOUNDATION SHIRAZ 2000, TATACHILLA WINERY South Australia – Bright acid and fine tannins. Bags of black fruit, spicy flavours. Generous structure and friendly coffee, caramel oak.	£18.00 NFW/NYW BWL
PETALUMA COONAWARRA 2001, PETALUMA AUSTRALIA South Australia – Ripe cassis fruit on the fore palate is balanced with rich, open oak and grippy tannins. Very long.	£21.80 BNK/NFW NYW/FLY ODD
THE GOMERSAL GRENACHE 2001, MAGPIE ESTATE South Australia – This had the judges excited: "An explosion of sundried raspberries… the sun-drenched maturity gathers momentum… invincible."	£22.00 NYW
PENLEY ESTATE RESERVE CABERNET SAUVIGNON 2000, PENLEY ESTATE South Australia – Rich, ripe, and juicy, with spicy, tarry cassis fruit, vanilla and caramel oak, and silky tannins.	£27.00 CCS/NYW
STONEWELL SHIRAZ 1998, PETER LEHMANN South Australia – Spicy fruit and Christmas cake flavours. Lush, with warm blackberry fruit and cocoa-oak and ripe, round tannins.	£28.90 WIDELY AVAILABLE
WOLF BLASS PLATINUM LABEL SHIRAZ 2001, BERINGER BLASS South Australia – Black fruit, spice, leather, crisp acidity, and fine tannins. A complexity of pepper, cedar, coconut, chocolate, and mint.	£35.00 NYW
PENFOLDS RWT BAROSSA VALLEY SHIRAZ 2001, SOUTHCORP South Australia – Intense inky power. Weighty, with juicy tannins and luscious berry, plummy concentration in a vanilla, mocha finish.	£39.50 WIDELY AVAILABLE
PENFOLDS BIN 707 CABERNET SAUVIGNON 2001, SOUTHCORP South Australia – Packed with chocolate oak, plummy, cedary ripe, ripe fruit. Minty notes emphasise the density and intensity of flavour.	£40.70 VDV/NYW ODD MWW

AUSTRALIAN RED GOLD / SILVER

EILEEN HARDY SHIRAZ 2001, BRL HARDY SOUTH AUSTRALIA – *Super ripe with leather, spice, smoky plums, raspberries, and violets. Dense tannins give a firmer texture than usual.*	**£43.40** HAX/HOU VDV/NYW
E&E BLACK PEPPER SHIRAZ 1999, BAROSSA VALLEY ESTATE SOUTH AUSTRALIA – *Big belting Barossa. An attack of cassis, mulberry, and eucalyptus. And yes, a profusion of pepper!*	**£46.20** VDV/VGN FEN/NYW

SILVER
AUSTRALIAN RED

☆ **EAGLEHAWK CABERNET SAUVIGNON 2003, BERINGER BLASS** SOUTH AUSTRALIA – *Sophisticated, with an integrated tannic structure. Laden with ripe cassis and chocolate oak. Boasts a lingering finish.*	**£5.00** ASD
☆ **DOVEDALE SHIRAZ 2002, STEP ROAD WINERY** SOUTH AUSTRALIA – *Black- and white-pepper powder nose. A cushion of damson and raspberry fruit lines the palate.*	**£6.00** SWS
☆ **OAK AGED SHIRAZ 2003, DE BORTOLI WINES** SOUTH AUSTRALIA – *Effortlessly elegant. Its robust tannic structure underpins plums drenched in chocolate. Sweet, fine oak.*	**£6.00** LAI
☆ **SERAFINO SHIRAZ 2000, SERAFINO WINES** SOUTH AUSTRALIA – *Smoke, darkest molasses, and mature blackberry fruit. A mellifluous, genteel palate with fresh flavours despite its maturity.*	**£6.00** NFW
☆ **YELLOW TAIL MERLOT 2003, CASELLA ESTATE** SOUTH AUSTRALIA – *An enchanting nose of vanilla, violets and toffee. Chewy tannins complement the ripe, bright summer-berry fruit flavours.*	**£6.00** SWS
☆ **HOUGHTON CABERNET SHIRAZ MERLOT 2001, HOUGHTON** WESTERN AUSTRALIA – *Damsons, loganberries, and blueberries compete with spicebox and saddle-leather elements. This blend is a modern Australian classic.*	**£6.50** FEN/MWW
★ **WAKEFIELD PROMISED LAND SHIRAZ CABERNET 2002, WAKEFIELD ESTATE** SOUTH AUSTRALIA – *Coconut oak decorates the rich, earthy bramble fruit scents and flavours, whilst pepper sprinkles the ultra-rich palate. Smooth.*	**£6.70** NFW/OZW SWS

78 AUSTRALIAN RED SILVER

☆ **DEEN VAT 4 PETIT VERDOT 2002, DE BORTOLI WINES** NEW SOUTH WALES – *Lavish oak complements many layers of chocolate, ripe blackberry, and red pepper flavours.*	£6.80 WIDELY AVAILABLE
☆ **PENFOLDS KOONUNGA HILL SHIRAZ CABERNET 2002, SOUTHCORP** SOUTH AUSTRALIA – *Unfettered dark vine fruits on nose and palate. Good depth and intensity, and more than a little complexity.*	£6.80 SOM/WSO TOS/JSM MWW
☆ **BIN 999 MERLOT 2002, WYNDHAM ESTATE** SOUTH AUSTRALIA – *Flowers, mint, smoke and berries vie for attention. The focused palate is structured, with a long finish.*	£7.00 CAX
☆ **RUTHERGLEN ESTATES DURIF 2003, RUTHERGLEN ESTATES** VICTORIA – *A port-like, rich, spicy molasses nose. The palate boasts dense plum fruit and chunky tannins.*	£7.00 WTS
☆ **TRYST CABERNET TEMPRANILLO ZINFANDEL 2002, NEPENTHE WINES** SOUTH AUSTRALIA – *Cassis and cherries intermingle with aromas of chocolate. Ripe, concentrated, warm and generous, and cosseted by soft tannins.*	£7.40 EDC/NFW OZW/SWS ODD
☆ **RED EARTH MERLOT 2002, TATACHILLA WINERY** SOUTH AUSTRALIA – *Richly oaked, its ripe red fruit possesses good concentration and balance. Chewy tannins crown it all.*	£7.50 NFW
☆ **RED EARTH SHIRAZ 2002, TATACHILLA WINERY** SOUTH AUSTRALIA – *Intense spices on the nose: cloves, cinnamon, and allspice. The textured, rich palate is packed with blueberry fruit.*	£7.50 NFW
CONTOUR 4 SANGIOVESE SHIRAZ 2001, CORIOLE SOUTH AUSTRALIA – *Bright and flavoursome, with excellent concentration. Bitter chocolate envelops juicy dark-fleshed cherries. Broad, sweetly ripe. A long finish.*	£7.90 WIDELY AVAILABLE
OMRAH MERLOT CABERNET 2001, PLANTAGENET WESTERN AUSTRALIA – *Lifted, with plenty of damson fruit, tobacco leaf aromas, and firm yet integrated tannins.*	£7.90 WIDELY AVAILABLE
WAKEFIELD CABERNET SAUVIGNON 2002, WAKEFIELD ESTATE SOUTH AUSTRALIA – *Ripe red fruit melds with herbs and white pepper on nose and palate. Fine balance, complexity, and length.*	£7.90 WIDELY AVAILABLE

AUSTRALIAN RED SILVER

BERESFORD SHIRAZ 2002, STEP ROAD WINERY **SOUTH AUSTRALIA** – *Pencil shavings, black-cherries, and cedar intermingle on the dense, sweetly ripe yet zippy palate.*	£8.00 WPR/NFW
INGOLBY SHIRAZ 2002, BERINGER BLASS **SOUTH AUSTRALIA** – *Fabulously fruity, with ripe, concentrated red and blackberry fruit flavours. Vanilla, chocolate and spicebox scents.*	£8.00 NYW
JAMIESONS RUN CABERNET SHIRAZ MERLOT 2001, BERINGER BLASS SOUTH AUSTRALIA – *Black-cherries, strawberries, eucalyptus, vanilla, and smoke rise from the glass. The palate is richly ripe and well-integrated.*	£8.00 MRN
RINGBOLT MARGARET RIVER CABERNET SAUVIGNON 2001, YALUMBA WESTERN AUSTRALIA – *Soft palate with fresh acidity and a round structure. Ripeness complemented by nutty and leafy notes. Robust finish.*	£8.00 TAU/NRW NFW/FLA NYW
ZONTES FOOTSTEP SHIRAZ VIOGNIER 2003, ZONTES FOOTSTEP SOUTH AUSTRALIA – *Youthful with zippy berries. Combines succulent, ripe, purple fruit with a dash of spice. Finishes with balanced crispness.*	£8.00 UNS/JSM
WARBURN ESTATE CABERNET SAUVIGNON 2003, RIVERINA WINES NEW SOUTH WALES – *A fabulously intense agglomeration of blackberries, liquorice, cassis, and bark. Creamy, bold, youthful, sumptuous, and ripe.*	£8.20 LAI
WARBURN ESTATE SHIRAZ 2003, RIVERINA WINES NEW SOUTH WALES – *Concentrated, with a dash of oak. Cool acidity combines with ripeness and elegance. Deep, dark, and promising.*	£8.20 LAI
FAMILY RESERVE PETIT VERDOT 2003, DE BORTOLI WINES SOUTH AUSTRALIA – *Inky black. Generous green pepper, truffles, and blueberries. Dense, its iron strength is tempered by lilting floral notes.*	£8.60 LAI
NINTH ISLAND PINOT NOIR 2003, PIPERS BROOK VINEYARD TASMANIA – *Clear and vibrant, a luxuriant jumble of raspberries and strawberries, Bourbon vanilla and touches of cinnamon.*	£8.70 WIDELY AVAILABLE
ANNIE'S LANE CABERNET MERLOT 2002, BERINGER BLASS SOUTH AUSTRALIA – *Whiffs of tobacco smoke lace a nose replete with raspberries, black-cherries, and herbs. A lengthy finish.*	£9.00 ODD

AUSTRALIAN RED SILVER

CAPEL VALE CABERNET SHIRAZ MERLOT 2001, CAPEL VALE WINES Western Australia – *Vivid loganberries, currants, and strawberries, lashings of leather and generous spicebox scents.*	£9.00 D&D
PENFOLDS THOMAS HYLAND SHIRAZ 2002, SOUTHCORP South Australia – *Ripe blackberry fruit, and grilled meat and olive aromas. Balanced and characterful; textured, yet open and appealing.*	£9.00 JSM/MWW
VINEYARD SELECT MCLAREN VALE SHIRAZ 2002, ANGOVE'S South Australia – *Very fine fruit was used in this mouthwatering, ripe, spicy wine.*	£9.00 D&D
BLEWITT SPRINGS SHIRAZ 2001, HILLSVIEW VINEYARDS South Australia – *Clean and ripe. The deep redcurrant and blackcurrant fruit is at once leafy and soft.*	£9.10 VDV/NFW ALL
YERING STATION PINOT NOIR 2001, YERING STATION WINES Victoria – *Liquid cherry and pepper on the nose. The palate has some seductive savoury red fruit with firm tannins.*	£9.20 SOM/FLA
PALANDRI SHIRAZ 2001, PALANDRI WINES Western Australia – *The nose offers brambles. The palate has a cushion of sweet fruit and balanced acidity. A spicy finish.*	£9.40 EDC/VIT OZW/INS
CAMPBELLS BOBBIE BURNS SHIRAZ 2002, CAMPBELLS OF RUTHERGLEN Victoria – *The palate has a nice weight of blackberry and blackcurrant fruit. The tannins are supple. A long finish.*	£9.80 HAX/CCS BOO/FLY WRW
PENFOLDS BIN 128 COONAWARRA SHIRAZ 2001, SOUTHCORP South Australia – *Complex, with saddle, poivre, cinnamon oak and damsons on the nose. The full-throttle palate is tannic and powerful.*	£9.80 WIDELY AVAILABLE
ST MARY'S SHIRAZ 2001, ST MARY'S South Australia – *The richness of ripe baked raspberry and mulberry flavours is lifted by white pepper and invigorating acidity.*	£9.80 ELV
MARGARET RIVER SHIRAZ 2002, EVANS & TATE Western Australia – *A youthful wine with silky oak and a complex array of mint, chocolate, and pepper.*	£9.90 HOU/HPW SMF/WRW ODD

AUSTRALIAN RED SILVER

BAILEYS GLENROWAN 1920S BLOCK SHIRAZ 2000, BERINGER BLASS Victoria – *A prominent, spicy, slightly sappy, minty nose. The medium-bodied palate's bursting with peppery fruit. A long liquorice finish.*	£10.00 ODD
CAPEL VALE CABERNET SAUVIGNON 2001, CAPEL VALE WINES Western Australia – *Firm yet fleshy currant and blueberry palate with plenty of concentration and a long finish.*	£10.00 D&D
CAPEL VALE MERLOT 2001, CAPEL VALE WINES Western Australia – *Soft and silky, with rich damson fruit, lifted tobacco aromas and hints of clove and cinnamon.*	£10.00 D&D
KANGARILLA ROAD SHIRAZ 2002, KANGARILLA ROAD South Australia – *Deep and textured, with layers of black bramble fruit, crushed peppercorns, sweet spice, and floral hints.*	£10.00 MWW
PIRRAMIMMA MCLAREN VALE SHIRAZ 2001, A C JOHNSTON South Australia – *Restrained, deep scents of mocha, olives, blackberries, and bark. The palate is lined with soft strawberries. Extremely elegant.*	£10.00 MWW
THE BACK SHED SHIRAZ 2002, REDHEADS STUDIO South Australia – *Fine plum fruit flavours and a handful of flowers on the nose. Concentrated, characterful, and intense.*	£10.00 LAI
IL BRICCONE 2001, PRIMO ESTATE South Australia – *Currants and loganberries drip from the palate of this chocolatey wine. Excellent mouthfeel, remarkable depth, and exceptional length.*	£10.20 WIDELY AVAILABLE
STELLA BELLA TEMPRANILLO 2002, STELLA BELLA WINES Western Australia – *Silky-smooth, with ripe, textured red-cherry fruit, vibrant acidity, and fine grainy tannins.*	£10.30 WIDELY AVAILABLE
HAMILTON'S STONEGARDEN GRENACHE SHIRAZ 2002, HAMILTON'S EWELL VINEYARDS South Australia – *Leather and spice, a superb depth of sweet fruit flavours, and a richly textured palate. A clean finish.*	£10.50 NFW/MOV SWS
SHOTFIRE RIDGE SHIRAZ 2001, THORN-CLARKE South Australia – *Made in a seductively creamy style, with good balance and robust alcohol. Intense blackberry flavours.*	£10.70 TAU/NFW

82 AUSTRALIAN RED SILVER

THE FERGUS 2001, TIM ADAMS WINES SOUTH AUSTRALIA – *Sweetly scented, with a fully developed nose and palate of baked loganberries and blackberries.*	**£10.70** AUC/NFW OZW
CORIOLE SHIRAZ 2002, CORIOLE SOUTH AUSTRALIA – *Big extract and whopping tannins lay the groundwork. Ripe, juicy mulberries, blackberries, and cinnamon bark. A powerful wine.*	**£11.10** WIDELY AVAILABLE
FUTURES SHIRAZ 2002, PETER LEHMANN SOUTH AUSTRALIA – *Bags of bramble fruit glow on the full palate, which has bright balancing acidity.*	**£11.40** EDC/VDV NFW/G&M ODD
WILLOWS VINEYARD SHIRAZ 2001, WILLOWS VINEYARD SOUTH AUSTRALIA – *Elegant loganberry fruit is given a dusting of cocoa and Madagascar vanilla. Long finish.*	**£11.40** AUC/NFW FLA/OZW MOV/NYW
HEWITSON L'OIZEAU SHIRAZ 2001, HEWITSON SOUTH AUSTRALIA – *Cassis and cherries, a seam of rosemary and a hint of nuttiness. Dark fruit and chunky tannins.*	**£11.60** VDV/NYW FLY
CLAIRAULT CABERNET MERLOT 2001, CLAIRAULT WINES WESTERN AUSTRALIA – *Deep crimson colour. Dark plum aromas, smoky oak, and tight currant fruit on the palate. Elegant, supple, and soft.*	**£11.90** WPR/MOV NYW/SWS
BLOCK 3 SHIRAZ 2002, SCARPANTONI ESTATE SOUTH AUSTRALIA – *Green apple skin tannins and savoury hints coupled with a spearmint, briar berries and undergrowth tones.*	**£12.00** LAI
ELDREDGE BLUE CHIP SHIRAZ 2002, ELDREDGE VINEYARDS SOUTH AUSTRALIA – *A tangle of undergrowth, violets, toast, and chocolate on the nose and the palate.*	**£12.00** AUC
PONDALOWIE SHIRAZ 2002, PONDALOWIE VINEYARDS VICTORIA – *Striking ripe fruits and pleasant charry oak. Firm tannins support the well-structured body.*	**£12.00** AUC/FLA OZW/MOV NYW
WAVECREST SHIRAZ 2002, NORFOLK RISE VINEYARD SOUTH AUSTRALIA – *The superbly balanced palate is loaded with damson fruit. Robust tannins underscore wild blueberries and herbs.*	**£12.00** VGN

AUSTRALIAN RED SILVER 83

Wine	Price / Codes
WOLF BLASS PRESIDENT'S SELECTION CABERNET SAUVIGNON 2001, BERINGER BLASS SOUTH AUSTRALIA – *Rich blackcurrant aromas meld with leather and smoke on the nose. A palate of berries and toasty oak.*	£12.00 SMF/FEN ODD
THE BONSAI VINE 2001, D'ARENBERG SOUTH AUSTRALIA – *Peppermint and Morello cherry; mocha and black fruit. Pure and resonant, with a ripe, lifted quality and a sustained finish.*	£12.10 NRW/NFW NYW/FLY ODD
HOWARD PARK SCOTSDALE SHIRAZ 2001, HOWARD PARK WINES WESTERN AUSTRALIA – *Young, yet deep. A cool, minty, leafy, textured, vividly fruity yet lively and fresh wine.*	£12.20 JNW/NYW FLY/BWL
PENFOLDS BIN 407 CABERNET SAUVIGNON 2001, SOUTHCORP SOUTH AUSTRALIA – *Another stellar wine from Penfolds, with plump cassis, lifted cigar scents and a saturated finish.*	£12.30 SOM/NYW ODD MWW
WOLF BLASS GOLD LABEL CABERNET SAUVIGNON CABERNET FRANC 2001, BERINGER BLASS SOUTH AUSTRALIA – *Spicy, ripe, and velvety. Pristine red-cherry fruit tumbles from the rich, refined palate. Excellent balance.*	£12.70 BNK/NYW JSM
THE LAUGHING MAGPIE 2002, D'ARENBERG SOUTH AUSTRALIA – *Floral notes, purple-blue berries and light spices on the nose. Dense sloes, savoury overtones, pepper and crisp acidity on the palate.*	£12.80 WIDELY AVAILABLE
BIMBADGEN ESTATE SIGNATURE SANGIOVESE 2003, BIMBADGEN ESTATE NEW SOUTH WALES – *Dates and prunes, roast walnuts, and cinnamon spill from this fabulous wine. Well-balanced and a long, fine finish.*	£13.00 HBJ
CABERNET MERLOT TRINDERS 2001, CAPE MENTELLE WESTERN AUSTRALIA – *A very polished wine, with clear ripe blackcurrant fruit, vivid acidity, and a taut tannic undercurrent.*	£13.10 BNK/EDC NYW/WTS MWW
SHADOWFAX SHIRAZ 2001, SHADOWFAX SOUTH AUSTRALIA – *Fresh, cool, well-handled black fruit is graced with vanilla bean and cracked pepper. Dense, fleshy, and layered.*	£13.30 WIDELY AVAILABLE
BOWEN COONAWARRA CABERNET SAUVIGNON 2001, BOWEN ESTATE SOUTH AUSTRALIA – *Lifted and sophisticated, with smoke aromas. A mouthwatering red-fruit palate propped up by sweet oak.*	£13.50 BEN/TAN AUC/OZW MOV/NYW

84 AUSTRALIAN RED SILVER

YARRA VALLEY SHIRAZ 2002, DE BORTOLI WINES **VICTORIA** – *Highly oaked and fruited, with attractive ripe raspberry, soy sauce, and undergrowth. Complex, soft, and long.*	£13.60 VDV/NFW FLY
KATNOOK ESTATE MERLOT 2001, WINGARA WINE GROUP **SOUTH AUSTRALIA** – *A mature, elegant red-berry palate laced with compelling whiffs of smoke and hints of game.*	£13.70 NFW/FLY
CLASSIC MCLAREN VALE SHIRAZ 2000, CLASSIC MCLAREN WINES **SOUTH AUSTRALIA** – *Bramble fruit flavours graced with oriental spices and touches of vanilla. Ripeness, elegance, structure, complexity, and power.*	£14.00 OZW
SHORT ROW SHIRAZ 2002, FOX CREEK WINES **SOUTH AUSTRALIA** – *Eucalyptus, damson fruit, allspice, nuts, and coconut oak decorate the ripe palate. A seam of youthful tannin.*	£14.00 SOM
THE STICKS & STONES TEMPRANILLO GRENACHE SAOZAO 2002, D'ARENBERG **SOUTH AUSTRALIA** – *A clever blend, spicy, saturated, and vivid, with white pepper notes and ripe cherry fruit.*	£14.10 NFW/NYW FLY
SHOTTESBROOKE MCLAREN VALE ELIZA SHIRAZ 2002, SHOTTESBROOKE **SOUTH AUSTRALIA** – *Rich fruit drips with bright mouthwatering acidity. Sugarplum fruit is laced with smoke and crushed green peppercorn aromas.*	£14.50 ROG
SHAW & SMITH SHIRAZ 2002, SHAW & SMITH **SOUTH AUSTRALIA** – *A wealth of complex aromatics is in evidence: violets, pepper, mulberries, coal, and vanilla spice.*	£14.80 BEN/TAU MOV/LIB FLY
H RESERVE SHIRAZ 2001, HASELGROVE WINES **SOUTH AUSTRALIA** – *Youthful and leathery, with plenty of gum tree bark. High tannins. A powerful, well-balanced wine.*	£15.00 D&D
ROSEMOUNT MCLAREN VALE RESERVE SHIRAZ 2001, SOUTHCORP **SOUTH AUSTRALIA** – *Blackcurrants and black cherries. The round structure is underpinned by ripe tannins. Glossy forward fruit flavours.*	£15.00 WTS
WOLF BLASS GOLD LABEL SHIRAZ VIOGNIER 2002, BERINGER BLASS **SOUTH AUSTRALIA** – *Velvety stone fruit lifts Victoria plum aromas and flavours. Carefully made, sophisticated, fresh, and fine.*	£15.00 NYW/ODD

AUSTRALIAN RED SILVER 85

OLD GARDEN MOURVÈDRE 2001, HEWITSON **SOUTH AUSTRALIA** – *A black beauty with farmyard aromas and touches of leather. Integrated oak and a long powerful finish.*	£15.30 VDV/WRK NYW/FLY WRW
FIFTEEN BARRELS XV 2001, TAPESTRY VINEYARDS **SOUTH AUSTRALIA** – *Grilled meats, spearmint, mocha, vanilla, and redcurrant fruit aromas. The palate is rich, balanced, and finishes long.*	£15.40 W2D
TAPESTRY THE VINCENT 2001, TAPESTRY VINEYARDS **SOUTH AUSTRALIA** – *Rich, smoky nose, soft tannins and peppery fruit. Plenty of oak augments opulent briar fruit palate.*	£15.40 W2D
YARRA VALLEY PINOT NOIR 2002, DE BORTOLI WINES **VICTORIA** – *Toast and oak are poised in perfect balance with delicate, soft, round strawberry fruit. Pronounced redcurrant jam and game nuances.*	£15.40 VDV/GHL NFW/FLY
PENLEY ESTATE SHIRAZ CABERNET SAUVIGNON 2000, PENLEY ESTATE **SOUTH AUSTRALIA** – *A developed bouquet, with worn leather, spicebox, and sweet damson fruit. A finely woven tannic texture.*	£15.50 CCS
WALTER'S CABERNET SAUVIGNON 2000, BREMERTON **SOUTH AUSTRALIA** – *Fabulous cassis flavours are graced with leafy aromatics and sustained by an integrated tannic web.*	£15.60 BNK/NFW CCS/NYW FLY
OLD BLOCK SHIRAZ 2000, ST HALLET WINES **SOUTH AUSTRALIA** – *Intense flavours of little black damsons and perfume of hedgerow flowers and pepper.*	£15.70 WIDELY AVAILABLE
KATNOOK ESTATE SHIRAZ 2002, WINGARA WINE GROUP **SOUTH AUSTRALIA** – *Cracked-pepper scents and flavours. An elegant palate of cigar leaves and strawberry fruit.*	£16.00 ESL/NFW FLY
FOUNDATION SHIRAZ 1998, TATACHILLA WINERY **SOUTH AUSTRALIA** – *Intensely purplish rouge. Rich menthol and blackcurrant nose, and big, full-bodied, mouthwatering chocolatey palate. Weighty, ripe and spicy.*	£16.30 EDC
THE HOLY TRINITY 2000, GRANT BURGE WINES **SOUTH AUSTRALIA** – *Strong, concentrated leather and red-berry flavours. Has a floral edge, bright acidity, and grippy, full tannins.*	£16.30 UNS/NFW FLY/WRW

AUSTRALIAN RED SILVER

Wine	Price
MENTOR 1999, PETER LEHMANN SOUTH AUSTRALIA – *Quality fruit meets superlative winemaking. With its mature, spicy red fruit flavours, this offering is big yet balanced.*	£16.40 EDC/UNS VDV/NFW G&M
ANNIE'S LANE COPPERTRAIL SHIRAZ 2000, BERINGER BLASS SOUTH AUSTRALIA – *Warm, wild heather and sweet vivid blueberries stud the nose. The palate is oaked, rich, and very smooth.*	£17.00 ODD
ST HALLETT OLD BLOCK SHIRAZ 2001, ST HALLETT WINES SOUTH AUSTRALIA – *A gorgeous velvety texture, that envelops a clean, spicy, smoky, and toasty mouthful of bilberry and blueberry fruit.*	£17.00 BNK/NRW NFW/OZW NYW
MOUNT BARKER SHIRAZ 2001, PLANTAGENET WESTERN AUSTRALIA – *The nose features just-roasted meat and burning mesquite. The palate is a jumble of bramble fruit flavours.*	£17.30 WIDELY AVAILABLE
ENTERPRISE CABERNET SAUVIGNON 2000, KNAPPSTEIN WINES SOUTH AUSTRALIA – *Sweet oak buttresses the dense wall of black fruit on the palate. Fine acidity lifts the ripe spiciness.*	£17.50 NFW
KNAPPSTEIN ENTERPRISE SHIRAZ 2000, KNAPPSTEIN WINES SOUTH AUSTRALIA – *The palate groans with mouthfilling black fruit compote flavours. Smoke, ginger, and clove rise from the lifted nose.*	£17.50 NFW
TATACHILLA FOUNDATION SHIRAZ 2001, TATACHILLA WINERY SOUTH AUSTRALIA – *Ripe red berries accented with notes of eucalyptus, and a textured palate of medium weight and concentration.*	£18.50 NFW/BWL
THE SIGNATURE CABERNET SAUVIGNON SHIRAZ 2000, YALUMBA SOUTH AUSTRALIA – *Sweet oak. Leafy notes. Dense fruit flavours. Leather and tar accentuate the richness of this earthy, spice-laden wine.*	£18.70 VDV/VIT SOM/NFW NYW
BALNAVES CABERNET SAUVIGNON 1999, BALNAVES OF COONAWARRA SOUTH AUSTRALIA – *Tremendous class: muted dark fruit, tea, tar, and bramble and a fresh, deep yet long palate.*	£18.80 BEN/VDV CCS/NYW LIB/FLY
HANNAH'S SWING SHIRAZ 2002, FOX GORDON WINES SOUTH AUSTRALIA – *Coal and spice on the nose. An undertone of oak races through the blackcurrant and smoky bacon palate.*	£18.80 VDV

AUSTRALIAN RED SILVER 87

KING LOUIS CABERNET 2002, FOX GORDON WINES SOUTH AUSTRALIA – *Cedar, spearmint, and ripe blackberry dominate the powerful palate. Sweet oak scents add lift. Balanced and very long.*	£18.80 VDV
THE STOCKS SHIRAZ 2000, WOODSTOCK WINERY SOUTH AUSTRALIA – *Watermint, red plum, and sweet, pink-flower scents. The ripe palate is tinged with smoke and tomato.*	£18.80 VDV/SOM NFW/RWM OWC
THE STOCKS SHIRAZ 2002, WOODSTOCK WINERY SOUTH AUSTRALIA – *Pepper, bramble fruit, and gum tree aromas. The dense plum fruit palate has a lifted eucalyptus note.*	£19.40 VDV/NFW OWC
LENSWOOD PINOT NOIR 2002, KNAPPSTEIN LENSWOOD VINEYARDS SOUTH AUSTRALIA – *Polished and focused, with bags of sweetly ripe strawberry fruit, firm dark earth, and gamey hints.*	£19.70 NYW WRW
RESERVE CABERNET SAUVIGNON 2000, YERING STATION WINES VICTORIA – *Fine fresh redcurrants, mocha, cloves, earth, cigar smoke, and vanilla cascade from this seamless wine.*	£20.00 FLA
YERING STATION RESERVE PINOT NOIR 2002, YERING STATION WINES VICTORIA – *Weighty, dark plums on the serious, oaky nose. The rounded palate has an aftertaste of vanilla and spice.*	£20.20 SOM/FLA NYW
BONESETTER SHIRAZ 2001, WILLOWS VINEYARD SOUTH AUSTRALIA – *Allspice and nutmeg grace the cranberry fruit, whilst a touch of espresso adds another dimension.*	£20.50 AUC/OZW
PICTURE SERIES BAD IMPERSONATOR SHIRAZ 2002, TWO HANDS WINES SOUTH AUSTRALIA – *Rich, with a ripe, sophisticated palate of red and black hedgerow fruits. Well-structured, with a long finish.*	£20.80 VDV/SOM NFW/CCS ALL
THE ABERFELDY 2001, TIM ADAMS WINES SOUTH AUSTRALIA – *The cranberry fruit palate is characterful, with fine-grained tannins, rich extract, and commendable balance.*	£20.80 AUC/WSO NFW/OZW NYW
CLASSIC CLARE CABERNET SAUVIGNON 1998, LEASINGHAM WINES SOUTH AUSTRALIA – *Ageing has encouraged leathery blackcurrant, licquorice, and tobacco aromatics, but there is still plenty of structure and fruit.*	£21.00 VDV

THE IRONSTONE PRESSINGS 2002, D'ARENBERG SOUTH AUSTRALIA – *A fabulous textured body. Leather and red berry on the nose. Grippy, punchy tannins balanced by crisp acidity.*	£21.50 NFW/FLY ODD
CRESTVIEW ESTATE RESERVE SHIRAZ 2001, STEP ROAD WINERY SOUTH AUSTRALIA – *The colour: ruby. The scents: toast, cherries, truffles, and mushrooms. The flavours: coffee, vine fruits, and cedar.*	£22.00 NFW
THE DEAD ARM SHIRAZ 2002, D'ARENBERG SOUTH AUSTRALIA – *A big wine. Stylish youthful tight black fruit is lavished with sweet spiced oak. Elegant flavours of fig and currant.*	£22.20 V&C/NYW FLY/ODD
YERING STATION RESERVE PINOT NOIR 2000, YERING STATION VICTORIA – *Leather, gamey notes, and baked strawberries on the nose. Silky palate with a rich array of dark fruits.*	£22.20 FLA/WTS
THE WARA MANTA RESERVE SHIRAZ 2002, NARDONE BAKER WINES SOUTH AUSTRALIA – *A restrained nose of charred currants and raisins. Textured, chocolatey, vibrant fruit laden with Indian spices.*	£23.00 NDJ
MITOLO GAM 2002, MITOLO SOUTH AUSTRALIA – *Dusty tannins and deep blackberry fruit flavours. Silky, very ripe, and full-bodied, and underscored with herbaceousness.*	£24.20 GRT/VDV NFW/NYW
LIMITED RELEASE SHIRAZ CABERNET 1999, JACOB'S CREEK SOUTH AUSTRALIA – *Deep and concentrated, with ground peppercorn scents, smoky blueberry fruit, and exotic coconut overtones.*	£25.00 CAX
YERING RESERVE SHIRAZ VIOGNIER 2002, YERING STATION WINES VICTORIA – *Spice, strawberries, and blackberries define the bouquet. The palate is sweetly ripe, intense and somewhat peachy.*	£25.00 FLA/NYW
SERPICO CABERNET SAUVIGNON 2003, MITOLO SOUTH AUSTRALIA – *Rich and ripe with a ruby hue. Herbs and eucalyptus lift the elegant palate of creamy blackberries.*	£25.50 GRT/VDV NFW/NYW
COMMAND SINGLE VINEYARD SHIRAZ 2000, ELDERTON WINES SOUTH AUSTRALIA – *Sweaty saddle-leather scents mixed with floral hints and minerals. Charred oak and mature red fruit flavours.*	£27.00 SOM/FLY

AUSTRALIAN RED SILVER 89

PENFOLDS MAGILL ESTATE SHIRAZ 2001, SOUTHCORP SOUTH AUSTRALIA – *Fine damson and cranberry fruit, spices, hints of loamy earth, integrated tannins and a long finish.*	£28.70 LAI/VDV SOM/ODD
MITOLO SAVITAR 2002, MITOLO SOUTH AUSTRALIA – *A muted nose of tar, mint, and coal. The medium-bodied palate has zingy acidity and bramble fruit.*	£29.20 GRT/VDV NFW/NYW
FOX CREEK RESERVE SHIRAZ 2002, FOX CREEK WINES SOUTH AUSTRALIA – *Coffee bean scents rise from the steely nose. Harmonious and restrained. Inky fruit and spice slowly unfold.*	£30.00 SOM
ROSEMOUNT ESTATE MCLAREN VALE BALMORAL SYRAH 2000, SOUTHCORP SOUTH AUSTRALIA – *Bourbon vanilla, espresso, and cocao scents. The mouth is saturated with blackcurrant and leather and sweet oak.*	£30.00 HAR/P&S
WOLF BLASS BLACK LABEL CABERNET SAUVIGNON SHIRAZ 2000, BERINGER BLASS SOUTH AUSTRALIA – *A nose of savoury damsons, its dense fruit interwoven with liquorice and chocolate. Sweet, firm, and spicy tannins.*	£30.00 NYW/JSM
WYNNS COONAWARRA ESTATE JOHN RIDDOCH CABERNET SAUVIGNON 1998, SOUTHCORP SOUTH AUSTRALIA – *A dense yet graceful, cassis- and mocha-infused wine. Excellent balance and striking individuality.*	£30.00 VDV/NYW MWW
PENFOLDS ST HENRI SHIRAZ 1998, PENFOLDS SOUTH AUSTRALIA – *Restrained aromas initially, alongside a seriously textured body. Cassis, dark fruits, chocolate, and ripe tannins on the palate.*	£30.90 WIDELY AVAILABLE
KATNOOK ESTATE ODYSSEY CABERNET SAUVIGNON 1998, WINGARA WINE GROUP SOUTH AUSTRALIA – *Fabulous minty notes on the nose and palate, and rich blackcurrant aromas follow on to the velvety palate.*	£31.30 SOM/NYW WTS
KATNOOK PRODIGY SHIRAZ 1999, WINGARA WINE GROUP SOUTH AUSTRALIA – *Lively yet soft; mouthwatering and complex. The mature cherry and cranberry flavours are big, full, textured, and very long.*	£31.80 SOM/NYW WTS/FLY ODD
KATNOOK ESTATE PRODIGY SHIRAZ 2000, WINGARA WINE GROUP SOUTH AUSTRALIA – *Fruited with sloes and ripe luxuriant damsons, and graced with toffee, coffee, and earthy spice.*	£35.00 NYW/FLY

AUSTRALIAN RED SILVER / BRONZE

THE RESERVE 1998, YALUMBA SOUTH AUSTRALIA – *An intense bouquet of mature purple fruits, spice, and chocolate. The chunky palate possesses structure and sweet tannins.*	£37.50 VDV/VIT SOM/NFW NYW
PENFOLDS RWT BAROSSA VALLEY SHIRAZ 2000, SOUTHCORP SOUTH AUSTRALIA – *Earthy and spicy notes, plus soft leather cushions on the nose. The palate holds gallons of sweet fruit.*	£39.30 WIDELY AVAILABLE
THE TALLY 2000, BALNAVES OF COONAWARRA SOUTH AUSTRALIA – *Glossy, ripe strawberry mingles with leather, vanilla pods, liquorice, cedar, and bittersweet chocolate. Concentrated, yet not remotely jammy.*	£48.00 LIB

BRONZE
AUSTRALIAN RED

☆ **LINDEMANS SOUTH AUSTRALIAN RESERVE CABERNET SAUVIGNON 2002, SOUTHCORP** SOUTH AUSTRALIA – *Green pepper notes accentuate forest fruit flavours. Spice scents. A crisp wine of medium length.*	£3.30 WIDELY AVAILABLE
☆ **BADGERS CREEK SHIRAZ CABERNET 2003, LES GRANDS CHAIS DE FRANCE** SOUTH AUSTRALIA – *This is a heavily oaked Australian wine, with powerful, warming coffee- and vanilla-infused mulberry fruit.*	£4.00 BGN
☆ **MHV SCENIC RIDGE CABERNET SAUVIGNON NV, REDELLO WINES** SOUTH AUSTRALIA – *Deep plum and cassis nose. This Cabernet Sauvignon's taut palate is developed, spicy, and crisp.*	£4.90 MHV
☆ **MHV SCENIC RIDGE MERLOT NV, REDELLO WINES** SOUTH AUSTRALIA – *A Merlot that's dark, muted reddish-purple in colour. Berries and chocolate oak pervade the nose and palate.*	£4.90 MHV
☆ **DB DURIF 2003, DE BORTOLI WINES** NEW SOUTH WALES – *Smoke and toast scent the nose. Ripe blackberries and mocha fill the exotically spiced palate.*	£5.00 BOR/SAF
☆ **KANGAROO RIDGE CABERNET SAUVIGNON 2002, BERINGER BLASS** SOUTH AUSTRALIA – *Restrained nose has hints of ripeness. Dried apricots, dates, and apples populate the palate. Deep, cedary, and spicy.*	£5.00 WFB

AUSTRALIAN RED BRONZE

☆ **VARIETAL RANGE SHIRAZ 2002, BRL HARDY** **SOUTH AUSTRALIA** – *Smoky berry flavours. Moderately complex wine yet light in body, with a medicinal cherry scent.*	£5.00 SMF/JSM
☆ **WOLF BLASS EAGLEHAWK SHIRAZ 2003, BERINGER BLASS** **SOUTH AUSTRALIA** – *A profoundly coloured wine, with fresh damsons and sweet spices on the soft, pleasing palate.*	£5.00 BNK/JSM
MHV SCENIC RIDGE RESERVE CABERNET SAUVIGNON 2002, REDELLO WINES **SOUTH AUSTRALIA** – *Raspberries and mint leaves grace this fresh, balanced, restrained wine from Australia. Firm, with good depth.*	£5.40 MHV
OPAL RIDGE SHIRAZ CABERNET 2003, BEELGARA ESTATE **SOUTH AUSTRALIA** – *A gentle giant, with herbaceous hints and intense red fruit. Suave touches of spice.*	£5.40 FFW/NFW JFE/CVE
YELLOW TAIL SHIRAZ 2003, CASELLA ESTATE **SOUTH AUSTRALIA** – *This showy, glamorous wine has sweetly ripe fruit and generous oak on its balanced, long palate.*	£5.50 SMF/NYW SWS/ODD JSM
JACOB'S CREEK CABERNET SAUVIGNON 2001, JACOB'S CREEK **SOUTH AUSTRALIA** – *Green mint and eucalyptus notes lace the nose. The palate has admirable brightness and clarity.*	£5.70 TOS/WTS JSM
LINDEMANS BIN 50 SHIRAZ 2003, SOUTHCORP **SOUTH AUSTRALIA** – *Deeply concentrated blackberry fruit, and the round yet structured palate has a pleasantly rustic character.*	£5.80 UNS/SOM FEN/TOS JSM/MWW
OXFORD LANDING SHIRAZ 2002, YALUMBA **SOUTH AUSTRALIA** – *Herbs, green damsons, and peppercorns on the nose. Persistent, slightly savoury, cherry-flavoured palate.*	£5.90 NRW/NFW TOS/NYW
BUCKINGHAM ESTATE SHIRAZ 2003, CELLARMASTER WINES **SOUTH AUSTRALIA** – *Easygoing, young, with red and purple fruit, ripe tannins, and a refreshing finish.*	£6.00 RWM/BUC
COPELAND ESTATE PRIVATE BIN SELECTION SHIRAZ 2003, CRANSWICK **SOUTH AUSTRALIA** – *Clear, attractive bilberry flavours; a Northern Rhône style echoes throughout the palate.*	£6.00 AVB

AUSTRALIAN RED BRONZE

HOUGHTON HRB 2002, HOUGHTON WINES **WESTERN AUSTRALIA** – *An intense, richly ripe, full-bodied offering with piles of cassis, chocolate, and clove scents.*	£6.00 BNK/WSO
KINGSTON SELECTION SHIRAZ 2001, KINGSTON ESTATE **SOUTH AUSTRALIA** – *Ready now, this is a soft, mature wine with pleasant strawberry jam flavours and a juicy finish.*	£6.00 RVA
MASTERPEACE SHIRAZ 2003, ANDREW PEACE WINES **VICTORIA** – *Herby, minty undertones. A warm palate with berry fruit and a dash of pepperiness.*	£6.00 UNS
MASTERPEACE SHIRAZ MALBEC 2003, ANDREW PEACE WINES **VICTORIA** – *Multi-layered, needing time to open up. Grainy tannins provide a structure and extend the finish.*	£6.00 SAF
NOTTAGE HILL SHIRAZ 2002, BRL HARDY **SOUTH AUSTRALIA** – *Lush black- and red-berry fruit flavours, hints of leather, bright acidity, and a medium body.*	£6.00 SMF/TOS
ROCK SHIRAZ BLEND 2002, HANGING ROCK WINERY **VICTORIA** – *This has vibrant red and black fruits on the palate, a linen-like texture, and a decent length.*	£6.00 ASD/THI
RUTHERGLEN ESTATES SANGIOVESE 2003, RUTHERGLEN ESTATES **VICTORIA** – *A moreish and forward "Oz-Ital" wine, with a refreshing, vivacious, lively strawberry- and raspberry-flavoured palate.*	£6.00 ASD
THE DELVER PETIT VERDOT 2003, MCGUIGAN SIMEON **SOUTH AUSTRALIA** – *Victoria plums and blackcurrants entwine with spicy oak. Warming and aromatic.*	£6.00 LAI
TRIMBOLI'S FAMILY RESERVE 15% SHIRAZ 2003, RIVERINA WINES **NEW SOUTH WALES** – *Dark plummy fruit on a ripe-tannined backbone. All is in balance with the warm alcohol.*	£6.20 LAI
DEAKIN SHIRAZ 2002, WINGARA WINE GROUP **VICTORIA** – *The concentrated juicy plum flavours more than hold their own against oak etched indelibly into the palate.*	£6.30 WIDELY AVAILABLE

AUSTRALIAN RED BRONZE

MOONDARRA RESERVE SHIRAZ 2003, SIMEON **SOUTH AUSTRALIA** – *Well-integrated oak backs up the fruit-driven palate. A straightforward, pleasantly moreish drop.*	£6.50 NFW
1502 BLACK SHIRAZ 2002, BEELGARA ESTATE **NEW SOUTH WALES** – *Vanilla and a wisp of acidity carry the raspberry, chocolate, and red-cherry fruit to a lengthy finish.*	£6.70 WIDELY AVAILABLE
THE MILL PETIT VERDOT 2002, WINDOWRIE ESTATE **NEW SOUTH WALES** – *Eucalyptus and mint hover above richly textured, aromatic, voluptuous black fruit. Fine tannins.*	£6.70 NRW/CPR NYW/BOO
DEEN VAT 1 DURIF 2002, DE BORTOLI WINES **NEW SOUTH WALES** – *Violets, toasty oak, and Straits of Malacca spices. The palate is packed with crisp crunchy black fruit.*	£6.80 BNK/VDV GHL/NFW FLY/INS
DEEN VAT 8 SHIRAZ 2002, DE BORTOLI WINES **NEW SOUTH WALES** – *An impressive nose and palate displaying a generous vanilla oak backbone. A wine to watch.*	£6.80 BNK/GHL NFW/FLY INS
FORBES ESTATE SHIRAZ 2003, ZILZIE WINES **VICTORIA** – *An elegant yet powerful and peppery Australian Shiraz with concentrated raspberry fruit. Take-no-prisoners tannins. One to keep.*	£6.80 LAI
THE MILL SANGIOVESE 2002, WINDOWRIE ESTATE **NEW SOUTH WALES** – *Charred, perfumed, mature damson fruit. This Sangiovese has a smooth texture, full body, and some complexity.*	£6.90 RNS/NRW CPR/NYW
BIN 444 CABERNET SAUVIGNON 2001, WYNDHAM ESTATE **SOUTH AUSTRALIA** – *Sweet fruit peeks through firm woody tannins, which enfold the developed, medium-bodied cassis flavours.*	£7.00 TOS
BOOARRA GRENACHE 2003, WESTERN RANGE WINES **WESTERN AUSTRALIA** – *Forward floral nose of summer fruits. Softly tannic palate of vibrant, perfumed cherries. Drink now.*	£7.00 ASD
PALANDRI CABERNET MERLOT 2002, PALANDRI WINES **WESTERN AUSTRALIA** – *Berry and spice aromas. The palate has good cassis fruit, balanced tannins, and decent weight on the finish.*	£7.00 VIT

94 AUSTRALIAN RED BRONZE

PALANDRI MERLOT 2002, PALANDRI WINES **WESTERN AUSTRALIA** – *Some development is displayed, although this wine is still young. Coconut, spice, and dark fruit seduce the taster.*	£7.00 VIT/SMF JFE
RUTHERGLEN ESTATES GRENACHE SHIRAZ MOURVEDRE 2003, RUTHERGLEN ESTATES **VICTORIA** – *A sweetly ripe floral nose, and a vivacious, almost jammy bramble fruit palate.*	£7.00 SMF
RUTHERGLEN ESTATES SHIRAZ 2003, RUTHERGLEN ESTATES **VICTORIA** – *Subtle jammy fruit alongside a touch of spice and liquorice. A fruitcake palate with spicy, peppery nuances.*	£7.00 VER
SINCLAIR ESTATE MERLOT 2003, MCPHERSON WINES **SOUTH AUSTRALIA** – *This approachable offering has a forward, slightly gamey nose, ripe tannins, and bright red fruit.*	£7.00 LAI
TAPESTRY SHIRAZ 2000, TAPESTRY VINEYARDS **SOUTH AUSTRALIA** – *Laden with sweet black fruit. The leather and smoke notes on the nose follow through on the palate.*	£7.00 SOM
THE BLACK SHIRAZ 2003, BEELGARA ESTATE **NEW SOUTH WALES** – *The palate has warm fruit, fresh acidity, moderate tannins and green mint all wrapped in creamy oak.*	£7.00 LAI
THE BLACK STUMP DURIF SHIRAZ 2003, CASELLA WINES **SOUTH AUSTRALIA** – *A burnt toffee aroma rises from the nose. Christmas spices lace the black damson fruit.*	£7.00 LAI
YALUMBA Y SHIRAZ 2002, YALUMBA **SOUTH AUSTRALIA** – *Powerful with violet and smoke aromas and a thick tarry palate showing good richness and weight.*	£7.10 CEB/VIT NFW/NYW
OLD WELL GRENACHE MOURVÈDRE SHIRAZ 2001, HILLSTOWE WINES **SOUTH AUSTRALIA** – *Following a jammy, tarry nose, plenty of sweet black fruits line the palate. Firm tannins.*	£7.20 LAI
PALANDRI ESTATE CABERNET SAUVIGNON 2002, PALANDRI WINES **WESTERN AUSTRALIA** – *A pronounced plum and cherry nose. The palate is clean with fine fruit, supple tannin. A harmonious finish.*	£7.20 VIT/OWC

AUSTRALIAN RED BRONZE **95**

WYNNS COONAWARRA ESTATE SHIRAZ 2001, SOUTHCORP SOUTH AUSTRALIA – *Full-bodied, with a soft glycerol texture and strawberry pie flavours. Nutmeg, cinnamon, and vanilla aromas.*	£7.20 BNK/HOU ODD/MW W
Y CABERNET SAUVIGNON 2002, YALUMBA SOUTH AUSTRALIA – *Very firm tannic structure binds the mulberry fruit palate. Lifted minty elements. Good varietal definition.*	£7.20 HOU/VIT NFW
PREECE CABERNET SAUVIGNON 2002, MITCHELTON WINES VICTORIA – *Youthful, deep, mouthfilling bramble-berry flavours. There's plenty of black fruit and mint on the palate.*	£7.30 FLY
PREECE MERLOT 2002, MITCHELTON WINES VICTORIA – *This wine has an exceptionally deep colour. Boot polish and blackberries on the nose. Full-bodied and intense.*	£7.30 FLY
BLEASDALE SHIRAZ CABERNET 2002, BLEASDALE SOUTH AUSTRALIA – *Eucalyptus, cherry compote, and vibrant spices. The intensity is good and the finish is balanced.*	£7.50 NFW/NYW FLY
FIDDLER'S CREEK CABERNET MERLOT 2000, BLUE PYRENEES VICTORIA – *Tobacco, mint, and spice envelop the wine's creamy black fruit. Maturing, with complex secondary aromas.*	£7.50 MKV
FIDDLER'S CREEK SHIRAZ CABERNET 2001, BLUE PYRENEES VICTORIA – *This ripe, mature wine has dusty tannins and opulent peppery blackberry fruit of moderate weight and concentration.*	£7.50 MKV
MIRANDA 1938 SHIRAZ 2003, MIRANDA WINES SOUTH AUSTRALIA – *Oak, redcurrants, pepper, and leather on the nose. The palate is full bodied, with spices and red fruit.*	£7.50 LAI
XANADU SECESSION SHIRAZ CABERNET 2002, XANADU NORMANS WESTERN AUSTRALIA – *Brightest ruby red. Juicy plums and rich prunes are overlaid with Christmas spices. Elegant, long, and fresh.*	£7.50 NFW/ODD
CLANCY'S 2002, PETER LEHMANN SOUTH AUSTRALIA – *A Barossa classic, with a medium-full palate of ripe plum, soft raspberry, and mouthwatering redcurrant flavours.*	£7.60 WIDELY AVAILABLE

AUSTRALIAN RED BRONZE

STEP ROAD CABERNET SAUVIGNON 2001, STEP ROAD WINERY South Australia – *Pronounced nose of blackcurrant and eucalyptus. The thick palate shows lush fruit with ripe tannins and sweet oak.*	£7.70 RAV/SMF WPR/NFW
TRENTHAM SHIRAZ 2001, TRENTHAM ESTATE South Australia – *A nose of Porty fruit. Sweet, prune fruit on the palate amid a swathe of tannins. Refreshing acidity.*	£7.70 BNK/NFW
WINDY PEAK CABERNET BLEND 2001, DE BORTOLI WINES Victoria – *The dry, evolved palate has warm, red fruit character and a firm tannic structure.*	£7.80 NFW/FLY
OMRAH SHIRAZ 2001, PLANTAGENET Western Australia – *Lushly fruited. Blackberries, blueberries, and sloes spill forth with abandon. Structured, judiciously oaked, and long.*	£7.90 WIDELY AVAILABLE
STEP ROAD SHIRAZ 2001, STEP ROAD WINERY South Australia – *With a subtle nose and a well-balanced palate with a smattering of spice and a lengthy finish.*	£7.90 RAV/WPR NFW
BAROSSA VALLEY ESTATE SHIRAZ 2001, BAROSSA VALLEY ESTATE South Australia – *Rich raspberry fruit, vanilla, cinnamon, and nutmeg aromas; hints of forest floor, grass, and leather.*	£8.00 VGN
HEARTLAND SHIRAZ 2002, HEARTLAND WINES South Australia – *Sumptuous ripe black-cherry palate. Alluring savoury meatiness and sweet oak.*	£8.00 GRT/NFW NYW
MAGNUS SHIRAZ CABERNET 2001, LEASINGHAM WINES South Australia – *Vibrant, sensuous, attractive, and rich, with damsons, cloves, and allspice underpinned by a web of grainy tannins.*	£8.00 NYW/JSM
MCPHERSON BASILISK SHIRAZ MOURVÈDRE 2002, MCPHERSON Victoria – *This has fresh, firm blueberry fruit, well-knit tannins, and coconut-vanilla oak. Fresh acidity and a grippy finish.*	£8.00 CTR/A&N CEP/FEN HOF
METALA SHIRAZ CABERNET SAUVIGNON 2001, BERINGER BLASS South Australia – *The deep colour is attractive, and the glorious forest fruit flavours are powerful and round. Elegant and well-integrated.*	£8.00 NYW

AUSTRALIAN RED BRONZE

OOMOO SHIRAZ 2001, BRL HARDY SOUTH AUSTRALIA – *Intense royal purple hue. Damsons and blueberries on the palate are lifted by peppery hints.*	£8.00 **CNT**
RESERVE SHIRAZ 2001, JACOB'S CREEK SOUTH AUSTRALIA – *Almost black in colour. Menthol, eucalyptus, and green-tea aromas dance over the ripe fruit.*	£8.00 **WTS/JSM**
SALTRAM BAROSSA CABERNET MERLOT 2002, BERINGER BLASS SOUTH AUSTRALIA – *Opaque. This is a well-crafted wine with a serious structure. Sweet fruit and integrated tannins.*	£8.00 **WFB**
SALTRAM BAROSSA SHIRAZ 2002, BERINGER BLASS SOUTH AUSTRALIA – *Smoky wine with tar and bramble aromas on the nose and palate. Supple structure and sweet fruit finish.*	£8.00 **WFB**
TESCO HOWCROFT ESTATE SHIRAZ 2002, SIMEON WINES SOUTH AUSTRALIA – *A nose of soft ripe fruit, with a light to medium-bodied palate of purple fruit. A fresh finish.*	£8.00 **TOS**
WAKEFIELD ESTATE SHIRAZ 2003, WAKEFIELD ESTATE SOUTH AUSTRALIA – *Ripe cherries and plums meld with toasty vanilla oak. Rich, full, and long, with grainy tannins.*	£8.00 **WIDELY AVAILABLE**
YARRA BURN SHIRAZ VIOGNIER 2002, YARRA BURN VICTORIA – *Feel the burn! Red- and white-fruit-salad flavours coalesce into a pure, silky, elegant whole.*	£8.00 **CNT**
MADFISH SHIRAZ 2002, HOWARD PARK WINES WESTERN AUSTRALIA – *Cherry-red colour and flavour. Fantastic grip and zippy acid buoy the attractive, ripe, spearmint-infused fruit.*	£8.20 **WIDELY AVAILABLE**
YALUMBA BAROSSA BUSH VINE GRENACHE 2002, YALUMBA SOUTH AUSTRALIA – *This wine has a distinctive silky cranberry fruit palate with warming alcohol, mature tannins, and peppercorn appeal.*	£8.20 **WIDELY AVAILABLE**
BROWN BROTHERS CABERNET SAUVIGNON 2001, BROWN BROTHERS VICTORIA – *This full-bodied wine has fine depth, with notes of cigar box, liquorice, juicy blackberries, and cream.*	£8.30 **EVI/JFE**

98 AUSTRALIAN RED BRONZE

BROWN BROTHERS SHIRAZ 2002, BROWN BROTHERS VICTORIA – *A beguiling, slightly smoky character on the nose while the palate brings fruit, spicy notes, and chunky tannins.*	£8.30 ESL/TOS JFE/JSM
FAMILY RESERVE BARREL AGED DURIF 2002, CASELLA WINES SOUTH AUSTRALIA – *Purplish black. A subdued nose leads to a rustic palate of baked plum tart.*	£8.30 LAI
PENFOLDS ORGANIC RED 2002, SOUTHCORP SOUTH AUSTRALIA – *Youthful tannins and fresh acidity, and notes of leather and smoke. Dried cherry fruit flavours.*	£8.30 BNK/SOM
PROMENADE OLD VINE SHIRAZ 2002, BEELGARA ESTATE NEW SOUTH WALES – *Deep colour and generous black fruit nose. A well-judged balance between rich, jammy fruit and spicy, vanilla-infused oak.*	£8.30 FFW/WOI WPR/NFW CVE
YALUMBA BAROSSA SHIRAZ 2001, YALUMBA SOUTH AUSTRALIA – *Packed with ripe fruit, this has a savoury side as well as supporting tannins and good oak.*	£8.30 WIDELY AVAILABLE
GSM GRENACHE SHIRAZ MOURVÈDRE 2002, PETER LEHMANN SOUTH AUSTRALIA – *A dark, deep, spicy wine, full of rich fruits. A peppery spine lurks beneath the fruit.*	£8.40 EDC/VDV NFW/G&M
HANGING ROCK AMAROO FARM SHIRAZ MOURVEDRE 2002, HANGING FARM WINERY VICTORIA – *Inky in colour. A big, bold sweet-fruited wine, with jammy blueberry fruit, vanilla oak, and a firm structure.*	£8.50 THI
FAMILY RESERVE DURIF 2003, DE BORTOLI WINES SOUTH AUSTRALIA – *Compelling notes of black molasses and banana on the nose; creamy vanilla and blackberry fruit in the mouth.*	£8.60 LAI
FAMILY RESERVE SHIRAZ 2003, DE BORTOLI WINES SOUTH AUSTRALIA – *Plums, spice, and smoke meld on the youthful, earthy palate, which is likely to develop further.*	£8.60 LAI
THE ROGUE CABERNET MERLOT 2001, NEPENTHE WINES SOUTH AUSTRALIA – *Cool mint and leafy blackcurrant scents. Touches of eucalyptus accentuate the rich black fruit flavours.*	£8.70 EDC/WPR NFW/OZW SWS

AUSTRALIAN RED BRONZE 99

MCLAREN VALE CABERNET SAUVIGNON 2002, SHOTTESBROOKE SOUTH AUSTRALIA – *Expressive mint and cassis nose leads to a powerful palate of ripe fruit and tannins.*	£8.90 ROG
ST HALLETT FAITH SHIRAZ 2002, ST HALLETT WINES SOUTH AUSTRALIA – *Peppery nose with sweet violet notes. The palate is fruit rich with soft tannins and structure.*	£8.90 BNK/NFW TOS/OZW NYW/JSM
ANNIE'S LANE SHIRAZ 2002, BERINGER BLASS SOUTH AUSTRALIA – *A classy wine, with bright-cherry and plum flavours.*	£9.00 NYW/ODD
BUSH VIEW MARGARET RIVER SHIRAZ 2002, EVANS & TATE WESTERN AUSTRALIA – *Weighty, with a very dry palate of bramble jam. Lengthy finish with a menthol lift.*	£9.00 M&S
GULF STATION PINOT NOIR 2003, DE BORTOLI WINES VICTORIA – *A nose of red berries and a touch of spice. The palate has fresh strawberries and soft, ripe tannins.*	£9.00 NFW
GULF STATION SHIRAZ 2002, DE BORTOLI WINES VICTORIA – *Dried savoury plums. In spite of its softness there's a kick of acidity on the finish.*	£9.00 NFW
RIDDOCH CABERNET MERLOT 2002, WINGARA WINE GROUP SOUTH AUSTRALIA – *The crisp yet soft palate proffers peppermint, espresso and tobacco notes, and blackcurrant fruit galore.*	£9.00 FLY
RIDDOCH CABERNET SAUVIGNON 2001, WINGARA WINE GROUP SOUTH AUSTRALIA – *Powerful eucalyptus and damson nose. The palate has cassis richness, solid tannins, and a creamy finish.*	£9.00 FLY
VICTORIA KINDRED SPIRITS MERLOT 2001, BEST'S WINES VICTORIA – *This Merlot's deep colour has a brick-red rim. Warm and inviting on nose and palate.*	£9.00 JNW/HOT
CORIOLE SANGIOVESE 2002, CORIOLE SOUTH AUSTRALIA – *Ripe, bramble fruit flavours. Weighty, with a broad, mouthfilling array of dates and cherries. Straightforward yet seamless.*	£9.10 WIDELY AVAILABLE

100 AUSTRALIAN RED BRONZE

BLEWITT SPRINGS MALBEC 2002, HILLSVIEW VINEYARDS South Australia – *The nose shows blueberry and spice aromas. The palate has masses of extract and the finish is powerful.*	£9.20 VDV/NFW BOO/ALL
PALANDRI MARGARET RIVER CABERNET SAUVIGNON 2002, PALANDRI WINES Western Australia – *Eucalyptus-driven nose with secondary cassis aromas. The palate is packed with spiced berry fruit checked by oak toast.*	£9.20 EDC/VIT JFE
THE HIGH TRELLIS CABERNET SAUVIGNON 2002, D'ARENBERG South Australia – *A supple, fleshy Cabernet with intense currant flavours and a firm tannic backbone.*	£9.20 RNS/NFW FLA/WES FLY/ODD
PENFOLDS THOMAS HYLAND CABERNET SAUVIGNON 2002, SOUTHCORP South Australia – *Gemstone red. Generously oaked yet balanced, with cassis and leaves on the nose and palate.*	£9.30 EVI/TOS
THE FOOTBOLT SHIRAZ 2001, D'ARENBERG South Australia – *Fiery cherry, tapenade, and capsicum aromas. An intoxicating palate of black plums. Very good intensity and complexity.*	£9.30 WIDELY AVAILABLE
BLUE PYRENEES CABERNET SAUVIGNON 2001, BLUE PYRENEES ESTATE Victoria – *Subtle nose of rosemary and cassis gives way to a mouthwatering palate of cool climate, sweetly ripe fruit.*	£9.50 BOO/INS
TREVELEN CABERNET MERLOT 2002, TREVELEN FARM Western Australia – *Mint and eucalyptus aromas. The palate is packed with squashy cassis fruit and tannins are soft and integrated.*	£9.50 ROG
WATER WHEEL SHIRAZ 2002, WATER WHEEL WINES Victoria – *Bold, rich and inky, with dark berries, vanilla oak, and a firm structure with a grippy finish.*	£9.50 OZW
FONTY'S POOL SHIRAZ 2001, FONTY'S POOL VINEYARDS Western Australia – *Oodles of black fruit, with a well-structured raft of grippy tannins keeping the warm alcohol in balance.*	£9.60 EDC/FFW NRW/CPR NYW/BOO
THE COVER DRIVE CABERNET SAUVIGNON 2002, JIM BARRY WINES South Australia – *Deep, dark, and brooding, its richness striving to balance the exuberant alcohol. Blackcurrants, plums, eucalyptus, and menthol.*	£9.70 VIT/NFW

AUSTRALIAN RED BRONZE

HAMILTON'S STONEGARDEN GRENACHE SHIRAZ 2001, HAMILTON'S EWELL VINEYARDS South Australia – *Dark and ripe, the palate screams red fruit, with integrated oak and acidity ensuring an elegant structure.*	£9.80 VDV/NFW MOV/SWS WRW
PREMIUM CABERNET SAUVIGNON MERLOT 2002, SANDALFORD Western Australia – *An elegant wine, its plummy nose ripe and round, its soft balanced palate spiked with peppercorns.*	£9.80 HAX
ST MARY'S HOUSE BLOCK CABERNET SAUVIGNON 2001, ST MARY'S South Australia – *The nose shows mint and eucalyptus notes. The palate is cassis rich with sweet vanilla oak and silky tannins.*	£9.80 ELV
STELLA BELLA CABERNET MERLOT 2000, STELLA BELLA WINES Western Australia – *Well-defined, with plenty of blackcurrant and redcurrant flavours, good intensity, and a long finish.*	£9.80 NFW/CCS ALL
BIN 61 SHIRAZ 2001, LEASINGHAM WINES South Australia – *Ripe, herbaceous and long. Additional cellaring will enable this lavish, muscular wine to display its charms fully.*	£10.00 NFW
HUNTER VALLEY SHIRAZ 2003, DE BORTOLI WINES New South Wales – *Concentrated and elegant, this black fruit beauty has plenty of sweet vanilla oak on the nose.*	£10.00 BOR/RSW
MCLAREN VALE CABERNET SAUVIGNON 2001, TATACHILLA WINERY South Australia – *Cassis-driven with berry and mint leaf aromas. The palate has good ripe fruit and tannins. Decent depth.*	£10.00 NFW
MCLAREN VALE MERLOT 2001, TATACHILLA WINERY South Australia – *A deeply coloured and intensely perfumed Australian wine. It is soft, medium-weight, poised, and balanced.*	£10.00 NFW
ORIGIN RESERVE SHIRAZ 2002, GRANT BURGE South Australia – *The nose shows tar and hedgerow aromas. The lush blackberry palate is balanced, supple, and concentrated.*	£10.00 THS
PIRRAMIMMA MCLAREN VALE CABERNET SAUVIGNON 2001, AC JOHNSTON South Australia – *Deep berry and minted nose leads to a lush fruit palate. Tannins and sweet oak are well-integrated.*	£10.00 MWW

102 AUSTRALIAN RED BRONZE

TESCO BAROSSA OLD VINES SHIRAZ 2002, MCGUIGAN SIMEON WINES SOUTH AUSTRALIA – A deep colour. The brisk alcohol sits well with the attractive, freshly-baked raspberry tart flavours.	£10.00 TOS
TYRRELL'S RUFUS STONE MCLAREN VALE SHIRAZ 2002, TYRRELL'S VINEYARDS PTY LTD SOUTH AUSTRALIA – Pungent aromatics of leather and briar lead to a dense black fruit palate. Strapping tannins and creamy oak.	£10.00 ODD
WIRRA WIRRA MCLAREN VALE GRENACHE 2002, WIRRA WIRRA VINEYARDS SOUTH AUSTRALIA – Perfumed with developed juicy plum fruit. The subtle soft fruit flavours are laced with vanilla.	£10.00 ODD
WYNNS COONAWARRA ESTATE CABERNET SAUVIGNON 2000, SOUTHCORP SOUTH AUSTRALIA – Dark rouge. The youthful black fruit aromas and flavours should develop further. Round tannic structure.	£10.00 HOU/NYW ODD
YARRA RIDGE PINOT NOIR 2002, BERINGER BLASS VICTORIA – Lifted black fruits dominate a streamlined palate, where the youthful fruit's fleshiness is balanced by good firm tannins.	£10.00 WFB
YERING CABERNET SAUVIGNON 2000, YERING STATION WINES VICTORIA – Plump, with cassis and mint aromas. The palate has fruit richness allied to a supple tannic structure.	£10.00 FLA
ALKOOMI SHIRAZ 2001, ALKOOMI WINES WESTERN AUSTRALIA – Good depth, with some development apparent on the leathery nose. Spiced red plum and cranberry flavours.	£10.20 BNK/JOB LAY
CHURCH BLOCK 2002, WIRRA WIRRA VINEYARDS SOUTH AUSTRALIA – Powerful cassis, mint and eucalyptus nose. Rich and supple palate with a touch of smoke on the finish.	£10.20 VDV/VIT SOM/WSO JSM
VASSE FELIX CABERNET SAUVIGNON MERLOT 2001, VASSE FELIX WESTERN AUSTRALIA – The nose shows a heady blend of wintergreen, eucalyptus, and vanilla oak. The lush damson palate is balanced.	£10.20 WIDELY AVAILABLE
PREMIUM CABERNET SAUVIGNON 2002, SANDALFORD WESTERN AUSTRALIA – Plums, cassis and strawberry fruit flavours radiate from this intensely flavoured, spicy, aromatic wine.	£10.40 HAX/NYW

AUSTRALIAN RED BRONZE 103

CLARE VALLEY CABERNET 2001, TIM ADAMS WINES **South Australia** – *Blackberries and redcurrants meld with lifted aromas of new-mown hay. A spicy, firm, and balanced wine.*	£10.50 AUC/NFW OZW
MCLAREN VALE COONAWARRA CABERNET SAUVIGNON 2001, CHAPEL HILL WINERY **South Australia** – *Classic Coonawarra menthol and gum tree nose; a palate of richly ripe currant fruit.*	£10.50 AUC/NFW TOS/FLA OZW
THE WALLACE 2002, GLAETZER WINES **South Australia** – *A smooth agglomeration of chocolate oak, green peppercorns, blackberries, and cherries.*	£10.50 GRT/VDV NFW/NYW ODD
TINTARA SHIRAZ 2000, BRL HARDY **South Australia** – *Intense and concentrated, with a dense wall of black fruit, flowers, spice and smoke.*	£10.50 CNT
STARVEDOG LANE SHIRAZ VIOGNIER 2003, RAVENSWOOD LANE **South Australia** – *Intense black fruit nose with toast and violet aromas. The palate is thick with depth to finish.*	£10.60 EDC/FFW NFW/CPR NYW
HEWITSON MISS HARRY 2002, HEWITSON **South Australia** – *Jammy, soft, and sweet-fruited on the nose, which leads to a ripe palate of vibrant red fruits.*	£10.70 BEN/WRK CCS/NYW FLY
THE FERGUS 2002, TIM ADAMS WINES **South Australia** – *Red-cherry jam and hints of nutmeg on the nose. Raspberry fruit flavours on the palate.*	£10.70 AUC/NFW OZW
CAPE JAFFA CABERNET SAUVIGNON 2001, CAPE JAFFA WINES **South Australia** – *Blueberries and blackcurrants line the palate. The nose has touches of violets and bay leaves.*	£10.80 HAX/VDV
CAPE JAFFA SHIRAZ 2001, CAPE JAFFA WINES **South Australia** – *Cooked tomatoey complexity. Well-balanced, with a sleek body and character in spades.*	£10.80 HAX/VDV
MCPHERSON RESERVE GOULBURN VALLEY SHIRAZ 2001, MCPHERSON **Victoria** – *Spicy, with a cool-climate palate of stewed prunes, a sprinkling of pepper, and a touch of mint.*	£11.00 CTR/A&N CEP/FEN HOF

104 AUSTRALIAN RED BRONZE

PHILLIPS ESTATE SHIRAZ 2002, PHILLIPS ESTATE **WESTERN AUSTRALIA** – *Black as night, with deep flavours of mature hedgerow fruit. Recommended for drinking now.*	£11.00 OZW
PONDALOWIE SHIRAZ CABERNET 2002, PONDALOWIE VINEYARDS **VICTORIA** – *Tobacco leaves, eucalyptus, leather, and liquorice radiate from this big, deep, ruby Australian wine.*	£11.00 AUC/FLA OZW
TINTARA CABERNET SAUVIGNON 1999, BRL HARDY **SOUTH AUSTRALIA** – *Vibrant redcurrant flavours meld with dark spices and cedar bark notes on the mouthwatering palate.*	£11.20 BNK/NFW
VOYAGER ESTATE SHIRAZ 2000, VOYAGER ESTATE **WESTERN AUSTRALIA** – *Taut and linear, with a dusty sweet oak nose, earthy berry flavours, and a deep vermilion tint.*	£11.20 NYW/J&B ODD
MCLEAN'S FARM RESERVE 2002, MCLEAN'S FARM WINES **SOUTH AUSTRALIA** – *Soft, elegant and juicy, with bold fruit, balanced oak, and a lengthy finish.*	£11.30 AUC/NFW TOS/OZW
ROBERT STEIN RESERVE SHIRAZ 2001, STEINS WINES **NEW SOUTH WALES** – *Black fruit and coffee on the nose. Savoury palate sports liquorice alongside robust tannins and a chewy finish.*	£11.30 ROG
CLAIRAULT CABERNET SAUVIGNON 2000, CLAIRAULT WINES **WESTERN AUSTRALIA** – *Victoria plum and black-cherry flavours and a hint of vanilla. Abundant fruit and spicy oak.*	£11.50 MOV/SWS
BAROSSA SHIRAZ 2002, HERITAGE WINES **SOUTH AUSTRALIA** – *Blackcurrants and redcurrants spill from the palate. The nose has plenty of woody, spicy oak.*	£11.60 AUC/NFW OZW/MOV NYW
COLDSTREAM HILLS PINOT NOIR 2002, SOUTHCORP **VICTORIA** – *Complex, soft, and ripe, with an enticing brick hue, cherry flavours and floral scents. Long, persistent finish.*	£11.60 EVI
WILLOWS CABERNET SAUVIGNON 2000, WILLOWS VINEYARD **SOUTH AUSTRALIA** – *Tones of vanilla and cedar bark grace the nose of this richly coloured, saturated Cabernet.*	£11.60 AUC/NFW OZW/MOV

AUSTRALIAN RED BRONZE 105

WILLOWS CABERNET SAUVIGNON 2001, WILLOWS VINEYARD SOUTH AUSTRALIA – *Opaque purple, with cedar, spice box and loam notes. Medium-bodied and powerfully structured.*	**£11.60** AUC/NFW OZW/MOV
HERITAGE CABERNET SAUVIGNON 2002, HERITAGE WINES SOUTH AUSTRALIA – *Inky black. Dried blackberries abound on the sweetly ripe, big, intense, spicy, and long palate.*	**£11.70** AUC/NFW OZW/MOV
PENLEY ESTATE HYLAND SHIRAZ 2002, PENLEY ESTATE SOUTH AUSTRALIA – *Young, minted, and forward. Likeable and leathery, with plenty of cranberry fruit. A bright finish.*	**£11.70** NRW/NFW CCS/NYW
TATACHILLA MCLAREN VALE SHIRAZ 2001, TATACHILLA WINERY SOUTH AUSTRALIA – *Pepper, dusky cherries, and spices; upfront and concentrated, with fruit galore, integrated tannins, and soft acidity.*	**£11.90** EDC/NFW BWL
EIGHT UNCLES CABERNET 2002, FOX GORDON WINES SOUTH AUSTRALIA – *A lifted, attractive nose of bark and eucalyptus, and firm young palate of black fruits.*	**£12.00** VDV
JUNIPER CABERNET SAUVIGNON 2000, JUNIPER ESTATE WESTERN AUSTRALIA – *Smooth tannins, appealing currant, and raspberry fruit and a hint of warm Indian spice.*	**£12.00** ADN
JUNIPER CABERNET SAUVIGNON 2001, JUNIPER ESTATE WESTERN AUSTRALIA – *Vibrant nose of burning leaves, gum trees, and ripe berries. The medium-weight palate is firm and fresh.*	**£12.00** ADN
JUNIPER ESTATE SHIRAZ 2001, JUNIPER ESTATE WESTERN AUSTRALIA – *Hedgerow fruit and flower nose. This wine is harmonious, balanced, and gentle with a subtly spicy finish.*	**£12.00** ADN
MITOLO JESTER 2002, MITOLO SOUTH AUSTRALIA – *Peppery black fruit. Powerful spiced plum flavours with a twist of mint. Lingering smoky finish.*	**£12.00** GRT/VDV NFW/NYW
NORFOLK RISE MOUNT BENSON SHIRAZ 2002, NORFOLK RISE VINEYARD SOUTH AUSTRALIA – *A generous, warm, ripe nose leads onto a great palate packed with crunchy fruit and decent tannins.*	**£12.00** VGN

AUSTRALIAN RED BRONZE

Wine	Price / Stockists
SCARPANTONI CABERNET SAUVIGNON 2002, SCARPANTONI ESTATE SOUTH AUSTRALIA – *Excellent varietal definition, with fresh blackcurrant fruit, notes of tobacco, and tones of clove spice.*	£12.00 LAI
WOLF BLASS PRESIDENTS SELECTION SHIRAZ 2001, BERINGER BLASS SOUTH AUSTRALIA – *A classic mint and gum tree aroma profile. Touches of spice and smoke accentuate the full-bodied cherry fruit.*	£12.00 FEN/ODD JSM
CLIFF EDGE SHIRAZ 2001, MOUNT LANGI GHIRAN VICTORIA – *Pepper and spice, crunchy black fruit, and smoky oak; grippy acidity and corduroy-textured tannins.*	£12.10 BEN/VDV MOV/NYW LIB/FLY
PHOENIX CABERNET SAUVIGNON 2002, PENLEY ESTATE SOUTH AUSTRALIA – *Cassis and menthol notes. The palate has hints of mocha and a seductive texture. Well-balanced oak.*	£12.10 NRW/NFW CCS/NYW
CORIOLE LALLA ROOKH 2001, CORIOLE SOUTH AUSTRALIA – *Still relatively young, with mint, blackberries, herbs, and an elegance that bodes well for the future.*	£12.20 VDV/SOM NFW/CCS NYW/FLY
HOWARD PARK SCOTSDALE CABERNET SAUVIGNON 2001, HOWARD PARK WINES WESTERN AUSTRALIA – *Classic example of Australian Cabernet: eucalyptus, coffee, chocolate, and sweetly ripe cassis. Fresh, firm, and cedary.*	£12.20 JNW/NYW FLY
LESTON CABERNET SAUVIGNON 2001, HOWARD PARK WINES WESTERN AUSTRALIA – *Leather, smoke, and ripe green peppers galore. Cedar, blackberries, and youthful tannins to the fore.*	£12.20 JNW/NYW FLY/BWL
THE DERELICT VINEYARD GRENACHE 2002, D'ARENBERG SOUTH AUSTRALIA – *Nothing's been neglected, we assure you. Sweet red plum fruit nose. The palate is soft, concentrated and medium-long.*	£12.20 NFW/NYW FLY
DIRECTOR'S CUT SHIRAZ 2001, HEARTLAND WINES SOUTH AUSTRALIA – *Brambly and oaky with a firm cushion of berries interwoven with masculine tannins.*	£12.50 GRT/NFW NYW/ODD
HAMILTON'S RAILWAY SHIRAZ 2000, HAMILTON'S EWELL VINEYARDS SOUTH AUSTRALIA – *Sweetly ripe, peppery nose. Delightful savoury balsamic notes. A firm tannic web supports the solid palate.*	£12.60 VDV/NFW OZW/NYW SWS

AUSTRALIAN RED BRONZE

Wine	Price
NEPENTHE PINOT NOIR 2002, NEPENTHE WINES **South Australia** – *Nepenthe just can't seem to put a foot wrong. Glamorous, soft, lush summer fruit flavours.*	£12.70 WIDELY AVAILABLE
PICTURE SERIES ANGELS SHARE SHIRAZ 2003, TWO HANDS WINES South Australia – *Massive colour. Intense rhubarb and raspberry flavours coalesce with chocolate in this Shiraz.*	£12.80 VDV/SOM NFW/CCS ALL
PLUNKETT SHIRAZ RESERVE 2002, PLUNKETT WINES Victoria – *Peppery spicy notes surround dark berry fruit and smoky oak. Juicy and jammy, with refreshing acidity.*	£12.80 NFW/CCS ALL
BROWN BROTHERS LIMITED RELEASE SHIRAZ 1997, BROWN BROTHERS Victoria – *A ripe, leathery nose and a palate of plum and blackberry fruit with hints of liquorice and spice.*	£13.00 NRW
CLASSIC MCLAREN VALE GRENACHE 1999, CLASSIC MCLAREN WINES South Australia – *There's a touch of maturity in the balanced, very dry, rich palate of mulberries and cinnamon.*	£13.00 OZW
LONGBOTTOM VINEYARD CABERNET SAUVIGNON 2002, TATACHILLA WINES South Australia – *A strongly coloured wine. Bourbon vanilla, liquorice, cigar box, and cocoa flavours of very good concentration.*	£13.00 LAI
SHOW RESERVE CABERNET MERLOT 1998, WYNDHAM ESTATE South Australia – *Rubber and blackcurrants on the nose. The palate has grainy tannins and a sweetly ripe finish.*	£13.00 CAX
HAMILTON'S RAILWAY SHIRAZ 2001, HAMILTON'S EWELL VINEYARDS South Australia – *A glycerine texture and an appealing mature colour enhance the mélange of truffle and blackberry flavours.*	£13.10 VDV/NFW OZW/SWS
SMITH & HOOPER WRATTONBULLY LIMITED EDITION MERLOT 2001, YALUMBA South Australia – *Mint-tastic. Excellent poise. Admirable bramble fruit definition has been achieved without too much concentration.*	£13.20 VDV/VIT SOM/NFW
CHATEAU REYNELLA SHIRAZ 2001, CHATEAU REYNELLA South Australia – *Smoothly textured, with smoky oak, mocha, and ripe cherry fruit on the structured nose and palate.*	£13.70 NFW/NYW WTS

AUSTRALIAN RED BRONZE

KATNOOK CABERNET SAUVIGNON 2001, WINGARA WINE GROUP SOUTH AUSTRALIA – *Supple and juicy, with violet perfume and rich blackcurrant fruit on the palate. The finish has depth.*	**£13.70** NFW/NYW WTS/FLY
NED AND HENRY'S SHIRAZ 2002, HEWITSON SOUTH AUSTRALIA – *A lightly wooded wine, with a lick of white pepper freshly ground over juicy red berries.*	**£13.70** BEN/VDV WRK/CCS NYW/FLY
PIPERS BROOK PINOT NOIR 2002, PIPERS BROOK TASMANIA – *Wild strawberry scents and flavours. A ruby red, ripe, dense, lush, and generously oaked wine.*	**£13.70** WIDELY AVAILABLE
BAROSSA SHIRAZ 2002, ELDERTON WINES SOUTH AUSTRALIA – *Earthy and savoury. Green vegetal hints score the deep rich blackberry palate. Concentrated and intense.*	**£13.80** FLY
FILSELL SHIRAZ 2002, GRANT BURGE WINES SOUTH AUSTRALIA – *Muted, with tantalising raspberry and pepper. A certain youthful richness is apparent. Will open further.*	**£13.80** UNS/NFW RWM/FLY WRW
SPEAR GULLY SHIRAZ 2002, SPEAR GULLY WINES VICTORIA – *Concentrated, developed and dark, this is a delicious mocha and Morello-cherry concoction.*	**£13.90** AUC/FLA OZW
MARIGINIUP SHIRAZ 2001, PAUL CONTI WINES WESTERN AUSTRALIA – *Ruby red. Peppers and spice on the nose. The palate is clean, fresh, ripe, and well-defined.*	**£14.00** MOV
WATERSHED CABERNET SAUVIGNON MERLOT 2002, WATERSHED PREMIUM WINES WESTERN AUSTRALIA – *Loaded with ripe-berry fruit flavours and tinged with leafy cedar and cigar box aromas.*	**£14.00** ORB
ST HALLETT BLACKWELL SHIRAZ 2001, ST HALLETT WINES SOUTH AUSTRALIA – *Fruit-driven and forward, with immediate appeal.*	**£14.20** NRW/NFW
ROSS CABERNET SAUVIGNON 2002, ROSS ESTATE SOUTH AUSTRALIA – *Minted bramble fruit mingles with cocoa powder and undergrowth on the ripe, juicy, concentrated palate.*	**£14.30** LAI

AUSTRALIAN RED BRONZE 109

NEPENTHE ZINFANDEL 2002, NEPENTHE WINES **South Australia** – *A minty character and supple tannins add structure to the ripe summer fruit flavours.*	**£14.90** EDC/HOU VDV/NFW OZW/JSM
BURTON 2000 MCLAREN VALE SHIRAZ 2000, BURTON PREMIUM WINES **South Australia** – *Pepper and smoke nose leads to a pungent blueberry palate. Tannins are supple and oak is well-judged.*	**£15.00** AHW
BURTON 2001 MCLAREN VALE SHIRAZ 2001, BURTON PREMIUM WINES **South Australia** – *Cherry liqueur on vanilla sponge cake nose. Spicy and jammy, with leathery notes on the long, sultry finish.*	**£15.00** AHW
COONAWARRA CABERNET SAUVIGNON 2000, BURTON PREMIUM WINES **South Australia** – *Dark ruby, with restrained yet lifted elements of cassis, cedar, and ripe tomato. Generous oak. Elegant.*	**£15.00** AHW
HOUGHTON PEMBERTON MERLOT 2002, HOUGHTON **Western Australia** – *An intense youthful purple colour. The soft nose possesses plums and leather; the palate is rich and firm.*	**£15.00** HOF
JOSEPH ANGEL GULLY SHIRAZ 2001, PRIMO ESTATE **South Australia** – *Violets, black-cherries and cracked pepper on the nose. Mocha, liquorice, and mint on the palate.*	**£15.00** AUC/FLA
MARGARET RIVER CABERNET SAUVIGNON 2002, HOUGHTON **Western Australia** – *Dense, layered, and packed with flavour, with ripe currants and blueberries, cedar, and mint.*	**£15.00** FEN
PENFOLDS BIN 389 CABERNET SHIRAZ 2001, SOUTHCORP **South Australia** – *So purple it's virtually black. Powerful oak tannins underpin elegant dark fruit on the palate.*	**£15.00** WIDELY AVAILABLE
WOLF BLASS GOLD LABEL SHIRAZ 2001, BERINGER BLASS **South Australia** – *Piles and piles of hedgerow fruits and a beautiful garnet gemstone colour. Balanced and approachable.*	**£15.00** WAV
ROSEMOUNT ESTATE TRADITIONAL MCLAREN VALE RED 2001, SOUTHCORP **South Australia** – *The heady berry and eucalyptus nose leads to a soft fruit palate showing nicely integrated oak and tannin.*	**£15.20** BNK

AUSTRALIAN RED BRONZE

YARRA VALLEY PINOT NOIR 2002, DE BORTOLI WINES **VICTORIA** – *Youthful, with minty black fruit and a fresh, open palate with spice and good structure.*	£15.30 BNK/VDV GHL/NFW FLY
MERUM SHIRAZ 2002, MERUM **WESTERN AUSTRALIA** – *Soft, youthful, approachable, and made for early drinking. Seductive flavours of Chinese duck with orange and allspice.*	£15.50 ROG
BREMERTON OLD ADAM SHIRAZ 2001, BREMERTON **SOUTH AUSTRALIA** – *Minty notes on the nose, while the palate has a beguiling richness of berries and sweet American oak.*	£15.70 VDV/SOM NFW/CCS NYW
SPECIALIZED SHIRAZ CABERNET MERLOT 2002, PENNY'S HILL **SOUTH AUSTRALIA** – *A complex nose of fruitcake and berries, and a palate where fruit compote balances gentle tannin layers.*	£15.90 FFW/NFW CVE/HOH ODD
TALTARNI CEPHAS 2001, TALTARNI VINEYARDS **VICTORIA** – *Harmonious, developed, and liberally spiced. Excellent concentration of brisk red berries and toasty oak. A long dry finish.*	£16.00 LAY
THE MENZIES COONAWARRA CABERNET SAUVIGNON 2000, YALUMBA **SOUTH AUSTRALIA** – *Deep wine with mint and eucalyptus aromas and a lush palate. Good concentration, richness and harmony to finish.*	£16.00 VDV/VIT SOM/NFW
BLEASDALE GENERATIONS SHIRAZ 1999, BLEASDALE **SOUTH AUSTRALIA** – *Spicy, earthy notes on the nose. A ripe-fruited palate with taut tannins in balance with gentle oak ageing.*	£16.80 VDV/NFW ODD
GEOFF MERRILL RESERVE SHIRAZ 1998, GEOFF MERRILL **SOUTH AUSTRALIA** – *A deep, developed, and warming wine, with strawberries, sweet spicebox scents, and woody tannins.*	£17.00 BNK /EVW HWL
CHAPEL HILL THE VICAR 2001, CHAPEL HILL WINERY **SOUTH AUSTRALIA** – *This quality wine is youthful and firm, with bramble fruit and green bell peppers in abundance.*	£18.00 AUC/FLA OZW
ROSS RESERVE SHIRAZ 2002, ROSS ESTATE **SOUTH AUSTRALIA** – *Dense, deep ruby red. Richly fruited, yet light and peppery, with firm, youthful fruit.*	£18.00 LAI

AUSTRALIAN RED BRONZE ■■■

JOSEPH CABERNET SAUVIGNON MODA 2001, PRIMO ESTATE WINES SOUTH AUSTRALIA – *Italian winemaking methods help add an extra dimension to the elegant cassis fruit.*	**£18.40** WIDELY AVAILABLE
THE ANGELUS CABERNET SAUVIGNON 2000, WIRRA WIRRA VINEYARDS SOUTH AUSTRALIA – *Powerful, with an intense berry, tar, and eucalyptus nose. The palate is deep and long with excellent structure.*	**£18.70** VDV/VIT SOM/WSO
ORIGIN CABERNET SAUVIGNON RESERVE SERIES 2001, WINERY EXCHANGE SOUTH AUSTRALIA – *Green pepper, tree bark, and youthful firm berries line the palate. Persistent and developed.*	**£19.00** WXC
ORIGIN SHIRAZ RESERVE SERIES 2002, WINERY EXCHANGE SOUTH AUSTRALIA – *Fruity, with blackberry and smoke aromas. Balanced ripe tannins and a lick of sweet oak.*	**£19.00** WXC
REIVER 2002, MITOLO SOUTH AUSTRALIA – *Lifted peppermint, creosote, plum, and lavender scents grace this intense, richly fruited, tightly-knit wine.*	**£19.00** GRT/VDV NFW/NYW
LANGI SHIRAZ 2000, MOUNT LANGI GHIRAN VICTORIA – *Christmas spices, leathery notes, ripe, vibrant damsons and a lengthy fresh finish. Exotic.*	**£20.20** WIDELY AVAILABLE
CURLY FLAT PINOT NOIR 2000, CURLY FLAT VICTORIA – *Vinous, ripe, and feminine, with seductive strawberries and cream flavours and understated barnyard aromatics.*	**£20.60** CCS/LIB FLY
CHARLES MELTON SHIRAZ 2001, CHARLES MELTON WINES SOUTH AUSTRALIA – *Fresh acidity buoys the lively chocolatey, peppery bilberry fruit. Moderately light colour and admirably sustained finish.*	**£20.90** WIDELY AVAILABLE
EIGHT SONGS SHIRAZ 1999, PETER LEHMANN SOUTH AUSTRALIA – *Very good varietal definition is in evidence: ripe raspberries, rich earth tones, and delicate floral notes.*	**£20.90** EDC/VDV NFW/G&M ODD
CLASSIC CLARE SHIRAZ 1998, LEASINGHAM WINES SOUTH AUSTRALIA – *Toasty oak and supple tannins swaddle ripe, opulent cassis fruit in a soothing blanket.*	**£21.00** VDV

AUSTRALIAN RED BRONZE

THE COPPERMINE ROAD CABERNET SAUVIGNON 2002, D'ARENBERG South Australia – *A typically full-blown affair from d'Arenberg, with big tannins balanced by ripe blackcurannts, plums, leather, tar, and oak.*	**£21.10** NFW/NYW FLY/ODD
ST ANDREWS CABERNET SAUVIGNON 1998, WAKEFIELD ESTATE South Australia – *Despite its age the fruit is still youthful, with a pleasing eucalyptus tinge. A big wine.*	**£21.30** LAI/RAV WPR/NFW RWM/SWS
WAKEFIELD ST ANDREWS SHIRAZ 2000, WAKEFIELD ESTATE South Australia – *A concentrated and dense wine, with ripe, supple flavours of caramel apples and blueberry pie.*	**£21.40** LAI/RAV WPR/NFW RWM/SWS
PETALUMA ADELAIDE HILLS SHIRAZ 2001, PETALUMA South Australia – *The nose is concentrated with perfumed blackberry aromas. A sweet and harmonious palate with good depth to finish.*	**£21.80** VDV/NFW NYW
EIGHT SONGS SHIRAZ 1998, PETER LEHMANN South Australia – *Inky wine with smoke and bramble aromas on the nose and palate. The finish is deep and harmonious.*	**£21.90** EDC/VDV G&M/WTS ODD
HOWARD PARK CABERNET SAUVIGNON 2001, HOWARD PARK WINES Western Australia – *Sweet and rich nose with lifted briar aromas. The palate shows cassis intensity married to supple tannic structure.*	**£22.40** JNW/WRK SOM/NYW FLY/BWL
CORIOLE LLOYD RESERVE SHIRAZ 2001, CORIOLE South Australia – *Spicy and earthy. Has good depth of flavour, with the crunchy fruit in balance with some appealing oak.*	**£23.20** WIDELY AVAILABLE
KINNAIRD SHIRAZ 2001, CAPEL VALE WINES Western Australia – *This deeply coloured wine, with its delicate nose of soy sauce and sun-warmed blackberries, is crisp and attractive.*	**£24.00** D&D
REDBROOK CABERNET SAUVIGNON 1999, EVANS & TATE Western Australia – *Brambles, blackberries, and cigar box. Generous and multi-dimensional, with a seamless, textured, silky core.*	**£27.00** P&S
PENFOLDS ST HENRI SHIRAZ 2000, SOUTHCORP South Australia – *Smoky coffee aromas amid the cassis. The palate has high tannins, ripe, and elegant fruit and pleasing complexity.*	**£27.50** VDV/SOM

AUSTRALIAN RED BRONZE / SEAL

WYNNS COONAWARRA ESTATE MICHAEL SHIRAZ 1998, SOUTHCORP SOUTH AUSTRALIA – *The soft understated caramel and cappuccino oak flavours smooth out the vibrant Morello cherry character.*	**£30.00** VDV/NYW
ROSEMOUNT ESTATE BALMORAL SYRAH 1998, SOUTHCORP SOUTH AUSTRALIA – *Some maturity is displayed in the brick-red colour of this wine. Chocolate mint flavours. Terrific mouthfeel.*	**£35.00** WTS
KATNOOK ODYSSEY CABERNET SAUVIGNON 1999, WINGARA WINE GROUP SOUTH AUSTRALIA – *Sweet currant nose, with hints of raisin and coconut. Ripe palate has mannered oak- and grape-derived tannins.*	**£35.70** NFW/NYW FLY
ROSEMOUNT ESTATE MOUNTAIN BLUE MUDGEE SHIRAZ CABERNET 2000, SOUTHCORP NEW SOUTH WALES – *Fine and deep, a rich smooth palate packed with purple fruit and balanced tannin.*	**£37.00** EVW
THE OCTAVIUS OLD VINE BAROSSA SHIRAZ 2000, YALUMBA SOUTH AUSTRALIA – *A dark, ripe, and long wine, with concentrated bramble flavours and an enviable creamy mouthfeel.*	**£37.50** VDV/VIT SOM/NFW NYW

SEAL OF APPROVAL
AUSTRALIAN RED

CABERNET SAUVIGNON 1998, SOUTHCORP SOUTH AUSTRALIA – *Mature wine that retains good density. With the complexity that comes from age, it's at its peak now.*	**£38.50** VDV/SOM WTS/ODD
JACK MANN CABERNET SAUVIGNON 1999, HOUGHTON WINES WESTERN AUSTRALIA – *Delightful sweet cassis merges seamlessly with supporting fine-tannined oak in this serious wine with a long finish.*	**£42.50** CNT
THOMAS HARDY CABERNET SAUVIGNON 1999, BRL HARDY SOUTH AUSTRALIA – *Deep in colour, with a peppery, exuberant nose and rich, succulent berry fruit in a friendly, well-oaked style.*	**£47.40** VDV/VGN
GEOFF MERRILL HENLEY 1997, GEOFF MERRILL SOUTH AUSTRALIA – *Orange-brick red colour. Farmyard character marries ripe bramble fruit. Drink this mature Australian wine now.*	**£50.00** NYW

AUSTRALIAN RED SEAL

☆ **SI JOLI PETIT AUSTRALIAN SHIRAZ CABERNET NV, PAUL SAPIN,** SOUTH AUSTRALIA – *Vibrant red- and black-hedgerow-berry flavours mingle with pepper notes.*	●£1.00 ROG
☆ **FIRST FLIGHT AUSTRALIAN DRY RED 2003, BRL HARDY** SOUTH AUSTRALIA – *Forward, approachable, and fruity, with piles of red apples, cranberries, and redcurrants.*	£3.00 SMF
☆ **BILLYGOAT SANGIOVESE 2003, CHIVERTON ESTATE** NEW SOUTH WALES – *Chewy black-cherry fruit with enchanting scents of cedar bark and tar.*	£4.00 NFW
☆ **FIRST FLIGHT AUSTRALIAN SHIRAZ CABERNET 2002, BRL HARDY** SOUTH AUSTRALIA – *A web of woody tannins underscores the cassis and white pepper palate.*	£4.00 SMF
☆ **KALGOORIE SHIRAZ CABERNET 2003, ANGOVES** SOUTH AUSTRALIA – *Leafy notes emanate from the ripe cassis and herb-strewn palate.*	£4.00 NTD
☆ **MASTERPEACE SHIRAZ CABERNET SAUVIGNON GRENACHE 2003, ANDREW PEACE WINES** VICTORIA – *Highly coloured. Notes of mint and flavours of plums and cinnamon.*	£4.00 NTD/SAF
☆ **MOONDARRA SHIRAZ 2003, SIMEON** SOUTH AUSTRALIA – *Rich purple hue. Flavours of damsons, blueberries, and clove buds.*	£4.00 MWW
☆ **MOONDARRA SHIRAZ CABERNET 2003, SIMEON** SOUTH AUSTRALIA – *Redcurrants meld with Victoria plums. Notes of cedar and leather.*	£4.00 WAV

SILVER
AUSTRALIAN SPARKLING

☆ **TASMANIA VINTAGE CUVÉE 1999, JANSZ YALUMBA** **TASMANIA** – *Apples, bananas, caramel, and almonds on the nose. The palate has a firm backbone and cleansing acidity. Mature and persistent.*	**£12.70** VDV/VIT TAU/SOM NFW/FLA
YARRABANK SPARKLING VINTAGE 1998, YERING STATION WINES **VICTORIA** – *Fresh fruit on the nose. Toasted almond and marzipan run through the appley palate. A creamy, long finish.*	**£15.30** FLA
CLASSIC CLARE SPARKLING SHIRAZ 1994, LEASINGHAM WINES **SOUTH AUSTRALIA** – *Dark crimson, with energetic mousse and ripe, perfumed fruit. A touch of chocolate oak adds richness to raspberry flavours.*	**£24.00** NYW/WTS

BRONZE
AUSTRALIAN SPARKLING

☆ **BANROCK STATION SPARKLING SHIRAZ NV, BANROCK STATION** **SOUTH AUSTRALIA** – *Foamy, lasting mousse. Concentrated plum fruit and spices; caramelly notes. Intensely aromatic.*	**£8.00** WIDELY AVAILABLE
☆ **DEAKIN SELECT SPARKLING SHIRAZ 2002, WINGARA WINE GROUP** **VICTORIA** – *Saddle-leather, chocolate and vanilla oak. The attractive palate heaves with bramble fruit and frothy mousse.*	**£8.00** FXT
☆ **WYNDHAM ESTATE BIN 555 SPARKLING SHIRAZ NV, WYNDHAM ESTATE** **SOUTH AUSTRALIA** – *Youthful fruit compote and herb aromas. Fresh, inviting blackberry fruit is dusted with fine tannins.*	**£8.00** MRN
☆ **SEAVIEW PINOT NOIR CHARDONNAY VINTAGE 1999, SOUTHCORP** **SOUTH AUSTRALIA** – *An attack of ripe toasty citrus fruit. One judge said: "Lemon meringue pie. With custard."*	**£8.50** SOM/EVI NYW
☆ **PREMIUM BRUT CUVÉE NV, JANSZ YALUMBA** **TASMANIA** – *Orange blossoms, freshly baked biscuits, peardrops, and apples. Delicate bubbles and a golden hue.*	**£9.90** WIDELY AVAILABLE

AUSTRALIAN SPARK. BRONZE / SEAL **/ SW.** SILVER / BRONZE

BROWN BROTHERS PINOT NOIR CHARDONNAY NV, BROWN BROTHERS MILAWA Victoria – *Russet apples, toast, and toffee flavours. Effervescent mousse. This enchanting, intense Australian sparkler has a rich ochre colour.*	£10.50 EVI/NRW JFE/WTS

SEAL OF APPROVAL
AUSTRALIAN SPARKLING

☆ **HARDY'S STAMP OF AUSTRALIA SPARKLING PINOT NOIR CHARDONNAY NV, BRL HARDY** South Australia – *Ripe strawberries, lush lemons, and hints of toast.*	£7.20 VGN/SMF TOS/JSM
☆ **NOTTAGE HILL CHARDONNAY BRUT 2001, BRL HARDY** South Australia – *Full-flavoured, with ripe lemons and green apples. Vigorous mousse.*	£7.30 VGN/FEN JSM

SILVER
AUSTRALIAN SWEET

☆ **PETER LEHMANN BOTRYTIS SEMILLON 2001, PETER LEHMANN** South Australia – *Tropical lychees, tangy marmalade and sweet stone fruits marry happily with notes of petrol and spiced oak. Wedded bliss.*	£7.30 EDC/VDV NFW/G&M
BROWN BROTHERS LATE HARVESTED NOBLE RIESLING 1999, BROWN BROTHERS Victoria – *Seville orange and botrytis scents. The luscious marmalade palate has a pretty acidic streak.*	£10.10 EVI/NRW JFE/WRW

BRONZE
AUSTRALIAN SWEET

CLARE VALLEY CORDON CUT RIESLING 2003, MOUNT HORROCKS South Australia – *Smoky notes rise from the nose. The palate has plenty of lemon mousse flavours and a velvety texture.*	£13.40 WIDELY AVAILABLE

NOBLE ONE 2001, DE BORTOLI WINES NEW SOUTH WALES – *Orange gold colour. Big botrytis on the nose; creamy lemon brûlée and candied oranges on the palate.*	**£14.00** WIDELY AVAILABLE
NOBLE ONE 2002, DE BORTOLI WINES NEW SOUTH WALES – *This golden-hued dessert wine has rich barley sugar flavours and scents of citrus blossom on the nose.*	**£14.40** WIDELY AVAILABLE

TROPHY
AUSTRALIAN FORTIFIED

☆ **STANTON AND KILLEEN CLASSIC RUTHERGLEN MUSCAT NV, STANTON AND KILLEEN** VICTORIA – *Sweet and rich, with caramel, nutty complexity and overlying Christmas cake, candied peel, tangy orange, and smoky characters.*	▲**£14.30** CCS/NYW FLY

GOLD
AUSTRALIAN FORTIFIED

☆ **BROWN BROTHERS LIQUEUR MUSCAT NV, BROWN BROTHERS MILAWA** VICTORIA – *Luscious and unctuously sweet. Packed with marmalade and orange syrup flavours, caramel, burnt toffee, and spice.*	■**£10.40** EVI/NRW JFE/OWC WRW MWW

SILVER
AUSTRALIAN FORTIFIED

☆ **SEPPELTS DP63 RUTHERGLEN MUSCAT NV, SOUTHCORP** VICTORIA – *Caramel, raisin and treacle aromas on the nose. Sweet, concentrated palate with multi-layered fruit. The finish has depth.*	**£8.00** NFW
☆ **SHOW LIQUEUR MUSCAT NV, DE BORTOLI WINES** NEW SOUTH WALES – *Toffee and caramel abound with good acidity leading to coffee and molasses swimming in a rich, voluptuous texture.*	**£9.60** BNK/VDV GHL/NFW FLY/INS

BRONZE
AUSTRALIAN FORTIFIED

AMPBELLS RUTHERGLEN MUSCAT NV, CAMPBELLS OF RUTHERGLEN VICTORIA – *Nutty tones, with toffee and spice; lifted notes of orange blossom, and a lingering sweet finish.*	£8.50 WIDELY AVAILABLE
TANTON AND KILLEEN RUTHERGLEN MUSCAT NV, STANTON AND KILLEEN VICTORIA – *A nose of orange blossom. Sweetness on the palate is well-balanced by acidity and tangerine fruit flavour.*	£10.90 WIDELY AVAILABLE
THE BLACK NOBLE NV, DE BORTOLI WINES NEW SOUTH WALES – *Coffee beans, caramel, and allspice on the nose. The palate is a warm blend of marmalade and molasses.*	■£15.80 WIDELY AVAILABLE

GOLD MEDALS HAVE SCORED the equivalent of at least 18.5/20 (or 95/100) and are exceptional. Silver has scored over 17/20 (or 90/100), bronze over 15.5/20 (or 85/100), and seals of approval over 14/20 (or 80/100).
☆ particularly good value
★ truly great value
▲ 50CL bottle
■ 37.5CL bottle
● 10CL bottle

FOR STOCKIST CODES turn to page 355. For regularly updated information about stockists and the International Wine Challenge, visit **wineint.com**. For a full glossary of wine terms and a complete free wine course, visit robertjoseph-onwine.com

AUSTRIA

No wine-producing country has reinvented itself as radically as Austria. The so-called anti-freeze scandal of twenty years ago centered on cheap, medium-sweet alternatives to Liebfraumilch. Today, this country is synonymous with rich and spicy dry whites made from grapes ranging from Riesling and Sauvignon Blanc to the local Grüner Veltliner; with luscious late-harvest wines that compete with the finest Sauternes; and with world-class reds, often made from varieties rarely found elsewhere.

TROPHY
AUSTRIAN WHITE

STEINMASSL RIESLING TROCKEN 2002, LOIMER **NIEDERÖSTERREICH** – *White flowers, satsumas, and earth on the nose. Fresh lemon rind acidity on the textured palate. Characterful.*	**£21.90** TWM NYW LIB/FLY

SILVER
AUSTRIAN WHITE

GRÜNER VELTLINER WÖSENDORFER KOLLMÜTZ 2002, RUDI PICHLER **NIEDERÖSTERREICH** – *Honeyed concentration is lifted by fresh, crisp orange peel. Tangy but tamed, and elegant. A great grapefruit length.*	**£18.30** GON

BRONZE
AUSTRIAN WHITE

GRÜNER VELTLINER SANDGRUBE PRIVATFÜLLUNG 2002, WOLFGANG AIGNER **NIEDERÖSTERREICH** – *A soft, creamily-textured wine with floral notes, whitecurrant, and orange zest essence and excellent length.*	**£10.20** HAM
WOHLMUTH SAUVIGNON BLANC 2003, GERHARD WOHLMUTH **STYRIA** – *Ground yellow spices and pickled lemons fill the nose and palate of this dry Styrian seductress.*	**£10.90** HAM

120 AUSTRIAN WHITE BRONZE

KAFERBERG GRÜNER VELTLINER 2002, LOIMER **NIEDERÖSTERREICH** – *Opulent orange scented nose and palate, with good weight, pith, blackcurrant leaves, minerality, and keen acidity.*	**£11.60** TAU/LIB FLY
UMATHUM GELBER & ROTER TRAMINER 2003, JOSEF UMATHUM **BURGENLAND** – *Ripe and concentrated, with rose oil and bitter peachstone scents. The palate displays very fresh acidity.*	**£12.50** FWW
UMATHUM PINOT GRIS 2003, JOSEF UMATHUM **BURGENLAND** – *The nose shows peach and apricot aromas. The palate displays intensity, balance, and a fine spicy finish.*	**£12.50** FWW
GRÜNER VELTLINER ALTE REBEN 2002, MARTIN NIGL **NIEDERÖSTERREICH** – *Aromatic and rich, showing lychee and musk aromas. The earthy palate is balanced with fresh acidity.*	**£13.40** GON
RIESLING PRIVAT SENFTENBERGER PIRI 2002, MARTIN NIGL **NIEDERÖSTERREICH** – *Slatey minerals and allspice aromas on the nose. Ripe bittersweet apples line the palate. Long finish.*	**£15.10** GON
SPIEGEL GRÜNER VELTLINER 2002, LOIMER **NIEDERÖSTERREICH** – *There is a good intensity of pink grapefruit on the nose and a toffee richness on the palate. Balanced citrus acidity.*	**£16.90** LIB/FLY
LOIMER RIESLING AL 2002, LOIMER **NIEDERÖSTERREICH** – *Glowing citrus flavours emanate from this medium-dry, glossy, balanced Austrian wine with tantalisingly soft acidity.*	**£22.00** WRK/TAU LIB/FLY
ZÖBINGER HEILIGENSTEIN RIESLING ALTE REBEN TROCKEN 2001, WEINGUT BRÜNDLMAYER **KAMPTAL** – *Toasted almonds and waxy orange flowers on the nose. The mouth fills with lushly textured sticky citrus fruit.*	**£24.00** HAX/NYW
RIESLING SMARAGD WEIENKIRCHNER ACHLEITCHEN 2002, RUDI PICHLER **NIEDERÖSTERREICH** – *A Riesling with a tang of honey and a touch of minerality. Elegant, mouthwatering bitter lemon flavours.*	**£24.60** GON

GOLD
AUSTRIAN RED

PRÄDIUM 2003, ERICH SCHEIBLHOFER BURGENLAND – *Smoky and toasty with notes of roasted vegetables and meat stew. A palate of raisins and rich oak.*	£19.00 NYW

SILVER
AUSTRIAN RED

SCHEIBLHOFER LEGENDS 2002, ERICH SCHEIBLHOFER BURGENLAND – *Silky, deep creamy fruits ooze from the juicy palate. Leather, blackberries, mint, and mocha flavours. A long finish.*	£13.00 NYW
SCHEIBLHOFER MERLOT 2002, ERICH SCHEIBLHOFER BURGENLAND – *A texture of chocolate-covered cherries melting in your mouth. Elements of mocha, earth, red fruit, and toast. Long.*	£19.00 NYW
SCHEIBLHOFER SHIRAZ 2002, ERICH SCHEIBLHOFER BURGENLAND – *A nose of gravadlax, dill, and blueberries. A full, rich and spicy palate showing ripe tannins. Lengthy finish.*	£22.00 NYW

BRONZE
AUSTRIAN RED

HAIDEBODEN 2002, JOSEF UMATHUM BURGENLAND – *Youthful, with an intense nose of succulent ripe cherry fruit, spices, violets, and pencil shavings.*	£12.00 FWW
BLEND I ZWEIGELT BLAUFRANKISCH 2002, WEINLAUBENHOF KRACHER BURGENLAND – *Sweet blackberries and cumin spice on the nose. The palate boasts a long, lushly fruited finish.*	£19.00 NYW
SCHEIBLHOFER CABERNET SAUVIGNON 2002, ERICH SCHEIBLHOFER BURGENLAND – *Pepper and cassis, coffee, and leaves. The wine's juicy palate is balanced, crisp, and pure.*	£19.00 NYW

GOLD
AUSTRIAN SWEET

TRAMINER TBA NO 1 NOUVELLE VAGUE 2001, WEINLAUBENHOF KRACHER BURGENLAND – *Immensely sweet. Benchmark Austrian acidity etches a path all the way to the incredibly long, spicy, complex finish.*	■£24.00 NYW
CHARDONNAY TBA NO 7 NOUVELLE VAGUE 2001, WEINLAUBENHOF KRACHER BURGENLAND – *Intensely sweet, with a textured, honeyed viscosity. Round, luscious, and extremely approachable, with liquorice notes.*	■£27.00 NYW

SILVER
AUSTRIAN SWEET

☆ **FISCHER BOUVIER TBA 1999, WEINGUT ALFRED FISCHER** BURGENLAND – *Sensual honey, citrus, and muscovado sugar nose. Layers of apples, oranges, lemons, and grapefruit unfurl on the palate.*	£8.40 CCS/ALL
UMATHUM BEERENAUSLESE 2002, JOSEF UMATHUM BURGENLAND – *Barley sugar, oranges, limes and honey entwine on this glorious, golden, very fresh, long wine.*	■£12.00 FWW
UMATHUM TBA 2001, WEINGUT JOSEF UMATHUM BURGENLAND – *Intense butterscotch and quince aromas. The treacly palate is unctuous with beautiful acid balance. Deep and long finish.*	■£15.00 FWW
SCHEUREBE TBA NO 4 ZWISCHEN DEN SEEN 2001, WEINLAUBENHOF KRACHER BURGENLAND – *Round and unctuous. A nose of sweet rose petals and mandarin oranges. The heady palate has a long finish.*	■£24.00 NYW
WELSCHRIESLING TBA NO 5 ZWISCHEN DEN SEEN 2001, WEINLAUBENHOF KRACHER BURGENLAND – *Complex quince and saffron aromas. The palate shows rich sweetness balanced by icy acidity. Persistent finish.*	■£24.00 NYW
GRANDE CUVÉE TBA NO 6 NOUVELLE VAGUE 2001, WEINLAUBENHOF KRACHER BURGENLAND – *Unmistakable botrytis aromas. The palate is deep and layered, with caramel and saffron notes. Complexity and great finesse.*	■£25.30 TAN/NYW

BRONZE
AUSTRIAN SWEET

CUVÉE BEERENAUSLESE 2002, WEINLAUBENHOF KRACHER BURGENLAND – *Hay bales and honey melt into butterscotch and caramel and russet-apple sweetness.*	■£10.00 TAN/NYW FLY
EISWEIN CUVÉE 2001, WEINLAUBENHOF KRACHER BURGENLAND – *Intensely pure. The palate is honeyed, with concentrated sweetness, searing acidity, and fine minerality.*	■£14.90 NYW/FLY
CHARDONNAY TBA NO 3 NOUVELLE VAGUE 2001, WEINLAUBENHOF KRACHER BURGENLAND – *Expressive caramel and citrus nose leads to a rich, round palate. Good weight. Concentrated finish.*	■£24.00 NYW
MUSKAT OTTONEL TBA NO 2 ZWISCHEN DEN SEEN 2001, WEINLAUBENHOF KRACHER BURGENLAND – *Pungent, aromatic and intense, with a luxuriant pillow of lychees and a long, crisp grapefruit finish.*	£24.00 NYW

CHILE

Look at the medal-winning white wines below and it is striking how many of the most successful wines were Sauvignon Blancs, Rieslings, and Viogniers. The awards won by these wines illustrate the dynamism of Chile's wine industry and a growing readiness to match different varieties to the regions in which they grow best. Look out for more exciting efforts from cooler areas like Casablanca and Bío-Bío (way down in the south). Cabernet more or less rules among the reds, but there are terrific Syrahs too and delicious examples of Merlot and Carmenère – the peppery grape once grown in Bordeaux, and, until recently known as "Chilean Merlot".

GOLD
CHILEAN WHITE

☆ **WHITE LABEL SAUVIGNON BLANC 2003, VIÑA CASABLANCA** ACONCAGUA VALLEY – *Gooseberry, green pepper character, and grassy aromatics with a bright intensity that runs through the very long persistence.*	£6.30 NRW/FLA NYW/INS MOR
☆ **CANTALUNA SAUVIGNON BLANC 2003, VIÑA CANTERA** ACONCAGUA VALLEY – *Blackcurrant leaf, nettles and fresh, ripe tomato leaf flavours. Perfect fruit acid balance, juicy and warm.*	£8.00 PAT
☆ **WINEMAKER'S LOT 20 RIESLING 2003, CONCHA Y TORO** BÍO-BÍO VALLEY – *Floral yet mineral, it displays classic lemon meringue pie flavour. Finely balanced and wistfully long.*	£8.00 ODD

SILVER
CHILEAN WHITE

☆ **CASILLERO DEL DIABLO VIOGNIER 2003, CONCHA Y TORO** ACONCAGUA VALLEY – *Ripe and scented with peaches and apricots. Creamy and fleshy, with a rich texture and a fresh finish.*	£5.40 HOU/VGN FLA/ODD

CHILEAN WHITE SILVER / BRONZE

☆ **EXPLORER SAUVIGNON BLANC 2003, CONCHA Y TORO** CENTRAL VALLEY – *Creamy, grassy apple, and lemon flavours with a fine depth of crisp juicy fruit on the full palate.*	**£5.50** WSO/WRW
☆ **ANAKENA RESERVADO VIOGNIER 2003, ANAKENA** RAPEL VALLEY – *Rich and heavy, with peach and passion-fruit flavours. Well knitted oak adds dimension and vanilla toast notes.*	**£6.30** JFE
☆ **TRIO GEWURZTRAMINER 2003, CONCHA Y TORO** ACONCAGUA VALLEY – *An intense array of apples and ruby grapefruit. Youthful, with a hint of lychee sweetness on the finish.*	**£7.00** ODD
CHARDONNAY SPECIAL RESERVE 2003, VIÑA TABALÍ LIMARÍ VALLEY – *Tarte tatin rushed from oven to table… that's what this spicy, enticing, sweetly oaked wine brings to mind.*	**£8.00** BUC
WILD FERMENT CHARDONNAY 2002, ERRAZURIZ ACONCAGUA VALLEY – *Muted, pale gold and elegant, the wine's butterscotch and pineapple aromas complement fresh, creamy flavours.*	**£10.20** EDC/FEN EVI/OWC JSM
WINEMAKER'S RESERVE CHARDONNAY 2003, VIÑA CARMEN ACONCAGUA VALLEY – *The yellow-apple, banana, and apricot fruit flavours and coconut oak aromas are voluptuous. Warm and very rich.*	**£11.60** FLY/SGL

BRONZE
CHILEAN WHITE

☆ **LOS CAMACHOS CHARDONNAY 2003, SAN PEDRO** CENTRAL VALLEY – *Lemon zest graces the nose. The palate has plenty of creamy lemon fruit and a dry finish.*	**£4.00** WRT
☆ **MHV SAN ANDRES SAUVIGNON CHARDONNAY 2003, SAN PEDRO** CENTRAL VALLEY – *Appears a little tight and grassy-appley on the nose, but explodes with ripe, peachy fruit flavours and crisp acids.*	**£4.20** MHV
☆ **35 SOUTH SAUVIGNON BLANC 2004, SAN PEDRO** CENTRAL VALLEY – *Pungent, lifted nettle, and guava aromas. A soft, medium-weight and fresh wine, with a pleasing roundness.*	**£4.90** SMF/RWM BUC/JSM

CHILEAN WHITE BRONZE

☆ **ANTU MAPU SAUVIGNON BLANC 2003, SAN JOSE DE APALTA** RAPEL VALLEY – *Ripe and perfumed with notes of fraises des bois and grassy gooseberries. Crisp and concentrated with great length.*	£5.00 MRN
MHV SAN ANDRES CHARDONNAY RESERVA 2002, SAN PEDRO ACONCAGUA VALLEY – *An integrated, balanced, pure, and dry wine with ripe plum, pear fruit, and vanilla essence.*	£5.60 MHV
INSIGNE GEWURZTRAMINER 2003, VIÑA CARMEN MAIPO VALLEY – *The understated character belies the pure, persistent pineapple and peach fruit on nose and palate.*	£5.70 FLY/SGL
VALDIVIESO SAUVIGNON BLANC 2004, VIÑA VALDIVIESO CURICÓ VALLEY – *Bright pale lemon yellow. The nose is floral and slightly honeyed, the palate is soft, and moderately weighty.*	£5.80 FLY
CHILENSIS RESERVA SAUVIGNON BLANC 2003, VIA WINE GROUP ACONCAGUA VALLEY – *There is a delicate barley water character with hints of apple and nettle, and a keen elegance.*	£6.00 BWL
MONOS LOCOS SAUVIGNON BLANC 2003, VIÑA CONCHA Y TORO CENTRAL VALLEY – *Grassy and lemony and a refreshing, clean style. It's crisp and clear with an elegance of fruit character.*	£6.00 VGN
TERRARUM SAUVIGNON BLANC 2003, VIÑA MORANDE ACONCAGUA VALLEY – *Very pale but full of aromatic, honeyed grassy flavours and there's a good depth of crisp, appley fruit.*	£6.00 VNO
TRIO SAUVIGNON BLANC 2003, CONCHA Y TORO ACONCAGUA VALLEY – *High tropical varietal character. Light, lifted, and ripe, with inviting grapefruit and lemon flavours.*	£6.00 WSO/FLA ODD/JSM
UNDURRAGA CHARDONNAY RESERVA 2002, VIÑA UNDURRAGA MAIPO VALLEY – *Delicate straw-gold colour. Coconut milk and ripe plantain nose; ripe and balanced, with a lengthy finish.*	£7.00 RAV
CASAS DEL TOQUI CHARDONNAY RESERVADO 2000, VIÑA DE LAROSE RAPEL VALLEY – *Bright gold. Ripe yellow starfruit and pear flavours coat the mouth. Candied lemon aromas. Good balance.*	£7.50 GRT

CHILEAN WHITE BRONZE / SEAL / RED TROPHY

SINGLE VINEYARD SAUVIGNON BLANC 2003, ERRAZURIZ Casablanca Valley – *Smooth pear and apple fruit and a lifted, perfumed nose that displays good ripeness. A clean finish.*	£8.00 HMA
VISIÓN VIOGNIER 2003, VIÑA CONO SUR Rapel Valley – *Complex creamy vanilla and peach kernel nose. Mineral hints add interest to the structured palate.*	£8.00 WST
CALITERRA CHARDONNAY RESERVA 2003, CALITERRA Aconcagua Valley – *Ripe, vibrant, with concentrated oak shining through the perfumed lemon fruit. Very attractive mouthfeel.*	£8.30 TAU/G&M
CHARDONNAY MAX RESERVA 2002, ERRAZURIZ Aconcagua Valley – *Fine fresh pear and juicy red-apple fruit flavours pour from the palate. Lively acidity. Long finish.*	£8.30 EDC
TERRUNYO SAUVIGNON BLANC 2003, CONCHA Y TORO Aconcagua Valley – *Fresh, appley, and grassy, with a depth of palate and fruit concentration that indicates its quality.*	£8.50 RAV/WSO WRW/ODD

SEAL OF APPROVAL
CHILEAN WHITE

☆ **SI JOLI PETIT CHILEAN SAUVIGNON BLANC NV, PAUL SAPIN,** Central Valley – *Gooseberries and starfruit dance on the nose and ripe palate.*	●£1.00 ROG

TROPHY
CHILEAN RED

CASA LAPOSTOLLE CUVÉE ALEXANDRE SYRAH 2002, CASA LAPOSTOLLE Rapel Valley – *Intense, herbal, and leathery, with floral overtones. Cedary tannin, crisp acid, toast, and good richness.*	£15.00 HAX

GOLD
CHILEAN RED

Wine	Price / Stockists
☆ **RESERVA CABERNET SYRAH 2003, VIÑA MISIONES DE RENGO** RAPEL VALLEY – *Masses of sweet, ripe blackcurrant fruit laden with round, mocha toffee oak, and chewy tannins. Big and rich.*	£6.00 EHL
☆ **RESERVE CABERNET SAUVIGNON 2003, VIÑA CONO SUR** MAIPO VALLEY – *Deliciously ripe and forward, with soft tannins and bags of fruit, bell pepper, mint, and chocolate oak.*	£7.00 ASD/WRC SMF
☆ **RESERVE CABERNET SAUVIGNON 2002, VIÑA CARMEN** MAIPO VALLEY – *A nose of redcurrants and mint. A deep palate and chewy tannins, all enveloped in smoky mocha oak.*	£8.20 FLY/WRW SGL
☆ **DON RECA LIMITED RELEASE MERLOT 2003, VIÑA LA ROSA** RAPEL VALLEY – *Inky plum colour and creamy black fruit flavours. Deliciously ripe and very fresh, with a touch of spice.*	£10.00 HOU/NYW WTS/JSM

SILVER
CHILEAN RED

Wine	Price / Stockists
☆ **VIÑA MAIPO RESERVA CABERNET SAUVIGNON 2003, CONCHA Y TORO** CENTRAL VALLEY – *Ripe cassis fruit melds with crunchy cranberry fruit on the palate. The nose has toast and vanilla notes.*	£5.00 CYT
☆ **RESERVE MERLOT 2003, VIÑA MAR** ACONCAGUA VALLEY – *Intriguing notes of charred wood, inkwell and undergrowth. A fine mouthfeel and deep, dark, and very long.*	£6.50 EHL
☆ **CUVÉE CABERNET SAUVIGNON RESERVA 2002, VIÑA MISIONES DE RENGO** RAPEL VALLEY – *Characterful, with blackcurrants, raspberries, and redcurrants. Its nose has a handful of thyme and hints of little wildflowers.*	£7.00 EHL
☆ **GRAND RESERVE MERLOT 2003, VISTAMAR WINES** MAIPO VALLEY – *Each judge remarked upon the concentration of this curranty, herby beast. Cellaring and/or decanting is recommended.*	£7.00 VNO

CHILEAN RED SILVER

☆ **LAS CASAS DEL TOQUI CABERNET SAUVIGNON RESERVADO 2001, VIÑA DE LAROSE** RAPEL VALLEY – *Burning leaf scents, redcurrants, tar, cloves, and sous bois on the nose. The palate has peppers and spice.*	£7.50 GRT
CABERNET SAUVIGNON LIMITED EDITION 2002, VIÑA MONTGRAS RAPEL VALLEY – *Cassis mingles with oak on the nose. A well-balanced palate of black forest fruits, leather, and oak.*	£8.00 WTS/ENO
CABERNET SAUVIGNON RESERVA 2002, CALITERRA RAPEL VALLEY – *Classic blackcurrant and crisp green bell pepper scents together with notes of mint and spice. A well-integrated palate*	£8.00 G&M
RESERVA SHIRAZ 2002, TERRAMATER MAIPO VALLEY – *A blockbuster with berries, plums, and wafts of smoke – they are all crammed into this long, elegant wine.*	£8.00 VER
MARQUÉS DE CASA CONCHA CABERNET SAUVIGNON 2002, CONCHA Y TORO MAIPO VALLEY – *Dark, intense colour hints at the riches to come. Deep, curranty flavours, and soft, seductive bouquet.*	£8.30 TAN/RNS FLA
VIU MANENT CABERNET SAUVIGNON RESERVE 2002, VIU MANENT RAPEL VALLEY – *Rich cassis and raspberries generously sprinkled with cinnamon scents. Enchanting smoke, leather, and soot elements.*	£8.30 ELV
CASA SILVA GRAN RESERVA LOLOL SYRAH 2002, VIÑA CASA SILVA RAPEL VALLEY – *Berry aromas. The lean plalate comprises ripe tannins with plummy flavours, smoky hints, and an elegant finish.*	£9.00 JKN
MORANDÉ EDICION LIMITADA SYRAH CABERNET 2002, VIÑA MORANDÉ MAIPO VALLEY – *A rich nose of black blackberries. Fleshy fruit, warm spices, and ripe tannins on the palate.*	£10.00 VNO
ERRAZURIZ MAX RESERVA SHIRAZ 2001, ERRAZURIZ ACONCAGUA REGION – *Vibrant jammy black fruits with a vanilla-coconut overlay on the nose. Creamily textured layers.*	£10.10 EDC/TOS MWW
VALDIVIESO CABERNET FRANC SINGLE VINEYARD 2001, VIÑA VALDIVIESO MAULE VALLEY – *Replete with smoky red stone fruit scents. The palate has oregano leaves and inky, lightly tannic fruit.*	£10.30 FLY

130 CHILEAN RED SILVER / BRONZE

20 BARRELS PINOT NOIR 2001, VIÑA CONO SUR **RAPEL VALLEY** – *A bouquet of raspberries and strawberries, compost, and mint. Meaty fruit, creamy oak, and good length.*	**£15.00** JSM/MWW WSO
ULTRA PREMIUM CABERNET SAUVIGNON 2002, VIÑA SANTA HELENA **RAPEL VALLEY** – *Freshy crushed spearmint leaves and mouthwatering redcurrant fruit grace the nose and palate.*	**£18.00** ILW

BRONZE
CHILEAN RED

☆ **35 SOUTH CABERNET SAUVIGNON 2003, SAN PEDRO** **CENTRAL VALLEY** – *Delicate eucalyptus coupled with deep damson flavours. Evolved, with tobacco notes and a smooth texture.*	**£4.90** SMF/RWM BUC/JSM
☆ **35 SOUTH CENTRAL VALLEY CARMENÈRE 2003, SAN PEDRO VINEYARDS & WINERY** **CENTRAL VALLEY** – *Ruby colour. Green bell pepper, chocolate, and cassis scents. Smooth, smoky, and lush. A classic.*	**£5.00** BUC
☆ **SIGLO DE ORO CARMENÈRE 2003, VIÑA SANTA HELENA** **RAPEL VALLEY** – *The ripe tannic structure enhances a palate of bramble fruit. Hints of cinnamon add a warm tone.*	**£5.00** ILW
☆ **VIÑA MAR PINOT NOIR 2003, VIÑA MAR** **ACONCAGUA VALLEY** – *Pale and delicate, this fine-boned Pinot Noir has smoky raspberry fruit and a smooth creamy finish.*	**£5.00** EHL
CASILLERO DEL DIABLO CARMENÈRE 2003, CONCHA Y TORO **RAPEL VALLEY** – *Pronounced bramble fruit flavours luxuriate on the intense, richly ripe palate. Touches of undergrowth.*	**£5.10** HOU/TOS FLA/JSM MWW
CASILLERO DEL DIABLO CABERNET SAUVIGNON 2003, CONCHA Y TORO **CENTRAL VALLEY** – *Robust tannins, chunky cassis, and crisp cleansing acidity all appear on this powerful Chilean wine.*	**£5.20** HOU/RAV TOS/WTS ODD/JSM
ESTAMPA CARMENÈRE MERLOT 2003, VIÑA ESTAMPA **RAPEL VALLEY** – *Vivid peppery berries on the nose. The palate features ripe black fruit, white spice, and leafiness.*	**£5.30** INS

CHILEAN RED BRONZE 131

VALDIVIESO CABERNET SAUVIGNON 2003, VIÑA VALDIVIESO CENTRAL VALLEY – *The nose is fine and aromatic, the palate radiates bell pepper and cherry flavours. Fresh, zingy, and clear.*	£5.40 TOS/FLY
CO-OP CHILEAN CABERNET SAUVIGNON RESERVE 2002, LUIS FELIPE EDWARDS RAPEL VALLEY – *Dense warm cassis is swathed in rich, warm chocolate flavours. Toasty oak comes through on the smoky finish.*	£5.50 CWS
CONCHA Y TORO CABERNET SAUVIGNON 2003, CONCHA Y TORO CENTRAL VALLEY – *Luxuriant cherry fruit, mocha notes, and whiffs of smoke all jumbled together on this zippy beauty.*	£5.50 HOU/RNS FEN/GHL
LA PALMA DORADA CARMENÈRE 2003, VIÑA LA ROSA RAPEL VALLEY – *Intense nose of fresh green bell pepper. Mulberries and plums. A flourish of warmth punctuates the finish.*	£5.50 HWL
TERRA NOVA CABERNET SAUVIGNON 2002, FREIXENET CURICÓ VALLEY – *The complex fruity bouquet leads to a palate replete with sweet fruit and classic Cabernet flavours.*	£5.50 BNK
TERRAMATER ZINFANDEL SHIRAZ 2002, TERRAMATER SANTIAGO DE CHILE – *Young and vinous with loads of cooked, preserved berries, and a black fruit complexity. Approachable tannins.*	£5.50 JSM
TOUCHSTONE MERLOT 2002, VIÑEDOS ORGANICOS EMILIANA RAPEL VALLEY – *Purplish ruby red, with a soaring herbal overtone. The youthful, medium-bodied palate has plenty of spicy fruit.*	£5.70 NYW/VRT
120 CARMENÈRE 2003, VIÑA SANTA RITA RAPEL VALLEY – *Dark savoury fruit dotted with pepper and worn leather. Bramble berries and bouquet garni.*	£6.00 BWC/JSM
ANAKENA RESERVADO CABERNET SAUVIGNON 2002, ANAKENA RAPEL VALLEY – *Bright redcurrant fruit on the elegant nose, and a powerful mouthful of savoury fruit supported by robust tannins.*	£6.00 WPR
CARTAGENA CABERNET SAUVIGNON 2001, XPOVIN CELLARS RAPEL VALLEY – *Black-purple colour, tomatoes and cherries dance on the nose. The medium-weight palate has toast and savoury elements.*	£6.00 LUV

132 CHILEAN RED BRONZE

CHILENSIS RESERVA SYRAH 2003, VIA WINE GROUP **CENTRAL VALLEY** – *Youthful, with a plush cushion of sweet cherry fruit, structured tannins, and a long, warm finish.*	£6.00 BWL
CREMASCHI FURLOTTI SYRAH RESERVE 2002, VIÑA CREMASCHI BARRIGA **MAULE VALLEY** – *Damson and cranberry fruit lines the firm palate. Hints of black pepper and tree bark pervade the nose.*	£6.00 CHN
ERRAZURIZ SHIRAZ 2003, ERRAZURIZ **ACONCAGUA VALLEY** – *Warm and luxuriant, with deep pockets of fruit, a medium-bodied palate, and a fresh finish.*	£6.00 TOS/WTS JSM
MONOS LOCOS MERLOT 2003, VIÑA CONCHA Y TORO **CENTRAL VALLEY** – *Red plums and cranberries coalesce on the fresh, vibrant palate of this warming, sweetly ripe blend.*	£6.00 VGN
PRODIGIO CARMENÈRE 2003, VIÑA CANTERA **RAPEL VALLEY** – *Scents and flavours of juicy ripe bell peppers and soy. Clean and firm. Crushed green leaf elements.*	£6.00 PAT
RAVANAL CARMENÈRE 2003, VIÑA RAVANAL **RAPEL VALLEY** – *Cracked black pepper and herbal tones grace the baked fruit. The lasting finish has a smoky tinge.*	£6.00 COK /GRT WNS/TRO
RESERVA CARMENÈRE 2003, VIÑA MISIONES DE RENGO **RAPEL VALLEY** – *Hints of the barnyard rise from the nose. Rosemary, perfumed damsons, and toasty oak on the palate.*	£6.00 EHL
RESERVE CABERNET SAUVIGNON 2002, VIÑA SANTA ALICIA **MAIPO VALLEY** – *Briar fruit and cedar notes entice the taster. This balanced Cabernet has elegance and a lasting finish.*	£6.00 BWS
SANTA INÉS RESERVA CABERNET SAUVIGNON 2003, DE MARTINO VINEYARD **MAIPO VALLEY** – *Hot, baked, and jammy. Massive tannins rein in the ripe, tightly knit blackberry, and juicy plum fruit.*	£6.00 SMF
TRIO CABERNET SAUVIGNON 2002, CONCHA Y TORO **MAIPO VALLEY** – *Perfumed with floral and spice aromatics, this intense, medium-bodied Chilean wine is upfront and pleasing.*	£6.00 FLA/ODD

CHILEAN RED BRONZE 133

SANTA DIGNA MERLOT 2003, MIGUEL TORRES **Curicó Valley** – *Ripe plums, tomatoes, and cherries please the nose. A silky soft, tannic web cocoons the fresh fruit flavours.*	**£6.10** RAV/FLY
ECHEVERRIA CARMENÈRE 2003, VIÑA ECHEVERRIA **Curicó Valley** – *Light-bodied red berry fruit. Bell peppers, spices, and a hint of cream on the nose.*	**£6.30** FFW/CVE
CASA LEONA CABERNET SAUVIGNON RESERVE 2002, VIÑA LA ROSA **Rapel Valley** – *Overtly pungent, with grass and spice aromas. Intense, minted blackcurrant fruit. High acidity and a drying finish.*	**£6.50** M&S
RESERVA MERLOT 2002, VIÑEDOS TERRANOBLE **Maule Valley** – *Smoke, fruits of the forest, and cherries vie for dominance. Dense and full, with a powerful tannic backbone.*	**£6.50** MCT
CABERNET SAUVIGNON RESERVA 2002, VIÑA MONTGRAS **Rapel Valley** – *Perfumed, vibrant cassis, and redcurrant elements are all well-defined on the nose and long palate.*	**£6.90** V&C/SOM ENO
CABERNET SAUVIGNON SYRAH RESERVA 2002, VIÑA MONTGRAS **Rapel Valley** – *Intensely inky, with minty notes and lots of chewy fruit on the palate. Layers of oak and spice.*	**£7.00** WTS/ENO
CARMENÈRE COLECCIÓN 2003, VIÑA CASA SILVA **Rapel Valley** – *Dark and brooding, with a glossy medium-bodied palate of dark fruit and cream.*	**£7.00** BOO
DOÑA DOMINGA RESERVA MERLOT 2002, VIÑA CASA SILVA **Rapel Valley** – *Dark-ruby red. Rich toasty overtones drape the upfront, chunky cherry fruit. A touch of provencal herb adds interest.*	**£7.00** GHL
DOÑA DOMINGA RESERVE CARMENÈRE 2002, CASA SILVA **Rapel Valley** – *This is a long, oaked, mouthwatering agglomeration of blackberries, mint, and cinnamon spice.*	**£7.00** WTS/JSM
GRAND RESERVE CABERNET SAUVIGNON 2003, VISTAMAR WINES **Maipo Valley** – *Orange rind and tree bark scent the nose. The palate has hedgerow berries and sweet spice.*	**£7.00** VNO

CHILEAN RED BRONZE

RESERVE MERLOT 2003, VIÑA CONO SUR RAPEL VALLEY – *Clear damson flavours, balanced acidity, and firm integrated tannins. Medium-long finish.*	£7.00 UNS/WTS
SELECCIÓN DEL DIRECTORIO CABERNET SAUVIGNON 2002, VIÑA SANTA HELENA RAPEL VALLEY – *The mouthwatering, fresh red-berry fruit palate is full-bodied, with good concentration and a lengthy finish.*	£7.00 ILW
SELECCIÓN DEL DIRECTORIO CARMENÈRE 2002, VIÑA SANTA HELENA RAPEL VALLEY – *Rich plum fruit, dry tannic structure, and a long, powerful finish. Intriguing caramel hints.*	£7.00 ILW
TERRARUM CARMENÈRE 2003, VIÑA MORANDE MAIPO VALLEY – *Pleasing summer fruit palate. Plenty of oak and peppery herbaceous fruit. Firm thrusting tannins.*	£7.00 SHB
TERRARUM RESERVE MERLOT 2003, VIÑA MORANDÉ MAIPO VALLEY – *Smoke and char on the nose. Vibrant, youthful, round red fruit aplenty. Likely to become more complex.*	£7.00 SHB
VERAMONTE CABERNET SAUVIGNON 2001, VERAMONTE MAIPO VALLEY – *A round wine, with astringent tannins, a mouthcoating texture, and plum and chocolate flavours. Concentrated.*	£7.00 SMF
RESERVA CABERNET SAUVIGNON 2002, VIÑA SANTA RITA MAIPO VALLEY – *It has blackcurrant leaves on the nose, and crunchy, overtly fruity juicy cranberries in the mouth.*	£7.20 VIT/TAU BWC/JSM MWW
PALO ALTO RESERVA CABERNET SAUVIGNON 2002, VIÑA FRANCISCO AGUIRRE LIMARÍ VALLEY – *This ripe, somewhat medicinal wine has juicy red and black fruits in abundance, creamy oak, and good balance.*	£7.30 FFW/CVE
ARBOLEDA CABERNET SAUVIGNON 2001, CALITERRA MAIPO VALLEY – *Sweet youthful cassis fruit beautified by a touch of oak. Chocolate flavours and grainy tannins.*	£7.50 HAX
VALDIVIESO CABERNET SAUVIGNON RESERVE 2001, VIÑA VALDIVIESO MAIPO VALLEY – *Subtle currant aromas meld with cocoa on the nose. Farmyard elements and firm tannins.*	£7.50 TOS/FLY JSM

CHILEAN RED BRONZE **135**

RESERVA MERLOT 2002, CASAS DEL BOSQUE **ACONCAGUA VALLEY** – *This has elegant weight and juicy, ripe plummy fruit leading to a long aromatic finish with an acidic tang.*	£7.60 UNS
ENVERO 2001, APALTAGUA RAPEL VALLEY – *Approachable juicy red fruit leads the attack. The flavours broaden onto a long, soft finish.*	£7.90 WRK/SOM CCS/MOV LIB/FLY
SECRETO CARMENÈRE 2003, VIU MANENT **RAPEL VALLEY** – *The nose has mulberry and tar notes. The palate shows sweet berry fruit allied to supple tannins.*	£7.90 ELV
CALITERRA MERLOT RESERVA 2002, CALITERRA **RAPEL VALLEY** – *This delicately smoky, fruit-filled wine has a soft, almost waxy texture, and a medium-long finish.*	£8.00 G&M
FINISIMO CABERNET SAUVIGNON 2001, CANEPA **MAIPO VALLEY** – *Tar, cordite, leather, and spicebox nose. Round, plummy, pungent fruit lines the saturated palate.*	£8.00 THI
LIMITED EDITION CABERNET SAUVIGNON COLCHAGUA VALLEY 2001, VIÑA MONTGRAS **RAPEL VALLEY** – *The nose displays warm berry and spice notes. The palate has richness, harmonious tannins, and sweet oak.*	£8.00 WTS
MARQUÉS DE CASA CONCHA MERLOT 2002, CONCHA Y TORO RAPEL VALLEY – *The ripe, juicy fruit is beginning to mature, yet retains its full-bodied, big bold style. Plenty of tannins.*	£8.00 JSM
TORREALBA MERLOT RESERVE 2001, VIÑA TORREALBA CURICÓ VALLEY – *A soft, big, full, and dry Merlot. Rubbery notes. Sweetly ripe strawberry fruit. Balanced and long.*	£8.00 PWW
COLINA NEGRA CABERNET SAUVIGNON 2002, MICHEL LAROCHE & JORGE CODERCH CENTRAL VALLEY – *High-toned strawberry on the nose leads to creamy red and black fruit flavours in the mouth. Youthful tannins.*	£8.10 NRW/FLY BWL
ARBOLEDA SYRAH 2002, CALITERRA RAPEL VALLEY – *Deep tar and blackberry aromas on the nose and lush fruit on the palate. Harmonious.*	£8.20 HAX/FLA

CHILEAN RED BRONZE

NATIVA CABERNET SAUVIGNON 2001, VIÑA CARMEN MAIPO VALLEY – *Purple, with an intense fragrance of mint and green plums. The fleshy palate has crisp acidity and oak.*	£8.20 WTS/FLY WRW/SGL
GRAN RESERVA LOS LINGUES CABERNET SAUVIGNON 2002, VIÑA CASA SILVA RAPEL VALLEY – *Intensely perfumed with red fruit and flora. Saturated, dense colour. The medium-weight palate has woody overtones.*	£9.00 BOO
TABALÍ SPECIAL RESERVE 2002, VIÑA TABALÍ LIMARÍ VALLEY – *Dark plum scents and flavours. Rich warm tobacco and spicebox overtones grace this robust, full-bodied wine.*	£9.00 BUC
VISIÓN CABERNET SAUVIGNON 2001, VIÑA CONO SUR MAIPO VALLEY – *A bouquet of currants, plums, and spicy oak. The sleek palate offers chewy tannins and a smoky finish.*	£9.00 WRC
VISIÓN PINOT NOIR 2002, VIÑA CONO SUR ACONCAGUA VALLEY – *Young, with a vegetal-tinged nose. Attractive baked fruit character and firm tannins.*	£9.00 WST
VITISTERRA GRAND RESERVA SYRAH 2002, VIÑA MORANDE MAIPO VALLEY – *The smoky nose leads to a generous palate showing elements of blackberry and plum.*	£9.00 VNO
VITISTERRA GRAND RESERVE MERLOT 2002, VIÑA MORANDE MAIPO VALLEY – *Sunny plums warm the ripe palate, which has a streak of herbiness. A medium-long finish.*	£9.00 VNO
CABERNET SAUVIGNON MAX RESERVE 2001, ERRAZURIZ ACONCAGUA VALLEY – *Well-balanced melange of blackcurrants and vanilla. A fruity nose and suave finish beguiles the taster.*	£9.20 EDC/FEN TOS
DON RECA LIMITED RELEASE MERLOT 2002, VIÑA LA ROSA RAPEL VALLEY – *Fresh autumnal fruits on the nose and a savoury nature to the palate. A softly tannic finish.*	£10.00 WTS/JSM
SINGLE VINEYARD SYRAH 2003, DE MARTINO VINEYARD RAPEL VALLEY – *Brimming with ripe soft, quite sweet briar fruit and fine enfolding freshness.*	£10.00 VGN

CHILEAN RED BRONZE 137

RESERVE SYRAH CABERNET SAUVIGNON 2001, VIÑA CARMEN MAIPO VALLEY – *An appealing nose of cassis and ripe fruits. Well-built structure, matching acidity and balanced oak.*	**£10.10** FLY/SGL
TERRUNYO CABERNET SAUVIGNON 2001, CONCHA Y TORO MAIPO VALLEY – *Toasty oak, black fruit, and a robust tannic structure. Spicy and ripe, with a resounding finish.*	**£10.30** RAV/WSO ODD
VALDIVIESO CABERNET SAUVIGNON SINGLE VINEYARD 2002, VIÑA VALDIVIESO CURICÓ VALLEY – *Elegant, aromatic cedar overtones. Several of our tasters commended this Chilean wine's complexity and balance.*	**£10.30** FLY
TERRUNYO CARMENÈRE 2002, CONCHA Y TORO RAPEL VALLEY – *Minty. Deep, glass-coating colour. A silkily textured palate of damson fruit. Very good balance.*	**£10.80** FLA/WRW ODD
1865 CARMENÈRE 2001, SAN PEDRO MAULE VALLEY – *Seductive prune and spicebox aromas assault the nose. The palate has fleshy fruit and touches of coconut oak.*	**£11.50** RWM/BUC
1865 MALBEC 2001, SAN PEDRO CURICO VALLEY – *The nose shows hints of leather and boysenberry. The palate is fruit driven with soft tannic structure.*	**£11.50** RWM/BUC
CUVÉE ALEXANDRE CABERNET SAUVIGNON 2000, CASA LAPOSTOLLE RAPEL VALLEY – *Densely packed with crisp cassis, this is a classy Chilean Cabernet of power and stamina.*	**£13.00** HOU/TAU
TERRUNYO PINOT NOIR 2003, CONCHA Y TORO ACONCAGUA VALLEY – *Plenty of soft fruit on this welcoming, well-balanced palate, with fine tannins and a subtle, lingering finish.*	**£13.00** ODD
SPECIAL SELECTION MALBEC 2001, VIU MANENT RAPEL VALLEY – *A nose of sweet plum fruit and a soft palate of dusty tannins and cherry flavours.*	**£13.90** ELV
QUINTA GENERACION CABERNET SAUVIGNON CARMENÈRE SHIRAZ PETIT VERDOT 2001, VIÑA CASA SILVA RAPEL VALLEY – *Black fruits and vanilla leap from the nose. The mouthwatering palate boasts plenty of cassis.*	**£14.00** JKN

138 CHILEAN RED BRONZE

ERRAZURIZ SINGLE VINEYARD CARMENÈRE 2001, ERRAZURIZ ACONCAGUA VALLEY – *Bell pepper and toast on the nose. The palate is a soft mouthful of plump hedgerow fruits.*	£14.10 EDC/HAX EVI
HOUSE OF MORANDÉ CABERNET SAUVIGNON 2001, VIÑA MORANDE MAIPO VALLEY – *The attractive blackberry palate is scented with a dark tangle of undergrowth. Balanced yet intense.*	£15.00 VNO
MANSO DE VELASCO 2000, MIGUEL TORRES CURICÓ VALLEY – *Cassis driven with berry and grass notes on the nose. A ripe, harmonious palate with good fruit persistence.*	£15.60 JFE/FLY
SOLENTE MALBEC 1999, VIU MANET RAPEL VALLEY – *Coaldust, blackberries, and plenty of toasty oak scents. A palate of sunny hedgerow fruits.*	£16.00 WAW
VALDIVIESO CABALLO LOCO NO 7 NV, VALDIVIESO CENTRAL VALLEY – *Cassis fruit dripping with zingy acidity, and a leafiness that adds interest to the vanilla-scented palate.*	£16.60 TOS/NYW FLY
D DONOSO 2001, CASA DONOSO MAULE VALLEY – *Ripe red damson fruit is lifted by notes of cedar. Bell pepper and blackcurrant aromas add another dimension.*	£20.00 CRI
DON MAXIMIANO FOUNDERS RESERVE 2001, ERRAZURIZ ACONCAGUA VALLEY – *Dense colour, powerful oak and vivid, sweetly ripe blackberry fruit. Pulls out the stops.*	£20.00 EDC/HAX TOS
CARMENÈRE RESERVA CASA LA JOYA 2001, VIÑAS BISQUERTT RAPEL VALLEY – *The nose shows cassis and cedar. The palate has dense black fruit and supple tannins.*	£24.00 MCT
CASA LA JOYA SYRAH RESERVA 2002, VIÑAS BISQUERTT RAPEL VALLEY – *With super-ripe purple fruits on the nose, soft red and black fruit flavours, and chunky tannins. Fresh acidity.*	£24.00 MCT
OCIO PINOT NOIR 2002, VIÑA CONO SUR ACONCAGUA VALLEY – *Raspberries and earth aromas mingle with leathery notes. Light, with savoury elements and a medium-long finish.*	£30.00 WSO

CHILEAN RED BRONZE / SEAL

VIÑEDO CHADWICK 2000, ERRAZURIZ Maipo Valley – *Supple, with blackcurrant and mint aromas. The palate is nicely balanced with well-integrated oak and tannins.*	£36.60 EDC/VIT FLA/WTS
VIÑEDO CHADWICK 2001, ERRAZURIZ Maipo Valley – *Cassis-driven wine with minty notes. The palate is balanced and harmonious with lush berry fruit to finish.*	£36.60 EDC/VIT FLA/WTS
CALITERRA SEÑA 2001, CALITERRA Aconcagua Valley – *Deep garnet. Herbal notes etch the peppery fruit and smoky oak on the nose. Menthol hints.*	£50.00 HAX/TAU

SEAL OF APPROVAL
CHILEAN RED

☆ **CASA ALVARES CHILEAN CABERNET SAUVIGNON NV, GRANDS VINS SÉLECTION** Central Valley – *Redcurrant jelly and blackberry pip flavours. Full yet balanced.*	£3.00 ALD
☆ **QUINTA LAS CABRAS 2002, VIÑA LA ROSA** Rapel Valley – *A flavourful blend of blackberries and strawberries wrapped in toasty oak.*	£3.00 SMF
☆ **LANDMARK VINTNER'S COLLECTION CHILEAN CABERNET SAUVIGNON 2003, VIÑOS SAN NICOLAS** Central Valley – *Undergrowth notes add interest to the bright ripe cassis fruit.*	£3.50 LCC
☆ **MHV SAN ANDRES TINTO NV, SAN PEDRO** Central Valley – *Clear and bright red-cherry fruit with whiffs of inkwell and pepper.*	£3.90 MHV
☆ **CHILEAN MERLOT 2003, VIÑA MORANDE** Central Valley – *Soft black plum flavours and a hint of menthol on the nose.*	£4.00 SMF
☆ **CO-OP CHILEAN CABERNET SAUVIGNON 2003, SANTA TERESA** Central Valley – *Robust blackcurrant fruit flesh is supported by firm tobacco leaf tannins.*	£4.00 CWS

CHILEAN RED SEAL / ROSÉ BRONZE / SWEET BRONZE

☆ **EL EMPERADOR MERLOT 2003, LES GRANDS CHAIS DE FRANCE** CENTRAL VALLEY – *Deeply coloured, with scents and flavours of black plums and red-cherries.*	£4.00 SPR
☆ **LOS CAMACHOS CABERNET SAUVIGNON 2003, SAN PEDRO** CENTRAL VALLEY – *Red-cherry fruit flavours meld with redcurrants on the firm, youthful palate.*	£4.00 WRT
☆ **MATISSES CABERNET SAUVIGNON 2001, XPOVIN CELLARS** CURICÓ VALLEY – *Masses of cassis and chocolate spill from this mouthwatering Cabernet.*	£4.00 LUV
☆ **O'HIGGINS RIDGE CABERNET SAUVIGNON 2003, SAN JOSE DE APALTA** RAPEL VALLEY – *Ripe, mouthfilling and rustic, with firm cassis and herb flavours.*	£4.00 G2W
☆ **PASO DEL SOL CABERNET SAUVIGNON 2003, TERRAMATER** CENTRAL VALLEY – *Bright, ripe, mouthwatering and fruit-driven cassis, and toast flavours.*	£4.00 MRN

BRONZE
CHILEAN ROSÉ

120 ROSÉ 2003, VIÑA SANTA RITA MAIPO VALLEY – *This perennial favourite is awash in sweetly ripe flavours and tinged with a note of leafiness.*	£5.80 BNK/TAU BWC/JSM

BRONZE
CHILEAN SWEET

LAS CASAS DEL TOQUI LATE HARVEST SEMILLON 2001, VIÑA DE LAROSE RAPEL – *Citrus peel aromas grace the nose. Notes of toffee enrich the long palate of apples and butter.*	■£8.00 GRT

EASTERN EUROPE

The countries to the east of the old Iron Curtain have, in recent years, been steadily overshadowed by the New World. The modernizing and privatizing of a collectivized industry has been a far more lengthy process than was anticipated and more investment is needed. But there are plenty of good inexpensive wines to be found in this area, and truly great sweet Tokajis in Hungary. Georgia is an ancient winemaking region that is worth looking out for.

BRONZE
EASTERN EUROPEAN WHITE

☆ **SPICE TRAIL WHITE 2003, NAGYREDE** HUNGARY – *Very ripe apples, allspice, and cloves assault the nose. The taut mineral palate has a long finish.*	£4.00 JSM
☆ **VIRGIN VINTAGE CHARDONNAY 2003, HILLTOP NESZMÉLY** HUNGARY – *A delicate straw gold. The developed aromas of candied-lemon fruit complement the ripe melon flavours.*	£5.00 VER

SEAL OF APPROVAL
EASTERN EUROPEAN WHITE

☆ **RECAS PINOT GRIGIO 2003, CRAMELE RECAS** ROMANIA – *Youthful, zippy, mouthwatering, and light-bodied, with a floral lift.*	£3.30 WOW
☆ **WOODCUTTERS WHITE 2003, HILLTOP NESZMELY** HUNGARY – *Bursting with peaches, white pepper, touches of rosehip, and nutmeg.*	£3.30 SAF
☆ **CO-OP BULGARIAN CHARDONNAY 2003, BOYAR SHUMEN** BULGARIA – *Ripe white-fleshed pear fruit flavours. Bright cleansing acidity.*	£3.50 CWS

EASTERN EUROPEAN WHITE SEAL / RED BRONZE / SEAL

☆ **BLUERIDGE CHARDONNAY 2003, BOYAR ESTATES** **BULGARIA** – *Warm toasty aromas grace the Granny Smith apple flavours.*	£4.00 SMF
☆ **NAGYREDE ESTATE PINOT GRIGIO 2003, NAGYREDE** **HUNGARY** – *Nuances of bitter almond, elderflower, quartz, and pear juice.*	£4.00 UNS
☆ **OLD TBILISI WHITE NV, GEORGIAN WINES AND SPIRITS** **GEORGIA** – *Structured yet fruit-driven, with vibrant sliced apple and mulberry flavours.*	£4.00 CAX
☆ **RIVERVIEW CHARDONNAY PINOT GRIGIO 2003, HILLTOP NESZMELY** **HUNGARY** – *Delicate white flower and peppery notes grace the green fruit flavours.*	£4.00 TOS/JSM

BRONZE
EASTERN EUROPEAN RED

☆ **RIVER ROUTE MERLOT 2003, CARL REH WINERY** **ROMANIA** – *Juicy bramble jelly fruit. Attractive acidity. A pleasing, forward, medium-bodied wine.*	£4.10 ASD/THS WRC/JSM
☆ **BLUERIDGE MERLOT SPECIAL SELECTION 2003, BOYAR ESTATES** **BULGARIA** – *Intensely flavoured and highly coloured, with chocolate and currant fruit flavours on the full-bodied palate.*	£5.00 DBO

SEAL OF APPROVAL
EASTERN EUROPEAN RED

☆ **MOUNT SOFIA MERLOT RUBIN NV, WINEZ** **BULGARIA** – *Black plum fruit flavours merge into royal-purple-coloured fruit.*	£4.00 CWS

EASTERN EUROPEAN RED SEAL / ROSÉ SEAL / SWEET GOLD

☆ **PRAHOVA VALLEY SPECIAL RESERVE PINOT NOIR 2000, HALEWOOD ROMANIA VINURI** ROMANIA – *Smoothly textured, with damson flesh and cedary tannins.*	£4.00 HAE/ASD BGN/JSM
☆ **TALARIS CABERNET SAUVIGNON 2003, WINEZ** BULGARIA – *Blackcurrants, herbs, tree bark, and spice-box aromas and flavours.*	£4.00 THS
☆ **VALLEY OF THE ROSES MERLOT 2003, STORK NEST ESTATES** BULGARIA – *Black-cherry flavours meld with bouquet garni on nose and palate.*	£4.00 WZD

SEAL OF APPROVAL
EASTERN EUROPEAN ROSÉ

☆ **RIVER ROUTE MERLOT ROSÉ 2003, CARL REH WINERY** ROMANIA – *Soft mouthfilling cherry flavours with a gentle cedary tone.*	£3.60 WTS
☆ **VALLEY OF THE ROSES CABERNET SAUVIGNON ROSÉ 2003, STORK NEST ESTATES** BULGARIA – *Crisp and structured, with crushed redcurrant flavours and firm tannins.*	£3.90 CWS/SAF
☆ **CABERNET SAUVIGNON ROSÉ 2003, NAGYREDE** HUNGARY – *Ruby pink. Dry, structured, herbaceous, full-bodied, and youthful.*	£4.00 UNS/JSM

GOLD
EASTERN EUROPEAN SWEET

DISZNÓKÖ TOKAJI ASZÚ 6 PUTTONYOS 1999, TOKAJ DISZNÓKÖ ESTATE HUNGARY – *Fresh orange zest, crystallised lemons, youthful pineapple and marmalade all spill from this modern, fresh Tokaji.*	▲£34.00 VIT

SILVER
EASTERN EUROPEAN SWEET

DOBOGO TOKAJI ASZÚ 6 PUTTONYOS 1999, DOBOGO Hungary – *Earl Grey tea on a nose laden with lemon marmalade. Zippy acidity cuts through dense, dried apricot syrup.*	▲£38.00 LIB

BRONZE
EASTERN EUROPEAN SWEET

DISZNÓKÖ TOKAJI 5 PUTTONYOS ASZÚ 1999, TOKAJ DISNOKO ESTATE Hungary – *Complex nose of saffron, honey, and quince. The palate has depth, intensity, and decent persistence.*	▲£20.20 VIT/FEN

For stockist codes turn to page 355. For regularly updated information about stockists and the International Wine Challenge, visit wineint.com. For a full glossary of wine terms and a complete free wine course, visit robertjoseph-onwine.com

FRANCE

Despite its recent slide down the UK pop parade, France remains the place to go when you are looking for variety and a truly interesting range of flavours that are not to be found anywhere else on earth. Champagne, Bordeaux, Burgundy, Rhône, Loire, and Alsace all remain the role models for producers around the world; and there are great examples at various price levels among the award winners below. But, just as interesting in their own way are the traditional and new wave wines that are now coming out of the south and southwest of France where a growing number of producers are taking a New World approach to their winemaking.

TROPHY
ALSACE WHITE

☆ **GEWURZTRAMINER GRAND CRU BRAND 2000, CAVE VINICOLE DE TURCKHEIM** ALSACE – *Soft and ripe with petals and peppery nuances, good weight, and racy acidity which punctuates the extended length.*	**£11.40** WRK/FEN NRW/PBA NYW

GOLD
ALSACE WHITE

☆ **GEWURZTRAMINER PRESTIGE 2002, PAUL ZINCK** ALSACE – *Distinctive waxy orange flower, rose petal, and lychee scents. Smooth and subtly spiced. Exotic and luxuriant, with a lasting finish.*	**£10.50** LAI
☆ **TURCKHEIM RIESLING BRAND 1999, CAVE VINICOLE DE TURCKHEIM** ALSACE – *Spice, grapefruit, lime, and honey battle it out on the nose for supremacy. Deliciously evolved petrol nuances.*	**£10.60** FEN/NRW PBA/JFE NYW
☆ **TOKAY PINOT GRIS GRAND CRU BRAND 2001, CAVE VINICOLE DE TURCKHEIM** ALSACE – *Honeysuckle, ripe Conference pears, and mint sprinkle the nose. The palate has plump satsuma, pink grapefruit, and lemon.*	**£11.30** WRK/NRW PBA/NYW

146 ALSACE WHITE GOLD / SILVER

☆ **GEWURZTRAMINER KESSLER GRAND CRU 2000, DOMAINES SCHLUMBERGER** ALSACE – *A rose garden in a glass. Perfumed and feminine with spicy undertones, it refrains from going over the top. Magnificent.*	£12.50 RWM
GEWURZTRAMINER VIEILLES VIGNES GRAND CRU FURSTENTUM 2001, DOMAINE PAUL BLANCK ALSACE – *Pure lychee, orange blossom, honey, and marmalade. Deep, fresh and rich, with balanced acidity and great length.*	£18.00 JBF
HERRENWEG DE TURCKHEIM GEWURZTRAMINER 2001, OLIVIER HUMBRECHT ALSACE – *True terroir typicity is expressed in this medal winner. Intense aromatic spice and powder puff perfume. Sustained, heady, and aristocratic.*	£18.00 WTS
BARMES BEUCHER RIESLING HENGST 2002, BARMES BEUCHER ALSACE – *Exotic fruit, roses, limes, and petrol. The stuff of the gods, powerful, with crisp acidity and sweetly ripe fruit.*	£21.90 GON
CUVÉE FRÉDÉRIC EMILE RIESLING 2000, TRIMBACH ALSACE – *Slightly scented with spicy notes and a grapefruit zing. It has the Riesling petrollyness and a honeyed texture.*	£24.90 ESL/LAI EVI/RWM
GEWURZTRAMINER HENGST 2002, OLIVIER HUMBRECHT ALSACE – *This biodynamic Gewurztraminer boasts lemony crispness, rambutan and honey flavours. Not too heavy, with moderate sweetness and an elegant richness.*	£39.80 SOM/GON NYW
PINOT GRIS RANGEN DE THANN CLOS SAINT-URBAIN 2002, OLIVIER HUMBRECHT ALSACE – *Intense and rich, with great aromatic definition. Hints of smoky game. Fresh, blindingly pure and focused. A classic.*	£43.30 GON

SILVER
ALSACE WHITE

☆ **RESERVE PINOT BLANC 2002, CAVE VINICOLE DE TURCKHEIM** ALSACE – *Exceptional concentration. Stone and lush apple aromas rise from the glass. Long and stylish, with a touch of botrytis.*	£6.30 WIDELY AVAILABLE
☆ **RESERVE PINOT GRIS 2002, CAVE VINICOLE DE TURCKHEIM** ALSACE – *Aromatic apricot, spice, and honey scents. Unctuous, its rich, ripe fruit balanced by a spine of acidity. Long.*	£7.10 HAX/PBA BOO/INS

ALSACE WHITE SILVER 147

TOKAY PINOT GRIS PATERGARTEN 2002, DOMAINE PAUL BLANCK Alsace – *Ripe, with peach and spice aromas on the nose. A rich and round palate with good fruit intensity.*	£12.00 JBF
PINOT BLANC RESERVE 2002, DOMAINE WEINBACH Alsace – *Unctuous aromas display richness, intensity, and spice. The generous, textured palate has toffee apple and pear flavours.*	£12.60 TAN/J&B
ZIND 1 DOMAINE ZIND HUMBRECHT 2001, OLIVIER HUMBRECHT Alsace – *Glinting delicate gold. A riot of guava and honeysuckle; glossy and balanced, with pungent lemongrass flavours.*	£13.00 WTS
GEWURZTRAMINER GRAND CRU STEINERT 2001, PIERRE FRICK Alsace – *Lush yet well-knitted, with stony mineral, rosewater, and musk scents. Apricot and peach flavours.*	£14.00 VER
RIESLING GRAND CRU FURSTENTUM 2001, DOMAINE PAUL BLANCK Alsace – *Heaving with elderflower aromas, honey and spice. Positively nectar-like, keenly balanced and a spicy finish.*	£17.00 JBF
PINOT GRIS GRAND CRU KITTERLÉ 1998, DOMAINES SCHLUMBERGER Alsace – *Opulent and finely textured, with poached pear elements. Big, luscious and powerful, with hints of quartzite minerality.*	£21.00 WIM
MUSCAT GOLDERT ZIND HUMBRECHT 2001, OLIVIER HUMBRECHT Alsace – *Seductive rose petal, honey, and clove-scented nose. The crisp, dry palate has peachy weight and a long finish.*	£22.00 WTS
TOKAY PINOT GRIS CUVÉE SAINTE CATHERINE 2000, DOMAINE WEINBACH Alsace – *Notes of apricot and spice. The palate is rich yet never cloying. The finish is long, minerally and harmonious.*	£22.50 J&B
RIESLING HEIMBOURG 2001, OLIVIER HUMBRECHT Alsace – *Ripe apricot and honeyed notes. Very rich with excellent depth and mineral overtones. Long and elegant.*	£23.80 SOM/GON WTS
CLOS DE CAPUCINS RIESLING GRAND CRU SCHLOSSBERG 2002, DOMAINE WEINBACH Alsace – *Gorgeously opulent, ripe, and spicy with a honeyed nose and exotic fruit. Complex and satisfying. An endless finish.*	£25.20 TAN/J&B

ALSACE WHITE SILVER / BRONZE

GEWURZTRAMINER HERRENWEG DE TURCKHEIM 2002, OLIVIER HUMBRECHT ALSACE – *Expressive, complex and burnt orange aromas. Fantastic concentration, earthy depth and excellent balance. The finish is long and harmonious.*	£26.10 GON/NYW

BRONZE
ALSACE WHITE

TESCO FINEST RIESLING 2002, VINS D'ALSACE KUEHN ALSACE – *Restrained and light, with good balance, elegant citrus fruit, and a refreshing bite of crisp acidity.*	£6.00 TOS
TESCO FINEST GEWURZTRAMINER 2002, VINS D'ALSACE KUEHN ALSACE – *Perfumed lychee and orange blossom nose. Rich, spicy, balanced, and fresh.*	£7.00 TOS
THE WAYDELICH COLLECTION GEWURZTRAMINER 2001, CAVE VINICOLE DE RIBEAUVILLÉ ALSACE – *White pepper, rosehips, Seville oranges, turkish delight, and white peaches on nose and palate.*	£8.00 WPR
RIESLING GRAND CRU EICHBERG 2002, PAUL ZINCK ALSACE – *Complex, big, ripe, and full-bodied. Vibrant and honeyed, with lime juice flavours and floral notes.*	£10.00 MWW
TOKAY PINOT GRIS 2003, DOMAINE PAUL BLANCK ALSACE – *Honeyed wine with a fat palate showing apricot and spice notes. Good weight and intensity to finish.*	£10.00 JBF
RIESLING SAERING GRAND CRU 2000, DOMAINES SCHLUMBERGER ALSACE – *Freshly sliced citrus fruit and honeycomb aromas. Long, fine, and elegant. Expresses its terroir beautifully.*	£10.80 JNW
PINOT BLANC ROSENBERG 2002, BARMES BUECHER ALSACE – *Bright green aromas. Heady, warming and lifted, with touches of honey softening its big bones.*	£11.90 GON
PINOT GRIS WINDSBUHL 2001, OLIVIER HUMBRECHT ALSACE – *The nose of this beauty is very honeyed, with excellent weight and a long, rich, off-dry finish.*	£34.00 WTS

BRONZE
BEAUJOLAIS RED

DOMAINE DE FONTALOGNIER BEAUJOLAIS VILLAGE 2003, GILLES ET NEL DUCROUX BEAUJOLAIS – *Plums and spice. Concentrated and intense, with excellent balance, youth, and a long, sweetly ripe finish.*	£6.40 / BBO
DOMAINE PELLETIER JULIÉNAS 2003, EVENTAIL DE VIGNERONS PRODUCTEURS BEAUJOLAIS – *Youthful and vibrant. Plum stewed fruit flavours and firm tannins. Hints of quartz dust and bubblegum.*	£6.50 / PLB
COMBE AUX JACQUES BEAUJOLAIS-VILLAGES 2003, LOUIS JADOT BEAUJOLAIS – *Buoyant cherry fruit on the nose. The palate has fine balanced tannins. Expressive, youthful, and deeply flavoured.*	£6.70 / FEN/WTS
HENRI LA FONTAINE BROUILLY 2003, FAYE BEAUJOLAIS – *A profusion of rich, ripe blueberry, damson, and raspberry fruit. Floral perfume. Soft texture and clear, buoyant acidity.*	£8.00 / MHV
SAINT AMOUR DOMAINE DES BILLARDS 2003, LORAN BEAUJOLAIS – *The deep red colour complements the palate of muted dark fruit, with its astringent tannins and long finish.*	£8.30 / ESL
MOULIN-À-VENT CLOS DU GRAND CARQUELIN CHÂTEAU DES JACQUES 2000, LOUIS JADOT BEAUJOLAIS – *Brick red. A touch of tree bark and a soft attack of red summer fruits. Dusty tannins.*	£13.00 / V&C

GOLD
BORDEAUX WHITE

☆ **CHÂTEAU DUCLA EXPERIENCE X 2002, YVON MAU** BORDEAUX – *Gooseberry, grass, and pea pods; waxy orange blossoms; a squeeze of lemon. Skilfully woven, it lingers for an eternity.*	£9.00 / FXT

SILVER
BORDEAUX WHITE

☆ **CHÂTEAU DE ROQUES SAUVIGNON BLANC 2003, CHÂTEAU LEZONGARS** Bordeaux – *Gorgeous gold. Smooth, its roundness crammed with lemon and pineapple fruit flavours. Herbs add lift to the richness.*	£6.00 HBJ
SENSUAL FRUIT WHITE 2003, CORDIER Bordeaux – *Soft. Sauvignon ripe lime, gooseberries, and a touch of green bean; Sémillon honey. Attractive, expressive, and velvet-textured.*	£8.00 VDO

BRONZE
BORDEAUX WHITE

☆ **CELLIER YVECOURT 2003, YVON MAU** Bordeaux – *Highly perfumed with lemon blossom aromas. Dry and round, with a medium-weight body and a silky texture.*	£5.00 UNS
☆ **CHÂTEAU BEAU MAYNE SAUVIGNON BLANC 2003, DOURTHE KRESSMANN** Bordeaux – *A balanced, consistent and weighty Sauvignon Blanc. Substantial mouthfeel and lengthy finish. Delicate herbal hints.*	£5.00 SAF/TOS
RADCLIFFE'S REGIONAL CLASSICS BORDEAUX BLANC 2003, DULONG FRÈRES Bordeaux – *Classic and restrained, with tea, pineapples, and lemons on nose and palate. Bright, young, and very attractive.*	£6.00 THS
CHÂTEAU FRÉDÉRIC BLANC 2003, FRÉDÉRIC ARINO Bordeaux – *Intense lemon fruit is sprinkled with a touch of sweet spice. Ripe, upfront, toasty, and inviting.*	£6.30 LAI
CHÂTEAU HAUT BONFILS 2003, CHÂTEAU HAUT BONFILS Bordeaux – *Dry, minerally and straw-pale, this delicate, grassy wine has a backbone of leafiness underpinning the citrus fruit.*	£6.40 LAI
DULONG FRÈRES SAINT SAVIN 2003, DULONG FRÈRES ET FILS Bordeaux – *Greenish gold. Restrained oak influence smooths out the green apple and ripe peach flavours.*	£7.00 SKW

GOLD LABEL BORDEAUX BLANC 2002, BARTON & GUESTIER Bordeaux – *Pale, with attractive white flowers on the nose and a rich, round, buttery mouthful of lemon flavour.*	£7.00 PFC
CHÂTEAU DU SEUIL GRAVES 2002, CHÂTEAU DU SEUIL Bordeaux – *A waxy texture coats the mouth with flavours of lemons, limes, and green melon fruit.*	£11.70 VGN/BIG

SEAL OF APPROVAL
BORDEAUX WHITE

☆ **SAUVIGNON BLANC NV, BOUEY ET FILS** Bordeaux – *Gooseberry and lime flavours spill from the fruit-rich palate.*	£3.90 MHV

TROPHY
BORDEAUX RED

CHÂTEAU PAPE-CLÉMENT 2001, CHÂTEAU PAPE-CLÉMENT Bordeaux – *Perfumed cassis fruit and overtones of smoky game. Soft chewy tannins on the lingering finish. Weighty and complex.*	£.00 NOT AVAILABLE IN THE UK

GOLD
BORDEAUX RED

☆ **CHÂTEAU MARTIN 2000, YVON MAU** Bordeaux – *Graves minerality and bright berry fruit flavours. Slightly fleshy with rich, ripe fruit and a warm fruitcake appeal.*	£10.00 TOS
CHÂTEAU LA GARDE 2000, DOURTHE KRESSMANN Bordeaux – *Elegant, fully ripe, and rich. Radiant coffee-bean oak complements the fruit rather than overwhelming it. Classy.*	£15.00 BBR
CHÂTEAU LA TOUR HAUT-BRION 1998, DOMAINE CLARENCE DILLON Bordeaux – *Displaying savoury game and primary fruit. Drinking now, this claret should continue to gain complexity without sacrificing freshness.*	£30.00 J&B

CHÂTEAU NENIN 1998, CHÂTEAU NENIN BORDEAUX – *Spicy fruitcake, tobacco, cedar, and game. Silky and balanced. Sensitive use of oak imparts a fine tannic structure.*	£45.00
	J&B

SILVER
BORDEAUX RED

☆ **CHÂTEAU LEON 2000, PHILIPPE PIERAERTS** BORDEAUX – *Earthy notes accompany black fruit on the nose. Savoury nuances, firm tannins, and ripe fruit on the palate.*	£7.00
	RNS
CHÂTEAU BARREYRES 2002, CASTEL FRÈRES BORDEAUX – *Classy cedary notes on the nose lead to a palate filled with sweet cassis fruit. A silky finish.*	£8.50
	JSM
CHÂTEAU CARIGNAN 2000, PHILIPPE PIERAERTS BORDEAUX – *The silky plum fruit palate has fine tannins, notes of undergrowth, and a sprinkling of cinnamon.*	£9.00
	DUN
CHÂTEAU DE LA GARDE 2001, CHÂTEAU DE LA GARDE BORDEAUX – *Cinnamon, nutmeg, and cigarillo scents. A mature tannic structure supports the tightly knit fruit. Excellent balance.*	£9.00
	JSM
WAITROSE SAINT EMILION 2002, YVON MAU BORDEAUX – *Well-balanced, with fragrant plums, spicy aromas, and coconut oak. The palate shows soft fruit. A grippy finish.*	£9.00
	FXT
CHÂTEAU D'ARCINS 2002, CASTEL FRÈRES BORDEAUX – *Pure fruit, lead pencil, spice, and delightful roast coffee bean characters perfume this French wine.*	£9.50
	ODD
AVERY'S FINE ST-EMILION 2000, AVERY'S OF BRISTOL BORDEAUX – *Blackcurrant fruit is invigorated by a dose of coffee, whilst firm yet integrated tannins sustain the medium-long finish.*	£10.00
	AVB
CHÂTEAU DE FRANCS LES CERISIERS 2002, D HEBRARD ET H DE BOUARD BORDEAUX – *Ripe fruit harmoniously intertwined with pleasing leafy notes and delicate menthol nuances. Some additional cellaring recommended.*	£10.50
	CHN

BORDEAUX RED SILVER

CHÂTEAU LA GRANGENEUVE DE FIGEAC 1997, LD VINS BORDEAUX – *A handsome rust red colour hints at the tertiary bouquet of spices, leather, and dried fruit.*	**£11.00** MWW
L'ENCLOS DU CHÂTEAU LEZONGARS 2001, CHÂTEAU LEZONGARS BORDEAUX – *This wine is youthful, with an absorbing nose, an elegant, light structure and a dense black fruit palate.*	**£11.00** VIT
CHÂTEAU GARRAUD 2002, VIGNOBLES LEON NONY BORDEAUX – *Fragrant cedary aromas lead to an elegant palate of cassis. Lightly tannic, with a balanced finish.*	**£14.00** CCS
CHÂTEAU LAROSE PERGANSON CRU BOURGEOIS 1998, CHÂTEAU LA TRINTAUDON BORDEAUX – *Cedarwood and blackberry aromas. The palate boasts grippy tannins, earth, herbs, game, toast, and black fruit.*	**£14.00** GRT
CHÂTEAU BELLEFONT BELCIER 2001, JACQUES BERREBI ET ALAIN LAGUILLAUNIE BORDEAUX – *The nose has plenty of modern oak and spice. The palate is succulent, with a pleasing chocolatey richness.*	**£15.00** CHN
CHEVALIER DE LASCOMBES 2001, CHÂTEAU LASCOMBES BORDEAUX – *Inky red, with an attractive cedar nose. Animal aromas and tanned leather elements. Blackberry fruit etched with graphite.*	**£16.00** WTS
CHÂTEAU LE BOSCQ 2000, DOURTHE KRESSMANN BORDEAUX – *Savoury roast meat and red fruit flavours and touches of cloves and cinnamon. Fleshy yet highly structured. Intense.*	**£17.00** BBR
CHÂTEAU L'ANCIEN 2002, VIGNOBLES LEON NONY BORDEAUX – *A profusion of silky cassis and plummy Merlot fruit populates the structured, well-balanced, long palate.*	**£25.00** CCS
CHÂTEAU TRIANON 2002, DOMINIQUE HEBRARD BORDEAUX – *Voluptuous nose of spicy berry fruits and plums. A richly complex palate of sweeter fruits. A long finish.*	**£32.00** ESL
COS D'ESTOURNEL 1997, COS D'ESTOURNEL BORDEAUX – *Sweet blackcurrants, patchouli, sandalwood, roast game, red cedar, and nutmeg swirl together. Mature, heady, and fine.*	**£45.00** J&B

BRONZE
BORDEAUX RED

☆ **CHÂTEAU MONTAUT GORRY 2003, ANDRÉ QUANCARD ANDRÉ** BORDEAUX – *Young, sweet fresh fruit on an elegant palate that finishes a touch on the green side.*	**£3.30** THI
☆ **MERCHANTS BAY MERLOT CABERNET SAUVIGNON 2003, GINESTET** BORDEAUX – *Hints of cigar box and mulberries alongside juicy fruit and a touch of sweet oak.*	**£4.80** IWS/WTS
☆ **CALVET LIMITED RELEASE 2002, CALVET** BORDEAUX – *Leafy characters on the nose mix with gentle fruit. The palate has hints of mint and soft fruit.*	**£5.00** GYW/JSM
☆ **RIGHT BANK 2003, PRODUCTA** BORDEAUX – *Young, with slightly green tannins, rich blackberry fruit, a firm structure and a long spicy finish.*	**£5.00** ADE/UNS
☆ **RIVERS MEET CABERNET MERLOT 2003, GINESTET** BORDEAUX – *A classic blend made in a modern style. Green pepper runs alongside sparkling redcurrant fruit on the palate.*	**£5.00** WAV
CHÂTEAU CLOS DE LA TOUR 2003, DOURTHE KRESSMANN BORDEAUX – *A vibrant crimson purple Merlot-dominated blend with ripe sweet fruit and polished tannins.*	**£6.00** DOU
COLLECTION PRIVÉE BORDEAUX MERLOT 2003, CORDIER BORDEAUX – *This wine has attractive fruit supported by a decent tannic backbone and a dry finish.*	**£6.00** VDO
PREMIUS 2002, YVON MAU BORDEAUX – *Currants, cedar, and blackberries on the nose and palate. Soft tannins, crisp acidity, and a chewy finish.*	**£6.70** UNS/TOS
L'ORANGERIE DE CARIGNAN 2001, PHILIPPE PIERAERTS BORDEAUX – *A lighter style of Merlot-dominated Bordeaux with an earthy plummy nose and a long inviting finish.*	**£7.20** JNW

BORDEAUX RED BRONZE 155

PRESTIGE CLARET 2000, AVERY'S OF BRISTOL **BORDEAUX** – *Forest floor, strawberries, rich clove buds, and mocha notes meld on this fleshy, flavourful offering.*	£8.00 AVB
RIGHT BANK 2000, PRODUCTA BORDEAUX – *A rich, gamey nose gives way to a silky palate of wild cherries, liquorice, vanilla, and currants.*	£8.00 ADE
SEIGNEURS D'AIGUILHE 2001, COMTES DE NEIPPERG **BORDEAUX** – *Focused, with good structure and aromatic definition. Its cushion of soft ripe cassis is bolstered by leather and tobacco.*	£8.00 WTS
DOURTHE LA GRANDE CUVÉE ST-EMILION 2001, CVBG DOURTHE KRESSMANN BORDEAUX – *Plums and tea leaves scent the nose. Medium-weight palate of redcurrant fruit wrapped in soft oaky vanilla.*	£9.00 DOU
CHÂTEAU CLOS DE LA TOUR RÉSERVE DU CHÂTEAU 2002, DOURTHE KRESSMANN BORDEAUX – *Enticing, with spicy oak on the nose and palate, and a good balance of freshness, oak, and fruit.*	£9.60 ODD
TREYTINS LALANDE DE POMEROL 2002, VIGNOBLES LÉON NONY BORDEAUX – *A wine with potential for early to medium drinking. Pencil shavings score the meaty, cherry fruit on the palate.*	£9.80 CCS
CHÂTEAU DE LANDIRAS 2001, MARSHALL BAILEY BORDEAUX – *Warm baked cherry tart aromas. Chewy, and complex. Needs to be drawn out to express fully its elegance.*	£10.00 LDS
CHÂTEAU REYSSON RESERVE DU CHÂTEAU 2002, DOURTHE KRESSMANN BORDEAUX – *A cru bourgeois with an inky colour, deep berry fruit, and robust tannins. Still needs time to reveal all.*	£10.00 DOU
CHÂTEAU DUCLA PERMANENCE VII 2001, YVON MAU BORDEAUX – *Faint sweet oak notes on the nose. Concentrated red fruit and creamy oak on the palate.*	£11.00 FXT
CHÂTEAU LABAT 2002, CHÂTEAU LABAT BORDEAUX – *Pure fruit unfettered by oak. A strawberry flavoured, vermilion hued wine with a long finish.*	£11.00 LAI

156 BORDEAUX RED BRONZE

CHÂTEAU LAPELLETRIE 2001, CHÂTEAU LAPELLETRIE BORDEAUX – *Chewy tannins are slightly overtaking the palate's fruit, but are in balance with the oak. A good finish.*	£12.00 TOS
CHÂTEAU PREUILLAC 2001, YVON MAU BORDEAUX – *Soft brambles on the nose. The sweet-fruited palate has some well-infused oak and a juicy finish.*	£12.00 FXT
LA PELOUSE 2001, CHÂTEAU CAMBON BORDEAUX – *A wine with smoky coffee scents and fresh blackberry fruit flavours of impressive concentration and length.*	£12.00 WTS
CHÂTEAU PREUILLAC 2000, YVON MAU BORDEAUX – *Juicy capsicum perfumes the nose. The palate combines bramble and cassis with mocha, all buttressed by sturdy tannins.*	£12.40 BNK/UNS
CHÂTEAU DU SEUIL GRAVES 2001, CHÂTEAU DU SEUIL BORDEAUX – *Ripe cassis and grassy notes. The palate is restrained with decent berry fruit allied to fine tannins.*	£15.00 VGN
CHÂTEAU PLAISANCE ST-EMILION 2001, CORDIER MESTREZAT BORDEAUX – *Attractive aromas of creamy brambles and mocha notes lead to a palate of Merlot opulence and silky tannins.*	£15.00 MWW
LA RESERVE DE LÉOVILLE-BARTON 2000, CHÂTEAU LÉOVILLE-BARTON BORDEAUX – *Restrained and feminine. Aromatically expressive and medium-bodied, with sweet spice, ripe blackberries, cedar, and Marmite.*	£19.50 ESL/JNW TAN/JFE
CHÂTEAU CANTEMERLE 1999, CHÂTEAU CANTEMERLE BORDEAUX – *Leather and cedar on the nose with cooked bramble fruit. A seductive palate with spicy oak. Dry finish.*	£20.00 MWW
AMAVINUM 2001, CHÂTEAU LA ROCHE BEAULIEU BORDEAUX – *Richly textured and coloured, this modern Bordeaux shows ripe red fruit and fine tannins on the lengthy palate.*	£23.00 GRT

BORDEAUX RED SEAL / **ROSÉ** SILVER / **SWEET** GOLD / SILVER **157**

SEAL OF APPROVAL
BORDEAUX RED

☆ **CHARLES DE MONTENEY 2002, CALVET** **BORDEAUX** – *Mulberries and cherries scent the nose. Full-flavoured, with firm tannins.*	£4.00 ALD
☆ **LANDMARK VINTNER'S COLLECTION CLARET 2002, CORDIER** **BORDEAUX** – *Dense damson and vibrant blackcurrant flavours and aromas.*	£4.00 LCC

SILVER
BORDEAUX ROSÉ

CHÂTEAU DE SOURS ROSÉ 2003, ESME JOHNSTONE **BORDEAUX** – *The nose is packed with ripe blackcurrants and the palate is deep and juicy, with a mineral backbone.*	£8.30 TAN/MW W

GOLD
BORDEAUX SWEET

CHÂTEAU RIEUSSEC SAUTERNES 1996, CHÂTEAU RIEUSSEC **BORDEAUX** – *Richly waxy, gently smoky, and in possession of a honeyed sweetness. The nectar of the gods: benchmark Sauternes.*	£34.50 GHL/J&B

SILVER
BORDEAUX SWEET

☆ **CHÂTEAU DU SEUIL CÉRONS 1999, CHÂTEAU DU SEUIL** **BORDEAUX** – *Botrytis and cinnamon spice combine to assail the nose. Smooth, oily, and very luscious.*	▲£10.00 BIG
TESCO FINEST SAUTERNES 2001, YVON MAU **BORDEAUX** – *Golden yellow. Ripest apples and raisins. Woody undertones and a jolt of acidity boost the rich flesh.*	£12.00 TOS

BORDEAUX SW. SILVER / BRONZE **/ BURGUNDY WH.** TROPHY / GOLD

CHÂTEAU LAFAURIE-PEYRAGUEY SAUTERNES 1997, CORDIER Bordeaux – *Intense saffron and honey on the nose and palate. Rich and ripe but harmonious. Complex and long finish.*	£36.00
	J&B

BRONZE
BORDEAUX SWEET

SAINSBURY'S CLASSIC SELECTION SAUTERNES 2002, VINTEX Bordeaux – *A pale yellow Sauternes with a soft, bright, youthful palate of lemons, grapefruit and gooseberries.*	■£8.00
	JSM
CLOS DADY SAUTERNES 2001, CLOS DADY Bordeaux – *Complex botrytis, honey, quince, and saffron nose. As the English are wont to quip: who's the Daddy?*	£21.00
	ENO

TROPHY
BURGUNDY WHITE

☆ **CHABLIS 1er CRU BROCARD 2002, DOMAINE JEAN-MARC BROCARD** Burgundy – *Bright lime, straw yellow. Chalky, crisp, balanced apple flavours. What is most impressive is its sinuous length.*	£12.20
	CEB/JSM
ST-AUBIN 1er CRU SUR GAMAY 2002, JEAN-CLAUDE BOISSET Burgundy – *This is more than Chardonnay: this is Burgundy. Ripeness, class, and elegance, and perfectly balanced, fine-grained oak.*	£19.00
	BEN/CCS MOV/NYW LIB/FLY

GOLD
BURGUNDY WHITE

☆ **BOURGOGNE CHARDONNAY EN SOL KIMMERIDGIEN 2002, DOMAINE JEAN-MARC BROCARD** Burgundy – *Pretty, round, and elegant, with soft ripe apricot and peach fruit over vanilla, butter, and honey notes.*	£7.00
	JBF/JSM
☆ **ST-VÉRAN BLASON DE BOURGOGNE 2001, BLASON DE BOURGOGNE** Burgundy – *Highly evolved creamy style with secondary flavours of toffee and nuts, loads of lemons, and white peach fruit.*	£8.00
	TOS

BURGUNDY WHITE GOLD 159

☆ **CHABLIS DOMAINE DES MANANTS 2002, DOMAINE JEAN-MARC BROCARD** BURGUNDY – *Light, chalky minerals, a restrained touch of oatmeal character, and elegant yet racy balancing acidity.*	**£9.20** JBF/G&M
☆ **POUILLY-FUISSÉ LES VIEUX MURS 2002, ETS LORAN ET FILS** BURGUNDY – *Full and weighty; oak clearly apparent yet well integrated. Attractive orange blossom and peach notes. Minerally and elegant.*	**£11.20** ESL
ANDRÉ SIMON CHABLIS 1ER CRU FOURCHAUME 2002, DOMAINE LAROCHE BURGUNDY – *Bright, pale-straw yellow, with pronounced mineral elements. Steely yet rich honeyed apple fruit buoyed by keen racy acidity.*	**£12.60** WRT
CHABLIS 1ER CRU MONTMAINS LES MANANTS 2002, DOMAINE JEAN-MARC BROCARD BURGUNDY – *Dry, lean, mineral character that suggests much more to come. Firm and crisp with a huge finish.*	**£14.10** JBF/G&M
MEURSAULT LOUIS JADOT 2000, LOUIS JADOT BURGUNDY – *A fine, concentrated Meursault with lemons, oatmeal, croissant, and noisette notes. Stupendous depth. A long, rambling finish.*	**£19.00** WTS/JSM
CHASSAGNE-MONTRACHET 1ER CRU LES CHENEVOTTES 2001, JEAN-NOËL GAGNARD BURGUNDY – *Star quality. The complex fruit is both concentrated and expressive, and emphasised by clear toasty oak. Superb.*	**£25.00** J&B
PULIGNY-MONTRACHET 1ER CRU LES FOLATIÈRES 2000, JOSEPH DROUHIN BURGUNDY – *Oatmeal, cream, toast, and butter notes lace ripe poached pear and yellow-apple fruit. Faultless and impeccably stylish.*	**£25.00** WTS
MEURSAULT 1ER CRU 2002, CHÂTEAU DE MARSANNAY BURGUNDY – *Refined, concentrated, and layered. Treacle, smoke, butterscotch, mushroom, and high toast. Immensely long. A wine of quality.*	**£27.00** PAT
PULIGNY-MONTRACHET CHAMPS CANET 2000, ETIENNE SAUZET BURGUNDY – *Excellent turbo-charged Burgundy. Smoky, mealy, and nutty, with mature savoury notes. Skilfully made, with an exceedingly long finish.*	**£48.00** TAN/WTS

SILVER
BURGUNDY WHITE

BEAU-MONDE PETIT CHABLIS 2002, J MOREAU	£8.00
BURGUNDY – *Very elegant mineral and burning leaf nose. Creamy citrus and seashell notes. Minerally, long, and harmonious.*	BWL
ASDA CHABLIS 1ER CRU 2002, DOMAINE LAROCHE	£9.50
BURGUNDY – *Leesy aromas, melons, apples, and white peaches. Savoury and mineral, with rapier acidity and a richly textured mouthfeel.*	ASD
CHABLIS PONT NEUF 2002, VAUCHER PÈRE ET FILS	£10.00
BURGUNDY – *Smoke, scents of rain, minerals, and white flowers; crisp green and yellow-apple flavours.*	NTD
CHABLIS VIEILLES VIGNES SAINTE CLAIRE 2002, DOMAINE JEAN-MARC BROCARD **BURGUNDY** – *Elegant, with a fresh nose and balanced palate. The mouthfeel is clean yet intense. Rich and concentrated finish.*	£10.00 JBF
RADCLIFFE'S CHABLIS 2002, LA CHABLISIENNE	£10.00
BURGUNDY – *The nose is restrained, with smoke and light citrus flavours. The creamy palate is pierced with minerals and acidity.*	THS
CHABLIS 1ER CRU GEORGES DESIRE 2001, GEORGES DESIRE **BURGUNDY** – *Excellent depth and richness. Luminous green. Comely, with chalky minerals, ripe aromatic pear, and hints of honeysuckle.*	£11.50 SMF
CHABLIS 1ER CRU 2001, CLAUDE CHONION	£12.00
BURGUNDY – *Powdery chalkdust and fresh key lime scents. Grassy and complex, with terrific grip. A lengthy finish.*	NTD
CHABLIS 1ER CRU CHANTRERIE 2002, MICHEL LAROCHE **BURGUNDY** – *Savoury, with dry chalky mineral elements and a long finish dripping with crisp citrus fruit. Very attractive.*	£13.00 BWL
CHABLIS VIEILLES VIGNES VAUROUX 2001, DOMAINE DE VAUROUX **BURGUNDY** – *Elegant and complex, with creamy chalk powder and flint scents. The palate is long, with finely wrought green apple acidity.*	£13.00 ENO

BURGUNDY WHITE SILVER / BRONZE

CHABLIS 1ER CRU VAUCOUPIN 2002, DOMAINE JEAN-MARC BROCARD BURGUNDY – *Fresh apple and seashell aromas. The palate combines ripe fruit with lean mineral acidity. Complex, elegant, and concentrated.*	£14.00 JBF/TAU ODD
AUXEY-DURESSES BLANC 2001, VALLET FRÈRES BURGUNDY – *Clean mineral and citrus aromas. The palate shows some fruit richness and vanilla oak. A finish of finesse.*	£15.00 PBA
PERNAND-VERGELESSES CHAMPY 2002, MAISON CHAMPY BURGUNDY – *Integrated, lively, and classic. A buoyant, perfumed offering. Creamy, open, and long, with seductive lemon zest flavours.*	£15.50 POL
POUILLY-FUISSÉ VIEILLES VIGNES 2002, VINS AUVIGUE BURGUNDY – *Creamy and full yet restrained, this developed, tight-knit beauty has smoke and green grass overtones.*	£17.00 CCS
MEURSAULT DU CHÂTEAU 2002, CHÂTEAU DE MARSANNAY BURGUNDY – *Vigour and exceptional texture. Roast hazelnuts, bags of elegant lemon fruit, butter, and wisps of smoke.*	£20.00 JSM
CHABLIS GRAND CRU LES CLOS 2002, DOMAINE DES MALANDES BURGUNDY – *Rich, white-fleshed peaches, apples, lemons, and melted butter. Cloves and cinnamon punctuate the big charry nose.*	£27.50 GHL
CHASSAGNE-MONTRACHET 1ER CRU TÊTE DU CLOS 2001, VINCENT DANCER BURGUNDY – *Very elegant mineral and brioche aromas. The palate is refined, its quality fruit underpinned by toasty oak.*	£28.00 J&B

BRONZE
BURGUNDY WHITE

CHABLIS LA LARME D'OR 2002, QUINSON BURGUNDY – *Refined, with creamy citrus and flint aromas. The crunchy green apple palate shows mineral intensity and freshness.*	£6.00 ALD
MÂCON-VILLAGES CHÂTEAU DE MIRANDE 2003, LORAN ET FILS BURGUNDY – *Crunchy citrus and flint aromas on the nose. The palate is clean, crisp, pure, and balanced.*	£6.50 ESL/BSL

BURGUNDY WHITE BRONZE

BOURGOGNE CHARDONNAY EN SOL JURASSIQUE 2002, DOMAINE JEAN-MARC BROCARD Burgundy – *Big pineapple fruit nose and a balanced, somewhat austere palate displaying good integration and length.*	£7.00 JBF
SAINT-VÉRAN LES MONTS 2002, CAVE DE PRISSE Burgundy – *Mineral rich, with a spritzy citrus nose and crunchy apple palate. The finish is clean and elegant.*	£7.50 M&S
BOURGOGNE HAUTES-CÔTES DE BEAUNE LES LARRETS BLANC 2002, DOMAINE LUCIEN JACOB Burgundy – *Some minerality is evident in this nutty wine packed with green berries. Exceedingly fresh.*	£8.00 3DW
MÂCON CHARDONNAY 2003, RAPHAEL ET GERARD SALLET Burgundy – *Clean, with clear green apple and flint aromas. The palate is light with good fruit purity and piercing acidity.*	£8.00 ROG
SALLET MÂCON-UCHIZY 2003, RAPHAEL ET GERARD SALLET Burgundy – *Textured yet light-bodied, this charmer of a wine has sweet apple and ripe pear flavours in abundance.*	£8.10 ROG
CÔTES DE NUITS VILLAGES BLANC 2002, DOMAINE DÉSERTAUX-FERRAND Burgundy – *Fruity nose. A long dry palate of citrus with seductive elements of warm straw, vanilla, and almonds.*	£8.80 3DW
CHABLIS BOISSET 2003, BOISSET Burgundy – *Pure citrus and apple nose. Hints of stony minerality, a relatively light structure and crunchy fruit.*	£9.00 MHV
CHABLIS JEAN-MARC BROCARD 2002, DOMAINE JEAN-MARC BROCARD Burgundy – *Fresh and fruity with citrus aromas and a linear palate showing some elegance and fine mineral acidity.*	£9.00 JBF
MARKS & SPENCER CHABLIS 2002, LA CHABLISIENNE Burgundy – *Flinty, with shell and citrus aromas. The palate is squeaky clean with good balance and crisp acidity.*	£9.00 M&S
ST-VÉRAN BLASON DE BOURGOGNE 2003, GROUPEMENT DE PRODUCTEURS DE PRISSE-SOLOGNY-VERZE Burgundy – *Clean, mineral style with starfruit and citrus notes on the nose and palate. Fine acidity.*	£9.00 TOS

BURGUNDY WHITE BRONZE 163

TESCO FINEST CHABLIS LABORIE ROI 2002, VAUCHER BURGUNDY – *The nose has flint and Granny Smith aromas. The palate is concentrated and steely with fine elegance.*	£9.00 TOS
POUILLY-LOCHÉ 2001, CAVE DES GRANDS CRUS BLANCS BURGUNDY – *Smoky scents curl upwards from the nose. Lemon and hints of fresh green bean on the palate. Soft mouthfeel.*	£9.30 ROG
BEAU-MONDE CHABLIS GRANDE RESERVE 2002, J MOREAU BURGUNDY – *Generous and inviting, with admirable balance, textured mouthfeel, and lively, fresh, ripe stone fruit finish.*	£10.00 BWL
TESCO FINEST CHABLIS 1ER CRU 2000, LA CHABLISIENNE BURGUNDY – *Water-pale, with a clean, flowery nose and a light-bodied yet concentrated palate possessing a long, bright finish.*	£10.00 TOS
CHABLIS VAUROUX 2002, DOMAINE DE VAUROUX BURGUNDY – *Creamy apple and citrus aromas and flavours; racy acidity on the palate. Elegant flinty finish.*	£10.50 ENO
MONTAGNY BLASON DE BOURGOGNE 2002, CAVE DES VIGNERONS DE BUXY BURGUNDY – *Concentrated apple, pineapple, and nut flavours line the herby, long, off-dry palate of this wine.*	£11.00 TOS
CHABLIS SAINT MARTIN 2002, MICHEL LAROCHE BURGUNDY – *The nose is clean and flinty. The palate contains fresh apple and citrus fruit. Mineral complexity to finish.*	£11.30 NYW/FLY BWL
BOURGOGNE HAUTES-CÔTES DE NUITS BLANC 2002, JEAN-CLAUDE BOISSET BURGUNDY – *Lavender honey, sweet white flowers, soft cashews, and ripe pear fruit characteristics.*	£12.10 BEN/CCS MOV/LIB FLY
CHABLIS 1ER CRU FOURCHAUME 2002, J MOREAU ET FILS BURGUNDY – *Conference pears, powdery oatmeal flakes, perfumed lemons, and honeysuckle scents and flavours.*	£12.30 JFE
RULLY 1ER CRU VIEILLES VIGNES 2002, VINCENT GIRARDIN BURGUNDY – *Pale in hue. Intense peachy fruit is buttressed by integrated oak. Persistent, bracing, and evolved, with elegant toastiness.*	£12.60 ESL/HAX MWW

BURGUNDY WHITE BRONZE

CHABLIS 1er CRU FOURCHAUME 2001, LA CHABLISIENNE Burgundy – Balanced, expressive, structured and long, with a developed profile of savoury green apples and rich yeasty complexity.	£13.00 M&S
CHABLIS 1er CRU VAILLONS BOISSET 2002, BOISSET Burgundy – Ripe and generously oaked, warm and tropical, with heady Russet apple and honey characteristics. Stylish.	£13.10 MHV
CHABLIS 1er CRU BEAUROY 2002, DOMAINE JEAN-MARC BROCARD Burgundy – Mineral rich, with fine apple and citrus fruit balanced by fresh acidity. Deep and intense.	£13.50 JBF
POUILLY-FUISSÉ THIBERT 2003, DOMAINE THIBERT Burgundy – Fresh and grassy, with an attack of green and yellow apples and juicy pear fruit. Persistent and aromatic.	£15.50 HAX/ABY
CHABLIS 1er CRU LES VAUDEVEY 2002, MICHEL LAROCHE Burgundy – A restrained, austere, lime-flavoured Chablis displaying excellent typicity. Admirable steeliness. Crisp apple acidity. Long finish.	£15.60 BNK/NYW FLY/BWL
POUILLY-FUISSÉ THIBERT 2002, CHRISTOPHE THIBERT Burgundy – Big nose. The palate is a pleasing mouthful of young white peach fruit with a warm finish.	£16.00 WTS
MEURSAULT LOUIS JADOT 1999, LOUIS JADOT Burgundy – Rich and buttery, its ripe fruit balanced by fine acidity and toasty oak. Elegant and mineral-infused, with good persistence.	£20.00 FEN
POUILLY-VINZELLES LES QUARTS 2002, THE BRET BROTHERS Burgundy – Pain grillé aromas assail the nose. Big, long, and leesy, with Champagne-like aromatics, this stunner's bright and bold.	£20.20 CCS/NYW FLY
CHABLIS GRAND CRU VAUDÉSIR 2002, DOMAINE DES MALANDES Burgundy – Dark oak and rich melon are juxtaposed with light citrus and steely minerals. Caramel apple elements.	£21.90 ESL/EVI BIG
CHABLIS GRAND CRU VAUDÉSIR 2000, WILLIAM FÈVRE Burgundy – Sicilian lemon and hawthorn blossom perfume scents this medium-bodied wine. Lengthy, with mineral stony hints.	£28.00 WTS

BURGUNDY WHITE BRONZE / RED TROPHY / GOLD

MARKS & SPENCER CHABLIS GRAND CRU GRENOUILLES 2000, LA CHABLISIENNE BURGUNDY – *Pleasing; lush yet light-bodied, with fresh acidity and subtle minerality. Pear and guava flavours abound.*	£30.00 M&S
CHABLIS GRAND CRU LES BLANCHOTS RÉSERVE DE L'OBÉDIENCE 2001, MICHEL LAROCHE BURGUNDY – *Luxuriant sweet soft oak melts into lime juice flavours. A wine with pronounced, well-defined, perfumed fruit.*	£45.80 FLY/BWL

TROPHY
BURGUNDY RED

GRANDS ECHÉZEAUX GRAND CRU 2002, MAISON ALBERT BICHOT BURGUNDY – *Intense. Cherry, spice, berry touches, and warm oak. Concentrated and velvety with a firm structure.*	£.00 NOT AVAILABLE IN THE UK

GOLD
BURGUNDY RED

GEVREY-CHAMBERTIN VIEILLES VIGNES 2001, DOMAINE HERESZTYN BURGUNDY – *Ripe, pure plummy fruit. Strawberry fruit and a maturing, beefy touch. Fruit complexity and concentration. Lots of potential.*	£20.00 WTS
ALOXE-CORTON DOMAINE MAILLARD 2001, DOMAINE MAILLARD PÈRE ET FILS BURGUNDY – *Elegant and light, with precision and purity in the fruit and an austere style. The mineral finish lasts.*	£23.00 NYW/ENO
BEAUNE 1ER CRU LES BRESSANDES 2002, JEAN-CLAUDE BOISSET BURGUNDY – *A nose of red fruits and caramel oak, and a textured, silky pillow of redcurrant and cherry fruit.*	£23.80 BEN/CCS MOV/NYW LIB/FLY
NUITS-SAINT-GEORGES DOMAINE MICHEL GROS 2002, DOMAINE MICHEL GROS BURGUNDY – *Very concentrated and perfumed. Sturdy, with a beguiling sweet ripeness and velvety warm tannins. Sophisticated and generously fruited.*	£24.00 JNW/NYW
CHAMBOLLE-MUSIGNY DOMAINE MICHEL GROS 2002, DOMAINE MICHEL GROS BURGUNDY – *Modern and powerful, with great concentration and a good dose of oak. It possesses a silky tannic structure.*	£24.60 JNW/NYW

BURGUNDY RED GOLD / SILVER

BEAUNE 1ER CRU LES TEURONS 2001, DOMAINE ALBERT MOROT BURGUNDY – *Ripe, confiture type red fruits, but the essence of the concentration is mineral. Depth and firm ripe tannins.*	£25.40 FFW/CVE
BEAUNE 1ER CRU LES TOUSSAINTS 2001, DOMAINE ALBERT MOROT BURGUNDY – *The perfumed berry fruits are very evident in the glass and they are underlaid with leafy, flowery notes.*	£26.20 CEB/FFW VIT/CVE
POMMARD 1ER CRU CLOS DE VERGER 2002, JEAN-CLAUDE BOISSET BURGUNDY – *High quality, concentrated Pinot flavours of redcurrant, raspberries, strawberries, and cream. It is lifted with vanilla oak.*	£32.50 BEN/MOV LIB/FLY
CORTON GRAND CRU RENARDES 2001, DOMAINE MAILLARD PÈRE ET FILS BURGUNDY – *Stylish, with density, old vine complexity and intensity to the raspberries. Supple, with grainy tannins. An extended finish.*	£43.00 ENO
CLOS VOUGEOT DOMAINE MICHEL GROS 2002, DOMAINE MICHEL GROS BURGUNDY – *Impressively deep black-cherry fruit and warm confiture notes. Big and concentrated with lots of extract.*	£47.30 JNW/TAN NYW

SILVER
BURGUNDY RED

SAVIGNY-LÈS-BEAUNE LUCIEN JACOB 2002, DOMAINE LUCIEN JACOB BURGUNDY – *Perfumed strawberry fruit, cedar, and vanilla greet the nose. Austere yet creamy, with a soft, ripe, mouthfilling palate.*	£8.80 3DW
GIVRY 1ER CRU LA GRANDE BERGE 2001, DOMAINE RAGOT BURGUNDY – *Delicate, light and perfumed, with a sylph-like body and bags of elegant red summer fruit. Silky tannins.*	£8.90 3DW
BOURGOGNE ROUGE 2002, DOMAINE PARENT BURGUNDY – *A pleasant fragrant nose. Refreshing cherry character shines alongside the fine tannins and cleansing acidity.*	£9.50 ESL
CHÂTEAU DE MARSANNAY ROUGE 2002, CHÂTEAU DE MARSANNAY BURGUNDY – *A wine with mouthwatering alpine strawberry flavours and scents of leaves, vanilla beans, coconut, and nutmeg.*	£10.00 MWW

BURGUNDY RED SILVER 167

GEVREY-CHAMBERTIN EN SONGE 2002, DOMAINE LUCIEN JACOB BURGUNDY – *Firmness meets elegance. Fine and complex, with many layers of soft vine fruits and balanced tannins.*	£12.20
	3DW
GEVREY-CHAMBERTIN PATRIARCHE PÈRE ET FILS 2002, PATRIARCHE PÈRE ET FILS BURGUNDY – *A tightly coiled beast, its intense, masculine cranberry fruit infused with saddle-leather and spiked with white pepper.*	£15.00
	PAT
LOUIS JADOT BEAUNE 1999, LOUIS JADOT BURGUNDY – *Developed game, earth, leather, mushrooms, and cherries. Well-integrated, with a slight herbaceous tinge.*	£16.00
	THS/LBS WIM/VKY DBY
BEAUNE 1ER CRU LES CENT-VIGNES 2001, DOMAINE ALBERT MOROT BURGUNDY – *Expressive, with good definition and impressive minerality. Expresses a sense of place while quenching one's thirst. Very satisfying.*	£24.50
	FFW/VIT CVE
CHAMBOLLE-MUSIGNY JEAN-CLAUDE BOISSET 2002, JEAN-CLAUDE BOISSET BURGUNDY – *Fine and elegant, its immaculate strawberry fruit possessing lifted perfume and the subtlest hint of grilled meat.*	£24.70
	BEN/CCS MOV/LIB FLY
GEVREY-CHAMBERTIN 1ER CRU CLOS DU FONTENY 1998, DOMAINE BRUNO CLAIR BURGUNDY – *The masterful Bruno Clair is firing on all pistons. Cherry, leather, and espresso flavours. Big, silky, and lifted.*	£29.00
	J&B
VOLNAY 1ER CRU LES CHEVRETS 2000, DOMAINE JEAN BOILLOT BURGUNDY – *A gamey nose with sweet and sour, smoky, red cherries. Cranberry and raspberry on the palate. Nutty finish.*	£29.00
	WTS
VOSNE-ROMANÉE 1ER CRU MALCONSORTS 2001, VALLET FRÈRES BURGUNDY – *Just the right amount of oak balances the fulsome, ripe cherries. An elegant wine with complexity and structure.*	£35.00
	PBA
GEVREY CHAMBERTIN 1ER CRU LAVAUX SAINT-JACQUES 2002, JEAN-CLAUDE BOISSET BURGUNDY – *Spicebox aromas and sparkling strawberry fruit flavours burst from this Super Premier Cru. A youthful, precocious beauty.*	£38.50
	MOV/LIB
VOSNE-ROMANÉE 1ER CRU AUX BRULÉES 2002, DOMAINE MICHEL GROS BURGUNDY – *Silky smooth tannins and vibrant acidity buttress aristocratic strawberry fruit. This is a stunning offering.*	£41.50
	JNW/NYW

RICHEBOURG GRAND CRU 2002, FRANCOIS PARENT **BURGUNDY** – *Linear, complex, and ripe. Grilled meats, currants, leather, and quartz. Still young, it should gradually evolve.*	£95.00 HHC/CHN

BRONZE
BURGUNDY RED

MÂCON ROUGE LOUIS JADOT 2003, LOUIS JADOT **BURGUNDY** – *Savoury scented red berry fruit. A seam of minerality lasts for the duration of the finish. Fresh.*	£6.00 ASD/WIM VKY/DBY
BOURGOGNE PINOT NOIR LOUIS JADOT 2000, LOUIS JADOT **BURGUNDY** – *Some eloquent complexity on the nose. Quite high acidity refreshes the palate of soft fruit and farmyardy nuances.*	£8.50 EDC/FEN FLA
MERCUREY 1ER CRU LES BYOTS 2002, DOMAINE MENAND **BURGUNDY** – *The rich, plummy nose marries well to a palate of savoury, tight, taut fruit with an earthy quality.*	£9.50 3DW
CÔTE DE BEAUNE VILLAGES HENRI LA FONTAINE 1999, HENRI LA FONTAINE **BURGUNDY** – *Earthy, with ripe prunes and integrated oak on the nose. The palate sports juicy fruit. A fine finish.*	£9.90 MHV
RULLY 1ER CRU LES CLOUX 2002, DOMAINE DE LA VIEILLE FONTAINE **BURGUNDY** – *A delicately coloured wine, with leather and peat notes gracing the black damson fruit flavours.*	£9.90 3DW
SAVIGNY-LÈS-BEAUNE BOUCHARD 2001, BOUCHARD PÈRE ET FILS **BURGUNDY** – *A plump nose, a lightish body, the right amount of fruit to balance gentle tannins, and pleasing acidity.*	£12.00 WTS
NUITS-SAINT-GEORGES LES PLANTES AU BARON 2001, R DUBOIS ET FILS **BURGUNDY** – *Elegant, with a rustic, open-knit palate and a floral nose, it should benefit from additional time in bottle.*	£12.40 3DW
BEAUNE BASTION 1ER CRU 2002, CHANSON PÈRE ET FILS **BURGUNDY** – *Ripe, red-cherry fruit spills from this textured, vivid wine with its firm tannins and brisk acidity.*	£14.90 ESL

BURGUNDY RED BRONZE

SAVIGNY-LÈS-BEAUNE 1ER CRU CLOS DES GUETTES 2001, LOUIS JADOT Burgundy – *The right amount of fruit balances the earthy, rustic palate. Softly spoken with expressive tannins and great length.*	£17.00 WTS
GEVREY-CHAMBERTIN DOMAINE MARCHAND 2001, DOMAINE MARCHAND Burgundy – *Sweet and perfumed with berry and cherry aromas and a supple palate of light tannin and ripe fruit.*	£18.00 TOS
VOLNAY 1ER CRU LES SENTEURS 2001, NICOLAS POTEL Burgundy – *Gentle supporting new oak, and a nice, plump mid-palate. With sweet fruit and fine-grained tannins. Fine and delicate.*	£18.00 M&S
GEVREY-CHAMBERTIN HENRI LA FONTAINE 2000, HENRI LA FONTAINE Burgundy – *A ripe, strawberry nose. A velvety palate of sour red fruit, a grainy texture, and a long finish.*	£19.20 BNK/MHV
ALOXE-CORTON 1ER CRU CLOS DU CHAPITRE 1998, DOMAINE FOLLIN-ARBELET Burgundy – *This wine has a seamless, fleshy, round palate with robust tannins, prominent fruit and fine minerality.*	£19.50 J&B
BEAUNE 1ER CRU LES EPENOTTES 2001, DOMAINE PARENT Burgundy – *Warming, lifted and intense, with scents of nutmeg and cinnamon gracing the palate of ripe summer fruits.*	£19.70 ESL
SAVIGNY 1ER CRU LA BATAILLÈRE AUX VERGELESSES 2001, DOMAINE ALBERT MOROT Burgundy – *Good depth on the nose and touches of spice alongside the bright fruit. Rustic tannins and medium length.*	£21.90 FFW/CVE
BEAUNE 1ER CRU AUX CRAS 2002, MAISON CHAMPY Burgundy – *Pure-berry nose leads to a supple palate of rich cherry fruit, friendly tannins, and light structure.*	£22.50 POL
SAVIGNY-LÈS-BEAUNE 1ER CRU LA DOMINODE 1998, DOMAINE BRUNO CLAIR Burgundy – *Smoky, leathery, and perfumed on the nose, the palate has a soft, silky feel and a fine balance.*	£24.50 TAN/J&B
POMMARD 1ER CRU LES RUGIENS 2002, FRANCOIS PARENT Burgundy – *Tannic, powerful, and robust. A wine's that's rich and mouthwatering, with plenty of lingering dark spice tones.*	£30.00 DEC

TROPHY
CHAMPAGNE

CHARLES HEIDSIECK BRUT MILLÉSIME 1989, CHAMPAGNES P&C HEIDSIECK Champagne – *Bright and toasty, with ebullient mousse and rich aromatic ruby grapefruit flavours. Mind-blowing complexity and layered elegance.*	**£.00** NOT AVAILABLE IN THE UK
BRUT CUVÉE DES DAMES NV, CHAMPAGNE GREMILLET Champagne – *Lemon and peach fruit and warm honey richness. The creamy texture is checked by balanced lively acidity.*	**£22.70** NRW/PBA NYW

GOLD
CHAMPAGNE

☆ **MHV LOUIS DE BELMANCE BLANC DE BLANC NV, CHAMPAGNES P&C HEIDSIECK** Champagne – *Continental breakfast nose with warm toast, brioche, and citrus fruit. Smoky, mouthfilling, buttery texture balanced with taut acidity.*	**£16.50** MHV
☆ **DRAPPIER BLANC DE BLANCS NV, CHAMPAGNE DRAPPIER** Champagne – *A feminine Champagne. Plenty of lemony overtones and peachy white fruit flavour. Light and elegant, with a creamy mousse.*	**£17.00** JNW/ABY
☆ **B BESSERAT DE BELLEFON NV, CHAMPAGNE LANSON** Champagne – *Notes of clover honey, brioche, and lime flowers. Delicious juicy ripe mandarin orange and ruby grapefruit. Mineral hints.*	**£18.00** MCD
★ **MILLÉSIME EXCEPTION 1999, CHAMPAGNE DRAPPIER** Champagne – *Subtle and restrained, with biscuit aromas and lemon and apple fruit. Pinhead mousse. Minerals lift the structured, creamy palate.*	**£19.00** ABY
FLEUR DE PRESTIGE BRUT 1997, CHAMPAGNE BEAUMONT DES CRAYÈRES Champagne – *Pure, textured, creamy and rich, with layers of complexity. Citrus flavours and hints of nuttiness. Slow, undulating mousse.*	**£19.50** JAR
☆ **ESTERLIN MILLÉSIMÉ 1995, CHAMPAGNE ESTERLIN** Champagne – *Starfruit and coconut aromas and understated earthy minerality. Layers of citrus and sweet delicate spice. Defined and persistent.*	**£19.80** CHS

☆ **HENRI BLIN VINTAGE BRUT 1998, CHAMPAGNE HENRI BLIN** CHAMPAGNE – *Young, with pippy green apple freshness. It's still tight, but is destined to develop into a swan.*	**£19.90** JBF/JFE ODD
☆ **ANDRÉ SIMON BRUT VINTAGE 1998, MARNE ET CHAMPAGNE DIFFUSION** CHAMPAGNE – *Full and round, with bready warmth and seductive notes of yeast autolysis. Elegant, structured, and long.*	**£20.00** WRT
☆ **LE BRUN DE NEUVILLE MILLÉSIMÉ BRUT 1997, CHAMPAGNE LE BRUN DE NEUVILLE** CHAMPAGNE – *Roasted nuts and baguette scents. Ripe black- and white-berry flavours. Drink this during the festive season.*	**£20.00** WAW
☆ **PIPER HEIDSIECK BRUT DIVIN NV, CHAMPAGNES P&C HEIDSIECK** CHAMPAGNE – *Very lemony. Citrus grove aromas. Elegant, mouthfilling white and yellow tropical fruit flavours with an edge of biscuity richness.*	**£20.00** FEN
☆ **VEUVE A DEVAUX BLANC DE NOIRS NV, CHAMPAGNE DEVAUX** CHAMPAGNE – *Notes of honeysuckle and flavours of wild strawberries. Full and firmly structured, with linear definition. Depth, texture, and backbone.*	**£20.00** HWL
CUVÉE FLORALE BRUT PRÉMIER CRU NV, MIGNON ET PIERREL CHAMPAGNE – *Broad, rich, round, weighty, and creamy, yet still in possession of fresh racy acidity. Leesy depth with doughy brioche flavours and a buttery texture. Outstanding.*	**£22.00** FCC
NOSTALGIE 1996, CHAMPAGNE BEAUMONT DES CRAYÈRES CHAMPAGNE – *Bold, bright apple fruit and crisp acidity. Yeast, orange blossom, and candied peel. Delicate and refined. Excellent balance.*	**£23.00** JAR
CHARLES HEIDSIECK BRUT RÉSERVE MIS EN CAVE EN 1998 NV, CHAMPAGNES P&C HEIDSIECK CHAMPAGNE – *Full, toasty and fine, with biscuit notes and crisp acidity. Candied grapefruit flavours. Long, textured finish.*	**£24.80** VGN/FEN TOS
BRUT MOSAÏQUE VINTAGE 1998, CHAMPAGNE JACQUART CHAMPAGNE – *Near perfect balance of fruit concentration lifted by racy acidity. Amazing complexity, evolving secondary elements, and what length.*	**£25.50** ODD MWW
HENRIOT MILLÉSIMÉ 1996, CHAMPAGNE HENRIOT CHAMPAGNE – *Pure, gorgeous pear and strawberry aromas, biscuity notes, and yeasty overtones. Full, rich, creamy, and utterly delicious.*	**£32.00** JEF

VEUVE CLICQUOT RICH RESERVE 1996, CHAMPAGNE VEUVE CLICQUOT Champagne – Classically styled, headily perfumed, and refreshingly jolly. Fat and smooth and full of pears, guava, and ruby grapefruit.	£37.70 FEN/OWC WRW/JSM
GOSSET GRAND MILLÉSIMÉ 1996, CHAMPAGNE GOSSET Champagne – Impressively hedonistic. Fruit firmly anchored to vivid acidic backbone. Meticulous winemaking + quality terroir + exceptional vintage = towering Champagne.	£38.00 EDC/SOM JFE/NYW RWM WRW
FEMME DE CHAMPAGNE VINTAGE 1990, CHAMPAGNE DUVAL-LEROY Champagne – Tropical fruit, butter, toast, and barley sugar. Creamy texture buoyed by never-ending mousse. Crammed with crisp lemons and cranberries.	£50.00 DUL/MCT
CUVÉE WILLIAM MILLESIMÉ 1996, CHAMPAGNE DEUTZ Champagne – Forceful red fruit backbone and texture and fresh apple-infused white fruit steeliness. A magnificent Champagne of great beauty and finesse.	£59.00 VIT/BWC
LANSON NOBLE CUVÉE 1995, CHAMPAGNE LANSON Champagne – Bramley apple and biscuit scents. Weighty grapefruit and strawberry flavours. Drinking now, its evolved complexity offset by fresh acidity.	£63.30 CVE/WTS ODD
TAITTINGER PRELUDE GRANDS CRUS NV, CHAMPAGNE TAITTINGER Champagne – Pale, fresh, and biscuity, with scents of white fruit, peaches, and honey. Rich and fruit-driven, with fresh, lifted acidity.	£65.00 EDC
LA GRANDE DAME 1995, CHAMPAGNE VEUVE CLICQUOT Champagne – Fresh, taut and well crafted, this soft creamy beauty has developed characteristics of yeast, croissants, and toast which emerge layer upon layer. Near-perfect.	£71.80 WIDELY AVAILABLE
DOM PÉRIGNON MILLÉSIMÉ 1996, CHAMPAGNE MOËT ET CHANDON Champagne – Multifaceted and concentrated, this is a huge Champagne, its fruit overlaid by rich toast. Certain to age well.	£73.80 WIDELY AVAILABLE
DOM RUINART VINTAGE 1993, CHAMPAGNE RUINART Champagne – Mushroomy, earthy, flinty, chalky, with classic autolytic flavours of yeasty creaminess, cinnamon spice, and nutty marzipan. Wonderfully layered.	£80.00 HAR/F&M NIC
COMTES DE CHAMPAGNE BLANC DE BLANC 1995, CHAMPAGNE TAITTINGER Champagne – A tight, fresh elegance defines this Champagne with its rich candied orange peel flavours and violet scents.	£80.50 EDC/HAX VIT/FEN CVE/MWW

SILVER
CHAMPAGNE

☆ **CHAMPAGNE BREDON NV, CHAMPAGNES P&C HEIDSIECK** CHAMPAGNE – *Clear, dry, and tight-knit. Attractive red berry flavours pervade the lively, yeasty palate. The finish is glamorous and ever so long.*	£13.00 WTS
☆ **MHV PAUL LANGIER BRUT NV, CHAMPAGNES P&C HEIDSIECK** CHAMPAGNE – *Seductive warm honeycomb and apple scents. The taut palate has greengage acidity and nectarine flavours.*	£14.00 BNK/MHV
☆ **MHV THE HOUSE CHAMPAGNE NV, CHAMPAGNES P&C HEIDSIECK** CHAMPAGNE – *Earthy notes and green apple fruit on the nose. The palate has a creamy texture and fresh bread notes.*	£14.00 BNK/MHV
☆ **PRINCE WILLIAM BLANC DE NOIRS NV, CHAMPAGNE ALEXANDRE BONNET** CHAMPAGNE – *Biscuit and hazelnut aromas, fine bubbles, and a complex array of apple and citrus flavours on the palate.*	£14.00 SMF
☆ **CUVÉE DE RÉSERVE BLANC DE BLANCS NV, CHAMPAGNE MAISON LENIQUE** CHAMPAGNE – *Packed with ripe white peach flavours, a seam of citrus acidity, and the merest nuance of yeast. Long creamy finish.*	£14.90 3DW
★ **TESCO PRÉMIER CRU BRUT NV, UNION CHAMPAGNE AVIZE** CHAMPAGNE – *Lemony green. The bouquet is broad and toasty. The palate resonates with ruby strawberries. Creamy, long, and rich.*	£15.00 TOS
CHAMPAGNE VICTOR BRUT NV, CHAMPAGNE VICTOR CHAMPAGNE – *Pale gold and positively streaming with fine bubbles. Elegant and delicate, with an intense bready finish.*	£17.00 UNS
TESCO BLANC DE BLANCS NV, CHAMPAGNE DUVAL-LEROY CHAMPAGNE – *Smoke and toast; yeast autolysis. Mouthfilling, bready mid-palate of full-bodied white peach and golden grapefruit Chardonnay fruit.*	£17.00 TOS
WAITROSE BLANC DE BLANCS BRUT NV, CHAMPAGNES P&C HEIDSIECK CHAMPAGNE – *Bright peach and pear fruit; razor acidity. Hazelnut, acacia blossom, stony minerals, and grass scent the nose.*	£17.00 WTS

CHAMPAGNE SILVER

GAUTHIER BRUT GRANDE ROSÉ RÉSERVE NV, MARNE ET CHAMPAGNE DIFFUSION Champagne – Pale pink with golden hints. Yeast, cinnamon, nutmeg, and wild strawberries scent the nose. Clean, with lively mousse.	**£18.00** INS
CANARD-DUCHÊNE BRUT NV, CHAMPAGNE CANARD-DUCHÊNE Champagne – Biscuit and butter aromas boost the palate of ripe golden apples, which is soft, round, fleshy, and intense.	**£18.50** WIDELY AVAILABLE
MASSÉ ROSÉ NV, CHAMPAGNE LANSON Champagne – Frothy, with a rose gold hue. Restrained, with green apple scents, warm ripe flavours, and good balance throughout.	**£19.00** CLA
PANNIER BRUT SELECTION NV, CHAMPAGNE PANNIER Champagne – An attack of lime cordial freshness. Chalk notes and autolytic development add complexity. A fresh, youthful Champagne.	**£19.00** HBJ
MHV LOUIS DE BELMANCE MILLÉSIMÉ 1996, CHAMPAGNES P&C HEIDSIECK Champagne – White peaches, Marmite, pears, and limes on the nose. A firm, elegant palate and fresh finish.	**£19.30** MHV
MERCIER BRUT ROSÉ NV, CHAMPAGNE MERCIER Champagne – Persistent foamy mousse, and a nose of almonds and ripe citrus. The palate offers toasty red summer fruits.	**£19.50** HOU/FEN
PIPER HEIDSIECK BRUT MILLÉSIMÉ NV, CHAMPAGNES P&C HEIDSIECK Champagne – Soft and lemony, with a creamy mousse. Grapefruit flavours and yeasty croissant characteristics. Layered complexity.	**£19.90** TOS/MWW
PAUL DÉTHUNE GRAND CRU ROSÉ NV, CHAMPAGNE PAUL DÉTHUNE Champagne – The nose is rich with butter, redcurrants and strawberries. The elegant palate has a yeasty, nutty tone.	**£20.00** CHS
WAITROSE BRUT VINTAGE 1996, CHAMPAGNES P&C HEIDSIECK Champagne – Elegance and finesse. Steely Bramley apple fruit, fresh baguette, and strawberry flavours. Firm backbone and a fabulously long finish.	**£20.00** WTS
BRUT PREMIERE CUVÉE NV, CHAMPAGNE BRUNO PAILLARD Champagne – Yeasty, toasty notes and enticing autolytic complexity. Stony minerality and lemon zest freshness penetrate the intense citrus fruit flavours.	**£22.70** LAI/NYW FLY

CHAMPAGNE SILVER

BESSERAT DE BELLEFON CUVÉE DES MOINES BLANC DE BLANCS NV, CHAMPAGNE LANSON CHAMPAGNE – *Fine bubbles rise through the pale gold liquid. Fresh and ripe, with youthful green fruit and poached pear richness.*	£23.00 MCD
CANARD DUCHÊNE VINTAGE 1993, CHAMPAGNE CANARD DUCHÊNE CHAMPAGNE – *Fresh and bright, with a nutty, creamy element and orange peel notes. Pearly, flowing mousse and a crisp backbone.*	£23.20 BNK/EDC NRW/WES
BLANC DE CHARDONNAY VINTAGE 1996, CHAMPAGNE DUVAL-LEROY CHAMPAGNE – *Spiced biscuits and candied citrus fruit nose and palate. Vivacity and energetic mousse. A very fine vintage.*	£24.50 L&W/MCT
EXTRA BRUT VINTAGE 1997, CHAMPAGNE DUVAL-LEROY CHAMPAGNE – *Mature. Nutty lees and fresh apple fruit. Fine, slow mousse and a tight structure. Apricot flavoured finish.*	£24.50 DUL
BLANC DE BLANCS 1995, CHAMPAGNE DE VENOGE CHAMPAGNE – *This class act still displays youthful clarity. Roast almond and cream richness melds effortlessly with an intriguing sweet-sour quality.*	£24.60 NRW/PBA BOO
VEUVE CLICQUOT DEMI-SEC NV, CHAMPAGNE VEUVE CLICQUOT CHAMPAGNE – *Certain to please the most discerning lover of sweet Champagne. Buttered brioche scents and a creamy texture.*	£26.10 WIDELY AVAILABLE
TAITTINGER DEMI-SEC NV, CHAMPAGNE TAITTINGER CHAMPAGNE – *Terroir is the key. Chalky elements clearly show under the rich sweetness. Persistent mousse and a long finish.*	£27.00 V&C/VIT
LANSON GOLD LABEL 1996, CHAMPAGNE LANSON CHAMPAGNE – *From an outstanding vintage, with complex, layered maturity. Apples, savoury notes and powerful blackberry elements.*	£28.50 TOS/WTS INS/MWW
PERRIER-JOUËT GRAND BRUT 1997, CHAMPAGNE PERRIER-JOUËT CHAMPAGNE – *Hints of strawberry and blackberry fruits overlay the toasty lees character. Lemon meringue pie flavours. Very refreshing and forward.*	£28.50 RAV/OWC ODD/MW W
NICOLAS FEUILLATTE GRAND CRU D'AY 1996, CHAMPAGNE NICOLAS FEUILLATTE CHAMPAGNE – *Admirable complexity and fine toasty development on the nose. The intense palate is rich, creamy, and mouthfillling.*	£29.50 LEW

MOËT ET CHANDON VINTAGE 1998, CHAMPAGNE MOËT ET CHANDON CHAMPAGNE – *Good linear drive and a fine racy acidity balance the fullness of the stylish fruit.*	**£31.20** WIDELY AVAILABLE
MOSAÏQUE BRUT BLANC DE BLANCS MILLÉSIMÉ 1997, CHAMPAGNE JACQUART CHAMPAGNE – *Buttered toast and lemon fruit layer the nose. The mid-palate has a hint of sweetness and brisk mousse.*	**£34.00** PAT/MWW
AUDOIN DE DAMPIERRE GRAND CRU 1998, COMTE AUDOIN DE DAMPIERRE CHAMPAGNE – *Green and yellow apple fruit, cranberry, and mineral. Vibrant and fresh, yet soft and approachable.*	**£35.50** COE
MOËT ET CHANDON VINTAGE RECENTLY DISGORGED 1990, CHAMPAGNE MOËT ET CHANDON CHAMPAGNE – *Rich yellow gold with a burbling mousse. Toasty and yeasty and leesy with a creamy texture lifted by racy acidity.*	**£36.00** MHU
VEUVE CLICQUOT VINTAGE RESERVE 1996, CHAMPAGNE VEUVE CLICQUOT CHAMPAGNE – *Toast and ripe red fruit nose. The palate has apple flavours, layers of nuts, and a marzipan finish.*	**£38.00** WIDELY AVAILABLE
MOËT ET CHANDON MILLÉSIMÉ ROSÉ 1998, CHAMPAGNE MOËT ET CHANDON CHAMPAGNE – *Pale salmon pink, its nose and palate a blend of aromatic sherbet and wild strawberries. Energetic mousse.*	**£38.30** HOU/CVE ODD
CHARLES HEIDSIECK RÉSERVE CHARLIE MIS EN CAVE EN 1990 NV, CHAMPAGNES P&C HEIDSIECK CHAMPAGNE – *Buttery and textured, with summer fruit, walnuts, patchouli, and guava. Fine, very ripe, and staggeringly complex.*	**£50.00** WTS
FEMME DE CHAMPAGNE 1995, CHAMPAGNE DUVAL-LEROY CHAMPAGNE – *Big and bready. Crisp citrus acidity imparts backbone to the full, creamy palate of white and red fruit.*	**£50.00** DUL/MCT
GRAND VIN DES PRINCES 1993, CHAMPAGNE DE VENOGE CHAMPAGNE – *A maturity which may only be derived from extended bottle ageing. Richness, classic elegance, and unmistakable quality.*	**£50.00** PBA
GOSSET CELEBRIS ROSE 1998, CHAMPAGNE GOSSET CHAMPAGNE – *Massive, with a palate of elegant strawberry fruit, fine spiralling mousse and superb length. Champagne doesn't get much classier.*	**£52.00** OWC WRW

CHAMPAGNE SILVER / BRONZE

GRAND SIÈCLE LA CUVÉE NV, LAURENT-PERRIER CHAMPAGNE – Crisp, fresh, and dry. Yeasty, with greengages and almonds and bright balanced acid. Creamy mousse.	£55.00 EDC MWW
COMTES DE CHAMPAGNE ROSÉ 1996, CHAMPAGNE TAITTINGER CHAMPAGNE – A terroir-driven Champagne with lean, chalky elegance and fresh fruit salad flavours. Developed aromas add complexity to the palate.	£86.70 EDC/CVE MWW

BRONZE
CHAMPAGNE

ASDA BRUT NV, NICOLAS FEUILLATTE CHAMPAGNE – Balanced, fresh apple and biscuit nose. The palate is well constructed, with good acidity and fine bubbles.	£10.40 ASD
BRUT CUVÉE DE RÉSERVE NV, CHAMPAGNE COMTE DE LANTAGE CHAMPAGNE – Concentrated and powerful. Fresh spring blossom, dark spice, and sliced pineapple flavours jostle for position.	£12.80 3DW
CUVÉE 3D WINES NV, CHAMPAGNE MAISON LENIQUE CHAMPAGNE – Good concentration of baked apple fruit on nose and palate. Fine mousse. Hints of minerality on the finish.	£12.90 3DW
ALBERT ETIENNE BRUT NV, CHAMPAGNE LANSON CHAMPAGNE – The pungent lemon and lime juice nose is coupled with a pear-flavoured palate bearing unstoppable mousse.	£14.00 SAF
ANDRÉ SIMON BRUT NV, MARNE ET CHAMPAGNE DIFFUSION CHAMPAGNE – Rich and biscuity, with a dry, mouthcoating texture, plenty of citrus fruit, and good balance.	£14.00 FEN/WRT
JEAN DE PRAISAC NV, CHAMPAGNES P&C HEIDSIECK CHAMPAGNE – Ripe pear fruit and yeast on the nose. Fresh acidity and chewy apple fruit on the palate.	£15.00 THS
LOUIS BOYIER BRUT NV, CHAMPAGNE HENRI BLIN CHAMPAGNE – Bold and toasty. Rich and full, its body bolstered by a seam of acidity and lifted by fine, long-lasting bubbles.	£15.00 ELV

178 CHAMPAGNE BRONZE

CHAMPAGNE LOUIS JAUNAY NV, CHAMPAGNES P&C HEIDSIECK Champagne – *Apple and pear fruit nose. The tart palate is packed with fresh fruit salad chunks. Long finish.*	£15.50 MWW
MAILLY GRAND CRU BRUT RESERVE NV, CHAMPAGNE MAILLY Champagne – *Green apple and lemon flavours are emphasised by aromas of nuts and minerals. Fine, characterful and saturated with flavour.*	£15.90 EOR
CHAMPAGNE BROSSAULT NV, CHAMPAGNES P&C HEIDSIECK Champagne – *Mineral hints score the concentrated palate of fresh green apple fruit. Fresh-baked bread and vanilla nuances scent the nose.*	£16.00 MWW
GAUTHIER BRUT GRANDE RÉSERVE NV, MARNE ET CHAMPAGNE DIFFUSION Champagne – *Pronounced yeasty notes, tight mousse, and a palate of fresh red fruit of weight and length.*	£16.00 INS
MHV PAUL LANGIER ROSÉ NV, CHAMPAGNES P&C HEIDSIECK Champagne – *Ripe, autolytic, and evolved, with nutty elements and intense herbal influences. Crunchy green apple flavour.*	£16.60 MHV
BRUT TRADITION NV, CHAMPAGNE JACQUART Champagne – *Clear and pungent. Ripe apple fruit attacks the nose and fills the mouth. Exceptionally dry and crisp.*	£17.00 TAU/SMF
CHAMPAGNE VICTOR NV, HISTORIC WINE COMPANY Champagne – *A fine mousse, elegant apple flavours, and biscuity depth. Crisp, bright, thirst quenching, and long.*	£17.00 JSM
ESTERLIN BRUT NV, CHAMPAGNE ESTERLIN Champagne – *Creamy, fresh and clear, with ripe limes, biscuits, and a handful of herbs on the palate.*	£17.10 CHS
ESTERLIN ROSÉ NV, CHAMPAGNE ESTERLIN Champagne – *Spiced summer fruit parades across the nose. A touch of cream smooths out the integrated, crisp palate.*	£17.10 CHS
HENRI BLIN BRUT NV, CHAMPAGNE HENRI BLIN Champagne – *Full and biscuity, with a touch of yeast and caramel on the nose and a crisp, lemony palate.*	£17.20 JBF/ODD

CHAMPAGNE BRONZE **179**

ALBERT ETIENNE MILLÉSIMÉ 1999, CHAMPAGNE LANSON Champagne – *Tightly knit and well-balanced, with rich croissant aromas, citrus fruit, raspberries, and evolved secondary elements.*	**£17.50** SAF
TESCO FINEST VINTAGE PREMIER CRU 1998, UNION CHAMPAGNE AVIZE Champagne – *Fresh apples and shortbread meld with a savoury character. Some complexity and weight.*	**£17.90** TOS
MERCIER DEMI-SEC NV, CHAMPAGNE MERCIER Champagne – *Attractive sweet strawberry compote fruit character. Elegant mousse and crisp acidity. Lifted perfume. Long finish.*	**£18.00** FEN/RWM
VEUVE A DEVAUX GRANDE RESERVE NV, CHAMPAGNE DEVAUX Champagne – *Deep toasty aromas. Attractive, evolved and pungent, with savoury hints. The sustained finish lingers on and on.*	**£18.70** EVI
CHAMPAGNE DE SAINT GALL BRUT TRADITION NV, UNION CHAMPAGNE Champagne – *Yeast, nuts, green apples, lime juice, and butter. Sweetly ripe, balanced, and fresh, with a mouthcoating texture.*	**£19.00** M&S
LE MESNIL BLANC DE BLANCS GRAND CRU BRUT NV, CHAMPAGNE LE MESNIL Champagne – *Bright, with floral notes, polished apricot and pear fruit, and a weighty, leesy, brioche character.*	**£19.00** WTS
CHAMPAGNE FLEURY ROSÉ NV, CHAMPAGNE FLEURY Champagne – *Delicate floral and citrus aromatics, and a palate of apples, crunchy biscuits, and roast nuts. Long finish.*	**£19.80** VRT
AYALA BRUT NV, CHAMPAGNE AYALA Champagne – *Apple and redcurrant flavours buoyed by a seam of chalky minerality. Firm, elegant, and honeyed.*	**£19.90** WIDELY AVAILABLE
BRUT PRÉMIER CRU NV, CHAMPAGNE FORGET BRIMONT Champagne – *Minute bubbles rise through pale lemon liquid. Elegant mouthfilling apple fruit and bread aromas. Long and creamy.*	**£20.00** VIT
EXTRA BRUT PREMIER CRU NV, CHAMPAGNE FORGET BRIMONT Champagne – *Full and rich, with autolytic aromas and melon and tropical characters. Smooth and creamy. Finishes well.*	**£20.00** VIT

180 CHAMPAGNE BRONZE

MARQUIS DE LA FAYETTE BRUT SELECTION NV, CHAMPAGNE PIERREL CHAMPAGNE – *Green apples and yeast lace the nose. The palate proffers a tight-knit mouthful of citrus fruit.*	**£20.00** FCC
MUMM CORDON ROUGE NV, CHAMPAGNE MUMM CHAMPAGNE – *Open and fresh in a fruit-driven, attractive style, with a touch of biscuity depth and a persistent finish.*	**£20.00** RAV/FEN TOS/MWW
PAUL DÉTHUNE GRAND CRU BRUT NV, CHAMPAGNE PAUL DÉTHUNE CHAMPAGNE – *A very fine mousse and racy acidity add interest to the luxuriant, autolytic, bready flavours.*	**£20.00** CHS
CUVÉE DES AMBASSADEURS NV, COMTE AUDOIN DE DAMPIERRE CHAMPAGNE – *Crisp honeyed citrus fruit flavours. Warm brioche and mineral nuances. Very fine mousse.*	**£20.50** UNS/COE
CUVÉE ROYALE BRUT NV, JOSEPH PERRIER CHAMPAGNE – *Mature, mellow and ripe, with a touch of earthy spice. Leesy aromatics; plump, medium-weight fruit.*	**£20.80** ESL/RWM FLY
LANSON BLACK LABEL NV, CHAMPAGNE LANSON CHAMPAGNE – *Very Champenois, with a creamy nose, rich bready complexity and sherbety acidity. Elegant and structured.*	**£20.80** WIDELY AVAILABLE
D DE DEVAUX NV, CHAMPAGNE DEVAUX CHAMPAGNE – *Pineapple fruit graces the nose. The dry biscuit palate has toasted walnuts and fresh citrus fruit on the lengthy finish.*	**£21.40** EVI/RWM
BRUT ROSÉ TRADITION NV, CHAMPAGNE JACQUART CHAMPAGNE – *Notes of brioche lace the nose. The palate has light-bodied red apple fruit flavours and a lasting finish.*	**£22.00** TOS
PHILIPPONNAT ROYALE RÉSERVE NV, CHAMPAGNE PHILIPPONNAT CHAMPAGNE – *The excellent Philipponnat terroir is amply displayed in the graceful baguette, lemon, raspberry, and mineral elements of this Champagne.*	**£22.00** CEL
IVORY LABEL DEMI-SEC NV, CHAMPAGNE LANSON CHAMPAGNE – *Deliciously fresh, delicately sweet and fruity, with lemon sherbet flavours. A classic, and it's simply marvellous.*	**£22.50** INS/MWW

CHAMPAGNE BRONZE

BESSERAT DE BELLEFON CUVÉE DES MOINES BRUT NV, CHAMPAGNE LANSON Champagne – *A rich honey colour pleases the eye. The yeasty character is lifted by bright citrus fruit.*	£23.00 MCD
BESSERAT DE BELLEFON CUVÉE DES MOINES ROSÉ NV, CHAMPAGNE LANSON Champagne – *Freshly baked biscuit scents rise from the nose. The palate sports cherry and strawberry fruit.*	£23.00 MCD
BLANC DE NOIRS NV, CHAMPAGNE DE VENOGE Champagne – *Light and fine with a creamy mousse and elegant floral scents. Bright acidity provides a firm backbone.*	£23.00 PBA
VIN DU PARADIS NV, CHAMPAGNE DE VENOGE Champagne – *The fruit is youthful, with complex nut and lime characters and a firm structure. Balanced.*	£24.00 PBA
CUVÉE SPECIALE BRUT VINTAGE 1997, CHAMPAGNE NICOLAS FEUILLATTE Champagne – *Aromatic and herbal, with biscuity notes and inimitable Champagne minerality. Yeasty, rich, and very complex.*	£25.00 TOS
VEUVE CLICQUOT YELLOW LABEL NV, CHAMPAGNE VEUVE CLICQUOT Champagne – *Cox's Orange Pippin and lemon zest flavours. Fantastic mousse and zippy acidity. Rich. Hazelnut hints.*	£25.30 WIDELY AVAILABLE
TAITTINGER BRUT RESERVE NV, CHAMPAGNE TAITTINGER Champagne – *Fine lively bubbles. Butter, brioche, and apple blossom scents on the nose. Lemon and lime flavours.*	£26.10 WIDELY AVAILABLE
CHAMPAGNE DE VENOGE VINTAGE 1995, CHAMPAGNE DE VENOGE Champagne – *Complex evolution is clear on the nose with mushroomy autolytic, yeasty aromas and a soft, creamy texture.*	£28.00 RNS/PBA BOO
CUVÉE ROYALE BRUT VINTAGE 1996, JOSEPH PERRIER Champagne – *Concentrated, with vibrant youthful fruit and a plethora of mineral and floral layers. Lasting mousse.*	£28.20 ESL/FLY
AYALA BRUT VINTAGE 1998, CHAMPAGNE AYALA Champagne – *Enticing lemon cheesecake and rich lees aromas. Loads of character and an immensely long finish.*	£28.90 BEN/V&C LIB/FLY

PHILIPPONNAT RÉSERVE MILLÉSIMÉE 1993, CHAMPAGNE PHILIPPONNAT Champagne – *Compelling date and greengage aromas mingle with raspberries on nose and palate. Fine acidity. Elegant structure.*	**£29.00** CEL
MOËT ET CHANDON BRUT IMPÉRIAL ROSÉ NV, CHAMPAGNE MOËT ET CHANDON Champagne – *Pale peach colour, with a steady stream of bubbles. Fresh and approachable, with apple fruit and yeasty tones.*	**£29.30** WIDELY AVAILABLE
BRUT PRESTIGE ROSÉ NV, CHAMPAGNE TAITTINGER Champagne – *Delicate onion skin hue. Ebullient mousse lifts the palate of redcurrant fruit, yeastiness, and fresh acidity.*	**£29.40** EDC/HAX FEN/OWC ODD MWW
AYALA BLANC DE BLANCS 1998, CHAMPAGNE AYALA Champagne – *Weighty white-fleshed fruit flavours with no small amount of complexity. Spicy notes on the nose. Lasting finish.*	**£30.30** V&C/LIB FLY
DOM RUINART ROSÉ VINTAGE 1990, CHAMPAGNE RUINART Champagne – *This is a superb mature rosé, gentle, persistent and full of savoury, meaty secondary flavours. Stylish.*	**£30.90** RAV/CVE
DEUTZ BLANC DE BLANCS 1996, CHAMPAGNE DEUTZ Champagne – *Lush, ripe, yellow apple fruit flavoured palate. The nose displays some evolution. Steely acidity supports the fruit.*	**£33.30** VIT/BWC ODD
MOËT ET CHANDON VINTAGE MILLÉSIMÉ BLANC 1988, CHAMPAGNE MOËT ET CHANDON Champagne – *Brilliantly fresh and clean, with a bright, attractive palate. Full of citrus fruit and a hint of sherbet.*	**£40.00** SEL
BOLLINGER GRANDE ANNÉE 1996, BOLLINGER Champagne – *Vintage Bolly: as good as ever. Forest floor and truffle aromas intermingle with citrus fruit. Taut and oh-so-powerful.*	**£47.10** WIDELY AVAILABLE
CUVÉE JOSÉPHINE 1990, JOSEPH PERRIER Champagne – *Developed, with powerful autolysis and Marmite elements. An eye-opening, rich, mature Champagne.*	**£57.00** ESL/FLY
EXTRA BRUT 1983, CHAMPAGNE DE VENOGE Champagne – *Deep gold. Mature. Hints of redcurrants and mayflowers. Earthy, displaying evolution, complexity, concentration, and superb length.*	**£75.00** PBA

GRAND SIÈCLE ALEXANDRA ROSÉ VINTAGE 1997, CHAMPAGNE LAURENT-PERRIER Champagne – *Coppery pink hue. Sweetly ripe redcurrant fruit on nose and palate. Leafy hints. Medium-weight.*	£145.00 EDC

SILVER
LANGUEDOC-ROUSSILLON WHITE

☆ **LA BAUME VIOGNIER VIN DE PAYS D'OC 2003, DOMAINE DE LA BAUME** Languedoc-Roussillon – *Straw yellow-green. Elegant melon scents on the nose; youthful lime flavours on the palate. Zesty, spicy, and fresh.*	£5.00 WTS
☆ **LE RIEUX D'OR CHARDONNAY 2002, CELLIER MERINVILLOIS** Languedoc-Roussillon – *Warm, powerful, and balanced. Green berries, fresh peaches, and ripe apples array the weighty, dry, intense palate.*	£6.40 LAI
★ **L'ECLUSE CHARDONNAY 2002, LAITHWAITES** Languedoc-Roussillon – *Perfumed and flavoured with ripe pears and yellow juicy apples. Very good depth and a fine finish.*	£6.70 LAI
CASSAIRE 2003, LAITHWAITES Languedoc-Roussillon – *A fine artisanal wine. This raving beauty boasts plenty of fresh ripe stone fruit and a graceful swathe of oak.*	£8.50 LAI

BRONZE
LANGUEDOC-ROUSSILLON WHITE

☆ **LE MAZET GRENACHE BLANC 2003, DOMAINES PAUL MAS** Languedoc-Roussillon – *Scented with fresh flowers, peaches, and bubblegum. The open, primary palate drips with fruit salad flavours.*	£4.00 SWS
☆ **CASTEL FRÈRES CHARDONNAY VIOGNIER 2003, CASTEL FRÈRES** Languedoc-Roussillon – *Pale lemon yellow. Peach aromas on the nose; the palate is an oily-textured affair with spices and citrus fruit.*	£5.00 JSM
☆ **LES ARGELIÈRES CHARDONNAY 2003, LGI** Languedoc-Roussillon – *Ripe melon and pineapple nose leads to a fresh palate showing richness and nicely integrated toasty oak.*	£5.00 MWW

184 LANGUEDOC-ROUSSILLON WHITE SEAL

☆ **VIRGINIE DE FRANCE CHARDONNAY 2003, CASTEL FRÈRES** LANGUEDOC-ROUSSILLON – *Ripe and well-made. Its quality fruit is allied to a fine acidic backbone and just a hint of sweet oak.*	£5.00 ODD
☆ **VIRGINIE DE FRANCE VIOGNIER 2003, CASTEL FRÈRES** LANGUEDOC-ROUSSILLON – *The straw yellow colour has a green hue. Fresh limes and nuts fill the nose; the peachy palate is round and soft.*	£5.00 ODD
☆ **WINTER HILL RESERVE CHARDONNAY 2003, FONCALIEU** LANGUEDOC-ROUSSILLON – *Long and refreshing, with a confident attack of red appleskins and cut grass. Brilliant yellow colour.*	£5.00 PLB
LES QUATRE CLOCHERS RESERVE CHARDONNAY LIMOUX 2000, AIMERY-SIEUR D'ARQUES LANGUEDOC-ROUSSILLON – *Concentrated, with mineral and toast on the nose. The palate is ripe and generous with elegant acidity.*	£7.00 TOS
MOULIN DE DAUDET VIOGNIER 2003, PAUL BOUTINOT LANGUEDOC-ROUSSILLON – *Menthol and spice aromas on the nose. The palate is very full-bodied and crammed with pears and peaches.*	£7.00 VGN
DOMAINE DE LA BAUME WHITE 2001, LA BAUME LANGUEDOC-ROUSSILLON – *Vibrant golden colour. The nose is huge, aromatic, and honeyed, and the glycerine-textured palate sports pear flavours.*	£10.00 WTS
MAS LA CHEVALIÈRE 2002, MICHEL LAROCHE LANGUEDOC-ROUSSILLON – *Clean pineapple and peach flavours sing on the medium-weight, crisp palate. A very long finish.*	£10.50 FLY/BWL JSM

SEAL OF APPROVAL
LANGUEDOC-ROUSSILLON WHITE

☆ **SI JOLI PETIT VINS DE PAYS D'OC CHARDONNAY NV, PAUL SAPIN 10CL** LANGUEDOC-ROUSSILLON – *Pineapples, pears, and green apple flavours and aromas.*	£1.00 ROG
☆ **ASDA CLASSIC CHARDONNAY 2002, FONCALIEU** LANGUEDOC-ROUSSILLON – *Bright citrus and apple flavours assail the nose and fill the mouth.*	£3.50 ASD

LANGUEDOC-ROUSSILLON WHITE SEAL / RED GOLD / SILVER

☆ **MHV VIN DE PAYS D'OC CHARDONNAY NV, PRODIS** LANGUEDOC-ROUSSILLON – *Guava, pineapple, lemon, and lime flavours line the refreshing palate.*	£4.00 MHV

GOLD
LANGUEDOC-ROUSSILLON RED

★ **VIRGINIE DE FRANCE SYRAH 2003, CASTEL FRÈRES** LANGUEDOC-ROUSSILLON – *Spicy fruit and liquorice notes. The palate is heaving with black fruit pastilles, olives, and garrigue.*	£5.00 ODD
☆ **CAZAL VIEL CUVÉE DES FEES 2002, LAURENT MIQUEL** LANGUEDOC-ROUSSILLON – *A winner from talented Monsieur Miquel. This wine is a greyhound, with visceral elegance, dusty fruit, and zingy acidity.*	£7.50 WTS
☆ **LAURENT MIQUEL BARDOU 2002, LAURENT MIQUEL** LANGUEDOC-ROUSSILLON – *The nose is an autumnal forest walk, squishy brambles aplenty. Luxuriant fruit. The oak confers complexity and length.*	£10.00 JSM

SILVER
LANGUEDOC-ROUSSILLON RED

☆ **CORBIÈRES TERRA VITIS 2003, MONT TAUCH** LANGUEDOC-ROUSSILLON – *The pronounced, unusual palate of rowan, strawberries, and blackberries is concentrated and balanced. Attractive smoked almond aromas.*	£5.00 MWW
☆ **WINTER HILL RESERVE CABERNET SAUVIGNON 2003, FONCALIEU** LANGUEDOC-ROUSSILLON – *This shows bright Cabernet fruit in a simple, fresh style, with a juicy palate and a good length.*	£5.00 PLB
☆ **WINTER HILL GRANDE RESERVE CABERNET SAUVIGNON 2003, FONCALIEU** LANGUEDOC-ROUSSILLON – *The oak has contributed a creamy aspect to the clear berry fruit. Pleasant, young, with a drying finish.*	£6.00 PLB
☆ **CHÂTEAU CRUSCADES HORTALA 2002, BESSIÈRE** LANGUEDOC-ROUSSILLON – *Developed, with rich secondary aromas of vanilla and spice. Balanced cherry fruit. Restrained.*	£7.00 ACW

186 LANGUEDOC-ROUSSILLON RED SILVER / BRONZE

☆ **TERRE D'OLIVIERS 2000, MAUREL VEDEAU** **LANGUEDOC-ROUSSILLON** – *Cassis, blackcurrant, and developed gamey notes lead swiftly onto a palate with ripe fruit flavours and juicy sweetness.*	**£7.00** THI
LES HAUTS DE L'ENCLOS DES BORIES LA LIVINIÈRE 2001, VIGNOBLES LORGERIL **LANGUEDOC-ROUSSILLON** – *Ripe soft black fruit flavours. A wine with bright acidity, grippy tannins, and a resounding finish.*	**£8.80** L&T
DOMAINE DE FONTSÈQUE CORBIÈRES 2001, GERARD BERTRAND **LANGUEDOC-ROUSSILLON** – *The nose is a mélange of black vine fruits tinged with saddles and spice. Underscored with powerful tannins.*	**£10.00** M&S
DOMAINES DES GARENNES MINERVOIS 2001, GERARD BERTRAND **LANGUEDOC-ROUSSILLON** – *Raspberries and strawberries galore. Cedar, cherries, and Cuban cigars. A balanced, genuinely complex, elegant wine.*	**£10.00** M&S
CHÂTEAU CAMPLAZENS LA RESERVE 2000, CHÂTEAU CAMPLAZENS **LANGUEDOC-ROUSSILLON** – *Savoury tones accompany fresh berries. The nose is clean, juicy, and peppery. Some silky, ripe, berry complexity.*	**£12.00** TAU
DOMAINE DU SILÈNE DES PEYRALS COTEAUX DU LANGUEDOC 2001, SILÈNE DES PEYRALS **LANGUEDOC-ROUSSILLON** – *An opulent nose of warm fruits, herbs, leather, and spice. A balanced palate of fruit, acid, and tannins.*	**£15.00** FTH

BRONZE
LANGUEDOC-ROUSSILLON RED

☆ **LE BRASSET GRENACHE SYRAH 2003, DOMAINES PAUL MAS** **LANGUEDOC-ROUSSILLON** – *Scents of leather and coal. Grainy tannins and tightly wound damson fruit with an acidic flourish.*	**£4.00** SWS
☆ **CASTEL FRÈRES MERLOT 2003, CASTEL FRÈRES** **LANGUEDOC-ROUSSILLON** – *After a light nose of smoky, tarry roses, the palate offers good ripe fruit and a spicy finish.*	**£5.00** BES/ODD
☆ **GOLD LABEL MERLOT 2003, DOMAINES VIRGINIE** **LANGUEDOC-ROUSSILLON** – *Fresh and appealing, with smoky plums on the nose. Firm tannins, full, ripe red fruit. A long finish.*	**£5.00** M&S

LANGUEDOC-ROUSSILLON RED BRONZE

☆ **LA CHÂSSE DU PAPE 2003, MEFFRE MÉDITERRANÉE** LANGUEDOC-ROUSSILLON – *Open, black fruits on the nose, with a toned body of brambles, white pepper, and firm tannins.*	£5.00 GYW
☆ **MAS D'EN BADIE SAINT ETIENNE DES VIGNES 2001, LES VIGNERONS DE PASSA** LANGUEDOC-ROUSSILLON – *Rich, with fascinating hints of lime and white pepper on the nose. Balanced. Intense. Youthful. Delicious.*	£5.00 ESL
☆ **OC CUVÉE 178 MERLOT 2003, LES CHAIS BEAUCAIROIS** LANGUEDOC-ROUSSILLON – *An elegant palate of smoky plums, with a balanced depth, firm structure and medium finish.*	£5.00 THI
☆ **WINTER HILL RESERVE SYRAH 2003, FONCALIEU** LANGUEDOC-ROUSSILLON – *A lot of soft, attractive berry fruit in evidence here on the soft, friendly palate.*	£5.00 PLB
☆ **CHÂTEAU GUIOT 2003, CHÂTEAU GUIOT** LANGUEDOC-ROUSSILLON – *Ripe, minty, and meaty with sweet fruit on the nose. Spice and berry fruit through to the finish.*	£5.30 MWW
DOMAINE DE BUADELLE 2002, CELLIER LAURAN CABARET LANGUEDOC-ROUSSILLON – *Rich prune flavours are lifted by an intriguing medicinal element. A soft, sweetly ripe, developed beauty.*	£6.00 LAI
DOMAINE DE PEYRAT MERLOT 2003, DOMAINE DE PEYRAT LANGUEDOC-ROUSSILLON – *Young and fruity, fresh and crisp, this wine is long, with a touch of spicy bitterness.*	£6.00 VER
LES JAMELLES SELECTION SPÉCIALE 2002, BADET CLEMENT LANGUEDOC-ROUSSILLON – *Oaky spice, chocolate and smoky red fruit on the nose. The palate sports ripe tannins. A peppery finish.*	£6.00 JSM
CUVÉE MARIELLE ET FREDERIQUE 2003, DOMAINE LA TOUR BOISÉE LANGUEDOC-ROUSSILLON – *Peppered raspberry and redcurrant fruit. Young, with a seam of acidity and taut, grainy tannins.*	£6.30 WAW
ABBOTTS PLATANUS MINERVOIS 2003, ABBOTT SNEYD ANDERSON LANGUEDOC-ROUSSILLON – *Thyme and lavender and rosemary notes. Earthy cherry fruit and spices. Good structure.*	£6.70 CCS/MOV BOO

188 LANGUEDOC-ROUSSILLON RED BRONZE

CHÂTEAU ELIMARIE SAINT-CHINIAN 2002, BESSIÈRE LANGUEDOC-ROUSSILLON – *A rich, ripe stewed plum nose. The plush cherry fruit on the palate is soft and full.*	**£7.00** ACW
GÉRARD BERTRAND TERRASSES DU QUATERNAIRES TERROIRS 2001, GERARD BERTRAND LANGUEDOC-ROUSSILLON – *The bouquet offers classy complexity, with jammy fruit and oaky tinges. The palate has sweet fruit.*	**£7.00** TOS
H ROUGE 2001, DOMAINE DE L'HOSPITALET LANGUEDOC-ROUSSILLON – *The nose offers a cornucopia of violets and smoky red fruit, leading to perfumed plums and blackcurrants.*	**£7.00** THI
ABBOTTS CIRRUS CABARDES 2000, ABBOTT SNEYD ANDERSON LANGUEDOC-ROUSSILLON – *Tarry notes, gamey, farmyardy undertones, and dense damson. Juicy berries and cherries, smooth tannins. A spicy tar finish.*	**£8.00** CCS/WES MOV/BOO
CHÂTEAU PAUL MAS COTEAUX DU LANGUEDOC 2002, DOMAINES PAUL MAS LANGUEDOC-ROUSSILLON – *Bright fruit on the nose and chunky fruit on the palate. Has firm tannins and a good finish.*	**£8.00** SWS
CHÂTEAU TOUR DE MONTREDON CUVÉE HUBERT AZAM 2000, LES VIGNERONS DE LA MÉDITERRANÉE LANGUEDOC-ROUSSILLON – *Hedgerow fruit flavours complement earthy farmyard and tar notes on nose and palate.*	**£8.00** VDO
VINUS DU CHÂTEAU PAUL MAS COTEAUX DU LANGUEDOC 2002, DOMAINES PAUL MAS LANGUEDOC-ROUSSILLON – *A nose of oak spice and berries. Oak is prominent on the palate, which has ripe black fruits.*	**£8.00** SWS
LAITHWAITES SYRAH 2002, LAITHWAITES LANGUEDOC-ROUSSILLON – *Juicy tinned cherries and berries abound, alongside grainy tannins and a spicy finish.*	**£8.20** LAI
LES HAUTS DE L'ENCLOS DES BORIES LA LIVINIÈRE 2001, VIGNOBLES LORGERIL LANGUEDOC-ROUSSILLON – *Soft attack is followed by a lightly tannic palate of savoury fruit and notes of the herb garden.*	**£8.50** V&C/TOS
MONT TAUCH FITOU L'EXCEPTION 2001, MONT TAUCH LANGUEDOC-ROUSSILLON – *Darkest chocolate and espresso notes on the nose. The lengthy finish is perfumed and balanced.*	**£10.00** TOS/MWW

LANGUEDOC-ROUSSILLON RED BRONZE / SEAL

CHÂTEAU DE LA NEGLY LA FALAISE 2001, CHÂTEAU DE LA NEGLY Languedoc-Roussillon – *Chunky. Intense fruit opens up on the palate. The complex nose has plentiful spicy aromas.*	£10.30 JNW/SOM MOV
ABBOTTS CUMULUS MINERVOIS 2001, ABBOTT SNEYD ANDERSON Languedoc-Roussillon – *Leafy and spicy, with whiffs of campfire, vanilla bean, and cinnamon. Tight and earthy.*	£12.30 CCS/MOV BOO
LE PRESTIGE 2001, DOMAINE MARCEVOL Languedoc-Roussillon – *Scents of wet earth after rain. Vanilla-infused cherry and strawberry flavours. Delicious and deep.*	£12.50 GRT
CHÂTEAU CAMPLAZENS PREMIUM 2001, CHÂTEAU CAMPLAZENS Languedoc-Roussillon – *Smoky, ripe black fruits marry with rich tarry notes on the nose. Smooth, fresh blueberries join well-integrated, smoky oak.*	£15.00 TAU
DOMUS MAXIMUS MINERVOIS LA LIVINIÈRE 2000, DOMAINE MASSAMIER LA MIGNARDE Languedoc-Roussillon – *Woody notes offset the fragrant black fruit flavours. The finish is taut and dry.*	£20.00 BBR

SEAL OF APPROVAL
LANGUEDOC-ROUSSILLON RED

☆ **VINS DE PAYS D'OC CABERNET SAUVIGNON SI JOLI PETIT NV, PAUL SAPIN** Languedoc-Roussillon – *Vibrant black-cherry flavours. Medium-bodied and pleasingly rustic.*	●£1.00 ROG
☆ **VINTNER'S COLLECTION CABERNET SAUVIGNON VIN DE PAYS D'OC 2003, FONCALIEU** Languedoc-Roussillon – *Vivid redcurrant and blackberry fruit flavours. Scents of thyme.*	£3.70 LCC
☆ **MHV CORBIÈRES 2003, TRESCH** Languedoc-Roussillon – *Deep flavours of red plums, blackberries, and a grinding of white pepper.*	£3.80 MHV
☆ **MHV CÔTES DU ROUSSILLON 2003, TRESCH** Languedoc-Roussillon – *Pomegranate and blackberry flavours. Scents of smoke and herbs.*	£3.80 MHV

☆ **CO-OP VIN DE PAYS D'OC CABERNET SAUVIGNON 2002, FONCALIEU** LANGUEDOC-ROUSSILLON – *Rustic, vibrant and intense, with plenty of cassis and poivre.*	£3.90 CWS
☆ **FITOU ROCHER D'EMBREE NV, MONT TAUCH** LANGUEDOC-ROUSSILLON – *Redcurrants, white pepper, and bilberries vie for attention.*	£4.00 SMF
☆ **LE BRASSET COTEAUX DU LANGUEDOC 2003, DOMAINES PAUL MAS** LANGUEDOC-ROUSSILLON – *Loganberries, leather and hints of herbs flavour this Hérault.*	£4.00 SWS
☆ **MHV MINERVOIS 2003, TRESCH** LANGUEDOC-ROUSSILLON – *Notes of coal, hints of rosehip, and black mulberries. Leather tones.*	£4.00 MHV

BRONZE
LANGUEDOC-ROUSSILLON ROSÉ

☆ **LES JAMELLES CINSAULT ROSÉ 2003, BADET CLEMENT** LANGUEDOC-ROUSSILLON – *Flavours of tiny ripe juicy wild strawberries explode onto the palate. Herb touches buoy the spicy finish.*	£5.00 JSM

BRONZE
LANGUEDOC-ROUSSILLON SPARKLING

☆ **CRÉMANT DE LIMOUX 2000, DOMAINE DELMAS** LANGUEDOC-ROUSSILLON – *Bready, with inviting autolytic yeasty aromas. Crisp acidity, biscuity tones, and fine swirling mousse.*	£9.00 VER
☆ **ROCHE LACOUR 2000, AIMERY SIEUR D'ARQUES** LANGUEDOC-ROUSSILLON – *The nose has ripe fleshy peaches, nuts, and brioche. A flush of fresh green apple flavour infuses the palate.*	£10.00 LAI

TROPHY
LOIRE WHITE

☆ **LA JALOUSIE 2002, DOMAINE DU CLOSEL CHÂTEAU DES VAULTS** Loire – *This phenomenal Savennières has lanolin, beeswax, and wool on the nose and a creamy, soft floral character.*	**£11.50** JNW

GOLD
LOIRE WHITE

☆ **RADCLIFFE'S SAUVIGNON BLANC 2002, CAVES DE HAUT-POITOU** Loire – *Light, bright, pale, and clear. Grassy, green apple flavours. Its taut elegance is very typical of the Loire. Racy.*	**£6.50** THS
☆ **CLOS DE NOUYS VOUVRAY SEC 2002, PIERRE CHAINIER** Loire – *Restrained lanolin hints, bright juicy apples, and white-fleshed pears vie with creamy elements on nose and palate.*	**£8.30** TAU/NRW PBA
☆ **POUILLY-FUMÉ CUVEÉ DE TRONSEC 2001, JOESPH MELLOT** Loire – *Pale lemony-green, resoundingly herbaceous, minerally Pouilly-Fumé with citrus and pea pod flavours and delicate floral notes.*	**£9.90** TAU/WPR
☆ **VOUVRAY LA COULÉE D'OR 2003, DOMAINE BOURILLON D'ORLÉANS** Loire – *Lemony, with hints of wet wool, white flowers, and wax. Full, sweet, and weighty, gently concentrated and persistent.*	**£10.00** FLY
☆ **CLOS DU PAPILLON 2002, DOMAINE DU CLOSEL CHÂTEAU DES VAULTS** Loire – *Big, waxy, and appley. Intense and honeyed, with a creamy, toasty texture and zingy lifted acidity.*	**£12.40** JFE
LE MONT VOUVRAY SEC 2002, HÜET Loire – *Lanolin and lemons and delicate fromage bleu overtones. Dry and intense, with excellent concentration and plenty of weight.*	**£13.00** J&B
VOUVRAY DEMI-SEC 2002, LE MONT Loire – *Racy minerality and lime cordial fruit. Rich and mouthfilling, with exotic fruits and fresh acidity. Gentle and harmonious.*	**£16.00** J&B

SILVER
LOIRE WHITE

☆ **TESCO FINEST VOUVRAY DEMI-SEC 2003, DOMAINE BOURILLON D'ORLÉANS** Loire – *The complex nose shows notes of honey and apple. The palate is ripe and round and finely balanced.*	**£6.00** TOS
DOMAINE DES BALLANDORS QUINCY 2003, DOMAINE DES BALLANDORS Loire – *Very minerally, its primary nose scented with Granny Smith apples and peaches. Delineated by bright acidity.*	**£7.90** SOM/MOV NYW/LIB
LA COULÉE D'ARGENT VIEILLES VIGNES VOUVRAY SEC 2003, DOMAINE BOURILLON D'ORLÉANS Loire – *The nose displays flint and toffee apple notes. The palate has richness and length allied to steely acidity.*	**£9.90** BEN/HAX
SANCERRE PERLE BLANCHE 2003, CHRISTIAN ET KARINE LAUVERJAT Loire – *The understated nose has sweet hay, cut grass, and ripe lemon fruit of great finesse. A classic.*	**£10.00** GWI

BRONZE
LOIRE WHITE

☆ **SAINSBURY'S ANJOU BLANC 2003, VINIVAL** Loire – *Initially subdued, this Chenin Blanc opens up to reveal apples, honey, and pears.*	**£3.00** JSM
☆ **MUSCADET DE SÈVRE-ET-MAINE SUR LIE CHÂTEAU LA TOUCHE 2003, VINIVAL** Loire – *Subdued fruit salad scents and lively melon and kiwi palate. A wine of style and substance.*	**£4.50** MWW
☆ **MUSCADET CÔTES DE GRANDLIEU SUR LIE 2003, LUC ET JÉROME CHOBLET** Loire – *Delineated lemon and Conference pear flavours. No green is showing on the ripe, balanced fruit.*	**£5.00** WTS
☆ **MUSCADET SÈVRE-ET-MAINE SUR LIE LE MOULIN DES COSSARDIÈRES 2003, VINIVAL** Loire – *A fresh nosegay of flowers, citrus, and asparagus. Elegance, concentration, complexity, and balance.*	**£5.00** M&S

LOIRE WHITE BRONZE 193

☆ **RADCLIFFE'S REGIONAL CLASSICS MUSCADET DE SÈVRE-ET-MAINE SUR LIE 2003, VINIVAL** Loire – *Attractive, fresh, and balanced, with a clean palate of light-bodied lanolin and candied-lemon characteristics.*	£5.00 THS
TOUCHSTONE SAUVIGNON BLANC 2002, CVOT Loire – *Bright and clean with a true varietal nose. Lean and grassy, with acidity imparting crispness to the finish.*	£5.50 VRT
SAUVIGNON BLANC DE LA TOURANGELLE 2003, CAVES DE LA TOURANGELLE Loire – *Blossoms and minerals dance on the subtly complex nose. Weighty and richly textured. A pleasure to drink.*	£6.70 LAI
LA TOUCHE SAUVIGNON BLANC 2003, CAVES DE LA TOURANGELLE Loire – *A sun-kissed, minerally and off-dry wine. Approachable and mellow, with good depth and a lasting finish.*	£6.80 LAI
SANCERRE DOMAINE DU CARROIR PERRIN 2003, PIERRE RIFFAULT Loire – *Bright, clean, and green. Lime juice and mineral lights shine on the elegant yet intense palate.*	£7.60 3DW
HENRI VALLON SANCERRE LES FRESNAIES 2003, JEAN BEAUQUIN Loire – *Mineral notes dust the warm nose. The palate has fat lime fruit and a fleshy dried apple finish.*	£8.50 WRT
ATTITUDE 2003, PASCAL JOLIVET Loire – *Soft, warm, and super-ripe; clear, focused, and layered, with yellow apple flavour on the persistent finish.*	£9.00 TAU
SANCERRE DOMAINE RAIMBAULT 2002, DOMAINE RAIMBAULT Loire – *Grassy green, with powerful lime oil character and a mineral edge. Linear, heady, and aromatic.*	£9.00 RAV/CWS
SIGNATURE CHARDONNAY VIN DE PAYS DU JARDIN DE LA FRANCE 2002, PAUL BOUTINOT Loire – *Rich, oily and pungent, with coconutty fatness, lime flavours and roast nut aromas. Honeyed and attractive.*	£9.00 RNS/PBA
MHV POUILLY-FUMÉ DOMAINE MINET LE BOIS CHAUD 2003, DOMINIQUE BAUD Loire – *Grass and guava fruit nose. Fresh, long, and textured, with a touch of minerality and a melon fruit palate.*	£9.80 BNK/MHV

194 LOIRE WHITE BRONZE / SEAL / **RED** GOLD

SANCERRE LES COLLINETTES 2003, JOSEPH MELLOT **LOIRE** – *The sophisticated nose has lees notes; the palate displays bright yellow-apple and pear fruit. Stylish.*	£9.80 TAU/WPR
POUILLY-FUMÉ LES CERISOTTES 2003, PAUL PABIOT **LOIRE** – *Star bright. Notes of smoke and green peaches on the nose. The palate boasts minerals, pineapples, and a long finish.*	£10.00 MWW
SANCERRE BROCHARD 2002, HUBERT BROCHARD **LOIRE** – *Ripe, grassy, and nutty. Elegant, with some mineral finesse to the gooseberry and straw bale palate.*	£11.00 M&S
POUILLY-FUMÉ LE CHAMPS DES VIGNES 2003, DOMAINE TABORDET **LOIRE** – *Lime fresh, with grassy notes and melon fruit. Clear, ripe, bright, and fresh, with good viscosity.*	£12.70 FFW/CVE
PASCAL JOLIVET POUILLY-FUMÉ 2002, POUILLY-FUMÉ **LOIRE** – *Neatly balanced, a keen seam of acidity under the nettle fruit. Pleasantly weighty, with a fresh finish.*	£13.50 SOH/GWI P&S/SEL BEL

SEAL OF APPROVAL
LOIRE WHITE

☆ **HENRI VALLON MUSCADET DE SÈVRE-ET-MAINE 2003, JEAN BEAUQUIN** **LOIRE** – *Delicate lemon and yellow-apple scents and flavours. Fresh and balanced.*	£3.50 WRT
☆ **MHV MUSCADET 2003, DOMINIQUE BAUD** **LOIRE** – *Starfruit, yellow grapefruit, and pear flavours. Light and refreshing.*	£3.80 BNK/MHV

GOLD
LOIRE RED

☆ **ANJOU ROUGE CUVÉE LES NOELLES 2003, DOMAINE DE SALVERT** **LOIRE** – *Laden with bright fruit supported by ripe tannins and a balance of acidity that offers a clean freshness.*	£7.40 3DW

SEAL OF APPROVAL
LOIRE ROSÉ

☆ **CABERNET ROSÉ LURTON 2003, ACKERMAN LAURANCE** Loire – *Coral pink, with bright, ripe strawberry flavours and hints of graphite.*	**£3.90** IWS/JSM
☆ **WAITROSE ROSÉ D'ANJOU 2003, VINIVAL** Loire – *Delicate and fine, with medium-sweet cherry fruit and minerally pencil shaving nuances.*	**£4.00** WTS

SILVER
LOIRE SPARKLING

☆ **CO-OP SPARKLING SAUMUR NV, CAVES DES VIGNERONS DE SAUMUR** Loire – *Biscuity, its medium-deep gold liquid bearing fine mousse. Balanced and fresh, with apple flavour on the finish.*	**£6.90** CWS

BRONZE
LOIRE SPARKLING

☆ **CRÉMANT DE LOIRE ROSÉ NV, ALLIANCE LOIRE** Loire – *Pale pink hue. Lavender and rosemary scents. The fresh palate is laden with soft raspberry fruit.*	**£9.30** LAI

SEAL OF APPROVAL
LOIRE SPARKLING

☆ **MARQUIS DE LA COUR SPARKLING BLANC BRUT NV, ACKERMAN LAURANCE** Loire – *Lifted aromas of white flowers. Flavours of lemons and starfruit.*	**£5.00** IWS
☆ **ACKERMAN SAUMUR BRUT NV, ACKERMAN LAURANCE** Loire – *Lifted lemon nose. Candlewax and pear flavours. Brisk mousse.*	**£6.70** ESL/IWS

GOLD
LOIRE SWEET

☆ **VOUVRAY DEMI-SEC LA BOURDONNERIE 2003, DOMAINE BOURILLON D'ORLÉANS** Loire – *Soft and lemony with wax and lanolin. Balanced high acidity, moderate sweetness and a refreshing, crisp finish.*	£7.00 MWW
☆ **CÔTEAUX DU LAYON ROCHEFORT CUVÉE LA GARDE 2002, EARL SORIN** Loire – *Sweet yellow roses and powdery mayflower notes. Clove buds and cumin hover on the sweetly honeyed palate.*	▲£15.00 3DW
LE MONT VOUVRAY MOELLEUX 1996, DOMAINE HUET Loire – *This wine is crammed with satsuma, sweet blossom, and peach elements, beautiful spokes on a wheel of achingly pretty acidity.*	£30.00 J&B

SILVER
LOIRE SWEET

☆ **VOUVRAY MOELLEUX CLOS DE NOUYS 2002, PIERRE CHAINIER** Loire – *Rich, with lanolin and honey aromas. The ripe palate has concentrated quince and saffron notes. Breathtaking acidity.*	£8.60 NRW/PBA NYW

SILVER
RHÔNE WHITE

CROZES-HERMITAGE CHÂTEAU CURSON 2001, ETIENNE POCHON Rhône – *Creamy nose sprinkled with the pollen scents of little white May flowers. Crisp, round apple-flavoured palate. Impressive length.*	£9.50 J&B

BRONZE
RHÔNE WHITE

CÔTES DU RHÔNE LES RABASSIÈRES 2003, MAISON BOUACHON Rhône – *Fresh peach and pepper powder scents. This characterful, fleshy, viscous wine should integrate further, given time.*	£7.30 FTH

TROPHY
RHÔNE RED

ALAIN GRAILLOT CROZES-HERMITAGE 2000, ALAIN GRAILLOT RHÔNE – *Masses of spice and a grind of white pepper and vibrant, powerful berries over a round tannin structure.*	**£15.50** RWM WTS

GOLD
RHÔNE RED

☆ **DOMAINE FERRATON CROZES-HERMITAGE MATINIÈRE 2001, FERRATON PÈRE ET FILS** RHÔNE – *Spicy, peppery, leafy, juicy, berryish. A grip of tannin and finesse in the layers of flavour and character.*	**£9.50** BBR
☆ **SABLET CHÂTEAU DU TRIGNON 2001, CHÂTEAU DU TRIGNON** RHÔNE – *Lifted and floral with a strawberry, raspberry Grenache nose. There is some concentrated oak complexity on the palate.*	**£9.80** BBR/FLY
☆ **GABRIEL MEFFRE GIGONDAS 2002, GABRIEL MEFFRE** RHÔNE – *Violets and minerals, sweet muted oak, coffee, fig, and Christmas pudding. Integrated tannins and a long finish. Powerful.*	**£10.00** GYW/JSM
CHÂTEAUNEUF-DU-PAPE 2000, CHÂTEAU MONT-REDON RHÔNE – *Lush black fruit spiced with coffee bean, liquorice, rosemary, thyme, and mulling spices. Silky and firm.*	**£14.50** J&B
MARQUISE DE LA TOURETTE HERMITAGE 1998, DELAS FRÈRES RHÔNE – *Farmy, gamey complexity over rich, extracted fruit. A big tannin structure and bright acidity. Leathery oomph adds weight.*	**£30.30** CEB/VIT BWC

SILVER
RHÔNE RED

DOMAINE DE LA MAURELLE 2001, LAITHWAITES RHÔNE – *Black-red colour. Gamey notes add interest to the black olives, cherry tomatoes, and leather flavours. Excellent length.*	**£11.00** LAI

CHANTE CIGALE CHÂTEAUNEUF-DU-PAPE 2000, CHANTE CIGALE Rhône – Red- and black-fruit nose. The palate is a smooth mouthful of Spanish chorizo sausages and ripe fruit.	£13.90 WIDELY AVAILABLE
CHÂTEAU DE BEAUCASTEL CHÂTEAUNEUF-DU-PAPE 1997, PERRIN ET FILS Rhône – Warm red raspberry fruit and white pepper nuances display their charms on the tightly knit nose and palate.	£30.00 WTS
CÔTE RÔTIE LES BECASSES 2001, M CHAPOUTIER Rhône – Restrained, with gamey notes, primary berries, and a white pepper kick. A long, complex wine.	£30.00 WRW
CÔTE RÔTIE SEIGNEUR DE MAUGIRON 2000, DELAS FRÈRES Rhône – Heady, powerful and creamy. Finely tuned coconut oak adds a third dimension and holds the length.	£31.50 VIT/BWC

BRONZE
RHÔNE RED

☆ **LA PIERRE DU DIABLE 2003, VIGNERONS DE BEAUMES DE VENISE** Rhône – Delicious spice, fine texture, and generous alcohol all enhance the liquorice and wild-cherry fruit.	£4.00 MRN
LOUIS BERNARD CÔTES DU RHÔNE-VILLAGES 2003, LOUIS BERNARD Rhône – Deep and ripe. Red sun-dried stone fruits are coupled with a stout dose of tannins.	£5.50 ESL/UNS
CARTE NOIRE 2001, VIGNERONS DE BEAUMES DE VENISE Rhône – Mineral and flower aromatics on the nose. The palate displays good evolution and delightful spiced jam flavours.	£5.80 SMF
DOMAINE DE LA GRANDE BELLANE VALRÉAS 2003, EARL GAIA Rhône – Ripe strawberries with vanilla pod sweetness. Full-bodied, with lively bright mouthwatering acidity.	£6.00 TOS/JSM CWS/THR
CHAPOUTIER BELLERUCHE CÔTES DU RHÔNE 2003, M CHAPOUTIER Rhône – A youthful, balanced wine, with a lifted nose of maquis and mulberries and a lasting finish.	£6.50 EDC

RHÔNE RED BRONZE 199

SABLET CÔTES DU RHÔNE-VILLAGES 2001, DOMAINE DE PIAUGIER Rhône – *Decisive leather notes. Very evolved, with well-judged use of oak and cranberry fruit on the balanced, mature palate.*	£6.50 MWW
GABRIEL MEFFRE CÔTES DU RHÔNE 2003, GABRIEL MEFFRE Rhône – *Vibrant mixed berry fruits with a touch of vanilla and cinnamon. Soft and juicy, with a little pepper.*	£7.00 GYW
JEROME QUIOT CÔTES DU RHÔNE-VILLAGES CAIRANNE 2001, JEROME QUIOT SELECTION Rhône – *Perfumed nose showing smoke, tar and violet notes. The sweet fruit palate is round and harmonious with decent length.*	£7.00 ELD /RIH ASH/MIW
DARRIAUD LA CÔTE SAUVAGE BARRIQUE CAIRANNE 2001, PAUL BOUTINOT Rhône – *Dense, dark-berry fruits, masses of creamy oak, coconut and pepper unfold in this captivating Cairanne.*	£7.50 PBA/FLA NYW/INS
NOBLES RIVES CROZES-HERMITAGE 2003, CAVE DE TAIN L'HERMITAGE Rhône – *A full-bodied wine. The delicious, exceedingly youthful raspberry liquor is lavishly laced with cedary tannins.*	£7.90 WRK/RNS SOM/PBA WES/BOO
COTEAUX DE SIGNAC CÔTES DU RHÔNE-VILLAGES 2003, LAITHWAITES Rhône – *Full, firm, and fruity. A vivid, rich, plummy wine with towering tannins and pepper spice.*	£8.20 LAI
LES GRANGES CÔTES DU RHÔNE-VILLAGES 2002, LAITHWAITES Rhône – *A wine with characterful damson and cherry fruit flavours, hints of the maquis and peppery notes.*	£8.20 LAI
LES PEYRIÈRES CÔTES DU RHÔNE-VILLAGES 2001, CAVE DE RASTEAU Rhône – *Firm leathery notes, tar and red cranberry fruit, all dusted with a generous sprinkling of white pepper.*	£8.40 LAI
LES PEYRIÈRES CÔTES DU RHÔNE-VILLAGES 2002, CAVE DE RASTEAU Rhône – *Deep purple colour, vivid peppery notes and a mouthful of cherry fruit enveloped in mouthwatering acidity.*	£8.40 LAI
TESCO FINEST GIGONDAS CHÂTEAU DE RAMIÈRES 2001, LES VIGNERONS DE BEAUMES DE VENISE Rhône – *A rust-red colour belies the maturity of this spicy, raisin-scented, slightly woody Gigondas.*	£9.00 TOS

200 RHÔNE RED BRONZE / SEAL

CLOS MONTIRIUS VACQUEYRAS 2001, MONTIRIUS Rhône – *Inkwell and black vine fruits feature on the concentrated, somewhat mature, and deeply coloured wine.*	**£10.00** VER
PERRIN VACQUEYRAS LES CHRISTINS 2002, PERRIN ET FILS Rhône – *Anise, sweet spice, and raspberry flavours grace the nose and permeate the palate.*	**£10.00** TOS
CROZES-HERMITAGE LES MEYSONNIERS 2002, M. CHAPOUTIER Rhône – *A tangy nose of ripe cherries. Chewy, fine-grained mocha tannins. Tarry finish.*	**£11.00** FEN
SÉGURET CUVÉE DE LA CASA BASSA 2000, DOMAINE DE CABASSE Rhône – *Smoky overtones waft from the cherry, prune, and plum fruit. Fresh acidity and dry, ripe tannins.*	**£11.70** JNW
NOBLES RIVES CORNAS 2001, CAVE DE TAIN L'HERMITAGE Rhône – *Blackberry and cassis with a leathery, gamey old world style and a sharp sneeze of pepper.*	**£12.50** WRK/PBA BOO
ALAIN GRAILLOT SAINT-JOSEPH 2000, ALAIN GRAILLOT Rhône – *Earthy and inky, with farmyard and tree bark aromas. The medium-weight palate is enlivened by cracked pepper.*	**£16.00** WTS
SAINT JOSEPH 420 NUITS 2002, ALAIN PARET Rhône – *Rich, oaky tobacco and berries on the nose. Ripe raspberry fruit with a creamy texture.*	**£16.50** WSG
NOBLES RIVES HERMITAGE 2001, CAVE DE TAIN L'HERMITAGE Rhône – *Development is beginning to show. A gamey character, herbal notes, and blueberry fruit.*	**£19.20** HAX/WRK PBA/WES BOO

SEAL OF APPROVAL
RHÔNE RED

☆ **CÔTES DU RHÔNE JEAN BERTEAU 2003, LA COMPAGNIE RHODANIENNE** Rhône – *Very dark reddish purple. Black and blue fruit flavours.*	**£4.00** IWS

GOLD
SOUTH WEST WHITE

☆ **BERGERAC BLANC SEC 2003, CHÂTEAU DES EYSSARDS** SOUTH WEST – *Lemon and grapefruit and a lean, elegant grassiness. A soft palate with ripe fruit and bracing acidity.*	**£6.00** V&C

SILVER
SOUTH WEST WHITE

☆ **LES VIGNES RETROUVÉES WHITE 2003, PRODUCTEURS PLAIMONT** SOUTH WEST – *Sun-warmed grass scents. The palate has rapier acidity, Granny Smith apple flavours and lashings of spice to finish.*	**£5.60** ESL/TAN
CHÂTEAU MONTDOYEN LA PART DES ANGES 2002, MONSIEUR HEMBISE SOUTH WEST – *Aromas of straw and lavender rise from the nose. The palate is an intense grapefruit, mandarin, and toast concoction. Powerful and full-bodied.*	**£11.80** GRT/EOR

BRONZE
SOUTH WEST WHITE

☆ **CHÂTEAU PIQUE SÈGUE MONTRAVEL 2003, MADAME MARIANNE MALLARD** SOUTH WEST – *Has soft ripe peach scents. Grassy elements complement the mouthwatering zippy lemon acidity.*	**£2.90** BBR
☆ **VIN DE PAYS DES CÔTES DE GASCOGNE 2003, DOMAINE DE SAINT-LANNES** SOUTH WEST – *Sweet lifted yellow honeysuckle scents. Tropical fruit and fresh herb flavours line the rich yet zingy palate.*	**£5.00** CCS/NYW LIB
CHÂTEAU LE RAZ 2003, VIGNOBLES BARDE SOUTH WEST – *This wine is pale yellow, with intense aromas of crushed leaves and asparagus spears. Fresh and balanced.*	**£5.80** TRO
LES NOUVEAUX GASCONS CÔTES DE ST MONT WHITE 2003, PRODUCTEURS PLAIMONT SOUTH WEST – *An austere nose slowly reveals pears, peaches, and powdery white blossoms. Fresh, full, intense apple flavours.*	**£6.50** HOU

SOUTH WEST WHITE BRONZE / SEAL / **RED** TROPHY / GOLD

PLAIMONT LE FAITE 2002, PRODUCTEURS PLAIMONT South West – Earthy tones, leaves, and little green crab apples intermingle on this expressive, harmonious, ripe wine. Weighty.	£9.60 JFE
JURANÇON SEC SÈVE D'AUTOMNE 2002, DOMAINE CAUHAPÉ South West – Huge, with rich, honeyed warmth, lively grapefruit acidity, and a hauntingly elegant, lasting mineral finish.	£10.70 WES/SGL

SEAL OF APPROVAL
SOUTH WEST WHITE

☆ **BARON ST JEAN , LES GRANDS CHAIS DE FRANCE** South West – Pretty floral aromatics add lift. Green and white berries line the palate.	£2.50 ALD
☆ **JP CHENET COLOMBARD CHARDONNAY 2003, LES GRANDS CHAIS DE FRANCE** South West – Tropical white fruit salad flavours. Aromas of little pink tea roses.	£3.90 BNK/JSM
☆ **JP CHENET SAUVIGNON BLANC 2003, LES CAVES DE LANDIRAS** South West – Crunchy pea pod and cut-grass characteristics. Clear and ripe.	£4.00 TOS

TROPHY
SOUTH WEST RED

☆ **MADIRAN CUVÉE CHARLES DE BATZ 2001, DOMAINE BERTHOUMIEU** South West – Solid tannins, black damsons, blueberries, and ripe currants. Deliciously smooth and concentrated with a never-ending finish.	£10.40 ALZ/NRW WES

GOLD
SOUTH WEST RED

☆ **LE PRESTIGE 2001, CHÂTEAU DU CÈDRE** South West – Discreet yet powerful, perfumed, and rich with damsons, plums, and leather. A powerful tannic structure.	£10.50 GRT

SILVER
SOUTH WEST RED

☆ **LES NOUVEAUX GASCONS CÔTES DE SAINT-MONT 2002, PRODUCTEURS PLAIMONT** South West – *Juicy fruit with sweet oak on the nose. Youthful. Savouriness and inky depth. Silky mineral influences.*	**£5.00** TOS
CHÂTEAU VIELLA VILLAGE 1999, PRODUCTEURS PLAIMONT South West – *Lifted and pronounced. Pure strawberry fruit is initially subsumed by huge tannins, but reappears on the finish.*	**£10.50** ADN/POR

BRONZE
SOUTH WEST RED

BERGERAC RÉSERVE DE CHÂTEAU GRINOU 2003, CHÂTEAU GRINOU South West – *Ripe cranberries, blueberries, and plums, with medium tannins. Plump and tasty, with a long finish.*	**£6.00** ALZ
FOLIE DE ROI MADIRAN 2001, CAVE DE CROUSEILLES South West – *Intense nose with blackberry and tar aromas. The palate has copious yet integrated tannins and an elegant finish.*	**£7.50** GWI
BERGERAC GRAND VIN DE CHÂTEAU GRINOU 2003, CHÂTEAU GRINOU South West – *Another inspiring wine from Guy Cuisset. Inky Merlot with aromas of raspberries and herbs. Supple and chocolatey.*	**£7.90** ALZ
CHÂTEAU DE MASCARAAS MADIRAN 2001, CAVE DE CROUSEILLES South West – *Intense and leathery with plums on nose and palate. The copious tannins are integrated; the finish, concentrated.*	**£12.00** GWI
CHÂTEAU PEYROS MADIRAN 2000, LEDA South West – *Powerful, with leather and bilberry aromas. The palate is thick with fruit and tannin. Good depth and weight.*	**£14.00** PAT

SEAL OF APPROVAL
SOUTH WEST RED

☆ **LA CUVÉE XY 2002, DULONG FRÈRES ET FILS** S<small>OUTH</small> W<small>EST</small> – *Scents of maquis and tar pepper the nose of this plum-flavoured wine.*	£4.00 SKW

SEAL OF APPROVAL
SOUTH WEST ROSÉ

☆ **CHÂTEAU PIQUE SËGUE BERGERAC ROSÉ NV, MADAME MARIANNE MALLARD** S<small>OUTH</small> W<small>EST</small> – *Structured and focused, with lifted aromas of cassis and cherry.*	£3.10 BBR
☆ **OLD TART ROSE 2003, ETS PAUL BOUTINOT** S<small>OUTH</small> W<small>EST</small> – *Vivid candyfloss pink colour. Intense cherry and blueberry flavours.*	£4.00 FEN/NRW PBA
☆ **PIAT D'OR ROSÉ NV, DIAGEO** S<small>OUTH</small> W<small>EST</small> – *Gently spicy, this strawberry-flavoured wine is luxuriantly fruited and medium-sweet.*	£4.00 JSM

GOLD
SOUTH WEST SWEET

☆ **JURANÇON MOËLLEUX SYMPHONIE DE NOVEMBRE 2001, DOMAINE CAUHAPÉ** S<small>OUTH</small> W<small>EST</small> – *Domaine Cauhape has produced a light marzipan and honey wine with non-cloying sweetness. Balanced zingy acidity.*	£12.60 JNW/CCS FLY/SGL
☆ **CUVÉE MARIE JEANNE SAUSSIGNAC 2001, CHÂTEAU LE PAYRAL** S<small>OUTH</small> W<small>EST</small> – *Honeyed botrytis aromas add layers of complexity, Sémillon breadth and Sauvignon gives a bite of freshness. Serious Saussignac.*	▲£13.10 SOM/NYW ENO
☆ **GRANDE MAISON 2001, THIERRY DESPRES** S<small>OUTH</small> W<small>EST</small> – *Stunning orange peel and marmalade flavours with a cinnamon spice nuance. Floral scents, minerals, and a seam of acidity.*	£14.00 SOM

BRONZE
SOUTH WEST SWEET

SAUSSIGNAC 2003, CHÂTEAU GRINOU South West – *Generous, deep, richly sweet bounty of nectarine, lemon, and honeysuckle aromas and flavours.*	▲£12.50 ALZ
COUP DE COEUR 2001, CHÂTEAU RICHARD South West – *Rich saffron and ripe quince nose. The palate displays sweetness countered by piercing acidity.*	▲£13.80 VRT
CHÂTEAU DE MONBAZILLAC 2001, MONSIEUR BARTOSZEK South West – *Quince, honey, and burnt orange aromas. The palate has intense sweetness married to fresh grapefruit acidity.*	£15.00 LAI

BRONZE
OTHER FRENCH WHITE

GARAGE WHITE NV, LAITHWAITES – *Golden. The nose has restrained sweet oak. The palate is weighty, with appealing pepper and butter characteristics.*	£9.00 LAI

SEAL OF APPROVAL
OTHER FRENCH WHITE

☆ **MHV MAISON BLANC MEDIUM DRY VIN DE TABLE FRANÇAIS NV, MARCEL HUBERT** – *A richly ripe, medium-sweet palate of juicy red apples and lychees.*	£3.20 BNK/MHV

BRONZE
OTHER FRENCH RED

GARAGE RED NV, LAITHWAITES – *Hedgerow fruit, some mineral notes, fine length, and no small amount of elegance.*	£9.30 LAI

SEAL OF APPROVAL
OTHER FRENCH RED

☆ **MHV MAISON ROUGE MEDIUM DRY VIN DE TABLE FRANÇAIS NV, DOMINIQUE BAUD** – *Velvety, and saturated with cassis and pomegranate flavours.*	£3.10 BNK/MHV
☆ **MHV MARCEL HUBERT MEDIUM DRY RED VIN DE TABLE FRANÇAIS NV, DOMINIQUE BAUD** – *Delicately peppery, luscious redcurrant flavours. Fresh lifted acidity.*	£3.10 BNK/MHV
☆ **MHV MAISON ROUGE DRY VIN DE TABLE FRANÇAIS NV, DOMINIQUE BAUD** – *Dark damsons, raspberries and ripe aromatic mulberry fruit.*	£3.30 MHV

GOLD MEDALS HAVE SCORED the equivalent of at least 18.5/20 (or 95/100) and are exceptional. Silver has scored over 17/20 (or 90/100), bronze over 15.5/20 (or 85/100), and seals of approval over 14/20 (or 80/100).
☆ particularly good value
★ truly great value
▲ 50CL bottle
■ 37.5CL bottle
● 10CL bottle

FOR STOCKIST CODES turn to page 355. For regularly updated information about stockists and the International Wine Challenge, visit wineint.com. For a full glossary of wine terms and a complete free wine course, visit robertjoseph-onwine.com

GERMANY

Ask most wine professionals to name the finest white wine in the world and the chances are that they'll opt for top-class German Riesling. The judges at this year's International Wine Challenge were so impressed by the examples that were set before them that they exercised their perogative and created several brand new trophies for the best of them. Of course, a number of stunning vintages have helped too, but we'd credit great winemaking.

TROPHY
GERMAN WHITE

HOCHHEIMER KIRCHENSTÜCK RIESLING SPÄTLESE 2003, WEINGUT KÜNSTLER RHEINGAU – *Rheingau impresario Künstler hits his stride. Intensely aromatic apple blossom, peaches, limes, honey, and kerosene elements.*	£14.60	RAY
GRAACHER HIMMELREICH RIESLING SPÄTLESE 1994, JJ PRÜM MOSEL-SAAR-RUWER – *A lime and grapefruit citrus punch; voluptuous sweetness. Magnificent fruit concentration; petrolly evolution. Expect no less from masterful JJ Prüm.*	£15.00	WTS
ESCHERNDORFER LUMP RIESLING SPÄTLESE TROCKEN 2003, WEINGUT HORST SAUER FRANKEN – *Floral and peppery, with citrus, a powerful streak of acidity, hints of smoke and spice, and a very long finish.*	£16.00	NYW

GOLD
GERMAN WHITE

☆ DÜRKHEIMER MICHELSBERG RIESLING 2003, DARTING ESTATE PFALZ – *Crisp, clean, fragrant nectarines, peaches, sweet spices, and minerals. Impressively dense and concentrated Pfalz richness. Distinctive.*	£6.00	M&S
☆ HOCHHEIMER HOLLE RIESLING KABINETT 2000, DOMDECHANT WERNERSCHES WEINGUT RHEINGAU – *Rich and well-balanced, with plenty of elegance and finesse and lots of fruit extract on the very long finish.*	£8.40	LAI

208 GERMAN WHITE SILVER

☆ **ROTSCHIEFER RIESLING SPÄTLESE TROCKEN 2002, FREIHERR HEYL ZU HERRNSHEIM** RHEINGAU – *Peaches, golden apricots, and racy key lime acidity that really lets it fly. Pretty and sophisticated.*	£9.50 WBN
☆ **OESTRICHER LENCHEN RIESLING KABINETT 2000, PETER JAKOB KÜHN** RHEINGAU – *The opulent nose has honeysuckle and apple perfume. The palate is creamy and crammed with tropical fruit.*	£10.00 WTS
☆ **ORIGIN RIESLING 2002, WINERY EXCHANGE** RHEINGAU – *Tropical pineapple and mango aromas; mineral hints. Voluptuous and impressive, its lush ripeness enlivened by balanced acidity.*	£11.00 WXC
☆ **HANS WIRSCHING IPHÖFER KRONSBERG SCHEUREBE SPÄTLESE TROCKEN 2003, WEINGUT HANS WIRSCHING** FRANKEN – *The lemon-drop nose gives way to the palate's racy chorus of bananas and peaches.*	£11.60 WBN
ESCHERNDORFER LUMP SILVANER SPÄTLESE TROCKEN 2003, WEINGUT HORST SAUER FRANKEN – *Honeyed, tropical ruby grapefruit nose. A palate of pineapples and lychees. Rich and luscious, with hints of spice.*	£15.00 NYW
ESCHERNDORFER LUMP SILVANER AUSLESE TROCKEN 2002, WEINGUT HORST SAUER FRANKEN – *Lemon zest, lime, almonds, and acacia scent the nose. Apples, apricots, and peaches line the palate. Phenomenally long.*	£20.00 NYW
RIESLING GREEN SEAL SPÄTLESE 2002, DOMAINE SCHLOSS JOHANNISBERG RHEINGAU – *Weighty yet graceful, with vibrant acidity underscoring the fresh lemon-lime fruit. Lean minerality. Immensely long.*	£21.20 FFW/NYW CVE

SILVER
GERMAN WHITE

DEINHARD AVANTGARDE 2001, DEINHARD KG RHEINHESSEN – *Bright gold colour. Spicy aromatics. An undercurrent of minerality hums throughout the medium-bodied apple and apricot palate.*	£10.30 FFW/CVE
RIESLING KABINETT MOSEL-SAAR-RUWER 2000, SA PRÜM MOSEL-SAAR-RUWER – *Slate soils at SA Prüm lend their wines a linear quality. Citrus and kerosene notes. Great focus.*	£10.30 VGN/GHL JFE

GERMAN WHITE SILVER / BRONZE

BERNKASTELER LAY RIESLING KABINETT 2003, DR LOOSEN MOSEL-SAAR-RUWER – *Delicate floral perfume, whiffs of smoke, and dark mineral hints. Rapier acid and lemon fruit.*	**£10.40** WIDELY AVAILABLE
ESCHERNDORFER LUMP RIESLING KABINETT TROCKEN 2003, WEINGUT HORST SAUER FRANKEN – *Pretty violet notes appear on the nose. Racy, vibrant lemon fruit fills the mouth. Long finish.*	**£11.00** NYW
IPHÖFER JULIUS-ECHTER-BERG SILVANER SPÄTLESE TROCKEN 2003, WEINGUT HANS WIRSCHING FRANKEN – *An aromatic nose showing citrus and mineral notes. The palate shows impeccable harmony between fruit and acidity.*	**£13.30** WBN/WSO
HOCHHEIMER KIRCHENSTUCK RIESLING SPÄTLESE 2002, WEINGUT KÜNSTLER RHEINGAU – *Inviting red grapefruit character. Good intensity and excellent acidity. Sharp minerality and fine balance. Drinks beautifully at present.*	**£14.00** WTS
ESCHERNDORFER LUMP RIESLING AUSLESE TROCKEN 2002, WEINGUT HORST SAUER FRANKEN – *This beauty is certain to reveal more in the future. Its tight fresh lime fruit is buttressed by minerality.*	**£20.00** NYW

BRONZE
GERMAN WHITE

☆ **VINTNER'S COLLECTION HOCK NV, SCHMITT SÖHNE** RHEINHESSEN – *A perfumed and luscious wine, with fresh acidity and a somewhat oily texture. Lengthy finish.*	**£3.00** LCC
DR L RIESLING 2003, WEINGUT DR LOOSEN MOSEL-SAAR-RUWER – *Lush, sweet, rich, candied pineapple fruit scents and flavours. Sweet and sour interplay unfolds on the shimmering palate.*	**£6.30** WIDELY AVAILABLE
VILLA WOLF PINOT GRIS 2003, JL WOLF ESTATE PFALZ – *Delicately spicy, with a fresh spritz to the crisp pear fruit. Hints of hazelnut and creamy apples.*	**£6.30** JNW
DRY RIESLING KALKSTEIN 2003, REH KENDERMANN PFALZ – *Very dry and well made, with neatly fused acidity. A modern, minerally, citrus-laden, floral Riesling.*	**£7.00** SAF

210 GERMAN WHITE BRONZE / SEAL

RADCLIFFE'S RIESLING KABINETT 2002, REH KENDERMANN MOSEL-SAAR-RUWER – *Honeyed fruit and light floral notes on the nose. The clean palate is fresh with excellent mineral definition.*	£8.00 THS
WERNER HOCHHEIMER KIRCHENSTUCK RIESLING SPÄTLESE 1997, DOMDECHANT WERNERSCHES WEINGUT RHEINGAU – *Droplets of honey scent the nose. The palate has ruby grapefruit and apricot flavours.*	£9.60 LAI
ESCHERNDORFER LUMP SILVANER KABINETT TROCKEN 2003, WEINGUT HORST SAUER FRANKEN – *Toffee apples, limes, flowers, and spices. A hint of green bell pepper keeps it interesting.*	£10.00 NYW
NIERSTEIN PETTENTAL RIESLING GROSSES GEWÄCHS 2002, FREIHERR HEYL ZU HERRNSHEIM RHEINHESSEN – *Soft toasty aromas on the nose. The palate has bright acidity and restrained, youthful, herby fruit.*	£15.00 WBN
NACKENHEIM ROTHENBERG RIESLING SPÄTLESE 2002, GUNDERLOCH RHEINHESSEN – *Light-bodied and attractive, with perfumed citrus fruit, fresh acidity and a pretty floral character.*	£16.60 JNW/CCS NYW
SEHNSUCHT 2002, WEINGUT HORST SAUER FRANKEN – *Hints of late harvest ripeness deepen the character of this caramelly wine with its long, balanced finish.*	£22.00 NYW

SEAL OF APPROVAL
GERMAN WHITE

☆ **ST AMANDUS NIERSTEINER GUTES DOMTAL 2002, ST AMANDUS** RHEINHESSEN – *Bright, ripe, and saturated with stone fruit and wildflower characters.*	£2.70 ALD
☆ **VINTNER'S COLLECTION NIERSTEINER GUTES DOMTAL 2003, SCHMITT SOHNE** RHEINHESSEN – *Ruby grapefruit, pear, pineapple, and tangerine aromas and flavours.*	£3.30 LCC
☆ **SOMERFIELD NIERSTEINER SPIEGELBERG 2002, SCHMITT SOHNE** RHEINHESSEN – *White-fleshed stone fruit, limes, gooseberries, and hedgerow flowers.*	£3.50 SMF

GERMAN WHITE SEAL / SPARKLING SEAL / SWEET TROPHY

☆ **CO-OP FOUR RS 2003, REH KENDERMANN** **RHEINHESSEN** – *Pretty wildflower scents and a lush, appley, medium-dry body.*	£4.00 CWS
☆ **GAU BICKELHEIMER KURFÜRSTENSTÜCK 2003, SCHMITT SOHNE** **RHEINHESSEN** – *Nectarines, white currants, lemons, and pineapples pour from this ripe wine.*	£4.00 SMF
☆ **MOSEL VALLEY 2003, MOSELBLICK** **MOSEL-SAAR-RUWER** – *Fresh and summery, with peach and nectarine fruit and floral scents.*	£4.00 JSM/WRT MRN

SEAL OF APPROVAL
GERMAN SPARKLING

☆ **DEINHARD MEDIUM DRY NV, DEINHARD** **MOSEL-SAAR-RUWER** – *Ripe and generously fruited. Laden with golden apples and white flowers.*	£6.80 FFW
☆ **DEINHARD LILA TROCKEN NV, DEINHARD** **MOSEL-SAAR-RUWER** – *Bountiful clean green flesh buoyed by neverending streams of bubbles.*	£7.30 FFW/EVI CVE
☆ **RIESLING SEKT BRUT NV, DEINHARD** **MOSEL-SAAR-RUWER** – *Fresh, youthful, intense, and aromatic, with very lively mousse.*	£7.30 FFW/FEN CVE

TROPHY
GERMAN SWEET

ESCHERNDORFER SILVANER AUSLESE 2002, BOCKSBEUTEL-HOF **FRANKEN** – *Freshly sliced golden apples and late-harvest aromas. The palate is intense, with acidity, earthy notes, and sweet spice.*	£.00 NOT AVAILABLE IN THE UK
BRAUNEBERGER JUFFER-SONNENUHR RIESLING AUSLESE 2002, KRANZ-JUNK **MOSEL-SAAR-RUWER** – *Stylish greengage nose. Layers of citrus fruit build to a crescendo and explode with a zing on the palate.*	£.00 NOT AVAILABLE IN THE UK

212 GERMAN SWEET TROPHY / GOLD / SILVER

ESCHERNDORFER LUMP RIESLING TBA 2002, WEINGUT HORST SAUER Franken – *Vibrant and powerfully concentrated. Astonishing minerality, satsuma and honey flavours. Wildly syrupy, yet perfectly balanced.*	▲£54.00 NYW
ESCHERNDORFER LUMP RIESLING EISWEIN 2002, WEINGUT HORST SAUER Franken – *Intense and impressive, with pure lemony lime fruit, honey, and apricots. Creamy caramel notes grace the long, vigorous finish.*	▲£55.00 NYW

GOLD
GERMAN SWEET

ESCHERNDORFER LUMP RIESLING AUSLESE 2002, WEINGUT HORST SAUER Franken – *Vibrant tropical citrus fruit aromas. Creamy and sweet, with mouthfilling grapefruit and limes, honeysuckle, guava, and apricots.*	▲£18.00 NYW

SILVER
GERMAN SWEET

HOCHHEIMER HÖLLE RIESLING AUSLESE GOLDCAP 2003, WEINGUT KÜNSTLER Rheingau – *Intense, with a complex pear blossom, turmeric, and lime nose. Searing acidity, near-perfect balance, and a very long finish.*	■£15.00 RAY
RIESLING EISWEIN 2001, WINZERVEREIN RUPPERTSBERG Pfalz – *Vivid citrus and nectarine aromas. Medium-bodied yet very concentrated with piercing minerality. The finish is long and elegant.*	■£15.00 JSM
NIERSTEIN BRUDERSBERG RIESLING AUSLESE GOLDKAPSEL 2001, FREIHERR HEYL ZU HERRNSHEIM Rheinhessen – *Complex honey, guava, and quince notes. The rich palate shows finesse and balance. Long and concentrated.*	£20.00 WBN
IPHÖFER JULIUS-ECHTER-BERG RIESLANER BEERENAUSLESE 2002, WEINGUT HANS WIRSCHING Franken – *Intense, with ripe fruit, mineral depth, and piercing acidity. The palate has balance, depth, and admirable length.*	■£40.80 WBN

GREECE + CYPRUS

Are Greece's go-ahead winemakers part of the Old World or the New World? Perhaps we should call them Ancient and Modern? In the year of the Olympics and the European Cup – and after a few years of hard work by Oddbins wine merchant – UK wine-drinkers have finally begun to discover that there is more to Greek wines than "Domestos" and Retsina, and that this country can offer wines made from "international" grapes and fascinating indigenous ones.

BRONZE
GREEK + CYPRIOT WHITE

☆ **CO-OP ISLAND VINES CYPRUS WHITE 2003, SODAP** **CYPRUS** – *Greenish colour. Pleasant nutty elements and tangy acidity. Youthful and modern, with a long finish.*	£4.00 CWS
☆ **CO-OP MOUNTAIN VINES SÉMILLON 2002, SODAP** **CYPRUS** – *Bright pale lemony green. Flowers and hints of candyfloss on the nose. Dry, round and approachable.*	£4.30 CWS
AMETHYSTOS WHITE 2003, DOMAINE CONSTANTIN LAZARIDI **MACEDONIA** – *Wildflowers and grasses scent the nose. This ripe, elegant wine is understated and supremely drinkable.*	£8.50 ODD
BIBLIA CHORA WHITE 2003, KTIMA BIBLA CHORA **MACEDONIA** – *Muted green fruit and mineral nuances. The aristocratic palate courses with vibrant zesty flavours. Long.*	£8.70 HAX/NYW FLY
CHÂTEAU JULIA SÉMILLON 2003, DOMAINE CONSTANTIN LAZARIDI **ADRIANI** – *Elegant floral and citrus notes on the nose. The palate has plenty of peaches, elderflowers, and lychees.*	£10.40 ODD

SEAL OF APPROVAL
GREEK + CYPRIOT WHITE

☆ **KOURTAKIS AEGEAN ISLANDS WHITE 2003, D. KOURTAKIS** RHODES – *Textured, elegant lemon zest flavours. Hints of minerality.*	**£4.00** ADE

SILVER
GREEK + CYPRIOT RED

PORTO CARRAS SYRAH 1999, DOMAINE PORTO CARRAS CHALKIDIKI – *Big, rich, and delectable. Exceptional black fruit. Deeply intense yet ripe. Fresh and lifted all the way through.*	**£20.60** YOD

BRONZE
GREEK + CYPRIOT RED

MOUNT ATHOS VINEYARDS TSANTALI 1999, EVANGELOS TSANTALIS MOUNT ATHOS – *From the mountain of the monasteries hails this fragrant, dark, brooding, structured wine. Unusual.*	**£7.50** LAI

ITALY

Sales of Italian wine in the UK dropped last year, but the value went up. In other words, we collectively shifted our sights upwards from basic "Valpol", Soave, and Lambrusco to wines with real character. And Italy is better placed to offer those than most other countries, thanks to its bewildering array of grapes, blends, and climates. This year, saw a greater number of Italian award winners than ever, and an impressive growth in the number of white wines. Whether you prefer classic Barolo and Chianti, or fancy exploring the uncharted territory of Arneis, Refosco, and Teroldego, the following pages should provide an invaluable guide.

TROPHY
PIEDMONT + NORTHWEST WHITE

☆ **CRISTINA ASCHERI ROERO ARNEIS 2003, ASCHERI** **PIEDMONT** – *Soft and grapey on the nose. Honey and lemon fruit complexity. Mouthfilling white peach flavour. Beautiful.*	£11.00 NYW/ENO

GOLD
PIEDMONT + NORTHWEST WHITE

☆ **GAVI DI GAVI MASSERIA DEI CARMELITANI 2003, TERREDAVINO** **PIEDMONT** – *Aromatic and grassy, its herbal complexity balanced with a soaring acidity. Powerful mineral notes score the palate and nose.*	£12.00 VIN

SILVER
PIEDMONT + NORTHWEST WHITE

☆ **GAVI DI GAVI TOLEDANA 2003, DOMINI VILLAE LANATA** **PIEDMONT** – *Lemon and almonds on the nose. A fresh palate with excellent balance and acidity. Complex, long finish.*	£7.00 D&D/MCT WRT

BRONZE
PIEDMONT + NORTHWEST WHITE

TESCO FINEST GAVI 2003, FRATELLI MARTINI SECONDO LUIGI Piedmont – The nose is fresh and aromatic with delicate floral notes. The palate is clean, with excellent acidity.	£6.00 TOS
LANGHE CHARDONNAY 2003, COSTA DI BUSSIA Piedmont – Greenish straw yellow hue. Lime zest attack; mouthcoating, almost oily texture. Some elegance. Developed.	£9.80 FFW/CVE
MONTALUPA LANGHE VIOGNIER 2001, ASCHERI Piedmont – Warm climate origins shine on this zingy tropical wine. Impressive, intriguing and honeyed, with a big finish.	£22.50 ENO

TROPHY
PIEDMONT + NORTHWEST RED

CANNUBI BAROLO 1999, PAOLO SCAVINO Piedmont – Pure style and elegance. The nose is perfumed with violets and roses and cherry tones come through on the palate.	£47.00 J&B

GOLD
PIEDMONT + NORTHWEST RED

☆ **BARBERA D'ASTI SUPERIORE TERE CAUDE 2001, CA' DEL MATT** Piedmont – Fine, restrained, spicy aromas. Ripe, red fruit behind balanced, well-structured oak and tannins. A tremendous finish.	£9.50 WIDELY AVAILABLE
☆ **BARBERA D'ASTI SUPERIORE LA LUNA E IL FALO 2001, TERREDAVINO** Piedmont – Warm, plummy berry fruit and a touch of spice to the palate. Amazing length. Wine with a future.	£11.50 V&C/VIN
SUDISFA ROERO NEBBIOLO 2000, NEGRO ANGELO E FIGLI Piedmont – Earthy, savoury palate with very Nebbiolo dry tannins and crisp acidity. Herbal undergrowth flavours and visible structure.	£21.20 GRT/NYW

PIEDMONT + NW RED GOLD / SILVER

BAROLO BUSSIA DARDI LE ROSE 1999, PODERI COLLA PIEDMONT – Subtle and supple. Dry tannins and bright acid. An ethereal elegance. Tar and roses, and savoury, developing flavours.	■ £25.70 FFW/HOU NRW/MER
BAROLO CEREQUIO SINGLE VINEYARD 1999, BENI DI BATASIOLO PIEDMONT – Light liquorice, cherries, overtones of raspberries, touches of spice, a leathery edge, and a grainy tannic texture.	£27.00 MON
BAROLO VIGNA ROCCHE 1998, GIOVANNI CORINO PIEDMONT – Intense ripe tannins, rich red berries, and delicate scents of wildflowers, white pepper, nutmeg, and hints of creosote.	£36.00 J&B
BAROLO CIABOT MENTIN GINESTRA 1999, DOMENICO CLERICO PIEDMONT – Packed with bright, cherry fruit, and cedar wood style. A flash of acidity, chewy tannins, and great depth of fruit.	£38.00 J&B
BAROLO VIGNA CONCA 1998, FRATELLI REVELLO PIEDMONT – A complex nose of cold cream, roses, and tar with jammy, plummy fruit on the palate, lively tannins, and bright acidity.	£43.00 NYW

SILVER
PIEDMONT + NORTHWEST RED

☆ **VALLE BERTA BARBERA D'ASTI 2003, ARALDICA** PIEDMONT – Jammy raspberries and cherries with mineral/herbal tinges on the nose. Bright, vibrant, raspberries and blackberries. Free-flowing tannins.	£7.30 VGN/MER BOO
EREMO FONTANAFREDDA LANGHE ROSSO 2002, FONTANAFREDDA PIEDMONT – Ripe berry and cherry aromas. Dense black fruit married to silky tannins and the merest hint of sweet oak.	£9.40 JNW/V&C VIT/JFE NYW/ENO
AIRONE MONFERRATO A1 2001, MICHELE CHIARLO PIEDMONT – Clean, with char, tar, and warm spiced oak. Savoury characteristics, soft tannins, and velvet cherry juice flavours.	£11.60 CEB/FFW CVE
BARBARESCO 2000, PRODUTTORI DEL BARBARESCO PIEDMONT – Perfumed nose showing floral and cooked meat aromas. Thick fruit and robust tannins. Length and complexity to finish.	£17.00 V&C

218 PIEDMONT + NW RED SILVER / BRONZE

ASCHERI BAROLO VIGNA DEI POLA 2000, ASCHERI PIEDMONT – *Whiffs of burning leaves, dried dates, and apricots scent the dry griotte palate, lifted by a big dry web of tannins.*	£22.80 TOS/ENO
TANTRA MONFERRATO ROSSO 2000, SCRIMAGLIO PIEDMONT – *The nose is full, with vanilla and blueberry notes. The palate is lush and creamy with a velvety mouthfeel.*	£23.50 FRI
ASCHERI BAROLO SORANO BRICCO E COSTE 1999, ASCHERI PIEDMONT – *Wild raspberry, floral, and spice aromas. Compact and structured with fruit intensity and tannic harmony.*	£37.00 ENO
BAROLO CASE NERE 1999, ENZO BOGLIETTI PIEDMONT – *Complex berry and spice aromas. Balanced rich fruit and silky tannins. Good depth and finesse to finish.*	£43.00 WSO
BARBARESCO CAMP GROS MARTINENGA 1999, MARCHESI DI GRESY PIEDMONT – *The palate is balanced and harmonious with lush blackberry fruit allied to silky tannins. The finish is long and concentrated.*	£48.60 FFW/MER BOO

BRONZE
PIEDMONT + NORTHWEST RED

LANGHE BACCANERA LO ZOCCOLAIO 2001, DOMINI VILLAE LANATA PIEDMONT – *Perfumed spicy oak, soft cherry fruit, chewy tannins, crisp acidity, and a lengthy finish.*	£8.00 MCT/WRT
RIVE BARBERA 2001, ARALDICA PIEDMONT – *Intense jam and berry nose leads to a lush blackfruit palate with supple tannins and decent weight.*	£9.80 FFW/MER FLA/INS
ASCHERI DOLCETTO D'ALBA NIRANE 2003, ASCHERI PIEDMONT – *Complex, with lifted, edgy sour cherry aromas and flavours. Peppercorns, fierce tannins, and just a touch of the farmyard.*	£10.00 ENO
BARBERA D'ASTI SUPERIORE LE ORME 2001, MICHELE CHIARLO PIEDMONT – *Deeply coloured, with a lush palate of super-ripe red-berries and cherries. Vibrant and well-balanced.*	£10.10 FFW/WPR CVE

PIEDMONT + NW RED BRONZE 219

BARBERA D'ALBA FONTANELLE 2002, ASCHERI **PIEDMONT** – *Textured ripe tannins, cherries, hints of spice, and a dash of liquorice.*	£11.00 ENO/JSM
BAROLO "REVELLO" 2000, ARALDICA PIEDMONT – *The nose has cherry and pancetta notes. The palate has concentrated fruit and a lick of creamy oak.*	£11.50 WIDELY AVAILABLE
CROERE BARBERA D'ALBA SUPERIORE 2001, TERREDAVINO PIEDMONT – *Soft and jammy with blackberry and violet notes. The palate shows sweet berries, supple tannins, and admirable persistence.*	£14.50 V&C/VIN
BRIC BERTU BARBERA D'ALBA 2001, NEGRO ANGELO E FIGLI PIEDMONT – *Sweet berry and cherry nose leads to a juicy palate showing well-integrated oak and tannins.*	£16.00 GRT
MALORA LANGHE NEBBIOLO 2001, TERREDAVINO PIEDMONT – *Perfumed with cherry and pancetta aromas. The palate is structured with fruit intensity, ripe tannins, and decent length.*	£17.00 VIN
BAROLO 1999, BENI DI BATASIOLO PIEDMONT – *The nose is berry-rich with light medicinal notes. The palate is warm and harmonious with supple tannins.*	£18.00 MON
ACSÉ BARBERA D'ASTI SUPERIORE 2000, SCRIMAGLIO PIEDMONT – *Supple with pronounced blackberry and toast notes. The palate is full and balanced with good fruit purity.*	£19.00 FRI
BARBERA D'ASTI MONTE COLOMBO 2001, MARCHESI DI GRESY PIEDMONT – *Spiced plumcake nose leads to a velvety palate of rich black fruit, ripe tannins, and sweet oak.*	£19.30 FFW/MER
GISEP BARBERA D'ALBA 2000, VIGNA RIONDA-MASSOLINO PIEDMONT – *Fruit-driven with intense blackberry aromas on the nose. The palate is lush with rich fruit and squashy tannins.*	£19.70 LIB/FLY
FONTANAFREDDA BARBARESCO COSTE RUBIN 2000, FONTANAFREDDA PIEDMONT – *The nose has berry and cherry blossom. The palate is balanced with notes of bacon and blueberry. Decent finish.*	£22.00 VIT/NYW ENO

220 PIEDMONT + NW RED BRONZE / SPARKLING GOLD / SILVER

BAROLO PODERI SCARRONE 1999, TERREDAVINO PIEDMONT – *Complex nose with raisin and medicinal character. The palate is elegant with persistent fruit allied to fine tannins.*	£29.00 VIN
BAROLO LA MORRA 1998, ELIO ALTARE PIEDMONT – *Cherry and smoked pancetta notes on the nose. The palate is intense, supple, and oak-spiced. Complex finish.*	£35.00 J&B
BAROLO LA CORDA DELLA BRICCOLINA SINGLE VINEYARD 1999, BENI DI BATASIOLO PIEDMONT – *Pronounced berry and pancetta nose leads to a rich palate of ripe fruit and integrated sweet oak.*	£36.00 MON
BAROLO FOSSATI 1999, ENZO BOGLIETTI PIEDMONT – *The nose is complex with medicinal and beetroot notes. The palate has sweet-berry fruit allied to elegant structure.*	£43.00 WSO

GOLD
PIEDMONT + NORTHWEST SPARKLING

☆ **ASTI SPUMANTE SANTORSOTA NV, SAN ORSOLA** PIEDMONT – *Scented with freshly crushed grapes. Sweet and jolly. Round, mellifluous, and packed with poached pears and rose petals.*	£5.30 WPR
★ **SPARKLING PINOT GRIGIO NV, BOSCA TOSTI** PIEDMONT – *Masses of pure, fresh, crisp lemon and peaches and pears. Approachable, yet aromatically complex. Who says Grigio lacks character?*	£6.00 PLB

SILVER
PIEDMONT + NORTHWEST SPARKLING

☆ **MOSCATO D'ASTI 2002, BENI DI BATASIOLO** PIEDMONT – *Delicate frothy mousse, perfumed fruit, and a long finish. Rich, with a long finish, good complexity, and evolution.*	£6.50 MON

BRONZE
PIEDMONT + NORTHWEST SPARKLING

☆ **MOMBELLO ASTI SPUMANTE NV, CAPETTA** PIEDMONT – *A concentrated, balanced and fresh wine. This well-made, classically grapey Asti has admirable zestiness and liveliness.*	£3.50 SMF
☆ **SOMERFIELD ASTI SPUMANTE NV, CAPETTA** PIEDMONT – *Pale, with delicate rose petal and ripe grape aromas on the nose. The palate is luscious, soft, and feminine.*	£4.00 SMF
ELECTO FRANCIACORTA 1998, MAJOLINI LOMBARDY – *Very fruity, with an attractive almond nose and a marzipan palate. A touch of sweetness lifts the finish.*	£18.00 BBL

SEAL OF APPROVAL
PIEDMONT + NORTHWEST SPARKLING

☆ **MOSCATO SPUMANTE , CAPETTA** PIEDMONT – *Fragrance of chalk and old roses. Sweet saturated palate of grapey fruit.*	£3.00 ALD/MRN
☆ **MHV ASTI NV, SANTERO** PIEDMONT – *Vivid rose petal and satsuma aromas. The palate is luscious and heady.*	£4.90 BNK/MHV
☆ **ASTI SPUMANTE NV, SANTERO** PIEDMONT – *Juicy apple flavours complement the nose of citrus and rosewater.*	£5.00 IWS
☆ **CANTI ASTI NV, FRATELLI MARTINI SECONDO LUIGI** PIEDMONT – *Turkish delight, honey, citrus blossom and tangerine scents and flavours.*	£5.00 TOS
☆ **MARTINI ASTI NV, BACARDI MARTINI** PIEDMONT – *Youthful and lively, with a perfumed floral nose and succulent ripe flavours.*	£7.50 EVI

SILVER
PIEDMONT + NORTHWEST SWEET

☆ **MOSCATO D'ASTI DI STREVI 2003, CONTERO** **PIEDMONT** – *Peachy, grapey, and frothy. Fresh acidity. An exotic and richly fruited wine with a perfumed quality.*	**£7.40** LIB/FLY

TROPHY
VENETO + NORTHEAST WHITE

☆ **PIAVE VECCHIA 2001, FASOLI GINO** VENETO – *Fine, rich honeyed depths. Perfumed lemon fruit accompanies a complex biscuity dimension imparted by understated oak.*	**£10.50** TWM/VRT

SILVER
VENETO + NORTHEAST WHITE

☆ **CANALETTO PINOT GRIGIO GARGANEGA 2003, CASA GIRELLI** VENETO – *Lime, lemon, and grapefruit flavours cleanse the mouth with purity and freshness. The nose is scented with heady meadowsweet.*	**£5.00** BGN
☆ **PINOT GRIGIO VALDADIGE 2003, PASQUA** VENETO – *Straightforward spritzy grapefruit flavours. Glamorous and soft, with zest and pith elements. Concentrated, elegant, and long.*	**£5.30** FLY
☆ **SOAVE CLASSICO SUPERIORE MONTE CLETHA 2002, CANTINA DI MONTECCHIA** VENETO – *Complex almond, olive, and light floral nose. Balanced, with clear acidity. The finish has length and elegance.*	**£7.00** ENO
☆ **MASO GUA PINOT GRIGIO TRENTINO 2003, CONCILIO** TRENTINO-ALTO ADIGE – *This northern beauty boasts white guava, bitter almond, nutmeg, and crisp yellow-apple scents and flavours.*	**£7.50** CIB
☆ **SAINSBURY'S CLASSIC SELECTION SOAVE 2002, INAMA** VENETO – *The nose has bitter almond and melon aromas. The palate is rich and well-balanced. Medium weight, with fresh acidity. Elegant.*	**£8.00** JSM

VENETO + NE WHITE SILVER BRONZE

TUFAIE SOAVE CLASSICO 2003, FRATELLI BOLLA **VENETO** – *Deeply aromatic, with complex herbal and floral notes. The palate is nutty and rich with fine acidity. Harmonious finish.*	£8.30 RAV
MASI MASIANCO 2003, MASI AGRICOLA **VENETO** – *The palate drips with ripe bitter melon juice. Creamy, round, and vivid. Original and exciting.*	£8.70 VIT/BWC
SAUVIGNON BLANC ISONZO DEL FRIULI 2003, I FEUDI DI ROMANS **FRIULI-VENEZIA GIULIA** – *Kiwis, scented lilies, and gooseberries assail the nose. Exciting, complex, and focused, with a seam of minerals.*	£8.80 DOD/V&C LIB/FLY
PINOT GRIGIO ISONZO DEL FRIULI 2003, I FEUDI DI ROMANS **FRIULI-VENEZIA GIULIA** – *Palest yellow. Herbs, spices, and glowing green apple flavours linger on the high-toned, harmonious palate.*	£9.70 DOD/V&C NYW/LIB FLY
ROSAZZO BIANCO 2003, RONCHI DI MANZANO **FRIULI-VENEZIA GIULIA** – *"Excellent and exciting," enthused the judges, and who are we to argue? Lychees, flowers, and white peaches.*	£15.00 VIN

BRONZE
VENETO + NORTHEAST WHITE

☆ **MHV VINO DA TAVOLA BIANCO NV, SARTORI** **VENETO** – *Some depth; soft pear and elderflower elements and a flourish of freshness on the finish.*	£3.50 MHV
☆ **SAINSBURY'S PINOT GRIGIO DELLE VENEZIE 2003, GRUPPO ITALIANO VINI** **VENETO** – *Soft, subtle, and elegant perfumed lemon fruit lines the textured palate and dances above it on the nose.*	£4.80 JSM
☆ **PINOT GRIGIO LA GIOIOSA 2003, LA GIOIOSA** **VENETO** – *Earthy and ripe green berries line the textured, spicy, nutty palate. On the full side for the genre.*	£5.00 TOS
☆ **SOAVE CLASSICO 2003, SARTORI** **VENETO** – *Classic bitter almond, lemon, pear, and elderflower notes appear on the textured nose and palate.*	£5.00 IWS

224 VENETO + NE WHITE BRONZE / SEAL / **RED** GOLD

PINOT GRIGIO DEL VENETO 2003, PERLAGE **VENETO** – *Ripe melon fruit aromas and flavours. Clear, correct, approachable, and slightly creamy, with lemon essence.*	£5.80 VER
FASOLI GINO LIBER 2001, FASOLI GINO **VENETO** – *The nose is creamy with almond notes. The palate shows fresh citrus fruit and a balanced finish.*	£8.50 VRT
CA DEI FRATI LUGANA 2002, CA DEI FRATI **VENETO** – *Vivid lemon yellow. Evolved elderflower and cucumber elements are scored with bright, green apple acidity.*	£8.90 WIDELY AVAILABLE

SEAL OF APPROVAL
VENETO + NORTHEAST WHITE

☆ **SOMERFIELD SOAVE 2003, GRUPPO ITALIANO VINI** **VENETO** – *Understated crushed nuts, hints of earth, and bright white fruit flavours.*	£3.30 SMF
☆ **MHV SOAVE 2002, SARTORI** **VENETO** – *Nuts and herbaceous notes on the nose. Fresh lemon fruit flavours.*	£3.70 BNK/MHV
☆ **MHV CHARDONNAY DELLA VENEZIE N/V, SCHENK ITALIA** **VENETO** – *Grapefruit, lemons, navel orange, and lime scents and flavours.*	£4.00 MHV

GOLD
VENETO + NORTHEAST RED

☆ **VIA NOVA AMARONE DELLA VALPOLICELLA 2001, VALPANTENA** **VENETO** – *Deep and concentrated with raisiny notes and black fruit character. Dry tannins, a hint of bitter fruit and clear acid.*	£11.00 JSM
PALAZZO DELLA TORRE 2001, ALLEGRINI **VENETO** – *A big chewy wine with cherry, plum fruit. Spicy, raisiny undertones give a satisfying complexity on the palate.*	£13.30 WIDELY AVAILABLE

VENETO + NE RED GOLD / SILVER

GRANDARELLA 2001, MASI AGRICOLA VENETO – *Beltingly concentrated and packing a punch. Crammed with chocolate and cassis. Roll on, indigenous grapes of Italy.*	**£16.10** VIT/NYW BWC
ALTEO AMARONE DELLA VALPOLICELLA CLASSICO 1999, FASOLI GINO VENETO – *Sweet richness and a ripe touch of integrated oak. Full of black-cherry fruit and dried fruit flavour.*	**£27.00** VRT
BOSAN AMARONE DELLA VALPOLICELLA 1998, GERARDO CESARI VENETO – *Ripe fruit, soft tannins, and deep velvet tannins. Primary fruit is giving way to farmy, raisiny, meaty flavours.*	**£37.30** AFI

SILVER
VENETO + NORTHEAST RED

☆ **TEROLDEGO ROTALIANO RISERVA 2000, MEZZACORONA** TRENTINO-ALTO ADIGE – *Freshly picked tobacco leaves, cloves, and cassis. Silky Morello cherries and wood on the palate with a lingering finish.*	**£6.80** CEB/UNS BWC
☆ **LISON PRAMAGGIORE REFOSCO DAL PEDUNCOLO ROSSO VALENTINO PALADIN 2003, PALADIN & PALADIN** VENETO – *Crimson in colour, perfumed cherries with hints of caramel and chocolate. Velvety and well-balanced.*	**£7.50** CMB
LA GROLA 2001, ALLEGRINI VENETO – *Sweet cherry fruit leads through to a balanced, blackcurrant-imbued palate enveloped in a dark cloak of rich oak.*	**£14.00** WIDELY AVAILABLE
AMARONE DELLA VALPOLICELLA CLASSICO 1999, FRATELLI BOLLA VENETO – *Intense nose of fig and molasses. The palate is deep and velvety with lush blueberry fruit allied to silky tannins.*	**£17.00** MCT
MERLOT RONC DI SUBULE 2001, RONCHI DI MANZANO FRIULI-VENEZIA GIULIA – *Deep colour and rich tannins. Delicious toast, chocolate, sous bois, and cherry characteristics. Grippy. Feral. Persistent. Very complex.*	**£18.00** VIN
LE ORIGINI AMARONE CLASSICO 1998, FRATELLI BOLLA VENETO – *A pungent damson, fig and meaty nose. The palate is savoury, punchy, and rich with juicy tannins.*	**£19.00** WPR

226 VENETO + NE RED SILVER / BRONZE

AMARONE 2000, ALPHA ZETA VENETO – *Densely structured and full-blooded. Walnut and oak aromas. The palate sports chewy, oaky fruit and a raspberry finish.*	**£19.80** NRW/CCS MOV/NYW LIB/FLY
CORTEFORTE AMARONE CLASSICO DELLA VALPOLICELLA 1998, CORTEFORTE VENETO – *Dried berry, truffle, and tar aromas. Rounded palate with velvety mouthfeel, lush fruit, and integrated tannins. Powerful finish.*	**£22.50** SMC
FALASCO AMARONE DELLA VALPOLICELLA 2000, VALPANTENA VENETO – *A complex bouquet of pepper, dried and soft fruits, with hints of cedar and tobacco and a long, clean finish.*	**£23.20** VIT/NYW ENO
VIGNETTI DI JAGO AMARONE CLASSICO DELLA VALPOLICELLA 1998, CANTINE SOCIALE VALPOLICELLA VENETO – *Developed raisin and blueberry aromas. Excellent ripe tannic structure and a lush damson finish.*	**£27.80** BRA
AMARONE DELLA VALPOLICELLA CLASSICO 2000, ALLEGRINI VENETO – *Intoxicating and inviting. Spicy, dried fruits on the nose. Sweet, dried fruits, tobacco, leather, spices, and exhilerating tannins.*	**£31.60** WIDELY AVAILABLE
LA POJA 2000, ALLEGRINI VENETO – *Medicinal notes linger above cedar and ripe cherries on the nose. High tannins drive the ripe plums palate.*	**£38.00** WIDELY AVAILABLE
RECIOTO DELLA VALPOLICELLA CLASSICO 2001, TOMMASO BUSSOLA VENETO – *Black-cherries, dark chocolate, and red cedar. This structured wine has elements of liquorice and sun-warmed bales of straw.*	**£46.00** VIT/NYW

BRONZE
VENETO + NORTHEAST RED

RUVELLO CABERNET SAUVIGNON PASSITO 2000, CANTINA DI SOAVE VENETO – *Its maturity is displayed in its tawny, garnet hue. Spicy oak, ripe fruit, and a mellow, lingering finish.*	**£6.00** ASD
SARTORI VIGNETI DI MONTEGRADELLA VALPOLICELLA CLASSICO SUPERIORE 2001, SARTORI VENETO – *Dark and brooding, the balanced, rounded palate is crammed with creamy black-cherry fruits, and finishes long.*	**£6.00** IWS/TOS

VENETO + NE RED BRONZE

CAPITEL DEI NICALÒ VALPOLICELLA CLASSICO SUPERIORE 2001, TEDESCHI VENETO – *Vivid and velvety, with wild cherry richness and silky tannins. The finish is long.*	**£6.30** WOI/SOM
ASDA EXTRA SPECIAL VALPOLICELLA RIPASSO 2001, SARTORI VENETO – *Inky black with some maturity, enticing aromas of cocoa and mocha leading into some concentrated richness.*	**£8.00** ASD
SARTORI REGOLO 2000, SARTORI VENETO – *Fine balance, where ripe fruit and hints of chocolate sit happily alongside a gentle dose of oak.*	**£8.00** IWS/UNS
CAPO DI TORBE VALPOLICELLA CLASSICO SUPERIORE 2001, FRATELLI BOLLA VENETO – *A lighter style of Valpolicella with a fresh, elegant palate showing some spicy and vegetal complexity.*	**£9.00** MCT
CONTI NERI RIPASSO VALPOLICELLA CLASSICO 2001, TENIMENTI ASSOCIATI VENETO – *A savoury wine with much complexity. Spices, raisins, and cocoa mingle with intense fruit and a fresh finish.*	**£9.00** LAI
MERLOT ISONZO DEL FRIULI 2001, I FEUDI DI ROMANS FRIULI-VENEZIA GIULIA – *A complex nose of violets, blueberries, and earthy plums and a streamlined palate with coffee and chocolate.*	**£9.00** V&C/LIB FLY
MERLOT CAMPO CAMINO BOSCO DEL MERLO 2001, PALADIN & PALADIN VENETO – *A light, slightly leafy nose with hints of liquorice leads to a medium-bodied style of Merlot, with pleasant, plummy fruit and a violet lift on the finish.*	**£9.50** CMB
MARA VALPOLICELLA VINO DA RIPASSO 2001, GERARDO CESARI VENETO – *Chocolate aromas. Elegant, succulent and rich, with a firm tannic backbone and good length.*	**£9.60** AFI
BARDOLINO CLASSICO SUPERIORE LE OLLE 2002, LENOTTI VENETO – *A riotous blend of juicy raspberries, strawberries and cherries follow aromas of dark chocolate and sweet black-cherry.*	**£10.00** MON
VALPOLICELLA CLASSICO SUPERIORE DI RIPASSO 2000, CORTE RUGOLIN VENETO – *Traditionally styled and drinking beautifully now, this ripasso has a balanced sweet fruit palate of length and elegance.*	**£12.70** BBR

AMARONE CLASSICO DELLA VALPOLICELLA DOMINI VENETI 2000, CANTINE SOCIALE VALPOLICELLA VENETO – *Exotic and savoury. Stewed fruit and tobacco mix with spicy prunes, ginger, and cinnamon. A rich, grainy finish.*	£13.00 BRA
FALASCO VALPOLICELLA RIPASSO 2002, VALPANTENA VENETO – *Young and strident, with intense flavours of plums, currants and raisins alongside well-integrated oak and a dash of spice.*	£13.00 VIT/ENO
CASTERNA AMARONE DELLA VALPOLICELLA CLASSICO 2000, PASQUA VENETO – *Light and modern with walnut and dried fruit aromas. A fresh, ripe palate with a pleasant, long finish.*	£15.00 PLB
CRESO CABERNET SAUVIGNON 1999, FRATELLI BOLLA VENETO – *Bitter black cherry and cloves on the palate. Velvety smooth, compact, and structured. Developed characteristics of sweet tobacco, earth, and wet leaves.*	£15.00 MCT
BOTTEGA VINAI TRENTINO LAGREIN DUNKEL 2001, CAVIT TRENTINO-ALTO ADIGE – *Ruby colour. Blackberries, beetroot, and nutmeg rise from the glass. Liquorice hints lurk within the grippy tannic structure.*	£15.20 MER
AMARONE DELLA VALPOLICELLA CLASSICO DOC 2000, TEDESCHI VENETO – *Forest complexity on the nose, with truffle, mushroom, and stewed fruit. The palate is spicy with sweet fruit.*	£17.60 BNK/FFW WOI/WPR EVI/CVE
MASO TORESELLA TRENTINO ROSSO 2000, CAVIT TRENTINO-ALTO ADIGE – *Leafy and mouthfilling, with cassis, spice, and vanilla on the nose. Full-bodied palate and a perfumed finish.*	£18.20 MER
LE VIGNE AMARONE DELLA VALPOLICELLA 2001, VALPANTENA VENETO – *Intense damson and raisin palate leads to a rich palate heavy on fruit and tannin. Good length and complexity.*	£19.00 NYW/ENO
QUATTRO VICARIATI TRENTINO ROSSO 1998, CAVIT TRENTINO-ALTO ADIGE – *Bottle age has encouraged animal, earthy notes on the nose. Fresh acidity balances the mature fruit. Long finish.*	£20.30 MER

SEAL OF APPROVAL
VENETO + NORTHEAST RED

☆ **SOMERFIELD VALPOLICELLA NV, PASQUA** **VENETO** – *Firm black-cherry fruit, mouthwatering acidity and scents of Christmas cake.*	£3.00 SMF
☆ **MHV VINO DA TAVOLA ROSSO NV, SARTORI** **VENETO** – *Raspberries scented with a handful of sweet spice powder.*	£3.50 MHV
☆ **SOMERFIELD BARDOLINO NV, PASQUA** **VENETO** – *Ripe redcurrants dusted with understated perfume of Indian spice.*	£4.00 SMF

SILVER
VENETO + NORTHEAST SPARKLING

☆ **RUGGERI SANTO STEFANO 2003, RUGGERI** **VENETO** – *Straw yellow, with an inviting nose of lemons and sweetly ripe apples. Soft-textured delicate fruit lingers on the finish.*	£10.50 V&C/VIT NYW/ENO

BRONZE
VENETO + NORTHEAST SPARKLING

☆ **RUGGERI QUARTESE 2003, RUGGERI** **VENETO** – *Fine mousse, a nose of marzipan and fresh hedgerow flowers. The palate has delicate yet zingy apple fruit.*	£9.90 DOD/V&C

SILVER
VENETO + NORTHEAST SWEET

TORCOLATO BREGANZE 2000, B BARTOLOMEO DA BREGANZE **VENETO** – *Deep lemon yellow. The nose is perfumed with caramelised bananas and sweet apples. Intense and luscious. Voluptuous.*	▲£16.00 FLW

BRONZE
VENETO + NORTHEAST SWEET

Wine	Price
COLLEZIONE DI CAVIT VENDEMMIA TARDIVA TRENTINO 2001, CAVIT Trentino-Alto Adige – *Candied lemon scents hover above the intense, unctuous, honeyed palate, which has sweet flowers and chunky marmalade flavours.*	▲£18.00 MER
COLLEZIONE DI CAVIT ARÈLE TRENTINO VIN SANTO 1995, CAVIT Trentino-Alto Adige – *Attractive walnut brown colour. Dates, sultanas and figs scent the nose of this wine. Bright acidity.*	▲£35.00 NRW

SILVER
TUSCANY + CENTRAL WHITE

Wine	Price
☆ **VERDICCHIO DEI CASTELLI DI JESI CLASSICO 2003, MONCARO** Marche – *Beautiful ruby grapefruit and pale-fleshed peach scents on the nose. Mouthcoating texture and lengthy finish.*	£4.30 WTS
VIN SANTO DI CAPEZZANA RISERVA 1998, TENUTA DI CAPEZZANA Tuscany – *Dark and deep. Lifted and warming. Plenty of toffee and caramel, figs, and toasted nuts. Sweet and intense.*	■£23.00 BEN/GHL MOV/LIB FLY

BRONZE
TUSCANY + CENTRAL WHITE

Wine	Price
☆ **LE VELE VERDICCHIO DEI CASTELLI DI JESI CLASSICO 2003, MONCARO** Marche – *This wine displays intense lemon fruit scents and a tangy, balanced palate of citrus fruit.*	£5.00 EUW
PAOLO MASI BIANCO VERGINE 2003, MASI RENZO Tuscany – *Richly fruited with ripe peaches. The bone-dry palate has a bolt of zingy acidity. Well-made, that wine.*	£5.60 LAI
TREBBIANO D'ABRUZZO 2003, FARNESE VINI Abruzzi – *Textured and delicate, with creamy apple flavours and soft scents of oak on the nose.*	£5.60 LAI

TUSCANY + CENTRAL WHITE BRONZE / SEAL / RED TROPHY

PALLIO DI SAN FLORIANO VERDICCHIO DEI CASTELLI DI JESI CLASSICO SUPERIORE 2003, MONTE SCHIAVO MARCHE – *Pale and green-hued, with a youthful, intense, lemony character and a discernably oily texture on the off-dry palate.*	£7.00 BWC
IL TORRIONE 2003, TERRE CORTESE MONCARO MARCHE – *Alluring pink-tinged lemon yellow. Flower petals and citrus fruit rise from the nose. The palate is zingy yet restrained.*	£7.20 LAI
VERDE CA' RUPTAE VERDICCHIO DEI CASTELLI DI JESI CLASSICO SUPERIORE 2002, MONCARO MARCHE – *Elderflowers and citrus fruit spring from the nose. The mouth fills with soft, ripe, green fruit flavours.*	£9.00 EUW
MALVASIA PASSITO SOLESTE 2002, MEDICI EMILIA ROMAGNA – *A vivid nose of honey and little wild violets. The sweetly ripe palate has excellent concentration.*	▲£15.00 VIN

SEAL OF APPROVAL
TUSCANY + CENTRAL WHITE

☆ **FRASCATI SUPERIORE 2003, FRATELLI MARTINI SECONDO LUIGI** LATIUM – *Nutty aromas rise from the golden glassful of yellow-apple fruit flavours.*	£4.00 WRT
☆ **MHV ORVIETO 2003, SCHENK ITALIA** UMBRIA – *Crushed hazelnut, white apple, and pear flavours. Good balance.*	£4.00 MHV

TROPHY
TUSCANY + CENTRAL RED

SCIRUS 2001, FATTORIA LE SORGENTI TUSCANY – *Enormous, with cherry-red fruit, chewy tannins, and brambly leather. Warm mocha oak emphasises the aromatic quality.*	£.00 NOT AVAILABLE IN THE UK
BRUNELLO DI MONTALCINO 1999, POGGIO SAN POLO TUSCANY – *Big tannins and integrated acids. It is beautifully balanced with all elements in perfect harmony.*	£35.70 WIDELY AVAILABLE

GOLD
TUSCANY + CENTRAL RED

☆ **TRE UVE MONTEPULCIANO 2003, MGM MONDO DEL VINO** Abruzzi – *Intense berries and deep blackcurrant. A decent whack of oak adds a coffee, mocha weight, and tarry complexity.*	£6.00 SAF
☆ **DOGAJOLO ROSSO TOSCANO 2003, CARPINETO** Tuscany – *Full-bodied. Packed with rich black fruit and perfumed violets. Concentrated, with a complexity of fruit and oak.*	£8.60 FFW/RNS CVE/JSM
☆ **EDIZIONE 4 CINQUE AUTOCTONI NV, FARNESE** Abruzzi – *Robust, rich, ripe fruit and a great acid balance. Heaving with herbal, heather, scrub-myrtle, and intense berry fruit.*	£9.00 LAI
☆ **PAOLO MASI ERTA E CHINA 2001, MASI RENZO** Tuscany – *Stylish and buoyantly fruity, with a floral aroma and a nutmeg-tinged finish that seems to last forever.*	£9.00 LAI
☆ **VIGNA MONTEPRANDONE 2001, SALADINI PILASTRI** Marche – *Chunky, chewy and packed with ripe red-and-black fruits and well judged oak. No-holds-barred, with a promising future.*	£10.50 MOV/LIB
VINO NOBILE DI MONTEPULCIANO CERRAIA 2001, AGRICOLTORI DEL CHIANTI GEOGRAFICO Tuscany – *A floral, plummy nose with cherry notes. A chewy palate with good mid-weight, juicy fruit, and tarry tannins.*	£14.00 AFI
VILLA CAFAGGIO SAN MARTINO 2001, BASILICA CAFAGGIO Tuscany – *A concentrated plum and cherry, summer pudding fruit profile. There is also some supporting chocolate, vanilla oak.*	£26.50 EVI
MEZZOPANE 2001, POGGIO SAN POLO Tuscany – *Pure cherries and summer pudding berries over the firm, tight tannins. Solid, with a lifting flash of acidity.*	£26.60 BEN/CCS MOV/LIB FLY
BRUNELLO DI MONTALCINO RISERVA 1998, TENUTA IL POGGIONE Tuscany – *Herbal, cherry fruit. The structure stands firm in classic style with a light oak prop and firmly gripping tannins.*	£37.00 VIT/NYW ENO

TESTAMATTA 2001, BIBI GRAETZ TUSCANY – *Dark and chocolatey. Masses of plummy cherries and a hint of thyme and rosemary. A big chewy wine.*	£46.00 FWL

SILVER
TUSCANY + CENTRAL RED

☆ **PAOLO MASI SANGIOVESE 2003, MASI RENZO** TUSCANY – *Simple yet pure Morello cherry and spice; restrained and uncluttered with some richness on the finish.*	£6.00 LAI
☆ **RIPAROSSO MONTEPULCIANO D'ABRUZZO 2002, DINO ILLUMINATI** ABRUZZI – *Restrained. Has a dry, tannic, youthful mouthful of sweet cherry fruit. Complex and extraordinarily elegant. Will age beautifully.*	£7.30 DOD/FFW CVE
☆ **MONTEPULCIANO D'ABRUZZO BUCARO 2001, CANTINE VOLPI** ABRUZZI – *The fine nose is redolent of grilled cashews and the perfume of wild scrub. Dark, creamy, cherry palate.*	£7.50 VER
BRUSCO DEI BARBI 2002, FATTORIA DEI BARBI TUSCANY – *Delicious fresh cherry and strawberry aromas. The palate is linear, light, and clean with wonderful fruit purity.*	£8.00 EVI/ENO
CHIANTI CLASSICO VILLA LA PAGLIAIA 2002, VILLA LA PAGLIAIA TUSCANY – *Plump fruitcake and mulled wine aromas. Thick with cherry fruit and succulent tannins. Good weight and elegance.*	£8.40 FFW/RNS MER
CHIANTI CLASSICO BASILICA CAFAGGIO 2002, VILLA CAFAGGIO TUSCANY – *Whiffs of smoke rise from the nose. Red and black elements, with strawberries, tar, cherries, and pepper. Concentrated.*	£9.00 M&S
POLIZIANO ROSSO DI MONTEPULCIANO 2003, POLIZIANO TUSCANY – *Cherries, cranberries, and blueberries follow an intense nose of plums and raisins, and lead to a long cherry-infused finish.*	£10.30 WIDELY AVAILABLE
CHIANTI RISERVA 2001, CANTINE LEONARDO TUSCANY – *Sweet Morello cherry and cream aromas. The palate has black fruit depth and ripe tannic structure. Impressive length.*	£10.70 V&C/SOM NRW/CCS LIB/FLY

234 TUSCANY + CENTRAL RED SILVER

CAMPO CENI IGT 2002, BARONE RICASOLI Tuscany – *Perfumed berry and violet nose. Lush palate strewn with blackberry fruit. The finish is sweet and concentrated.*	£11.00 VIT/NYW ENO/JSM
MANTELLO SANGIOVESE SYRAH 2000, FRATELLI SENSI Tuscany – *Briar, leather and espresso aromas. The palate has rich fruit intensity, velvety tannins, and exceptional harmony. Concentrated finish.*	£11.00 CTL
TRE ROSE VINO NOBILE DE MONTEPULCIANO 2000, TENIMENTI ANGELINI Abruzzi – *Plenty of red-cherry fruit flavour spiked with freshly ground black pepper, thyme, and dried bay leaf aromas.*	£11.00 H&H
TERRE DI MAESTRALE 2001, MEDICI Emilia Romagna – *Bracing acidity and powerful tannins. A ripe palate of hedgerow fruits and roast nuts. Broad, characterful, and textured.*	£12.00 VIN
BROLIO CHIANTI CLASSICO 2002, CASTELLO DE BROLIO Tuscany – *Rich cherry and Dundee cake aromas. The palate shows rich black fruit, fine tannic backbone, and integrated oak.*	£12.10 DOD/VIT SOM/ENO JSM
VILLA CAFAGGIO CHIANTI CLASSICO 2002, BASILICA CAFAGGIO Tuscany – *Perfumed berry and savoury notes. Sweet damson fruit, balanced sweet tannins, and well-integrated oak.*	£13.00 EVI/WRW ODD
ROSSO DI MONTALCINO 2002, TENUTA IL POGGIONE Tuscany – *Plum and Morello cherry aromas. The spiced palate shows fruit intensity, supple tannins, and decent structure. Nice perfumed finish.*	£13.50 VIT/ENO
VILLA CAFAGGIO CHIANTI CLASSICO RISERVA 2001, BASILICA CAFAGGIO Tuscany – *Coffee, raisin, and fruitcake aromas. Wonderful plum fruit, silky tannins, and a nice touch of creamy vanilla oak.*	£15.40 EVI
VILLA DI CAPEZZANA CARMIGNANO 2000, TENUTA DI CAPEZZANA Tuscany – *Intensely fruit-driven. The vegetal notes on the nose and palate add complexity. Stewed fruit lends a lengthy, savoury finish.*	£15.40 WIDELY AVAILABLE
RIPA DELLE MORE 2001, CASTELLO VICCHIOMAGGIO Tuscany – *Structured and spicy, with leather and liquorice over the bright cherries. Deep, rich, and opaque. Elegance and stylish.*	£15.90 HOH

TUSCANY + CENTRAL RED SILVER

SAN ZIO ROSSO DI TOSCANA 2001, CANTINE LEONARDO TUSCANY – *The nose shows herb and savoury salami. The palate has damsons married to silky, prominent tannins. Spicy finish.*	**£15.90** V&C/GHL LIB/FLY
ALLEANZA 2000, CASTELLO DI GABBIANO TUSCANY – *This historic winery's offering is made in collaboration with California's Beringer. Creamy savouriness and spicy cherries dominate throughout.*	**£16.00** WFB
CA' MARCANDA PROMIS 2002, ANJELO GAJA TUSCANY – *Leafy tones and a cloak of oak. A dense carpet of cherry and dark fruits, with intense tannins.*	**£19.40** V&C/JAR
CASTELLO DI FONTERUTOLI CHIANTI CLASSICO 2000, CASTELLO DI FONTERUTOLI TUSCANY – *Juicy savoury fruit mixes with leather and apricot notes. Well-structured with damsons and plums, firm tannins, and well-integrated oak.*	**£20.80** DOD/JNW NYW/ENO
VILLA DI CORSANO ROSSO DI TOSCANA 2000, CANTINA DI MONTALCINO TUSCANY – *Concentrated. Black-stone-fruited nose and full-bodied palate. Plenty of extract well-wrapped up in majestic oak.*	**£22.70** LIB/FLY
BRUNELLO DI MONTALCINO 1999, POGGIO TEMPESTA TUSCANY – *Opulent, with a damson and cigar box nose. The truffled palate is ripe and intense with succulent blueberries.*	**£23.00** LIB
FRABUSCO 2001, TENUTA CORINI UMBRIA – *Deep, with plum and spice aromas. The palate is soft-hearted with sweet cherries, fine tannins, and creamy oak.*	**£25.00** HIL
GHIAIE DELLA FURBA 2000, TENUTA DI CAPEZZANA TUSCANY – *Complex, with marmite, oak, and dried fruits. The palate is big, with muscular tannins and plenty of backbone.*	**£25.30** WIDELY AVAILABLE
BRUNELLO DI MONTALCINO 1999, CASTELLO BANFI TUSCANY – *Succulent, with cherry and spice aromas. The palate shows lush fruit, velvety mouthfeel, and well-integrated oak and tannins.*	**£27.80** TAU/VIN MWW
CASTELLO DI BROLIO CHIANTI CLASSICO 2000, CASTELLO DI BROLIO TUSCANY – *Sweet and savoury fruit on the nose, the palate packed with attractive fruit, well-integrated oak, and soft, spicy tannins.*	**£28.50** DOD/VIT NYW/ENO

236 TUSCANY + CENTRAL RED SILVER

BRUNELLO DI MONTALCINO TENUTA NUOVA 1998, CASANOVA DI NERI Tuscany – *Complex Morello cherry, tar and damson aromas. Beautiful fruit depth and harmony with a nice lick of creamy vanilla oak.*	**£30.00** WTS
POLIZIANO VINO NOBILE DI MONTEPULCIANO ASINONE 2000, POLIZIANO Tuscany – *Delicious prunes, raisins and plum fruit, with a stone fruit intensity on the palate, allied to a hint of coconut.*	**£31.00** EDC/NYW ENO
VINO NOBILE DI MONTEPULCIANO ASINONE 2001, POLIZIANO Tuscany – *Superb balance between the wood and fruit points to a good future, with plush soft fruits balancing ripe, fine-grained tannins.*	**£31.00** EDC/V&C ENO
LE STANZE DEL POLIZIANO 2001, AZIENDA AGRICOLE POLIZIANO Tuscany – *Spicy, cedary oak on the nose, the palate is dark-cherry fruit supported by a seamless tannic structure.*	**£31.70** DOD/V&C SOM/ENO
SUMMUS SANT'ANTIMO 2000, CASTELLO BANFI Tuscany – *Mature. Prunes and currants weigh on this silky-textured wine with its fresh acidity and broad spectrum of flavour.*	**£35.00** VIN
BRUNELLO DI MONTALCINO CAMPO DEL DRAGO 1999, CASTIGLION DEL BOSCO Tuscany – *A powerful vanilla, blueberry, and savoury spice nose with an intense fruit palate showing good extraction, complexity, and balance.*	**£36.60** FFW/HOU MER
VINO NOBILE RISERVA GRANDI ANNATE 1999, AVIGNONESI Tuscany – *A dense wall of chocolate, smoky cherries, and prunes hemmed in by firm cedary tannins. Spiced with cinnamon.*	**£38.50** BEN/CCS MOV/NYW LIB/FLY
DESIDERIO 1999, AVIGNONESI Tuscany – *A fiery tannic structure dominating the leathery bramble fruit. Given time, the tannins should integrate further.*	**£38.80** WIDELY AVAILABLE
SOLENGO 2001, TENUTA DI ARGIANO Tuscany – *The nose reveals autumnal fruit. The palate has black fruits, serious tannins and a hefty dose of oak.*	**£40.70** WIDELY AVAILABLE
BRUNELLO DI MONTALCINO RISERVA POGGIO ALL'ORO 1997, CASTELLO BANFI Tuscany – *A pungent blueberry and vanilla nose. The palate shows lush cherries. Tannins are silky, the finish is harmonious.*	**£51.00** V&C/VIN

BRONZE
TUSCANY + CENTRAL RED

☆ **MONTICELLO NV, CANTINA CLITERNIA** **VINO DA TAVOLA** – *Jammy wine with currant and spice aromas. The palate is ripe with good berry fruit purity to finish.*	**£5.00** LAI
LA TORRETTA 2003, CANTINA CLITERNIA **MOLISE** – *The nose has berry richness and savoury depth. The palate has fine tannins and a harmonious finish.*	**£5.20** LAI
VILLA ICONA SANGIOVESE 2003, TERRE CORTESE MONCARO **MARCHE** – *Rich and ripe with berry and spice aromas. The palate is supple with well-integrated tannins. A clean finish.*	**£5.20** LAI
BOSCOVENTO ESINO ROSSO 2003, TERRE CORTESE MONCARO **MARCHE** – *Warm and spicy with currant and white pepper aromas. The palate has juicy fruit and gentle tannins.*	**£5.50** LAI
FARNESE MONTEPULCIANO D'ABRUZZO 2003, FARNESE **ABRUZZI** – *Fruity and very clean, with delicate, expressive strawberry fruit. A balanced and very long wine.*	**£5.90** LAI
LEONARDO CHIANTI 2003, CANTINE LEONARDO **TUSCANY** – *Juicy, with cherry and berry aromas. The palate shows pure red fruit and a lick of spice.*	**£6.50** WIDELY AVAILABLE
TENUTA DI BURCHINO CHIANTI SUPERIORE 2001, CASTELLANI **TUSCANY** – *Warm, savoury wine showing berry and thyme on the nose. A lush palate with concentrated damsons. Friendly tannins.*	**£7.00** BUC
PAOLO MASI CHIANTI 2003, MASI RENZO **TUSCANY** – *Summer fruit character. The palate is balanced, with a light tannic structure and long clean finish.*	**£7.60** LAI
VILLA VETRICE CHIANTI RUFINA RISERVA 2001, FATTORIE GALIGA E VETRICE **TUSCANY** – *Smooth, tannic and long, with piles of sweet cherry and summer strawberry fruit. Powerful and faintly savoury.*	**£7.90** G&M/ENO

TUSCANY + CENTRAL RED BRONZE

SOLO SHIRAZ 2002, CANTINE SAN MARCO Latium – Sweet berry fruit and spice. Dry grippy tannins impart balance. It has a lengthy finish.	£8.00 BUC
JORIO' MONTEPULCIANO D'ABRUZZO 2001, UMANI RONCHI Abruzzi – Ripe raspberry and coffee aromas. The palate is intense and velvety with juicy fruit and supple tannins.	£8.30 EDC/JNW ENO
PREGIO DEL CONTE ROSSO 2001, SALADINI PILASTRI Marche – Deeply coloured with sweet berry and spice aromas. The palate has fruit depth and supple tannins.	£9.00 MOV/LIB
ROSSO CONERO MARCHE FATTORIA LE TERRAZZE 2001, FATTORIA LE TERRAZZE Marche – Charry and very ripe on the nose. The palate is generous, with red berries and well-resolved tannins.	£9.00 BBR
PAOLO MASI CHIANTI RISERVA 2000, MASI RENZO Tuscany – Suave herb and pancetta notes. The palate displays savoury cherry fruit allied to a fine tannic structure.	£9.60 LAI
CIMERIO ROSSO CONERO RISERVA 2000, MONCARO Marche – The nose is quite charry, while the palate is firm-structured yet juicy. Nicely balanced with a fresh finish.	£10.00 EUW
ROCCAVIVA ROSSO PICENO SUPERIORE 2000, MONCARO Marche – Spicy with blackberry jam and black pepper aromas. The palate is warm with fruit richness and soft tannins.	£10.00 EUW
BADIA A COLTIBUONO CHIANTI CLASSICO 2001, BADIA A COLTIBUONO Tuscany – Savoury style with herb and cherry notes on the nose and lush Morello cherry fruit on the palate. Good richness to finish.	£10.30 TOS
CHIANTI CLASSICO CONTESSA DI RADDA 2001, AGRICOLTORI DEL CHIANTI GEOGRAFICO Tuscany – Taut, with toasty oak etching the black-cherry fruit. Attractive floral notes; the finish is long and powerfully tannic.	£10.80 AFI
BAROCCO MARCHE ROSSO 2000, MONCARO Marche – Fleshy wine with spiced currant and pepper aromas. The palate has good tannic structure and fruit purity.	£11.00 EUW

TUSCANY + CENTRAL RED BRONZE 239

ESIO MARCHE ROSSO 2001, MONTE SCHIAVO **MARCHE** – *The nose has violet and cherry perfume. The mouthfeel is round and structured with friendly tannins.*	**£12.00** BWC
CHIANTI CLASSICO RISERVA MONTEGIACHI DOCG 2000, AGRICOLTORI DEL CHIANTI GEOGRAFICO **TUSCANY** – *With an enticing nose of sweet, spicy fruit, minerals, and herbs; the lengthy palate offers light fruit cloaked in spice.*	**£13.00** AFI
ROBERTO STUCCHI CHIANTI CLASSICO 2001, BADIA A COLTIBUONO **TUSCANY** – *Savoury, with rich Morello cherry notes on the nose and palate. The finish has depth, harmony. Decent length.*	**£13.40** DOD/FFW WPR/CVE
MANDRONE DI LOHSA 2002, AZIENDA AGRICOLE POLIZIANO **TUSCANY** – *Well-made with a somewhat green tinge throughout. Some of the fruit dominated by oak, needing time to open up.*	**£14.50** ENO
CARPINETO VINO NOBILE DI MONTEPULCIANO RISERVA 1999, CARPINETO **TUSCANY** – *Dark, baked fruit on the nose, followed by a mouthful of plums, cherries, soft acidity, and balanced tannins.*	**£16.60** FFW/CVE
ROSSO DI MONTALCINO 2001, CASTELLO BANFI **TUSCANY** – *The nose shows berry and oak notes. The palate shows good fruit hung on supple tannic structure.*	**£17.00** VIN
POLIZIANO VINO NOBILE DI MONTEPULCIANO 2001, POLIZIANO **TUSCANY** – *A medley of nutty flavours mix with the rich dried fruit. Serious tannins and a long raisin-imbued finish.*	**£17.40** DOD/EDC JNW/V&C NYW/ENO
CAMPO DELLA MURA ROSSO PICENO SUPERIORE 2000, MONCARO **MARCHE** – *Sumptuous, with a brooding nose of black cherry and violets. A rich, velvety-textured palate with ripe black fruits.*	**£17.50** EUW
ADEODATO ROSSO CONERO 2001, MONTE SCHIAVO **MARCHE** – *Huge, showy, and toasty. A powerful palate of smoke- and vanilla-laced cherry fruit. Leather and rosemary add depth.*	**£18.00** BWC
NENFRO 2001, MOTTURA **LATIUM** – *The wild-cherry nose leads to a plum palate with a dash of nutmeg and a slight greenness.*	**£18.00** VIN

240 TUSCANY + CENTRAL RED BRONZE

VIGNETI DEL PARCO ROSSO CONERO DOC RISERVA 2000, MONCARO Marche – *Savoury, cedary notes on the nose and vigorous cherries on the palate. A rustic style of red.*	**£18.00** EUW
SANTO IPPOLITO ROSSO DI TOSCANA 2001, CANTINE LEONARDO Tuscany – *Hints of oak grace the dense palate of plums, spices and strong tannins. The finish is sweetly fruited.*	**£19.80** V&C/MOV LIB/FLY
CASTIGLION DEL BOSCO BRUNELLO DI MONTALCINO 1999, CASTIGLION DEL BOSCO Tuscany – *A leafy tone is evident, as is some development. The prune-flavoured palate possesses a resounding streak of tannin.*	**£20.30** FFW/NRW MER
CASALFERRO SANGIOVESE DI TOSCANA 2001, BARONE RICASOLI Tuscany – *Morello cherry and bay leaf nose. Harmonious, with a long, savoury finish.*	**£24.90** WIDELY AVAILABLE
BRUNELLO DI MONTALCINO IL POGGIONE 1999, TENUTA IL POGGIONE Tuscany – *Savoury nose showing herb and Morello cherry notes. The deep palate is intense with subtle oak and ripe tannins.*	**£25.40** V&C/VIT WSO/ENO
BARBI BRUNELLO DI MONTALCINO 1998, FATTORIA DEI BARBI Tuscany – *The nose shows complex spice and cedar aromas. The palate is deep and lush with a creamy finish.*	**£25.70** V&C/ENO
VILLA CAFAGGIO CORTACCIO 2001, BASILICA CAFAGGIO Tuscany – *Fresh acidity and some sour cherry character. With sufficient body and balanced weight of fruit to improve with time.*	**£27.50** EVI
FLACCIANELLO DELLA PIEVE 2000, TENUTA FONTODI Tuscany – *Black cherries and well-charred oak on the nose. The chewy palate shows fine acidity and spicy, savoury fruit.*	**£32.90** WIDELY AVAILABLE
FONTALLORO 2000, FELSINA BERARDENGA Tuscany – *A delicious, creamy, savoury nose with a tightly-structured palate. Cherry, plum, and damson fruits, with a lingering finish.*	**£33.00** NYW/LIB
SANGIOVETO DI COLTIBUONO 1999, BADIA A COLTIBUONO Tuscany – *Complex nose with sage, berry, and coffee notes. The palate is elegant with fruit intensity and harmonious tannins.*	**£36.40** FFW/CVE

TUSCANY + CENTRAL RED BRONZE / SEAL / **ROSÉ** BRONZE

VINO NOBILE DI MONTEPULCIANO SALCO 2000, SALCHETO TUSCANY – *A delicate floral edge, where creamy purple fruits are enhanced by light notes of tar and bitter spices.*	£36.50 / L&W
TENUTA BELGUARDO 2001, TENUTA BELGUARDO TUSCANY – *A charry, oak-dominated nose, with dense black fruit behind. Powerful and ripe with a high acidity and a bitter finish.*	£41.00 / ENO
BRUNELLO DE MONTALCINO POGGIO ALLE MURA 1998, CASTELLO BANFI TUSCANY – *Intense nose showing mocha and Morello cherry notes. The rich palate is harmonious. Plenty of depth to finish.*	£50.00 / V&C/VIN

SEAL OF APPROVAL
TUSCANY + CENTRAL RED

☆ **SOMERFIELD SANGIOVESE DAUNIA NV, DONELLI VINI** TUSCANY – *Deep blackberry flavours, bay leaves, and whiffs of tar.*	£2.50 / SMF
☆ **COLLEZIONE ITALIANA MONTEPULCIANO D'ABRUZZO 2003, CASA GIRELLI** ABRUZZI – *Delicate spice, fresh cherries, plums, and hints of charcoal.*	£2.80 / ALD
☆ **MHV TUSCAN RED 2002, CASTELLANI** TUSCANY – *Blueberry and loganberry fruit flavours and hints of herbaceousness.*	£3.80 / MHV

BRONZE
TUSCANY + CENTRAL ROSÉ

MONTEPULCIANO D'ABRUZZO CERASUOLO VIGNA CORVINO 2003, AZIENDA AGRICOLA CONTESA ABRUZZI – *A balanced wine with lifted raspberry fruit flavours, crisp acidity, and a touch of creaminess.*	£6.10 / FFW/RNS MER/FLA INS

BRONZE
TUSCANY + CENTRAL FORTIFIED

☆ **BARONA BIANCO NV, WSE** – Spices and bouquet garni leaves perfume the nose. Flavours of pears and grapefruit shine on the faultless palate.	**£3.30** BNK/MHV

SILVER
SOUTH + THE ISLANDS WHITE

FIANO DI AVELLINO TERRE DI DORA 2003, TERREDORA DI PAOLO Campania – Vivid greenish hue. Intense floral aromas, pears, and apricots. The medium-bodied palate is textured, long, and perfumed. Gorgeous.	**£12.50** DOD
★ **D'ISTINTO CATTARRATO CHARDONNAY 2002,** Calatrasi – Melting butter, moist vanilla beans and citrus fruit. The crisp yet warming palate is big, balanced, concentrated, and full.	**£4.50** MRN

BRONZE
SOUTH + THE ISLANDS WHITE

☆ **INYCON CHARDONNAY 2003, CANTINE SETTESOLI** Sicily – Sweet honey and melon aromas. Some minerality graces the fleshy palate of limes and peaches.	**£5.00** TOS/WTS ENO/JSM
☆ **INYCON GRECANICO 2003, CANTINE SETTESOLI** Sicily – Celery and green melon scents and flavours. Long and refreshing, with a swathe of wild herbs.	**£5.00** ENO
INYCON FIANO 2003, CANTINE SETTESOLI Sicily – Deep gold, with a very full, ripe, aromatic nose. Zesty acidity meets butterscotch palate. Long citrus finish.	**£6.30** VIT/ENO JSM
GRECO DI TUFO LOGGIA DELLA SERRA 2003, TERREDORA Campania – A light-bodied style, with a touch of oak providing smoothness and spice. Pears and vanilla pods appear on the finish.	**£12.00** ATM

SOUTH + ISL. WHITE BRONZE / SEAL **/ RED** TROPHY / GOLD **243**

FIANO DI AVELLINO CAMPORE 2003, TERREDORA **CAMPANIA** – *A somewhat subdued tropical nose. Medium-bodied, with lively acidity, complexity, and weight. Pineapple tones.*	£12.20 ATM/HAX

SEAL OF APPROVAL
SOUTH + THE ISLANDS WHITE

☆ **IL PADRINO CATARRATO CHARDONNAY 2003, MGM MONDO DEL VINO** SICILY – *Fresh toasted almond and lemon flavours. Delicate herbal tones.*	£4.00 WTS
☆ **MHV SICILIAN WHITE 2002, CONCILIO** SICILY – *A zippy seam of acidity tears through ripe yellow-fruit flavours.*	£4.00 MHV

TROPHY
SOUTH + THE ISLANDS RED

AGLIANICO DEL VULTURE ROSSO DI COSTANZA 2001, TENUTA LE QUERCE BASILICATA – *Dark-cherry oak and intricate spice balanced by creamy, rounded oak. Impressively serious with a grippy, juicy finish.*	£21.50 ATM

GOLD
SOUTH + THE ISLANDS RED

☆ **TENUTE AL SOLE SALENTO NEGROAMARO 2001, CANTINE DUE PALME** PUGLIA – *Juicy, ripe fruit, and blackberry flavours balanced by friendly new oak flavours of spice and vanilla.*	£4.60 HAX/CTL
☆ **BRINDISI ROSSO 2001, CANTINE DUE PALME** PUGLIA – *Warm and full of fruit, with raisined notes and smoky, coffee bean complexity over a firm, tannin structure.*	£5.50 CTL/JSM
☆ **VILLA QUINZIANA 2002, CANTINE DUE PALME** PUGLIA – *Still restrained on the nose but shows promise of opening up. Brambly, leathery, peppery, and fruit flavours.*	£6.90 LAI

SILVER
SOUTH + THE ISLANDS RED

☆ **IL PADRINO SYRAH 2003, MGM MONDO DEL VINO** SICILY – *The fruit opens up beautifully on the nose, leading to an easygoing mouthful with silky black fruits.*	£5.00 SMF/ODD UWM
☆ **SALICE SALENTINO ROSSO 2002, CANTINE DUE PALME** PUGLIA – *Robust and vivid. Firm black-cherry fruit, hints of cracked pepper, and lifted acidity. Medium-full in body.*	£5.00 HAX
☆ **BRINDISI ROSSO 2002, CANTINE DUE PALME** PUGLIA – *Vibrant red- and black- summer fruits tumble from the palate. The finish has brisk acidity and firm tannins.*	£6.00 JSM/V&C
☆ **SQUINZANO ROSSO 2002, CANTINE DUE PALME** PUGLIA – *Spicebox and sweet oak on the nose. The palate's a super ripe agglomeration of dessicated cherries and blueberries.*	£6.00 L&T
☆ **IL BASSO PRIMITIVO 2003, MGM MONDO DEL VINO** PUGLIA – *Spicy red and purple fruit aromas. A rich, fleshy palate packed with soft fruit. A long, balanced finish.*	£6.30 LAI
APOLLONIO SALENTO ROSSO VALLE CUPA 2000, APOLLONIO PUGLIA – *Very appealing, clear, intense and concentrated. Medium-bodied red-cherry fruit, touches of spice, and a balanced tannic structure.*	£7.70 CCS/BOO ALL
APOLLONIO SALENTO PRIMITIVO DOC TERRAGNOLO 2000, APOLLONIO PUGLIA – *A bouquet of tobacco, cedar, and spicy, earthy aromas. A sweet, tarry palate with soft attractive fruit.*	£7.90 CCS/MOV BOO/ALL
DON ANTONIO NERO D'AVOLA 2002, MORGANTE SICILY – *Ripe blue fruits dominate the full, fleshy palate. The tannins are ripe and fine-grained. The acidity is fresh.*	£15.70 MOV/NYW LIB/FLY

BRONZE
SOUTH + THE ISLANDS RED

☆ **ANCORA BENEVENTANO ROSSO 2003, ADRIA VINI** CAMPANIA – *Ripe nose showing dark fruit and savoury spice aromas. The palate is rich and velvety with decent structure.*	**£4.00** FFW/NRW MER/BOO INS
☆ **MHV SICILIAN RED 2000, CONCILIO** SICILY – *Spice and nutmeg flavours add an exotic allure, with its sweet bramble fruit and tightly structured palate.*	**£4.00** MHV
☆ **CO-OP PUGLIA PRIMITIVO/SANGIOVESE 2002, MGM** PUGLIA – *The Sangiovese adds an earthy touch to the spicy fruit on this light-bodied Primitivo.*	**£4.50** CWS
☆ **ZAGARA NERO D'AVOLA CABERNET 2003, CONCILIO** SICILY – *Delightful figgy flavours join the raisined fruit on the palate, accompanied by good acidity and dry tannins.*	**£4.50** IWS
☆ **ZAGARRA NERO D'AVOLA SANGIOVESE 2003, CONCILIO** SICILY – *Exuberant, with vibrant blue fruit on the nose and spice accompanying the fresh berry and cherry fruit.*	**£4.50** IWS/SMF
☆ **INYCON MERLOT 2003, SETTESOLI** SICILY – *An easygoing Merlot, this wine has nice fruit on a sleek body with matching acidity and a pleasant finish.*	**£5.00** TOS/ENO
☆ **MEZZOMONDO NEGROAMARO SALENTO 2003, MGM MONDO DEL VINO** PUGLIA – *The nose is pronounced with baked fruit and spice aromas. The palate is rich and ripe with a savoury finish.*	**£5.00** WTS
☆ **TRULLI SALICE SALENTINO 2001, CANTELE** PUGLIA – *The heady jam and smoke nose leads to a savoury palate thick with ripe black fruit. Powerful finish.*	**£5.00** WAV
ACCADEMIA DEL SOLE CABERNET SAUVIGNON SHIRAZ 2003, CALATRASI – *Perfume of violets and ripe cherries. Ripe fruit flavours are supported by refreshing acidity and grippy tannins.*	**£6.00** SMF

ITALIAN SOUTH + THE ISLANDS RED BRONZE

VERETO ROSSO SALICE SALENTINO 2001, AGRICOLE VALLONE PUGLIA – Earthy wine with tar, jam, and ripe berry aromas. The palate is thick and supple with lots of spicy fruit intensity.	**£6.10** WIDELY AVAILABLE
POTENZA PRIMITIVO 2003, MGM MONDO DEL VINO PUGLIA – The wine's spicy cherry and plum aromas lead to a fruity palate, supported by grippy tannins.	**£6.60** LAI
PILLASTRO PRIMITIVO 2002, CANTINE DUE PALME PUGLIA – Dark and dense, this offers spice, plums, chocolate and oak on the nose. A rich, sweet, soft-fruited palate.	**£6.80** LAI
TENUTA ALBRIZZI 2002, CANTINE DUE PALME PUGLIA – Cabernet Sauvignon mixes well with Primitivo, as the spicy, savoury aromas dance off the sweet, black-cherry palate.	**£6.80** LAI
FORTIUM SALICE SALENTINO 2002, CANTINE DUE PALME PUGLIA – A pungent mulberry, vanilla, and baked earth nose. The intense palate has fruit married to sturdy tannins.	**£7.00** LAI
ORIGIN SYRAH 2002, MENINI SICILY – Raspberry confit nose. Fresh, with sweet juicy fruit and a firm, rather dry finish.	**£7.00** THS
SELVAROSSA SALICE SALENTINO ROSSO DOC RESERVA SPECIALE 2000, CANTINE DUE PALME PUGLIA – A pronounced cherry and spice nose. The palate is thick with ripe fruit. The long finish is savoury.	**£8.00** HAX
NERO D'AVOLA 2003, MORGANTE SICILY – Figs and mocha dominate an opulent nose. A soft, creamy-textured palate with spicy oak. A balanced, tight structure.	**£8.10** CEC/DOD MOV/NYW LIB/FLY
AGLIANICO IRPINIA 2003, TERREDORA CAMPANIA – Savoury wine with notes of bay and red meat. The palate is thick and spicy with a long powerful finish.	**£9.50** ATM
VIRTUOSO PRIMITIVO DI PUGLIA 2001, CASA GIRELLI PUGLIA – Hints of smoke and eucalyptus join on the nose, leading to a sweet, berry-fruited palate with firm tannins.	**£9.50** EVI/ODD

SOUTH + THE ISLANDS RED BRONZE / SEAL 247

VIRTUOSO SYRAH DI SICILIA 2001, CASA GIRELLI **SICILY** – *A spicy, berry, oak-infused nose. Powerful dark fruit on the palate and strong but soft tannins.*	**£10.00** VLW/☆&R
CANNONAU DI SARDEGNA SELEZIONE 2000, SANTA MARIA LA PALMA **SARDINIA** – *Intense spicebox and celeriac aromas. Medicinal hints lift the intriguing palate of blackberries and oak.*	**£10.50** MON
IL PRINCIPIO AGLIANICO IRPINIA 2001, TERREDORA **CAMPANIA** – *Deep wine with aromas of red-cherries and spice. Mouth-filling with lush damson fruit and a savoury finish.*	**£11.00** ATM
IL FALCONE RISERVA CASTEL DEL MONTE 2001, RIVERA **PUGLIA** – *Full-bodied, with a ruby red colour and an array of black stone fruits, peppers, and spice.*	**£13.00** MON
CABÁNICO ALOVINI BASILICATA 2001, ALOVINI **BASILICATA** – *This Aglianico-Cabernet blend yields violets and plums on the nose and a lingering smoky finish.*	**£15.00** CVE
MORGANA ALTA SALICE SALENTINO RISERVA 2000, LI VELI **PUGLIA** – *Inky, with rich blackberry and cinnamon aromas. The palate is spiced with creamy vanilla notes and juicy fruit.*	**£21.00** LIB
IL PATRIGLIONE IGT DEL SALENTO 1997, COSIMO TAURINO **PUGLIA** – *Deep, with burnt earth, raisin, and blackberry aromas. The palate is thick and ripe with a powerful finish.*	**£24.80** FFW/CVE

SEAL OF APPROVAL
SOUTH + THE ISLANDS RED

☆ **ROSSO DI PUGLIA 2003, CANTELE** **PUGLIA** – *Dark prunes, black cherries, mulberries, and hints of loam.*	**£3.50** IWS

NEW ZEALAND

Proving that it's not a one-trick pony, New Zealand is now making a growing range of wines that have nothing to do with Sauvignon Blanc. Of course, there are plenty of examples of that grape among the awards below, but there are great Rieslings, Chardonnays, and Gewürztraminers among the whites and Pinot Noirs, Cabernet Sauvignons, Merlots, Syrahs, and even Zinfandels among the reds. As elsewhere in the New World, regionality is increasingly important, but there are also some delicious multi-regional blends. Notice too, the success of the Villa Maria Pinot Noir which is one of a number of award-winning screwcap-sealed New Zealand wines.

TROPHY
NEW ZEALAND WHITE

WAIRAU RESERVE SAUVIGNON BLANC 2003, SAINT CLAIR ESTATE MARLBOROUGH – *Weighty, shimmering ripe fruit. This is a great example of the voluptuous, vivid Kiwi style. Grass and gooseberry notes.*	£13.00 CVE

GOLD
NEW ZEALAND WHITE

☆ **OLD RIVER RIESLING 2002, CAIRNBRAE WINES** MARLBOROUGH – *Razor acidity offsets the off-dry, minerally palate with its lemon and lime flavours. Fragrant, bright, and peachy.*	£8.00 UNS/NYW
☆ **PRIVATE BIN SAUVIGNON BLANC 2003, VILLA MARIA** MARLBOROUGH – *Fantastically herbaceous, its rich gooseberry and new-mown hay elements paired with a touch of asparagus. Just off dry.*	£8.00 WIDELY AVAILABLE
☆ **RIVERVIEW HAWKE'S BAY CHARDONNAY 2000, MORTON ESTATE WINES** HAWKE'S BAY – *Mineral Chardonnay with austere grapefruit and citrus peel flavours. Toasty new wood provides rich, modern vanilla. Superbly made.*	£9.20 CEB/VIT TWM NYW BWC/NZH

NEW ZEALAND WHITE GOLD / SILVER

☆ **MARLBOROUGH CHARDONNAY 2002, ISABEL ESTATE** MARLBOROUGH – *Ripe, peachy, tangy fruit and rich buttery oak. Spicy overtones and a ripe nutty complexity of oak and fruit.*	£12.00 WIDELY AVAILABLE
☆ **RESERVE CLIFFORD BAY SAUVIGNON BLANC 2003, VILLA MARIA** MARLBOROUGH – *Rich, ripe, and earthy. Evolved smoky notes and primary whitecurrant fruit. Pepper nuances. Sturdy fruit tannins. Long finish.*	£12.00 UNS/VGN ODD

SILVER
NEW ZEALAND WHITE

☆ **OYSTER BAY CHARDONNAY 2002, OYSTER BAY WINES** MARLBOROUGH – *Stylish, with flint, citrus, and biscuit aromas. The palate is tightly structured with depth and mineral complexity. Balanced.*	£6.80 UNS/NRW JSM/MWW
☆ **PRIVATE BIN EAST COAST CHARDONNAY 2003, VILLA MARIA** EAST COAST – *Clean, zingy, and packed with fruit, this lemony, floral, fresh, mineral wine pushes all the right buttons.*	£6.90 UNS/FEN WTS/ODD JSM/NZH
☆ **MARLBOROUGH SAUVIGNON BLANC 2002, GIESEN WINES** MARLBOROUGH – *Asparagus and gooseberries dance on the nose. Mineral hints and a fine mellow mouthfeel last forever.*	£7.00 TOS
☆ **KONRAD SAUVIGNON BLANC 2003, KONRAD & CO WINES** MARLBOROUGH – *Light gooseberry aromas. An attack of dry, fresh, balanced, medium-bodied classic varietal green fruit flavour on the palate.*	£7.50 DUN
RESERVE MARLBOROUGH CHARDONNAY 2002, MONTANA WINES MARLBOROUGH – *Restrained yet rich, with complex oak and melon flavour elements duetting on the energetic, ripe, soft, and buttery palate.*	£8.00 WTS/ODD JSM MWW NZH
CANTERBURY HOUSE CHARDONNAY 2002, CANTERBURY HOUSE WINERY CANTERBURY – *Clear flavours of lemons, lychees, guava, and kiwi. Laced with sweet vanilla pod aromas. Vivid and very elegant.*	£9.00 NZD
MARLBOROUGH SAUVIGNON BLANC 2003, VIDAL ESTATE MARLBOROUGH – *Noticeable currant leaf notes on the tropical nose and palate. Crisply balanced, with good New Zealand typicity.*	£9.00 VGN

250 NEW ZEALAND WHITE SILVER

PALLISER SAUVIGNON BLANC 2003, PALLISER ESTATE **MARTINBOROUGH** – *This nectar has a classic, pungent nose of grass and gooseberry fruit. Dry, with zingy acidity and a restrained quality.*	**£9.00** HOU/WSO NYW/J&B NZH
BOYSZONE VINEYARD MARLBOROUGH PINOT GRIS 2003, KIM CRAWFORD **MARLBOROUGH** – *Spices and citrus command the nose. An array of flowers, herbs, and key limes appears on the palate.*	**£9.20** WIDELY AVAILABLE
BLACK LABEL RIESLING 2003, ESK VALLEY **HAWKE'S BAY** – *Many layers of juicy apple fruit unfold on the palate. Fresh and ripe, with a hint of honey.*	**£9.50** VIT/FLA
CLIIFORD BAY SAUVIGNON BLANC 2003, CLIFFORD BAY ESTATE **MARLBOROUGH** – *Straw yellow, with intense asparagus aromas. The palate is a rounded array of candied lemons, green peas, and spangly gooseberry fruit.*	**£9.80** FRI
MATUA VALLEY JUDD ESTATE CHARDONNAY 2002, BERINGER BLASS **GISBORNE** – *Voluptuous, with a buttercream nose and textured citrus and guava fruit holding its own against the generous oak.*	**£10.00** NYW
RESERVE WAIRAU SAUVIGNON BLANC 2003, VILLA MARIA **MARLBOROUGH** – *Wairau Reserve is special. It has restraint, but then bursts out into crunchy citrus with a touch of spice.*	**£10.00** FEN/NYW JSM/MWW NZH
VIDAL RESERVE CHARDONNAY 2002, VIDAL ESTATE **HAWKE'S BAY** – *Complex, with good aromatics on the nose and a refined palate which shows ripe fruit, sweet oak, and piercing acidity.*	**£10.00** LBS /WIM VKY/DBY
OMAKA RESERVE CHARDONNAY 2002, SAINT CLAIR ESTATE **MARLBOROUGH** – *The tropical clementine and peach fruit is sweetly ripe and rich. Smoke, oatmeal, and butter unfurl on the nose.*	**£11.80** FFW/VIT NYW/CVE NZH
SINGLE VINEYARD SEDDON SAUVIGNON BLANC 2003, VILLA MARIA **MARLBOROUGH** – *The quince nose is acrid and ripe. The palate features lush melons and a long finish.*	**£12.00** WIM/DBY LBS/VKY
SINGLE VINEYARD FLETCHER CHARDONNAY 2002, VILLA MARIA **MARLBOROUGH** – *Clear, vibrant, elegant white-fleshed fruit flavours merge with powerful butterscotch oak. Rich, tropical, and vivid green-gold.*	**£15.00** V&C

NEW ZEALAND WHITE SILVER / BRONZE

ESK VALLEY RESERVE CHARDONNAY 2002, ESK VALLEY HAWKE'S BAY – *Complex noisette, butter, and citrus elements. The palate is rich yet zesty. The finish displays power and admirable persistence.*	**£15.20** VIT/FLA NZH
MARGRAIN GEWURZTRAMINER 2002, BOUTIQUE WINE OF NEW ZEALAND WAIRARAPA – *Concentrated and full-bodied, with a bold lychee, cream, and baked apple fruit character. Powerful alcohol and significant length.*	**£16.00** BWN
ULTIMO GISBORNE CHARDONNAY 2002, RONGOPAI WINES GISBORNE – *Vanilla pod aromatics. The palate is a lime-green glassful of grapefruit and guava fruit bearing a jolt of acidity.*	**£20.00** SGL

BRONZE
NEW ZEALAND WHITE

MATUA VALLEY CHARDONNAY 2003, BERINGER BLASS GISBORNE – *Pineapples and lime juice nose; the light-bodied palate is a crisp yet ripe array of citrus flavours.*	**£6.00** TOS
MARLBOROUGH SAUVIGNON BLANC 2003, MONTANA MARLBOROUGH – *Gooseberryish and nettley in style, with citrus and tropical fruit complexity on the saturated palate.*	**£6.20** WIDELY AVAILABLE
CO-OP EXPLORERS VINEYARD SAUVIGNON BLANC 2003, SAINT CLAIR ESTATE MARLBOROUGH – *Crisp apple fruit and piercingly bright acidity make a good structure for the classic gooseberry palate.*	**£6.50** CWS
FAIRLEIGH ESTATE SINGLE VINEYARD CHARDONNAY 2002, WITHER HILLS MARLBOROUGH – *Lanolin and grapefruit scents. The mouth is filled with big buttery citrus, whilst the finish has a hint of hay.*	**£7.00** MWW
MATUA VALLEY MARLBOROUGH SAUVIGNON BLANC 2003, BERINGER BLASS MARLBOROUGH – *Clean, green, and fresh, its bright citrus fruit palate possessing a jagged grassy edge. Zesty, with very good typicity.*	**£7.00** TOS
STONELEIGH MARLBOROUGH RIESLING 2003, MONTANA WINES MARLBOROUGH – *A powerful nose of freshest lemons and barley sugar, and a palate that's rich without being too sweet.*	**£7.00** AD1

NEW ZEALAND WHITE BRONZE

STONELEIGH MARLBOROUGH SAUVIGNON BLANC 2003, MONTANA WINES Marlborough – Bright delicate hue. Ripe sticky ochre physalis radiates from the nose. Slightly savoury, balanced, and fresh.	£7.00 AD1
PRIVATE BIN RIESLING 2003, VILLA MARIA Marlborough – Honeydew melon and lemon sherbet on the nose. The palate has clear, balanced, plentiful, and weighty lime fruit flavour.	£7.30 HOU/FEN EVI/WTS NZH
MARLBOROUGH SAUVIGNON BLANC 2003, BABICH WINES Marlborough – Delicate green hue. Marjoram hints rise above the mouthwatering ruby grapefruit and gooseberry flavours.	£7.80 FEN/EVI G&M/NZH
PREMIUM SELECTION SAUVIGNON BLANC 2003, SELAKS Marlborough – Delicate green bell pepper and rich pungent asparagus flavours and scents meld. Seamless, rich and very classy.	£7.80 SGL
PRIVATE BIN MARLBOROUGH CHARDONNAY 2003, VILLA MARIA Marlborough – Clean and fresh with bright citrus and melon fruit. The palate is balanced with good acidity.	£7.90 HOU/UNS ODD/NZH
CO-OP EXPLORERS VINEYARD CHARDONNAY RESERVE 2001, SAINT CLAIR ESTATE Marlborough – Fine white and yellow fruit flavours fill the mouth. Coconut and vanilla scents.	£8.00 CWS
RESERVE EAST COAST VINEYARD SELECTION GEWURZTRAMINER 2003, MONTANA WINES East Coast – Fruit salad scents and mouthwatering flavours. Approachable and dry, with a delicately spiced finish.	£8.00 WTS
RESERVE SAUVIGNON BLANC 2003, MONTANA WINES Marlborough – The green-hued, velvety palate has white guava fruit and freshly shelled green pea flavours.	£8.00 BNK/ODD MWW NZH
SHEPHERDS RIDGE CHARDONNAY 2002, WITHER HILLS VINEYARDS Marlborough – Elegant wine showing fresh lemon zest on the nose. The palate is buttery with good balance and refreshing acidity.	£8.00 M&S
RESERVE DRY RIESLING 2003, SHERWOOD ESTATE Marlborough – Pale hue. Perfume of rose, nutmeg, and citrus. The bright velvet white peach palate is underscored by minerality.	£8.20 CCS/NYW INS/ALL

NEW ZEALAND WHITE BRONZE 253

THE STONES SAUVIGNON BLANC 2003, CAIRNBRAE WINES MARLBOROUGH – *Pronounced and intense, with asparagus, currant leaf and gooseberry fruit layers and a light smoky touch for added interest.*	**£8.30** SOM/NYW
ALLAN SCOTT PRESTIGE SAUVIGNON BLANC 2003, ALLAN SCOTT WINES MARLBOROUGH – *Ripe and concentrated, with creamy tropical fruit and an attractive lush palate. Very fresh fruit with persistence.*	**£8.50** BNK/FLA
WITHER HILLS SAUVIGNON BLANC 2003, BRENT MARRIS MARLBOROUGH – *Mangoes and crunchy fresh green bean aromas rise from the glass. Sweetly ripe, with a tart lift on the finish.*	**£8.60** ESL/VIT ODD/NZH
PALLISER RIESLING 2003, PALLISER ESTATE MARTINBOROUGH – *Ripe, full-bodied mouthful of lime skin, flint and lemon oil. Excellent concentration without veering into over-sweetness.*	**£8.70** WSO/NYW J&B/NZH
ESK VALLEY SAUVIGNON BLANC 2003, ESK VALLEY MARLBOROUGH – *Appley and lemony with a mineral hint and restrained elegance. Light, with a soft palate and clean acidity.*	**£8.80** HOU/LAI VIT/FLA NZH
BARREL FERMENTED CHARDONNAY 2002, BLACK BARN VINEYARDS HAWKE'S BAY – *This is a coconut- and lemon-scented wine with soft, pleasing, open-textured, pippy appeal. Creamy and moreish.*	**£8.90** MUW
MARLBOROUGH SAUVIGNON BLANC 2003, KIM CRAWFORD MARLBOROUGH – *A resounding thwack of guava fruit and blackcurrant leaves. A real crowd-pleaser, with splendid length.*	**£8.90** WIDELY AVAILABLE
CELLAR SELECTION MARLBOROUGH CHARDONNAY 2002, VILLA MARIA MARLBOROUGH – *Biscuity and complex. Lots of mandarin orange flavours and toasty oak on nose and palate.*	**£9.00** NYW/ODD NZH
KOTARE SAUVIGNON BLANC 2003, RIVERSLEIGH ESTATE MARLBOROUGH – *Peaches and cream and green bean aromas on the nose. Intensely flavoured, with a pale blonde hue.*	**£9.00** CAO
MARLBOROUGH SAUVIGNON BLANC 2003, TOHU WINES MARLBOROUGH – *Subdued and herby, with a fine citrus palate, notes of gooseberry, and tea leaves. Fine acidity.*	**£9.00** CEB/NZH

NEW ZEALAND WHITE BRONZE

MARLBOROUGH VINEYARDS SAUVIGNON BLANC 2003, SACRED HILL WINES Marlborough – *Intense asparagus scents. Some minerality and a pleasing grassy element. Smooth texture. Very fresh.*	£9.00 DWL
STONELEIGH RAPAURA SERIES MARLBOROUGH CHARDONNAY 2001, MONTANA WINES Marlborough – *Sweet pears, new wood, and spicebox aromatics meld with ripe fresh banana and nectarine fruit flavours.*	£9.00 AD1
STONELEIGH RAPAURA SERIES MARLBOROUGH SAUVIGNON BLANC 2002, MONTANA WINES Marlborough – *Warming nose, and a full-bodied palate of concentrated, sweetly ripe green fruit. Very fresh finish.*	£9.00 AD1
COLEFIELD HAWKE'S BAY SAUVIGNON BLANC 2003, MORTON ESTATE WINES Hawke's Bay – *Grassy, tropical profile, with plenty of green crunchy Granny Smith apple fruit on the nose and palate.*	£9.10 VIT/FEN NYW/BWC NZH
WITHER HILLS CHARDONNAY 2002, BRENT MARRIS Marlborough – *Full and round, with butterscotch roundness and lemon fruit. Pears, sherbet, green berries, and flowers entwine on the nose.*	£9.10 ESL/VIT ODD/NZH
BLACK LABEL CHARDONNAY 2002, ESK VALLEY Hawke's Bay – *Lively and fresh with citrus and mineral notes on the nose. The palate is restrained with ripe fruit checked by bright acidity.*	£9.20 VIT/FLA NZH
CELLAR SELECTION RIESLING 2002, VILLA MARIA Marlborough – *Just a tad off-dry, this is deliciously citric with lemon and lime notes and a keen mineral edge. Wonderfully fragrant.*	£9.20 ODD
GROVE MILL SAUVIGNON BLANC 2003, THE NEW ZEALAND WINE COMPANY Marlborough – *Fresh, crisp gooseberry fool flavours and leafy herbaceousness. Well-made, with finely tuned, keen acidity.*	£9.20 FLA/ODD NZH
MUD HOUSE CHARDONNAY 2003, MUD HOUSE Marlborough – *Ripe Comice pear juice bursts from the vivid palate, whilst cinnamon graces the nose.*	£9.20 SOM/NZH
SAINT CLAIR SAUVIGNON BLANC 2003, SAINT CLAIR ESTATE Marlborough – *Nettles and gooseberry fruit on the nose; an intense citrus palate. Structured and long, with zingy acidity.*	£9.20 WIDELY AVAILABLE

NEW ZEALAND WHITE BRONZE 255

MARLBOROUGH DRY RIESLING 2003, KIM CRAWFORD **MARLBOROUGH** – *Flowers and a touch of botrytis on the nose; a pleasantly sweet palate of ruby grapefruit and spicebox flavours.*	£9.50 WIDELY AVAILABLE
SOWMAN SAUVIGNON BLANC 2003, SOWMAN ESTATE **MARLBOROUGH** – *Bright greeny lemon yellow colour. Pronounced and dry, with a long, savoury, civilised finish. Drink now.*	£9.60 LAI
GROVE MILL CHARDONNAY 2002, THE NEW ZEALAND WINE COMPANY **MARLBOROUGH** – *Elegant cashew tones meld with vanilla beans, toast, and golden apples on nose and palate.*	£9.90 SBS/ODD SAF/WIM NZH
MELNESS RIESLING 2002, MELNESS WINES **CANTERBURY** – *Petrol and honeysuckle grace the nose; lychees and apples saturate the palate. Bright acidity. Long finish.*	£9.90 MUW
BLIND RIVER SAUVIGNON BLANC 2003, BLIND RIVER WINES **MARLBOROUGH** – *Excellent varietal definition. Fresh Cape gooseberry aromas and flavours on the balanced, zippy nose and palate.*	£10.00 ODD
BLUE RIDGE CHARDONNAY 2002, WEST BROOK WINERY **MARLBOROUGH** – *Full, creamy, and elegant, with pear, lemon, green apple, and guava scents and flavours.*	£10.00 GRT/NYW
CELLAR SELECTION SAUVIGNON BLANC 2003, VILLA MARIA **MARLBOROUGH** – *Another star in the Villa Maria galaxy. Grassy and gooseberryish with a fresh style and grilled asparagus scents.*	£10.00 ODD
CLOCKTOWER SAUVIGNON BLANC 2002, WITHER HILLS **MARLBOROUGH** – *Pungent, grassy, and tropical, with stone fruit and greengage flavours. Powerful and long. Excellent balance and concentration.*	£10.00 M&S
MARLBOROUGH CHARDONNAY 2002, NAUTILUS ESTATE **MARLBOROUGH** – *Pale gold, with a greengage and toast and citrus rent by almond, spice, and resinous nuances.*	£10.00 NYW/NZH
MOUNT RILEY SAUVIGNON BLANC 2003, MOUNT RILEY WINES **MARLBOROUGH** – *Subdued and mineral. There is a leafy asparagus tone with tropical notes which places this wine firmly in Marlborough.*	£10.00 V&C

NEW ZEALAND WHITE BRONZE

Wine	Price / Codes
RESERVE MARLBOROUGH CHARDONNAY 2002, VILLA MARIA Marlborough – Lemon yellow. More lemons on the perfumed nose and yet again on the lifted, integrated, citrussy palate.	£10.00 BEC/DBY ODD/WIM NZH
VAVASOUR SAUVIGNON BLANC 2003, VAVASOUR WINES Marlborough – Sautéed green beans on the nose. The palate has hints of ripe satsumas and a mineral lift on the finish.	£10.00 ODD
WAIPARA WEST CHARDONNAY 2001, TUTTON SIENKO & HILL Canterbury – Lychees, pear-drops, and Russet apples intermingle on this round, buttery, lime green wine.	£10.00 WAW/ODD
ESTATE SELECTION THE CIRCLE SEMILLON 2003, SILENI ESTATES Hawke's Bay – Lifted, with lanonlin and limes in abundance. Appealing pale green colour. Touches of rosemary on the nose.	£10.20 JAV/BCF GHL/WSO DVY/NZH
BRIGHTWATER SAUVIGNON BLANC 2003, BRIGHWATER VINEYARDS Nelson – Crisp green bell pepper and pineapple scents. Lemon zest and green apple flavours mingle in the mouth.	£10.30 LAI
MARLBOROUGH SAUVIGNON BLANC 2003, DRYLANDS Marlborough – Very ripe with summer asparagus and fresh peas type fruit. It is concentrated and rich with a clean freshness.	£10.50 ODD/NZH
CANTERBURY MARLBOROUGH DRY RIESLING 2003, WAIPARA HILLS Canterbury/Marlborough – Crushed lavender leaves on the nose. Earthy touches add weight to the palate of ripe lemons and grapefruit.	£11.00 OZW
MARLBOROUGH SAUVIGNON BLANC 2003, WAIPARA HILLS Marlborough – Pale green. The nose has a superripe grapefuit character. Straightforward, pretty and thirst quenching.	£11.00 OZW
PATUTAHI ESTATE GEWURZTRAMINER 2002, MONTANA WINES Gisborne – Big, inviting, spicy, and lively. This wine should be chilled down and consumed over the next two years.	£11.10 HAX/FEN JFE
ESTATE SELECTION CHARDONNAY 2002, SILENI ESTATES Hawke's Bay – Lightly toasted nose coupled with a fresh palate of lime juice, hazelnuts, and hints of allspice.	£11.20 JAV/BCF GHL/WSO DVY/NZH

NEW ZEALAND WHITE BRONZE / RED GOLD

AVERY SAUVIGNON BLANC 2003, CRAGGY RANGE **MARLBOROUGH** – *Restrained and minerally with a mouthwatering grapefruit style. Weighty green apple and gooseberry fruit and a long pure finish.*	£11.30 EDC/FFW CPR
ORMOND ESTATE CHARDONNAY 2002, MONTANA WINES **GISBORNE** – *Bright straw-yellow, with a riot of mango, lime, and grapefruit flavours. Creamy nuances smooth out the flavours.*	£11.50 BNK/FEN ODD/NZH
SINGLE VINEYARD TAYLOR'S PASS SAUVIGNON BLANC 2003, VILLA MARIA **MARLBOROUGH** – *Fully ripe, with quince and honey and gooseberry flavours, and a hint of residual sugar. Grassy notes.*	£12.00 WIM/DBY LBS/VKY
ALLAN SCOTT PRESTIGE CHARDONNAY 2001, ALLAN SCOTT WINES **MARLBOROUGH** – *Aromatic green apple and citrus nose. The palate has rich fruit balanced by cool acidity. Refined finish.*	£12.10 BNK/CCS
MARLBOROUGH PINOT GRIS 2003, NAUTILUS ESTATE **MARLBOROUGH** – *Gently spiced, perfumed white and green berries give way to a palate of fresh, restrained fruit.*	£13.20 NYW/NZH
TE MUNA ROAD CHARDONNAY 2002, CRAGGY RANGE **MARTINBOROUGH** – *Golden colour. Notes of lychee, toast, and cream on the nose. The palate is round, stylish, and long.*	£14.70 FFW/WSO CPR
CRAIGHALL CHARDONNAY 2002, ATA RANGI **MARTINBOROUGH** – *Accessible, powerful, and fruity. Judicious amounts of oak and an inviting, zesty mouthful of ripe peach and pear flavours.*	£20.00 WIDELY AVAILABLE

GOLD
NEW ZEALAND RED

☆ **CELLAR SELECTION PINOT NOIR 2002, VILLA MARIA** **MARLBOROUGH** – *Sweet strawberry and raspberry flavours, a touch of farmyard development and a lavish dose of oak.*	£11.80 VGN/FEN NYW
NEWTON FORREST CORNERSTONE CABERNET MERLOT MALBEC 2002, FORREST ESTATE WINERY **HAWKE'S BAY** – *Intensely inky and minty, with ripe blackcurrants, cedar notes, and gritty tannins that add texture.*	£12.60 JNW

NEW ZEALAND RED GOLD / SILVER

THE RESERVE ZINFANDEL 2002, KEMBLEFIELD ESTATE WINERY HAWKE'S BAY – *Vibrant raspberry fruit and a touch of spice and farmy development. Clear and pure with a soft structure.*	£20.70 HBJ/MHW NZH

SILVER
NEW ZEALAND RED

MATUA VALLEY MARLBOROUGH PINOT NOIR 2003, BERINGER BLASS MARLBOROUGH – *Soft summer fruits with a touch of mint. Powerful tannins and mouthwatering acidity on the lasting palate.*	£8.00 YOB
RESERVE CABERNET SAUVIGNON MERLOT 2001, DELEGAT'S WINE ESTATE HAWKE'S BAY – *Cedar and white pepper added to blackcurrant flavours. Powerful yet integrated tannins sustain the generous fruit.*	£8.00 MWW
CELLAR SELECTION MERLOT CABERNET SAUVIGNON 2002, VILLA MARIA HAWKE'S BAY – *Good mouthfeel augmented by firm tannins on the long, lush, and spicy palate.*	£8.70 VGN/NZH
RESERVE MARLBOROUGH PINOT NOIR 2002, MONTANA WINES MARLBOROUGH – *A stunning array of raspberries, sous bois, mint, and cedar. Bright acidity and firm tannins complement the fruit.*	£10.00 RAV/JFE WTS/ODD NZH
VIDAL ESTATE SYRAH 2002, VIDAL ESTATE HAWKE'S BAY – *Luxuriant, velvety, and full, with a floral nose and an integrated tannic structure. A quality wine.*	£10.00 NYW/JSM
VIDAL PINOT NOIR 2002, VIDAL ESTATE HAWKE'S BAY – *Refined strawberry and raspberry fruit flavours, silky tannins, balanced acidity, and a full body. The finish is long and refreshing.*	£10.00 LBS /WIM VKY/DBY
HUNTER'S PINOT NOIR 2002, HUNTER'S WINES MARLBOROUGH – *Elegant, silky, and long, with mulberries, a delicate floral perfume and understated roast and mineral aromatics.*	£11.70 BNK/CEB JOB/LAY NZH
MURDOCH JAMES MARTINBOROUGH CABERNET FRANC 2002, MURDOCH JAMES ESTATE WAIRARAPA – *Bitter chocolate scents complement a palate of mature yet bright bramble fruit flavours. Stunning.*	£12.00 CAV

PALLISER PINOT NOIR 2002, PALLISER ESTATE **WAIRARAPA** – *Savoury roast game aromas interwoven with elegant mulberry fruit flavours. Ripe, with glossy black coal notes.*	**£12.70** HOU/NYW J&B/NZH
RESERVE PINOT NOIR 2002, VILLA MARIA **MARLBOROUGH** – *Delicate strawberry fruit flavours and a touch of bitter toast on the long, sophisticated finish.*	**£15.20** NYW/NZH
GIMBLETT GRAVELS MERLOT 2002, CRAGGY RANGE **HAWKE'S BAY** – *Spicebox notes enhance the compact, firm palate of classy black fruit and cedar. Grippy tannins and bright acidity.*	**£15.30** FFW/CPR NYW
GIMBLETT GRAVELS BLOCK 14 SYRAH 2002, CRAGGY RANGE **HAWKE'S BAY** – *Gravelly mineral notes, ripe fresh red cherry flavours, thyme aromas, and a zing of acidity. Long.*	**£15.60** FFW/CPR NYW
OMAKA RESERVE PINOT NOIR 2002, SAINT CLAIR ESTATE **MARLBOROUGH** – *Caramel oak notes and pretty strawberry fruit glow on the rich, racy palate. Medium-bodied, with a lasting finish.*	**£16.60** FFW/VIT CVE/NZH
DAVISHON PINOT NOIR 2002, ALEXANDRA WINE COMPANY **CENTRAL OTAGO** – *Wildflowers, toasty oak, and game notes. The palate is loaded with plums and cherries and a thicket of undergrowth.*	**£17.00** SWG
AKARUA PINOT NOIR 2002, BANNOCKBURN HEIGHTS **CENTRAL OTAGO** – *Rich, juicy mulberry fruit. Profoundly ripe, with a flush of alcohol on the bold, luxuriant palate.*	**£18.00** OWL
MOUNT MICHAEL PINOT NOIR 2003, MOUNT MICHAEL **CENTRAL OTAGO** – *Fresh strawberries and blueberries, hints of espresso and coconut, vanilla, and dusky undergrowth.*	**£19.50** EWW
THE QUARRY 2001, CRAGGY RANGE **HAWKE'S BAY** – *Focused, fragrant and clear, with damsons, cassis, minerals, cigars, pepper, and a helping of earth.*	**£22.10** FFW/CPR NYW

BRONZE
NEW ZEALAND RED

MARLBOROUGH PINOT NOIR 2002, MONTANA WINES **MARLBOROUGH** – *This polished Pinot has mounds of summer fruit flavour coupled with silky integrated tannins.*	**£7.00** WAV
SHINGLE PEAK PINOT NOIR 2003, BERINGER BLASS **MARLBOROUGH** – *A smooth texture, fine tannins, and clear raspberry fruit flavours meld on this youthful offering.*	**£7.00** JSM
STRATUM RED MERLOT PINOT NOIR PINOTAGE 2003, SHERWOOD ESTATE **MARLBOROUGH** – *The attractive nose features violets, cherries, and plums. Spices accentuate the ripe, juicy red and black fruits.*	**£7.00** ALL
KAITUNA HILLS CABERNET MERLOT RESERVE 2002, MONTANA **HAWKE'S BAY** – *The nose shows plum and spice. The palate has lush blueberry notes, supple tannins, and decent concentration on the finish.*	**£8.00** M&S
STONELEIGH MARLBOROUGH PINOT NOIR 2002, MONTANA WINES **MARLBOROUGH** – *Perfumed and flavoured with sweetly ripe red bramble fruits, Madagascan vanilla, and tree bark. Gamey notes.*	**£8.00** AD1
PRIVATE BIN MERLOT CABERNET SAUVIGNON 2002, VILLA MARIA **EAST COAST** – *Very ripe dark vine fruits and lashings of creamy oak. Good balance and weight throughout.*	**£8.70** FEN/ODD
HAWKE'S BAY CABERNET SAUVIGNON MERLOT 2001, TRINITY HILL **HAWKE'S BAY** – *Full of juicy redcurrant and cherry fruit with plenty of warmth and tannins. A good food wine.*	**£9.00** HOU
SEIFRIED PINOT NOIR 2002, SEIFRIED ESTATE **NELSON** – *Meaty and fleshy, with a vigorous attack of firm wild strawberry fruit, fresh acidity, and grippy tannins.*	**£9.30** FLA
CELLAR SELECTION SYRAH 2002, VILLA MARIA **HAWKE'S BAY** – *Blackberry scented, with a rich fruit palate showing firm tannins and smoky intensity. The finish has depth.*	**£10.00** ODD

NEW ZEALAND RED BRONZE 261

MARLBOROUGH PINOT NOIR 2001, CAIRNBRAE WINES MARLBOROUGH – *Ripe, glamorous, and long, with glowing red fruit flavours and bay leaf and thyme aromas.*	£10.00 H&H
MATUA VALLEY BULLRUSH MERLOT 2002, BERINGER BLASS HAWKE'S BAY – *Red fruit, a touch of cream and light green pepper notes on the palate in this medium-bodied wine.*	£10.00 WFB
OYSTER BAY PINOT NOIR 2001, OYSTER BAY WINES MARLBOROUGH – *Harmonious cherry and raspberry nose. The palate displays clear fruit purity and a soft tannic web.*	£10.00 SMF
OYSTER BAY PINOT NOIR 2002, OYSTER BAY WINES MARLBOROUGH MARLBOROUGH – *Supple style with berry and black pepper aromas. The palate has silky tannins and a touch of pancetta spice.*	£10.00 SMF/ MWW
WAIMEA PINOT NOIR 2002, WAIMEA ESTATES NELSON – *Deep colour, seductive nose, lively acidity, and excellent grip. This deserves more time to develop its charms.*	£10.00 MWW
SPY VALLEY PINOT NOIR 2002, SPY VALLEY WINES MARLBOROUGH – *Berry-rich nose with vegetal notes. The palate is balanced with ripe fruit, silky tannins, and a decent finish.*	£10.20 WES/NYW FLY/JSM
VICARS CHOICE PINOT NOIR 2002, SAINT CLAIR ESTATE MARLBOROUGH – *Powerful aromas of strawberries and blueberries; a rich, somewhat gamey wine already displaying some evolution.*	£10.70 FFW/VIT WOI/NYW CVE/NZH
GLADSTONE PINOT NOIR 2003, GLADSTONE VINEYARDS WAIRARAPA – *Raspberries galore. Ruby red, with a hint of earth, a spike of rosemary, and a longish finish.*	£10.80 JNW
VINEYARD SELECTION PINOT NOIR 2002, MUD HOUSE MARLBOROUGH – *Sweetly perfumed strawberry fruit on the nose and palate; elegant, of medium weight, and silky texture.*	£10.80 JNW/SOM NZH
STONELEIGH RAPAURA MARLBOROUGH PINOT NOIR 2002, MONTANA WINES MARLBOROUGH – *Deep black and red berry flavours, hints of sous bois, tinges of smoke, and cinnamon spice.*	£11.00 AD1

NEW ZEALAND RED BRONZE

BORTHWICK PINOT NOIR 2002, BORTHWICK ESTATE **WAIRARAPA** – *A classic nose of meat juices and ripe fruit; a mulberry palate underscored by youthful tannins. Elegant.*	**£12.00** JAR
GIMBLETT ROAD HAWKE'S BAY CABERNET SAUVIGNON MERLOT 2002, TRINITY HILL **HAWKE'S BAY** – *Opaque. Mulberries and lashings of spice. Packed with open-knit fruit. Firm tannins on the finish.*	**£12.00** BTH
WAIPARA SPRINGS PINOT NOIR 2002, WAIPARA SPRINGS **CANTERBURY** – *Sweet cherry fruit and tree bark flavours. Mouthwatering acidity, medium body, and a web of dusty tannins.*	**£12.00** HAY
FAIRHALL ESTATE MERLOT CABERNET SAUVIGNON 1999, MONTANA WINES **MARLBOROUGH** – *Sumptuous peppermint spice hovers over morello fruit, which is suspended in a web of supple tannins.*	**£12.10** FEN/NZH
PRESTIGE PINOT NOIR 2001, ALLAN SCOTT WINES **MARLBOROUGH** – *Perfumed with lifted cherry and vegetal aromas. The palate shows pure berry fruit allied to silky tannins.*	**£12.30** HDS/GGR GSL
CANTERBURY PINOT NOIR 2002, WAIPARA HILLS **CANTERBURY** – *Delicately coloured. Violets coalesce with squashed strawberries in this textured, fresh, structured wine.*	**£13.00** OZW
DOCTORS CREEK PINOT NOIR 2002, SAINT CLAIR ESTATE **MARLBOROUGH** – *This mouthwatering offering has piles of strawberries and raspberries and roast meat juice hints.*	**£13.00** FFW/VIT RNS/CVE NZH
TERRACES ESTATE PINOT NOIR 2002, MONTANA WINES **MARLBOROUGH** – *Pure, lean and mouthwatering, with meaty aromas, strawberry compote flavours, and lashings of oak.*	**£13.00** ODD
ANDERSON VINEYARD PINOT NOIR 2002, KIM CRAWFORD **MARLBOROUGH** – *Barnyard, straw, and raspberry fruit melange. Clean, intense, and medium-bodied, with a fresh long finish.*	**£14.40** WIDELY AVAILABLE
WITHER HILLS PINOT NOIR 2002, BRENT MARRIS **MARLBOROUGH** – *Heavy toast and smoky bacon aromas blend beautifully with the hedgerow fruit. Corsetted by generous amounts of oak.*	**£14.50** ESL/VIT WTS/ODD MWW NZH

NEW ZEALAND RED BRONZE

Wine	Price / Availability
RESERVE CABERNET SAUVIGNON MERLOT 2001, VILLA MARIA Hawke's Bay – Blackcurrant fruit with minty hints on the dark, spicy palate with its balanced oak.	£14.70 EDC/NZH
ISABEL PINOT NOIR 2002, ISABEL ESTATE Marlborough – Fresh, toasty, and elegant, with tinned strawberry fruit flavours and a foundation of soft, seductive tannins.	£14.80 WIDELY AVAILABLE
MARLBOROUGH PINOT NOIR 2002, NAUTILUS ESTATE Marlborough – Beautifully crafted, its oak seamlessly integrated, and layer upon layer of summer fruits. Balanced, with a long finish.	£14.80 NYW MWW NZH
VIDAL RESERVE MERLOT CABERNET SAUVIGNON 2000, VIDAL ESTATE Hawke's Bay – A mouthful of damsons and currants. This beauty should develop further given more time.	£14.80 LBS /WIM VKY/DBY NZH
MARTINBOROUGH VINEYARD PINOT NOIR 2002, MARTINBOROUGH VINEYARD Wairarapa – Classic and elegant, this medium-bodied wine is crammed with sustained cherry fruit flavours.	£16.50 NYW/NZH
RESERVE MERLOT CABERNET SAUVIGNON MALBEC 2000, ESK VALLEY Hawke's Bay – Restrained and mineral-infused crisp crunchy black fruit flavours and a toasty finish.	£17.00 LAI/VIT FLA/NYW NZH
DRY GULLY PINOT NOIR 2002, DRY GULLY Central Otago – Medium-deep indigo red colour. A resounding attack leads to a full-bodied palate of strawberry fruit with fine acidity.	£18.00 SWG
WOOING TREE PINOT NOIR 2003, WOOING TREE VINEYARD Central Otago – Notes of undergrowth tangle with soft ripe raspberry fruit on the nose and palate. Deep colour and good length.	£19.50 EWW
PASK RESERVE MERLOT 2002, CJ PASK WINERY Hawke's Bay – Deep, dark and somewhat muted on the nose. Ripe and racy, with a mouthful of bitter cherry fruit.	£20.00 G&M
ULTIMO GISBORNE MERLOT 2002, RONGOPAI WINES Gisborne – A savoury nose leads to fine depth and richness on the palate with soft fruit and good length.	£20.00 SGL

NEW ZEALAND RED BRONZE **SPARKLING** SILVER / BRONZE

JACKSON BARRY PINOT NOIR 2002, OLSSEN'S GARDEN VINEYARD CENTRAL OTAGO – *Full and savoury, with a long palate of dry, intense raspberry fruit flavours. Good mouthfeel. Chalky finish.*	£20.50 BON
MARTINBOROUGH BLUE ROCK PINOT NOIR 2002, MURDOCH JAMES ESTATE WAIRARAPA – *Sweet vanilla oak aromas. With plenty of concentration on the attack, this is an elegant Martinborough Pinot Noir.*	£21.00 ODD
CJ PASK RESERVE DECLARATION 2002, CJ PASK WINERY HAWKE'S BAY – *Soft dark berries and flowers on the nose. Plenty of fruit and firm tannins in the mouth.*	£21.30 G&M
SINGLE VINEYARD SEDDON PINOT NOIR 2002, VILLA MARIA MARLBOROUGH – *Fresh, pure strawberry fruit spills from this ripe wine with its hints of the barnyard.*	£22.00 V&C
SLAP JACK CREEK PINOT NOIR 2002, OLSSEN'S GARDEN VINEYARD CENTRAL OTAGO – *Thrusting acidity, loganberry, and damson fruit, and a rich yet restrained nose all define this wine.*	£29.90 BON

SILVER
NEW ZEALAND SPARKLING

☆ **LINDAUER SPECIAL RESERVE NV, MONTANA WINES** – *The fresh palate has pineapples, cherries, limes, and jackfruit flavours. Complex, spicy, and long.*	£8.90 RAV/FEN TOS/ODD MWW NZH

BRONZE
NEW ZEALAND SPARKLING

☆ **LINDAUER BRUT NV, MONTANA WINES** – *Fresh stone fruit nose with lots of nutty aromas, and a soft, developed tropical fruit palate of some complexity.*	£8.30 WIDELY AVAILABLE
DEUTZ MARLBOROUGH CUVÉE NV, MONTANA WINES MARLBOROUGH – *This classy fizz has a candied citrus fruit nose and a youthful, lively, long finish.*	£11.20 WTS/ODD MWW/NZH

NEW ZEALAND SPARKLING / SWEET BRONZE

HUNTER'S MIRU MIRU 2000, HUNTER'S WINES **MARLBOROUGH** – Vibrant and bright with ripe lemony notes of good ripeness, fine mousse, and well-balanced acidity.	£11.90 BNK/TAN JOB/LAY NZH
LINDAUER GRANDEUR NV, MONTANA WINES – Melted butter, guava, pears, and strawberries, with delicate hints of spice. A blast of lemon rind acidity keeps it fresh.	£12.20 AD1/MWW

BRONZE
NEW ZEALAND SWEET

LATE HARVEST RIESLING 2003, FORREST ESTATE WINERY **MARLBOROUGH** – Delicate orange blossom notes scent the nose. The palate is a light-bodied blend of citrus and pear fruit.	£10.00 ADN

FOR STOCKIST CODES turn to page 355. For regularly updated information about stockists and the International Wine Challenge, visit wineint.com. For a full glossary of wine terms and a complete free wine course, visit robertjoseph-onwine.com

NORTH AMERICA + CANADA

Sadly, far too few of California's best wines reach the shores of the UK; they are mostly snapped up by US and Asian wine-lovers who are readier to pay the (generally high) prices they command than their counterparts in this country. The wines we are more likely to see here are the heavily marketed brands – most of which are particularly disappointing when compared to offerings from elsewhere around the world. In this section, we pick out a range of truly worthwhile wines from established stars like Ridge and Beaulieu, and from some newer names such as Boulders, that offer value for money as well as great drinking.

TROPHY
CALIFORNIA WHITE

GEYSER PEAK RESERVE CHARDONNAY 2002, GEYSER PEAK WINERY CALIFORNIA – *Quality oak imparts butterscotch and sweet date flavours; the lemony fruit is lush; crisp acidity keeps the richness in check.*	£.00 NOT AVAILABLE IN THE UK

GOLD
CALIFORNIA WHITE

CLOS DU BOIS ALEXANDER VALLEY RESERVE CHARDONNAY 2002, CLOS DU BOIS CALIFORNIA – *Bright, shimmering golden fruit and silky nutty oak flavours intermingle on the dense, saturated palate. Rich, layered, and characterful.*	£16.00 AD1

SILVER
CALIFORNIA WHITE

FATHER OAK CHARDONNAY 2002, EOS ESTATE WINERY CALIFORNIA – *Pronounced toast and fresh cantaloupe melon on the nose. The palate shows ripeness held in check by fine acidity.*	£8.00 M&S

CALIFORNIA WHITE SILVER / BRONZE

COASTAL VINEYARDS CHARDONNAY 2001, ERNEST & JULIO GALLO CALIFORNIA – *A compelling combination of toffee and sliced green bean aromas assails the nose. Juicy pineapple flavours permeate the palate.*	£10.00 TOS/JSM
SONOMA COUNTY CHARDONNAY 2001, ERNEST & JULIO GALLO CALIFORNIA – *Toasty, persistent, and complex, its lifted lemon and cantaloupe fruit swaddled in a spiced oak blanket.*	£12.00 HBJ
LAGUNA RANCH CHARDONNAY 2001, ERNEST & JULIO GALLO CALIFORNIA – *Clear, bright buttery oak graces the palate of candied lemon fruit. Firm acidity, excellent ripeness, and a long finish.*	£14.00 JSM
NAPA VALLEY FUMÉ BLANC 2002, ROBERT MONDAVI CALIFORNIA – *Delicate sweet smoky notes integrate well into the clean, crisp, very dry gooseberry, melon, apple, and peach fruit.*	£20.00 RMO

BRONZE
CALIFORNIA WHITE

BERINGER FOUNDERS ESTATE CHARDONNAY 2002, BERINGER BLASS CALIFORNIA – *Sweet rich orange and nectarine fruit nose. Smoky notes and a zesty tang of acid enliven the palate.*	£8.00 ODD/THS
FETZER BARREL SELECT CHARDONNAY 2001, FETZER VINEYARDS CALIFORNIA – *Vanilla and smoke aromas. The soft palate has richness, warmth, a buttery texture, and melon fruit.*	£8.00 JSM MWW
SELECT VINEYARDS SAUVIGNON BLANC 2002, CONCANNON VINEYARD CALIFORNIA – *Sweet ripe fruit tones. Crisp, spicy, and grassy, with warming alcohol and good integration.*	£8.00 THS
CLOS DU BOIS CHARDONNAY 2002, CLOS DU BOIS CALIFORNIA – *Sweet icing sugar, campfire, and spices pepper the complex nose, whilst fruit salad flavours fill the mouth.*	£8.70 RAV
BONTERRA CHARDONNAY 2002, BONTERRA VINEYARDS CALIFORNIA – *Rich and buttery with a whiff of toast on the nose. Ripe and spicy with a nice lick of sweet oak.*	£8.90 VGN/TAU WTS MWW

CALIFORNIA WHITE BRONZE

BERINGER NAPA VALLEY CHARDONNAY 2001, BERINGER BLASS CALIFORNIA – *Appealing, vivid, and fresh, the peach and apricot palate is full and structured, with cinnamon toast notes.*	**£10.70** BWC/WAV MWW
LA CREMA SONOMA COAST CHARDONNAY 2002, KENDALL JACKSON CALIFORNIA – *Warm tropical fruit lines the super soft fleshy palate. A touch of almond skin flavour adds another dimension.*	**£11.00** KJW
RIVERSTONE CHARDONNAY ARROYO SECO 2001, J LOHR CALIFORNIA – *Green plum flavours start the mouth watering, and creamy vanilla paves a smooth path to the finish.*	**£12.00** ENO
SIMI SONOMA CHARDONNAY 2002, SIMI CALIFORNIA – *Big fruit salad aromas on the nose. Deep and ripe, with melon, lemons and warm vanilla characteristics.*	**£12.00** CNT
ST FRANCIS CHARDONNAY 2002, ST FRANCIS CALIFORNIA – *Ripe and spicy with melon and toast aromas. The rich fruit is balanced by fine acidity.*	**£12.90** EDC/VIT
TWO ROCK CHARDONNAY 2001, ERNEST & JULIO GALLO CALIFORNIA – *Rich and ripe with tropical melon notes. The palate is opulent with good balance and a lick of spicy oak.*	**£14.00** WAV
HEITZ NAPA VALLEY CHARDONNAY 2001, HEITZ CELLARS CALIFORNIA – *Acid green-yellow hue. Rich toffee and vanilla ice cream nuances swathe bright pineapple chunk flavours.*	**£15.00** J&B
SANTA BARBARA COUNTY CHARDONNAY 2001, AU BON CLIMAT CALIFORNIA – *Bright lemon and lime scents entwine with buttered peach and tropical guava fruit flavours.*	**£16.70** CCS/NYW FLY
RUSSIAN RIVER RANCHES CHARDONNAY 2002, SONOMA CUTRER CALIFORNIA – *Expressive citrus and brioche nose leads to a harmonious palate which displays richness checked by steely acidity.*	**£17.00** LEA
ARROYO VISTA CHARDONNAY 2001, J LOHR CALIFORNIA – *Honeyed buttery oak softens the fresh, lively grapefruit flavours. The seductive finish is a force to be reckoned with.*	**£18.00** NYW/ENO

CALIFORNIA WHITE BRONZE / SEAL **/ RED** TROPHY / GOLD **269**

RAMEY RUSSIAN RIVER VALLEY CHARDONNAY 2000, RAMEY WINE CELLARS CALIFORNIA – *Pale and buttery, with great helpings of spice. The honey and banana flesh drapes itself over an oaky skeleton.*	**£27.50** CCS/FLY
ESTATE BOTTLED CHARDONNAY 2000, ERNEST & JULIO GALLO CALIFORNIA – *Intense. Notes of crushed almonds add lift to the round, weighty, opulent palate of citrus fruit.*	**£30.00** E&J

SEAL OF APPROVAL
CALIFORNIA WHITE

☆ **CO-OP CALIFORNIA THE BIG CHILL CHARDONNAY COLOMBARD 2002, GOLDEN STATE VINTNERS** CALIFORNIA – *Vivid and ripe, with an open, approachable palate of lemon fruit.*	**£4.00** CWS
☆ **SIERRA VALLEY WHITE 2003, ERNEST & JULIO GALLO** CALIFORNIA – *Fruit-salad flavours and attractive scents of flowers.*	**£4.00** JSM

TROPHY
CALIFORNIA RED

GEORGES DE LATOUR PRIVATE RESERVE CABERNET SAUVIGNON 2000, BEAULIEU VINEYARD CALIFORNIA – *Masses of minty cassis, cedary fruit and multi-layered smoky oak. The palate has earthy undertones and soft yet firm tannins.*	**£.00** NOT AVAILABLE IN THE UK

GOLD
CALIFORNIA RED

☆ **AMADOR COUNTY ZINFANDEL 2001, RAVENSWOOD** CALIFORNIA – *Rich, thick berry fruit with layers of blackberries and loganberries. An intense and powerful mouthful with a dense tannin structure.*	**£10.00** SMF/NYW
☆ **LA CREMA CARNEROS PINOT NOIR 2000, KENDALL JACKSON** CALIFORNIA – *Fresh primary fruit blends nicely with maturing vegetal, savoury notes to form layers of flavour and an intense complexity.*	**£12.00** KJW

CALIFORNIA RED GOLD / SILVER

RIDGE GEYSERVILLE 2001, RIDGE VINEYARDS CALIFORNIA – *Ripe blackberry and raspberry fruit and a complex spiciness over round, soft tannins and a little lift of acidity.*	£22.60 WIDELY AVAILABLE
RIDGE LYTTON SPRINGS 2001, RIDGE VINEYARDS CALIFORNIA – *A pure, serious wine with rhubarb and soya complexity and perfumed notes. Typical bramble notes and a generous texture.*	£22.70 WIDELY AVAILABLE
ATLAS PEAK ZINFANDEL MEAD RANCH 2001, TURLEY CALIFORNIA – *Layers of complexity with soy sauce, rhubarb, raspberries, and brambles. The tannins are huge but ripe.*	£30.00 NYW
FORT ROSS SONOMA COAST PINOT NOIR 2001, SCHERRER CALIFORNIA – *A toasty, spicy hedgerow fruit nose with mint overtones. Weighty soft black fruit and a smooth tannic structure.*	£31.80 TWM/NYW LIB

SILVER
CALIFORNIA RED

★ **THE BOULDERS PETITE SIRAH 2002, KINGSLAND WINES & SPIRITS** CALIFORNIA – *Delightful mocha notes score crystal-clean redcurrant fruit. Wisps of smoke and nutty elements complete its aromatic profile.*	£5.00 CWS
☆ **SONOMA COAST PINOT NOIR 2002, SEBASTIANI** CALIFORNIA – *Intense smoky charcoal scents bolster the vibrant palate of sun-warmed raspberries. Liberally oaked, yet balanced and attractive.*	£7.00 BWC
MONTEVIÑA AMADOR COUNTY BARBERA 2001, MONTEVIÑA CALIFORNIA – *This has fine, black-cherry fruit imbued with a touch of liquorice and well-balanced with silky tannins.*	£8.00 PLB
ESTANCIA PINOT NOIR 2001, ESTANCIA CALIFORNIA – *Sweet wild alpine strawberry and cedar flavours delight the taster.*	£10.00 BNK/FEN
PRIVATE SELECTION PINOT NOIR 2001, ROBERT MONDAVI CALIFORNIA – *Polished strawberry flavours, a mouthfilling texture, good ripeness, and fine aromatic definition.*	£10.00 RMO

CALIFORNIA RED SILVER 271

ALEXANDER VALLEY CABERNET SAUVIGNON 2001, SIMI CALIFORNIA – *This Cabernet is full, with some evolution, good concentration and balance, spices, minerals, grippy tannins, and plenty of purple fruits.*	£15.00 **CNT**
AVANT GARDE PINOT NOIR 2002, DOMAINE CARNEROS CALIFORNIA – *Wild strawberry flavours. Mint and cedar hints waft from the nose, and the palate is swathed in silky tannins.*	£15.00 **V&C/VIT**
BARRELLI CREEK ZINFANDEL 1999, ERNEST & JULIO GALLO CALIFORNIA – *Richly textured clean berry fruit. Big, with depth and weight, and a balanced, warming finish.*	£15.00 **WAV**
FREI RANCH ZINFANDEL 2000, ERNEST & JULIO GALLO CALIFORNIA – *Integrated, creamy, textured, and big, with lively berry fruit and good complexity.*	£15.00 **HBJ**
ALEXANDER VALLEY RESERVE MERLOT 2000, CLOS DU BOIS CALIFORNIA – *Earthy notes join restrained black fruit on the nose. A mature balance of red and purple fruits, light tannins and crisp acidity.*	£16.00 **AD1**
PRIVATE COLLECTION PINOT NOIR 1999, FETZER VINEYARDS CALIFORNIA – *Tar, leather, and cloves entwine with summer fruits on the nose and palate. Sophisticated, mouthcoating and long.*	£17.00 **ODD**
SEGHESIO BARBERA 2001, SEGHESIO CALIFORNIA – *Sweet, spicy black cherry fruit lies on top of smoky oak, a touch of tar and profuse but balanced tannins.*	£18.60 **WIDELY AVAILABLE**
Q NAPA VALLEY CABERNET SAUVIGNON 2002, WINERY EXCHANGE CALIFORNIA – *Intense spice, blackcurrants and a streak of minerality. Judicious oak, integrated tannins, and an aromatic touch of smoke.*	£20.00 **WXC**
OLD VINE ZINFANDEL 2002, SEGHESIO CALIFORNIA – *The deep black-fruited nose is laced with lashings of spiced wood. A serious wine, with a mellifluous mouthfeel.*	£23.00 **WIDELY AVAILABLE**
NAPA VALLEY MERLOT 1999, CAFARO CALIFORNIA – *Blackcurrant leaf aromas on the nose. Slowly unfolding layers of juicy fruits. Weighty and beefy. Very drinkable.*	£32.20 **CCS/LIB**

CALIFORNIA RED SILVER / BRONZE

ESTATE BOTTLED CABERNET SAUVIGNON 1997, ERNEST & JULIO GALLO Cᴀʟɪꜰᴏʀɴɪᴀ – *Sweet cigar and bell pepper, blackcurrant, and tobacco flavours. Prominent tannins. A long velvety finish.*	£60.00 E&J

BRONZE
CALIFORNIA RED

BERINGER STONE CELLARS MERLOT 2001, BERINGER BLASS Cᴀʟɪꜰᴏʀɴɪᴀ – *A bouquet of bright menthol and blackberry fruit leads to a smooth palate oozing forest fruit jam.*	£6.00 ODD/WAV
DELICATO SHIRAZ 2003, DELICATO FAMILY VINEYARDS Cᴀʟɪꜰᴏʀɴɪᴀ – *Perfumed dark pastille fruit on nose and palate. A delicious touch of treacle creeps in.*	£6.00 SMF/JSM
KENDALL JACKSON COLLAGE CABERNET MERLOT 2001, KENDALL JACKSON Cᴀʟɪꜰᴏʀɴɪᴀ – *Displaying evolution. An attack of spice leads to sweet ripe plums, chewy tannins and a lingering finish.*	£6.40 SMF/G&M KJW
EAGLE PEAK MERLOT 2002, FETZER VINEYARDS Cᴀʟɪꜰᴏʀɴɪᴀ – *Enticing fruit cake character on the nose leads to a smooth and oaky palate with pleasing grippy tannins.*	£7.00 SMF/JSM
VINTNERS BLEND ZINFANDEL 2001, RAVENSWOOD Cᴀʟɪꜰᴏʀɴɪᴀ – *There is a great depth of layered juicy fruit and mixed red berries. Well-balanced with enough acid to lift it.*	£7.10 BNK/SMF WSO/WTS MWW
BARREL SELECT ZINFANDEL 2001, FETZER VINEYARDS Cᴀʟɪꜰᴏʀɴɪᴀ – *Bags of warm rich cherry gateau flavours bounce out of the glass. A tinge of farmyard development.*	£8.00 TAU
SELECT VINEYARDS MERLOT 2001, CONCANNON VINEYARD Cᴀʟɪꜰᴏʀɴɪᴀ – *Aromas of fresh, plummy fruit with a dash of pencil lead, followed by a pleasant palate with rounded berry fruits.*	£8.00 THS
BERINGER FOUNDERS ESTATE MERLOT 2000, BERINGER BLASS Cᴀʟɪꜰᴏʀɴɪᴀ – *Sweet brambly fruits on the nose lead into an engaging medium-bodied palate, with juicy plums and cherries, gentle acidity, and a good oaky backbone.*	£9.00 BWC

CALIFORNIA RED BRONZE

BERINGER FOUNDERS ESTATE ZINFANDEL 2001, BERINGER BLASS CALIFORNIA – *Enchanting perfume lifts the mouth-filling raspberry fruit. Soft, ripe, and inviting; a very approachable wine.*	**£9.00** ODD
BONTERRA CABERNET SAUVIGNON 1999, BONTERRA VINEYARDS CALIFORNIA – *Rich purple fruits on a fruity palate in a streamlined style. Fresh acidity and ripe but firm tannins.*	**£9.00** BTH/JSM ODD/WRC
SONOMA COUNTY CABERNET SAUVIGNON 2000, SEBASTIANI VINEYARDS CALIFORNIA – *Attractive fruit with some obvious oak on the nose. Elegant curranty fruit is balanced by vanilla oak.*	**£9.00** BWC
BONTERRA SYRAH 2000, BONTERRA VINEYARDS CALIFORNIA – *Dark tarry cherry fruit. Restrained and medium-bodied, with an evolved, concentrated, very dry palate of wild blueberries.*	**£10.00** ODD/WRC
COASTAL VINEYARDS CABERNET SAUVIGNON 1999, ERNEST & JULIO GALLO CALIFORNIA – *Pure cassis, with a touch of fragrant oak imparting chewy tannins and a smoky finish.*	**£10.00** TOS/JSM
CROSSPOINT MERLOT 2001, J LOHR CALIFORNIA – *A lighter, more juicy style of California Merlot with bright plum and currant fruit on the nose and palate, and a refreshing finish.*	**£10.00** ENO
JENICA PEAK SYRAH 2002, WINERY EXCHANGE CALIFORNIA – *A Rhône-style nose, ripe, pure, and chock-a-block with developing damson fruit. Enviably fine mouthfeel.*	**£10.00** WXC
PASO ROBLES CABERNET SAUVIGNON 2001, ESTANCIA CALIFORNIA – *Medium full, with good length and balance, a touch of oak and a cushion of ripe cassis fruit with a smoky finish.*	**£10.00** THS
SONOMA COUNTY CABERNET SAUVIGNON 2001, CLOS DU BOIS CALIFORNIA – *Herbs, spices, and warm jammy fruit. Soft tannins and spicy oak engage with plummy fruit on the palate.*	**£10.60** RAV
CLOS DU BOIS ZINFANDEL 2001, CLOS DU BOIS CALIFORNIA – *Keenly dry, beautifully balanced and just a little edge of maturity in the farmy spice.*	**£11.50** RAV

CALIFORNIA RED BRONZE

SONOMA COUNTY PINOT NOIR 2000, ERNEST & JULIO GALLO CALIFORNIA – *Berry and cherry nose leads to a supple palate showing black fruit intensity and ripe tannins.*	£12.00 HBJ
SONOMA COUNTY ZINFANDEL 2001, ERNEST & JULIO GALLO CALIFORNIA – *Deep red and black juicy fruit flavours. Hay scents punctuate the full, sweetly ripe palate.*	£12.00 HBJ
LA CREMA SONOMA COAST PINOT NOIR 2002, KENDALL JACKSON CALIFORNIA – *Vivid strawberry fruit flavours radiate from the palate of this ripe, cedary wine. Concentrated and long.*	£12.50 G&M/KJW
LOS OSOS MERLOT 2001, J LOHR CALIFORNIA – *Supple with plum and allspice aromas on the nose. The palate has fruit purity allied to integrated oak and tannins.*	£12.50 ENO
SEVEN OAKS CABERNET SAUVIGNON 2001, J LOHR CALIFORNIA – *A big, brambly bear on the nose, with ripe mouthfilling fruit on the palate. Fine-grained tannins and a juicy finish.*	£12.50 ENO
SONOMA COUNTY ZINFANDEL 2002, SEGHESIO CALIFORNIA – *A well-made wine with a powerful tannic substructure, sweet jammy blackberry fruit, and a mouthwatering finish.*	£14.30 WIDELY AVAILABLE
SONOMA OLD VINE ZINFANDEL 1999, ST FRANCIS CALIFORNIA – *Very dry and deeply concentrated, with notes of undergrowth and tea leaves gracing the exceptionally ripe fruit.*	£14.50 EDC/FEN
FREI RANCH CABERNET SAUVIGNON 1997, ERNEST & JULIO GALLO CALIFORNIA – *Spicy purple fruit and mushroom nose. Plenty of brambles, firm tannins, and a long finish.*	£15.00 JSM
SEGHESIO SANGIOVESE 2001, SEGHESIO CALIFORNIA – *Very full, with a palate tinged with toasty oak. Powerful, concentrated and heavy, with white chocolate, prunes, and tar.*	£18.00 WIDELY AVAILABLE
STATE PINOT NOIR 2000, MARIMAR TORRES CALIFORNIA – *Juicy wine with cherry and toast on the nose. The palate has silky tannins, lush fruit, and a spiced finish.*	£19.50 FLY

CALIFORNIA RED BRONZE

HEITZ CABERNET SAUVIGNON 1995, HEITZ CELLARS **CALIFORNIA** – *This is a classic mature California Cabernet, with ripe berry fruit nose and a gracious, lighter, softer palate.*	£19.90 J&B
ST FRANCIS RESERVE BEHLER MERLOT 1998, ST FRANCIS **CALIFORNIA** – *Ripe fruit, spicy leather, and a touch of undergrowth. Complex, elegant, and grippy. Enjoy now.*	£22.00 LBS /WIM VKY/DBY
HOME RANCH ZINFANDEL 2002, SEGHESIO **CALIFORNIA** – *A very modern Zinfandel with a big structure and plenty of chewy fruit and a touch of oak.*	£23.20 WIDELY AVAILABLE
LE CIGARE VOLANT 2001, BONNY DOON VINEYARD **CALIFORNIA** – *Heady nose of berry spice and leather. A supple yet structured palate of ripe fruit and integrated oak.*	£23.40 JNW/CCS NYW/FLY WRW
FAMOUS GATE PINOT NOIR 2000, DOMAINE CARNEROS **CALIFORNIA** – *Lush wine with plum and cherry fruit, silky tannins, and fresh acidity. Good weight and intensity to finish.*	£23.50 VIT/NYW
NAPA VALLEY CABERNET SAUVIGNON 2000, ROBERT MONDAVI **CALIFORNIA** – *Perfumed black-cherry scents on the nose. Rich, dark, and upfront, with a sensuous ruby red colour.*	£30.00 RMO
RUSSIAN RIVER VALLEY PINOT NOIR 2001, SCHERRER **CALIFORNIA** – *Medium-bodied, with bags of strawberries and vanilla beans. Powerful alcohol and a lasting finish.*	£30.00 LIB
PINOT NOIR KNOX ALEXANDER 2000, AU BON CLIMAT **CALIFORNIA** – *Exceptionally ripe and very intense, with plenty of savoury black-cherry flavours. Powerful and layered.*	£36.80 CCS/NYW FLY
PINOT NOIR ISABELLE 2000, AU BON CLIMAT **CALIFORNIA** – *Mature, full-bodied, and firm, with a ripe, pungent tangle of forest fruit flavours and undergrowth accents.*	£41.80 CCS/NYW FLY

BRONZE
CALIFORNIA ROSÉ

FETZER VALLEY OAKS SYRAH ROSÉ 2003, FETZER VINEYARDS California – *Intense and structured, with buoyant acidity, sun-warmed raspberries, strawberries, and pretty rose petal aromas.*	**£6.10** BNK/UNS SMF/TOS JSM MWW

SEAL OF APPROVAL
CALIFORNIA ROSÉ

☆ **ECHO FALLS ZINFANDEL ROSÉ 2003, CONSTELLATION WINES** California – *Crisscrossed with blueberries, raspberries, and leafy hints.*	**£4.00** MRN MHV LCC/NTD OST

GOLD
CALIFORNIA SPARKLING

☆ **DOMAINE CARNEROS BRUT 2000, DOMAINE CARNEROS** California – *Cool, stylish, and enticing. Packed with sweetly ripe lemon fruit and biscuit notes. Finely integrated crisp fizz of impeccable quality.*	**£16.00** VIT/NYW

BRONZE
CALIFORNIA SPARKLING

ROEDERER ESTATE QUARTET NV, ROEDERER ESTATE California – *Pale lemon gold. Fresh crisp Bramley apples, raspberry nuances, and vanilla touches. Breadth and complexity.*	**£16.50** HAX
DOMAINE CARNEROS LE RÊVE 1997, DOMAINE CARNEROS California – *Elegant, with some maturity. A wine of finesse; only quality fruit was used. Harmonious, fresh, creamy, and very long.*	**£28.00** VIT/NYW

SILVER
CALIFORNIA FORTIFIED

☆ QUADY ELYSIUM BLACK MUSCAT 2002, QUADY WINERY **California** – *Seductive flavours of cranberry, raspberry, and cherry. Medium-full body, with fresh acidity, floral perfume, and a vibrant vermilion colour.*	■£7.70 WIDELY AVAILABLE

BRONZE
PACIFIC NORTHWEST RED

WILLAMETTE VALLEY PINOT NOIR 2001, FIRESTEED **Oregon** – *Robust wood treatment sits compatibly with juicy red cherry fruit. Sweetly spiced and tinged with cedar nuances.*	£16.00 LIB

SILVER
CANADIAN SPARKLING

INNISKILLIN SPARKLING VIDAL ICEWINE 2001, INNISKILLIN WINES **Ontario** – *Exciting and unique, combining startling purity with amazingly sweet fruit and delicate bubbles. The palate is elegant and concentrated.*	■£48.00 LAI

TROPHY
CANADIAN SWEET

INNISKILLIN OAK AGED VIDAL ICEWINE 2002, INNISKILLIN WINES **Ontario** – *Intensely sweet pineapple and apricot fruit, whiffs of smoke, barley sugar, and toffee-apples. Soaring acidity and exceptional balance.*	■£54.00 VIT

GOLD
CANADIAN SWEET

CAVE SPRING RIESLING ICEWINE 2001, CAVE SPRING CELLARS **Ontario** – *A truly great Canadian Riesling Icewine with elegance and concentration and bright, refreshing acidity. Incredibly pure.*	■£25.00 BBR

278 CANADA SPARKLING SILVER / BRONZE

CAVE SPRING RIESLING ICEWINE 2002, CAVE SPRING CELLARS Ontario – Big, powerful, and concentrated. Refined nose of luscious orange peel. Fine texture and balance. Ripe and exceptionally long.	■£30.00 BBR

BRONZE
CANADIAN SWEET

MISSION HILL RIESLING ICEWINE 2001, MISSION HILL FAMILY ESTATE British Columbia – The palate is clean, crisp, and balanced and the finish has excellent weight and complexity.	■£20.00 VIT/TAU

Gold medals have scored the equivalent of at least 18.5/20 (or 95/100) and are exceptional. Silver has scored over 17/20 (or 90/100), bronze over 15.5/20 (or 85/100), and seals of approval over 14/20 (or 80/100).
☆ particularly good value
★ truly great value
▲ 50CL bottle
■ 37.5CL bottle
● 10CL bottle

For stockist codes turn to page 355. For regularly updated information about stockists and the International Wine Challenge, visit wineint.com. For a full glossary of wine terms and a complete free wine course, visit robertjoseph-onwine.com

PORTUGAL

A decade or so ago, Portugal's tally of top International Wine Challenge medals would have been almost exclusively made up of port and madeira. Nowadays, as elsewhere in the world, Portuguese winemakers are introducing New World expertise and openness of mind to their traditional wine regions. This has resulted in a reward in the shape of six gold medal reds from the Douro, Estremadura, and Ribatejo – three regions that were barely associated with classy red table wines as recently as a decade or so ago. Another interesting development is the skill with which the Portuguese have both mastered "imported" grapes such as Syrah, and local ones such as Touriga Nacional.

SILVER
PORTUGUESE FORTIFIED MUSCAT

☆ **JP VINHOS MOSCATEL DE SETÚBAL 1995, JP VINHOS** PENINSULA DE SETÚBAL – *Deep tangerine colour. The luxuriant palate has plenty of marmalade and mature, maderised flavours. Warming, inviting, and accessible.*	**£10.00** EHL

TROPHY
MADEIRA

SERCIAL 10 YEARS OLD RESERVE NV, BARBEITO MADEIRA Madeira – *Nutty and gingery, with acrid orange peel and sweet fruit cake aromas. Fine rancio character.*	**£20.40** HAX/WPR EVI/FLY

SILVER
MADEIRA

☆ **BLANDY'S HARVEST MALMSEY COLHEITA 1997, MADEIRA WINE COMPANY** Madeira – *A touch of molasses on the nose. Balanced, persistent Madeira with an elegant palate of citrus and raisins.*	**£12.20** FEN/NYW

BLANDY'S 15 YEAR OLD MALMSEY NV, MADEIRA WINE COMPANY Madeira – *Luminous deep-brown with glints of green. This mouthcoating Madeira boasts roast coffee beans, toffee, cloves, and smoke.*	▲£16.60 SOM/G&M
HENRIQUES & HENRIQUES BUAL 15 YEAR OLD NV, HENRIQUES & HENRIQUES Madeira – *Intense aromas of roast nuts, coffee, and fruitcake. On the dry side for a Bual, with vivid, fine acidity.*	▲£17.20 ESL/VIT NYW
HENRIQUES & HENRIQUES VERDELHO 15 YEAR OLD NV, HENRIQUES & HENRIQUES Madeira – *Whiffs of espresso and autumn bonfires. The mature, warm, lush palate has excellent balance and a long, long finish.*	£18.50 VIT/EVI NYW/WTS
HENRIQUES & HENRIQUES 15 YEAR OLD MALMSEY N/A, HENRIQUES & HENRIQUES Madeira – *Elegant and voluptuous. A riot of rancio, citrus, vanilla, and incense and ginger cake flavours. A crisp, tannic finish.*	▲£18.90 VIT/WOI WPR/WTS
VERDELHO OLD RESERVE 10 YEAR OLD NV, VINHOS BARBEITO Madeira – *Elegant, soft, and inviting. The medium-weight palate features muscovado sugar, Christmas stollen, walnuts, and oranges.*	£19.50 HAX
BLANDY'S BUAL VINTAGE 1964, MADEIRA WINE COMPANY Madeira – *Lifted and intense. Spirity aromas of coffee and caramel and a soft, silky mouthfeel. Luscious and powerful.*	£70.00 JEF
BLANDY'S TERRANTEZ VINTAGE 1975, MADEIRA WINE COMPANY Madeira – *Star bright mahogany. Vivid lemon and lime scents; earthy tree bark flavours add depth to the smooth palate.*	£80.00 JEF

BRONZE
MADEIRA

☆ **COSSART GORDON 5 YEAR OLD SERCIAL NV, MADEIRA WINE COMPANY** Madeira – *Fresh orange and honey nose leads to a palate of golden fruit. The finish is dry with good freshness.*	▲£10.00 C&B/HVN L&C
BLANDY'S 5 YEAR OLD BUAL NV, MADEIRA WINE COMPANY Madeira – *The coour of molasses, an intense palate of demerara sugar, oranges, and caramel, with coffee bean hints.*	£12.30 SOM/GHL G&M

BLANDY'S 10 YEAR OLD RICH MALMSEY NV, MADEIRA WINE COMPANY Madeira – The nostrils fill with rich aromas of figs, chocolate, toffee, and charred wood. Sweet, with a long finish.	▲£14.20 FEN/G&M SHB
COSSART GORDON BUAL SERCIAL COLHEITA 1988, MADEIRA WINE COMPANY Madeira – Subtle and elegant, yet intense. A complex array of citrus peel, raisins, dates, and cashews. Christmas pudding finish.	▲£15.00 PGR
COSSART GORDON HARVEST MALMSEY 1997, MADEIRA WINE COMPANY Madeira – Light golden brown. The nose and palate are focused, with elegant, pure candied peel, and apricot flavours.	▲£15.00 LAI
BLANDY'S 10 YEAR OLD BUAL NV, MADEIRA WINE COMPANY Madeira – Rich and intense, with enviable rancio characteristics. Mocha, toffee, and dried apricot flavours and scents. Very long.	▲£16.00 SHB

TROPHY
PORT

SMITH WOODHOUSE VINTAGE 2000, SMITH WOODHOUSE Douro – Full of black fruit and brandy with figgy flavours and a spirity lift.	£34.50 ESL/TAN FLY
TAYLORS 40 YEAR OLD TAWNY NV, THE FLADGATE PARTNERSHIP Douro – Fragrant, with a clear rancio character. Full of hazelnuts and walnuts, sweet richness, and a long nutty finish.	£69.00 FEN

GOLD
PORT

☆ **WARRE'S OTIMA 10 YEAR OLD TAWNY NV, WARRE'S** Douro – Great integration of layers of marzipan and nuts, dried fruits and raisins, coffee, and caramel. Heady stuff.	▲£9.90 SMF/FEN NRW/TOS NYW/ODD
☆ **QUINTA DA ERVAMOIRA 10 YEAR OLD TAWNY NV, RAMOS PINTO VINHOS** Douro – Soft and round, with gentle aromatics of fruit cake and almond, dried peel and raisins, and a crisp mouthwatering finish.	£19.50 HAX/WPR GHL/EVI

KROHN 20 YEAR OLD TAWNY NV, WIESE & KROHN **Douro** – *Full of toffee and caramel and raisined fruit and candied peel. Richly sweet, with terrific balancing acidity.*	£25.60 FFW/HAX MER/JFE
DOW'S 20 YEAR OLD AGED TAWNY NV, SILVA & COSENS **Douro** – *Orange rind, nuts and spice, touches of sandalwood, amplified by the warming alcohol and lifted acidity.*	£26.00 FEN
GRAHAM'S 20 YEAR OLD TAWNY NV, W&J GRAHAM **Douro** – *Red fruit character and a clean cut of acid. Warm and full, with sleepy dried fruit flavour.*	£27.70 FEN/TOS OWC
CHURCHILL'S VINTAGE 1991, CHURCHILL GRAHAM **Douro** – *Immense purity of fruit coupled with sweet spice and ginger, cherry and plums, and a touch of eucalyptus.*	£41.70 RAV/CCS FLY

SILVER
PORT

☆ **SMITH WOODHOUSE FINEST RESERVE NV, SMITH WOODHOUSE** **Douro** – *Medium-deep garnet. Quite complex, with dense plum, spice, and chocolate on the nose. Flavours of sweet fruit and orange spice.*	£5.90 ASD
☆ **MHV SPECIAL RESERVE NV, SILVA & COSENS** **Douro** – *Perfect balance, velvet tannins, and good acidity. Fruitcake spice and cedar notes. The finish has a chocolate mint character.*	£7.60 MHV
☆ **QUINTA DO PORTAL VINTAGE 2000, QUINTA DO PORTAL** **Douro** – *Lush, layered, and smoky, with tonnes of strawberry fruit and graceful floral and earth hints.*	£8.00 TWM
☆ **OSBORNE LBV 1999, GRUPO OSBORNE** **Douro** – *Plummy, figgy, generous fruit on the palate. The elegant nose is imbued with hints of violets and Morello cherry.*	£9.50 HBJ
☆ **SANDEMAN LBV 1999, SOGRAPE** **Douro** – *Textured, powerful and extracted, with an array of smoky black bramble fruits and a touch of clove.*	£10.00 CAX

★ **GRAHAM'S LBV 1999, W&J GRAHAM** **Douro** – *Ruby red, seductively sweet, and full-bodied, with bilberries, nutmeg, star anise, and hazelnuts.*	**£10.30** WIDELY AVAILABLE
☆ **THE LATE BOTTLED VINTAGE 1999, NIEPOORT** **Douro** – *A slowly unfolding mouthful of strawberries scored with pencil shavings, espresso, lavender, and cinnamon.*	**£13.00** WIDELY AVAILABLE
☆ **DOW'S CRUSTED BOTTLED 1999 NV, SILVA & COSENS** **Douro** – *Scents of soot and black damsons. Lifted and vigorous, this is immature, but will gain complexity in time.*	**£14.20** FEN/NRW TOS
WARRE'S LBV BOTTLE MATURED 1995, WARRE'S **Douro** – *With an alluring nose, fine density, and powerful structure. Rich, sweet cherry fruit, spice, and cedar flavours mingle effortlessly.*	**£15.40** GHL/NRW
WARRES TRADITIONAL LBV 1992, WARRE'S **Douro** – *A fresh, spicy plum and mint nose. The palate shows complexity, spice, grip, and a lengthy, mellow finish.*	**£15.50** FEN/NRW TOS/NYW
10 YEAR OLD AGED TAWNY NV, QUINTA DO PORTAL **Douro** – *Lush yet balanced by fine acidity, this tawny has floral notes and approachable yet aristocratic fruit.*	**£15.80** ESL/TWM
TAYLORS 10 YEAR OLD TAWNY NV, THE FLADGATE PARTNERSHIP **Douro** – *A seductive nose cloaked in spice and caramel. Full and well balanced, resonant fruit keeping the alcohol in check.*	**£16.60** TAN/UNS FEN/EVI JSM/MWW
PORTAL COLHEITA 1994, QUINTA DO PORTAL **Douro** – *The bouquet offers cedary notes and spicy almond scents. The palate is rich with plums, prunes, and baked raisins.*	**£17.00** GRT
GRAHAM'S MALVEDOS VINTAGE 1996, W&J GRAHAM **Douro** – *Damson fruit flavours, with chocolate elements on the long finish. This needs more time to display its finest.*	**£21.00** SOM
CALEM COLHEITA 1961, AA CALEM & FILHOS **Douro** – *This elder statesmen bears a pale colour, nutty character, and delicate structure. To admire and drink over the short term.*	**£22.00** VIT

OSBORNE VINTAGE 2000, GRUPO OSBORNE Douro – *Bitter chocolate, smoke, tobacco, violets, raspberry fruit, and pencil lead aromas and flavours pour from the nose and palate.*	£22.00 HBJ
FERREIRA DUQUE DE BRAGANCA 20 YEAR OLD TAWNY NV, SOGRAPE Douro – *Elegant apricot and treacle flavours fill the mouth. The nose has wildflowers and walnut skin.*	£30.00 BWC
QUINTA DE RORIZ VINTAGE 2001, QUINTA DE RORIZ Douro – *Full of ripe dark plums; streaming with the juice of crushed cherries. Very good concentration. Upfront and big.*	£30.00 DVY/PAL
DOW'S 30 YEAR OLD TAWNY NV, SILVA & COSENS Douro – *Fruitcake, coffee, and caramel nose; palate of firm sweet fruits, hints of dried orange peel and spices and generous alcohol.*	£35.00 BBR/F&M RS2/G&M
DOW'S QUINTA DA SENHORA DA RIBEIRA VINTAGE 2001, SILVA & COSENS Douro – *Sumptuous, with sandalwood, golden raisins, and raspberry pips galore. Magnificent cherries and oriental bazaar spice notes.*	£35.00 DVY/THO N&P
QUINTA DO BOM RETIRO 20 YEAR OLD TAWNY NV, RAMOS PINTO Douro – *Layer upon layer of rich aromas and flavours of tree bark, undergrowth, truffles, and marmalade.*	£36.00 MMD
CHURCHILL'S VINTAGE 1985, CHURCHILL GRAHAM Douro – *Elegant and balanced, this port has dry dusty tannins and a big lifted palate of richly smoky strawberry fruit.*	£38.50 WOI
QUINTA DO VESUVIO VINTAGE 2001, SYMINGTON FAMILY Douro – *This port is enormous. Stern, mammoth crunchy hedgerow fruit, leather, spice, and prune flavours. Incredible power.*	£39.00 WOI
BARROS COLHEITA 1978, BARROS ALMEIDA Douro – *Smooth and elegant – time in bottle was time well spent. Honeyed and nutty, with a superb creamy finish.*	£41.50 VIT
FONSECA VINTAGE 1985, THE FLADGATE PARTNERSHIP Douro – *Mature mahogany hue. Coffee and wild strawberries explode onto the palate, which is structured, aristocratic, and stylish.*	£45.00 MOV

GRAHAM'S 30 YEAR OLD TAWNY NV, W&J GRAHAM **Douro** – *Pale golden amber. Glorious bouquet of figs, dark berries, and spices. An elegant dowager with big tannins and rich fruit.*	£49.30 FEN/RWM
CALEM VINTAGE 1983, AA CALEM Douro – *Striking garnet colour fading to amber. Cedar, cigar leaf, and cinnamon notes accent tight spicy plum pudding flavours.*	£50.00 VIT
GRAHAM'S 40 YEAR OLD TAWNY NV, W&J GRAHAM **Douro** – *A mature tawny which floors the taster with its figs, butterscotch, tangerines, hazelnuts, almonds, and cloves.*	£65.00 FEN

BRONZE
PORT

☆ **NAVIGATORS VINTAGE CHARACTER NV, REAL COMPANHIA VELHA Douro** – *Very mature and cedary, its rasined palate possessing a smattering of chocolate and black pepper.*	£6.00 SMF
☆ **NAVIGATORS LBV 1996, REAL COMPANHIA VELHA** **Douro** – *Attractive brambly fruit mixes with chocolate on the nose, while the palate sports nuts and spice.*	£7.00 SMF
☆ **SMITH WOODHOUSE LBV 1998, SMITH WOODHOUSE Douro** – *Young, with spicy peppery fruit, a voluptuous mouthfeel, and a structured, sustained finish.*	£7.60 ASD/ODD
☆ **CO-OP LBV 1997, SMITH WOODHOUSE Douro** – *With youthful berry fruit and mint chocolate on the nose, this is an approachable, concentrated wine.*	£7.80 CWS
☆ **CROFT DISTINCTION NV, THE FLADGATE PARTNERSHIP Douro** – *Deep crimson. Clear and forward, with black pepper and plums. Mouthcoating texture.*	£8.00 SMF/JSM
☆ **WAITROSE LBV 1998, SILVA & COSENS Douro** – *An interesting LBV, where walnuts on the nose lead to a palate packed with soft plummy fruit and figgy flavours, too.*	£8.50 WTS

☆ **DOW'S LBV 1999, SILVA & COSENS** Douro – *Sweet, with plumcake intensity on the nose and blueberry richness on the palate. The finish is supple.*	**£9.70** SMF/FEN
☆ **FONSECA 10 YEAR OLD TAWNY NV, THE FLADGATE PARTNERSHIP** Douro – *Slightly pink, with spiced fruit, nutty notes, good grip, and sumptuous smoothness.*	**£10.00** MOV
☆ **OFFLEY LBV 1999, SOGRAPE** Douro – *Sweet and round with deep plum and damson aromas. The mouthfeel is velvety, the finish warm and spirity.*	**£10.00** TDC
TAYLORS LBV 1998, THE FLADGATE PARTNERSHIP Douro – *Showing maturity. Hints of chocolate and tapenade mingle with spices. Generous soft berry fruit.*	**£10.30** WIDELY AVAILABLE
GRAHAM'S LBV 1998, W&J GRAHAM Douro – *With a burnt raisiny nose, this has rich Christmas cake fruit on the palate and a medium length.*	**£10.80** WIDELY AVAILABLE
TRADITIONAL LBV 1998, QUINTA DO NOVAL Douro – *A rich port from one of the Douro's stars, lively, deeply coloured and vibrant.*	**£11.30** BNK/ESL FEN/WPR WES
MAJARA FINEST RESERVE NV, CASAL DOS JORDÕES Douro – *Fresh spiced plum and huckleberry fruit on the palate. Exceedingly rich and well-balanced.*	**£11.50** VER
CHURCHILL'S LBV 1998, CHURCHILL GRAHAM Douro – *Chocolate covered cherry chracter. Juicy, balanced, and scored with zesty acidity.*	**£11.70** HAX/CCS
LATE BOTTLED VINTAGE 1998, QUINTA DE LA ROSA Douro – *Unctuous. Spiced damson fruit with a spirity lift on the nose and palate. Sweet and concentrated.*	**£12.10** JNW/RAV WRK/NRW CCS/NYW
QUINTA DO CRASTO LBV 1998, QUINTA DO CRASTO Douro – *Much complexity is found in this graceful aged LBV. Smooth, balanced, and integrated, with rich fruitcake and chocolate flavours.*	**£13.00** SOM/ENO

RAMOS PINTO LBV 1998, RAMOS PINTO VINHOS **Douro** – Loads of character. Hints of violet and turmeric on the nose. A superbly rich velvety mouthfeel.	£13.50 WPR/GHL
SMITH WOODHOUSE LBV BOTTLE MATURED 1994, SMITH WOODHOUSE Douro – A nutty nose and baked, raisined fruit alongside bitter chocolate and spicy notes.	£13.50 SOM/FEN NRW/NYW
GRAHAM'S CRUSTED BOTTLED 1999 NV, W&J GRAHAM Douro – An evolved, creamy style, with complex berry, caramel, and nutty flavours and aromas. Sumptuous milk chocolate hints.	£13.70 ESL/JSM
TESCO VINTAGE 1995, SYMINGTON FAMILY Douro – Plummy, with clove and cinnamon aromas. The palate has very rich, deep blackberry fruit and a syrupy finish.	£14.00 TOS
INFANTADO LBV 1998, QUINTA DO INFANTADO Douro – Hints of black pepper and olive. Fruit shines on the mid-palate before leading to an austere finish.	£14.30 BEN/V&C LIB
TEN YEAR OLD TAWNY NV, QUINTA DO NOVAL Douro – Scents of walnuts and citrus blossoms, and flavours of runny honey scored with orange rind acidity.	£14.40 BNK/FEN WTS
WARRE'S LBV BOTTLE MATURED 1994, WARRE'S Douro – Reminiscent of Christmas pudding, with good clean fruit and a spicy middle-palate. Fine complexity and a pleasing depth.	£15.20 FEN/GHL NRW/JSM
FONSECA QUINTA DO PANASCAL 1988, THE FLADGATE PARTNERSHIP Douro – This robust, structured port has fabulous concentration, tangy red fruit, and a firm tannic backbone.	£19.00 WPR/MOV
BARROS COLHEITA 1989, BARROS ALMEIDA Douro – Pale tawny colour. Marked nuttiness mixes well with fruit and spice on the fine, lasting finish.	£20.20 VIT/WOI
QUINTA DO VALE D. MARIA VINTAGE 2001, JOSÉ MARIA DA FONSECA & VAN ZELLER Douro – Lush wine with a plum and spirit nose. The palate creamy and the finish has depth and intensity.	£20.30 LAI/TAN

DOW'S QUINTA DO BOMFIM 1996, SILVA & COSENS **Douro** – *Savoury farmyard aromas. Velvet-textured and sweet; big and round, but with good grip.*	£20.70 FEN/NRW TOS
WARRE'S QUINTA DA CAVADINHA 1995, WARRE'S **Douro** – *Gum tree and chocolate hovers over a bed of concentrated cassis. Blockbuster Port at its most quintessential.*	▲£22.30 HOU/FEN GHL
TAYLOR'S QUINTA DE VARGELLAS 1988, FLADGATE PARTNERSHIP Douro – *Lush and deep with rich damson and cherry fruit on the palate. The finish is powerful and heady.*	£22.70 HAX/TOS MOV
HEREDIAS VINTAGE 2001, SOCIEDADE DE VINHOS SENHORA DO CONVENTO Douro – *A huge armful of wildflowers on the nose, and generous quantities of figs, dates, and mocha flavours.*	£24.50 GON
TAYLORS QUINTA DE VARGELLAS 1996, THE FLADGATE PARTNERSHIP Douro – *A brooding port which in spite of its youth is serious indeed. Powdery cinnamon bark tannins.*	£24.80 TAN/EVI TOS
INFANTADO VINTAGE 1997, QUINTA DO INFANTADO Douro – *Some evolution, good concentration and deep liquorice flavours. Edgy tea leaf aromas.*	£28.00 LIB
QUINTA DO CRASTO VINTAGE 2001, QUINTA DO CRASTO Douro – *Big and rich, with inky black fruits, fresh orange peel, fig, and marmite aromas that just won't quit. Fabulous.*	£29.50 ENO
FERREIRA VINTAGE 1982, SOGRAPE Douro – *Vivid red colour. Chilli pepper, spice, and chocolate flavours flesh out the warm palate of toast and damson jam.*	£30.00 BWC
TAYLORS 20 YEAR OLD TAWNY NV, THE FLADGATE PARTNERSHIP Douro – *Dried apricots, marmalade, meadowsweet, and sweet chestnut honey scents the nose. Lush, long, and satisfying.*	£32.30 FEN/RWM JSM
KROHN COLHEITA 1995, WIESE & KROHN Douro – *Caramel and stewed raisin nose and a complex palate of orange peel and mulling spices.*	£34.00 FFW/MER

PORT BRONZE / SEAL **289**

CHURCHILL'S VINTAGE 1994, CHURCHILL GRAHAM **Douro** – *Deep, luscious, and spicy, with dried fruit, inkwell, white pepper, and tar scents and flavours.*	£38.90 HOU/RAV CCS
CHURCHILL'S VINTAGE 2000, CHURCHILL GRAHAM **Douro** – *Wow! Spicebox, pencil lead, blueberry, and violet elements tumble together on nose and palate.*	£39.00 TAN
QUINTA DA GRICHA VINTAGE 1999, CHURCHILL GRAHAM **Douro** – *Vermilion. The herbaceous nose is complemented by a palate of earthy blackberries and raspberries.*	£42.00 CCS
TAYLORS VINTAGE 1985, THE FLADGATE PARTNERSHIP **Douro** – *Oregano punctuates the nose of oranges, vanilla pod, and bitter chocolate. Spicy and generous.*	£44.00 TAN/GHL JSM
QUINTA DO NOVAL VINTAGE 1995, QUINTA DO NOVAL **Douro** – *Clean, concentrated, and structured, with coffee, stone fruit, and chewy raisin characters.*	£47.00 WPR
CROFT VINTAGE 1977, THE FLADGATE PARTNERSHIP **Douro** – *Amber-hued, with coffee bean and ripe purple-fig character. Big, velvety, balanced, and long.*	£55.00 MOV

SEAL OF APPROVAL
PORT

☆ **NAVIGATORS RUBY NV, REAL COMPANHIA VELHA** **Douro** – *Velvety sweet cherry fruit and warming sandalwood essence.*	£5.00 SMF
☆ **NAVIGATORS TAWNY NV, REAL COMPANHIA VELHA** **Douro** – *Ripe apricot, toasted walnut, and golden syrup characteristics.*	£5.00 SMF
☆ **MHV REGIMENTAL FINE RUBY NV, SILVA & COSENS** **Douro** – *Crimson red. Voluptuous loganberries and a sprinkle of white pepper.*	£5.90 BNK/MHV

PORT BRONZE **/ PORTUGUESE WHITE** BRONZE

☆ **TAYLOR'S FINEST RESERVE NV, TAYLOR'S** DOURO – *Robust spice, firm blackberry fruit, and hints of granite.*	£6.00 M&S
☆ **SAINSBURY'S LATE BOTTLED VINTAGE 1998, SYMINGTON'S** DUORO – *Garnet red. Lush ripe strawberry fruit flavours spiced with cinnamon.*	£7.00 JSM
☆ **CO-OP VINTAGE CHARACTER NV, SMITH WOODHOUSE** DOURO – *Bilberries, strawberries, and cloves. Luscious and powerful.*	£7.20 CWS

BRONZE
PORTUGUESE WHITE

☆ **SEGADA 2003, DFJ VINHOS** RIBATEJO – *Soft, elegant, and balanced. A fresh floral nose, and a dry, somewhat fat palate of apricots and peaches.*	£4.70 UNS/SMF ODD
☆ **BELA FONTE BICAL 2002, DFJ VINHOS** BEIRAS – *Fresh lemon scents greet the nose. Broad, rich, and heavy, with a long clean finish. Big.*	£5.00 D&F
☆ **JP VINHOS CATARINA 2002, JP VINHOS** PENINSULA DE SETÚBAL – *Plenty of vanilla oak smooths out the palate, which is lifted by zingy acidity. Layered flavour. Good concentration.*	£5.00 EHL
ESPORÃO MONTE VELHO WHITE 2003, ESPORÃO ALENTEJO – *Citrus, gooseberries, and flowers, with some weight and spice. Refreshing, warm, and lively.*	£5.50 WRW
QUINTA DO VALE PERDIDO WHITE 2003, CASA SANTOS LIMA ESTREMADURA – *The bouquet has white flowers, sage, and citrus fruit. Dry, with fresh acidity, mineral influence, and a persistent finish.*	£5.50 LAI
GRAND' ARTE ALVARINHO 2003, DFJ VINHOS ESTREMADURA – *Pale, with delicate citrus blossoms on the nose. Beautifully integrated oak, bright spangly acidity, and a long finish.*	£6.50 BOO

PORTUGUESE WHITE BRONZE / SEAL / **RED** TROPHY / GOLD **291**

CASTELLO D'ALBA RESERVA BRANCO 2002, VINHOS DOURO SUPERIOR Douro – *Tropical pineapples, passionfruit, melon, and macadamia nuts. Pretty creamy notes add the finishing touch.*	£8.00 REY

SEAL OF APPROVAL
PORTUGUESE WHITE

☆ **SERRAS DE AZEITÃO 2003, JP VINHOS** Peninsula de Setúbal – *Deeply fragrant, with lavender and rose notes. Dry, ripe citrus flavours.*	£4.00 EHL

TROPHY
PORTUGUESE RED

QUINTA DO PORTAL AURU 2001, QUINTA DO PORTAL Douro – *Lots of rich oak, plenty of ripe fruit, and a complexity of spice, currant, damson, and raisin fruit character.*	£25.00 CHN

GOLD
PORTUGUESE RED

☆ **DFJ TOURIGA NACIONAL TOURIGA FRANCA 2001, DFJ VINHOS** Estremadura – *Stuffed with damson and summer berry fruit flavours. A creamy texture and chocolate oak notes.*	£6.50 TOS/MOV
☆ **GRAND' ARTE ALICANTE BOUSCHET 2003, DFJ VINHOS** Estremadura – *This beauty is packed to the gunnels with sweet spice, spearmint, flowers, liquorice, and black-cherry fruit.*	£6.50 D&F
☆ **GRAND' ARTE TRINCADEIRA 2003, DFJ VINHOS** Ribatejo – *Splendid floral perfume and menthol notes. Full blackcurrant, blueberry, and plum flavours; tight-knit oak and integrated round tannins.*	£10.00 MOV
QUINTA DO CRASTO DOURO RESERVA 2001, QUINTA DO CRASTO Douro – *Rather like port without the fortification. Dense raisined fruit; chunky tannins. This is one powerful wine, with massive fruit intensity.*	£13.50 NYW/ENO JSM

PORTUGUESE RED GOLD / SILVER

QUINTA DOS QUATRO VENTOS RESERVA 2001, CAVES ALIANCA Douro – *Bags of black fruit, a very fine texture, and a mouthcoating texture. Prominent vanilla oak and spicebox scents.*	£19.10 FFW/MER NYW
QUINTA DO VALE MEAO 2001, F OLAZABAL & FILHOS Douro – *Powerful Touriga Nacional spice, cloves, currant, and black fruit style. Acidity gives lift and braces the fruit weight.*	£29.00 HAX

SILVER
PORTUGUESE RED

☆ **QUINTA DO LAGOALVA RESERVA 2001, QUINTA DA LAGOALVA DE CIMA** Ribatejo – *A fragrant nose of black-cherry and bramble fruit. Pleasingly complex, with layers of damsons, cherries, and well-integrated oak.*	£5.00 FWW
☆ **SEGADA 2002, DFJ VINHOS** Ribatejo – *A distinctive bouquet of spice, minerals, violets, and fruity cherries. Firm and spicy. This would make a good food wine.*	£5.10 RAV/SMF ODD
☆ **DFJ CALADOC ALICANTE BOUSCHET 2001, DFJ VINHOS** Estremadura – *Ripe cherry fruit flesh tightly bound in fine tannins. Balanced, juicy, and lifted, its richness enlivened by zingy acidity.*	£6.00 D&F
☆ **QUINTA DA SETENCOSTAS 2003, CASA SANTOS LIMA** Estremadura – *Perfumed with caramel apples and blackberries. A beguiling magenta hue and a forward, fruit-packed, rich, massively ripe palate.*	£6.00 JSM
☆ **TESCO FINEST TOURIGA NACIONAL 2003, DFJ VINHOS** Estremadura – *True Portuguese style shines from this modern wine with its rich fruit compote flavours, menthol, and sweet Parma violet notes.*	£6.00 TOS
☆ **GRAND'ARTE MERLOT 2001, DFJ VINHOS** Estremadura – *Well-balanced, with medium tannins, sweetly ripe plummy fruit, and a touch of liquorice. Kudos to master winemaker José Neiva.*	£6.50 D&F
ESPORÃO RESERVA 2001, ESPORÃO Alentejo – *Huge, ripe and rich cherry flavours with robust charm. Elegant tannins and oak integration. Considerable length.*	£9.40 SOM/GHL BOO/WRW

PORTUGUESE RED SILVER 293

ESPORÃO ARAGONES 2002, ESPORÃO Alentejo – *Acrid spent match scents harmonise with sweet oak. Delicious raspberry ripple flavours. Bright, smooth, and elegant.*	£10.00 NYW/WAW
ESPORÃO SYRAH 2002, ESPORÃO Alentejo – *Ripe, tangy raspberry fruit, with sweet, spicy, chewy tannins. The oak is well-judged, conferring both complexity and a powerful finish.*	£10.00 JEF
CORTES DE CIMA 2002, HANS KRISTIAN JORGENSEN Alentejo – *With its toasty, ripe red fruit, this wine is seriously sumptuous. Integrated oak, spicy fruit, and a long finish.*	£11.00 ADN/ODD JNW/MWW
QUINTA DO CRASTO TOURIGA NACIONAL 2001, QUINTA DO CRASTO Douro – *Vivid upfront oak notes, chocolate and cherries. Huge power and richness. Plenty of vanilla and cinnamon toast.*	£11.00 ENO/JSM
QUINTA DAS BACELADAS SINGLE ESTATE 2001, CAVES ALIANCA Beiras – *Earthy, oaky, spicy and laden with berries. The tannins are marked but balanced, suggesting that ageing should benefit this wine.*	£12.00 FFW/MER
QUINTA DA GARRIDA 2001, CAVES ALIANCA Dão – *Pimentos and sundried tomatoes glow on nose and palate. Fine chalky tannins and a dark purple hue.*	£12.40 FFW/L&S NRW/MER
POST SCRIPTUM 2002, PRATS & SYMINGTON Douro – *Made from the traditional Port grape trilogy. Round, full, concentrated dark fruit is infused with a subtle oak injection.*	£14.00 JEF
CORTES DE CIMA SYRAH 2002, HANS KRISTIAN JORGENSEN Alentejo – *A tarry nose alongside ripe, tangy raspberry fruit well balanced by the judicious use of oak.*	£15.50 ADN
QUINTA DO PORTAL TOURIGA FRANCA 2001, QUINTA DO PORTAL Douro – *The dark liquid clings to the glass. Attractive deep blackcurrant fruit flavours and scents of tobacco leaves and coaldust.*	£19.00 TWM
CORTES DE CIMA INCÓGNITO 2002, HANS KRISTIAN JORGENSEN Alentejo – *Crimson purple, with damsons on the nose. Tangy, fresh and youthful, with fine-grained, integrated tannins.*	£19.50 ADN

ESPORÃO GARRAFEIRA 2001, ESPORÃO Alentejo – The palate has huge intensity of berry fruits, coupled with a fair thwack of oak on a medium to full-bodied framework.	£19.50 JEF
QUINTA DO PORTAL GRANDE RESERVA 2001, QUINTA DO PORTAL Douro – Rich dark fruit nose with a soft creamy edge and orange blossom aromas. Concentrated, with powerful tannins.	£20.00 TWM
QUINTA DA LEDA 2000, SOGRAPE Douro – Spice, truffles and sea salt. Taut, rich and intense, with flavours of bramble fruit and wild herbs.	£21.00 BWC
DUAS QUINTAS RESERVA 2001, RAMOS PINTO VINHOS Douro – Juicy yet very dry, this has upfront dark-fleshed cherry flavours, Indian spices, and a long grippy finish.	£21.30 HAX/JNW TAU/WPR
TDA TERRUGEM ALENTEJO 2001, CAVES ALIANCA Alentejo – Powerful bouquet and palate. Rich, dense and meaty, the palate of tinned strawberries carrying its oak well. Still young.	£32.40 FFW/MER
VINHA MARIA TERESA 2001, QUINTA DO CRASTO Douro – The piercing nose offers woody spices and date scents, progressing inevitably towards a dried fruit palate.	£43.00 VIT/ENO

BRONZE
PORTUGUESE RED

☆ **VINHA DO MONTE 2002, SOGRAPE** Alentejo – Plums, cherries, and chocolate flavour this deep, rich wine. A tight tannic web reins in the fruit.	£5.00 SGL
DFJ MERLOT TINTA RORIZ 2003, DFJ VINHOS Estremadura – Medicinal notes, sweet strawberry fruit, a handful of liquorice and a ripe brambly finish.	£5.40 D&F
ROCHA DO MONTE 2003, DFJ VINHOS Terras do Sado – Expressive, soft, mature fruit with earth and leather notes. Savoury, ripe, and powerful.	£5.40 D&F

PORTUGUESE RED BRONZE 295

CASA DO LAGO 2002, DFJ VINHOS RIBATEJO – A warm, ripe palate of rich cherry flavours. Structured, with integrated tannins, solidly ripe fruit, and balanced, soft oak.	**£5.50** D&F
DUQUE DE VISEU 2000, SOGRAPE DOURO – Deep and earthy, with clear berry fruit and a supple tannic structure. Medium weight and length.	**£5.60** WES MWW
DFJ CABERNET TINTA MIUDA 2000, DFJ VINHOS ESTREMADURA – A full-bodied wine with a restrained, mature nose, and a fine palate with cranberry, plums, and hints of coffee.	**£5.80** D&F/BGN
ESPORÃO MONTE VELHO RED 2003, ESPORÃO ALENTEJO – A huge nose of curry spices and wild thyme, and a palate of earthy, peppery raspberries dotted with flowers.	**£5.80** GHL/BOO WRW
PEDRAS DO MONTE 2003, DFJ VINHOS TERRAS DO SADO – Forward, with mature, complex aromas, exceedingly ripe, clean redcurrant fruit, and earthy, tannic quality.	**£5.80** RAV/SMF MOV
BELA FONTE TOURIGA FRANCA TINTA RORIZ 2001, DFJ VINHOS BEIRAS – A light, modern wine with soft red fruits, medium tannins, and a refreshing finish.	**£6.00** BOO
GRAND' ARTE CALADOC 2001, DFJ VINHOS ESTREMADURA – Very ripe crushed berry flavours. Perfume of violets and menthol. Lush mouthcoating texture.	**£6.00** D&F/JSM
BELA FONTE JAÉN 2003, DFJ VINHOS BEIRAS – The judges loved this mature beauty with its open-knit texture and pretty savoury raspberry fruit.	**£6.10** RAV
GRAND' ARTE CABERNET SAUVIGNON 2000, DFJ VINHOS ESTREMADURA – One to enjoy now, this inky, rustic wine has an interesting, well-balanced palate of mulberry, mint, and fresh fruit.	**£6.50** D&F
MANTA PRETA 2003, DFJ VINHOS ESTREMADURA – With a lively minty lift, this youngster offers soft black fruit and a lick of sweet coconut oak.	**£6.50** MOV/WTS

PORTUGUESE RED BRONZE

FONTE DO BECO 2003, DFJ VINHOS PALMELA – This quintessential Portuguese wine has grippy ripe tannins, earth, tar, and a drying finish.	£6.70 MOV/BOO
CASA DA ALORNA COLHEITA SELECCIÓNADA 2001, QUINTA DA ALORNA RIBATEJO – A complex nose and rich ripe palate of black fruit. Balanced, soft, round, and long.	£6.80 HAX/L&S BOO
CHAMINÉ 2002, CORTES DE CIMA ALENTEJO – Graphite and vegetation scent the nose. The palate has heaps of dark fruit flavour on its pungent, plummy palate.	£7.00 ODD
VINHOS SOGRAPE RESERVA ALENTEJO 2001, SOGRAPE ALENTEJO – Spiced plum and berry nose leads to an intense palate of ripe fruit, sweet oak, and soft tannin.	£8.00 MWW
DOURO RED 2001, QUINTA DO VALLADO DOURO – The nose shows elements of earth, plum, and spice. Intense, with a ripe, ample structure. Long finish.	£8.40 NYW
QUINTA DA URZE TINTA RORIZ 2002, ROBOREDO MADEIRA DOURO – Juicy cherry and crushed almond aromas. Concentrated, youthful, and mouthwatering. Deep purple.	£9.00 REY
QUINTA DA URZE TOURIGA FRANCA 2002, ROBOREDO MADEIRA DOURO – Complex and inviting, with a smooth texture, integrated tannins, and lasting finish.	£9.00 REY
QUINTA DA URZE TOURIGA NACIONAL 2002, ROBOREDO MADEIRA DOURO – Warm, lifted, and packed with red fruit preserves. Taut tannins and brisk bayleaf aromas.	£9.00 REY
DOURO TINTO 2002, QUINTA DE LA ROSA DOURO – Plenty of poise and aplomb. Creamy black-cherry palate imbued with hints of chocolate and liquorice.	£9.30 JNW/SOM CCS/FLY OWC
VALLE PRADINHOS 2000, CASAL VALLE PRADINHOS TRÁS-OS-MONTES – Aromas of cassis and fine woody spice. Exceptionally well-balanced, and replete with sweet, spicy fruit, fresh acidity, and great depth.	£9.70 BEN/HAX WPR

PORTUGUESE RED BRONZE 297

GRAND' ARTE TOURIGA FRANCA 2002, DFJ VINHOS **ESTREMADURA** – *A sweetly ripe nose and a mouthful of raspberry fruit. Lifted acidity. Perfumed, youthful, and quaffable.*	£10.00 MOV
HERDADE DO ESPORÃO TOURIGA NACIONAL 2002, ESPORÃO **ALENTEJO** – *The fragrant nose is dusted with cinnamon and nutmeg, and the very dry palate is laden with firm cherry fruit.*	£10.00 NYW/POR
SÓ TOURIGA NACIONAL 2001, JP VINHOS **TERRAS DO SADO** – *Pure, fresh and straightforward, this fragrant wine bursts with perfume of red fruit, green pepper, and hints of the barnyard.*	£10.00 EHL
VALLE PRADINHOS 2001, CASAL VALLE PRADINHOS **TRÁS-OS-MONTES** – *A wine needing time to bring exuberant tannins into balance with ample fruit. The rich nose has smoky black fruits.*	£10.00 HAX
MÁ PARTILHA 2000, JP VINHOS **TERRAS DO SADO** – *The palate is already displaying some maturity as tobacco joins the somewhat dried berry fruit.*	£10.50 EHL
CORTES DE CIMA 2001, HANS KRISTIAN JORGENSEN **ALENTEJO** – *Warm and spicy with a peppery nose. Ripe, sweet fruit and a refreshing tang on the finish.*	£11.00 ADN/ODD JNW MWW
QUINTA DA BACALHOA 2001, JP VINHOS **TERRAS DO SADO** – *Medium-full in body, this wine from the historic Bacalhôa estate is fresh and round with soft tannins and complex cedar, cigar box, and blackberry fruit aromas.*	£11.00 EHL
QUINTA DO VALE D. MARIA DOURO RED 2001, JOSÉ MARIA DA FONSECA & VAN ZELLER **DOURO** – *Spicebox and celeriac scents on the nose. Powerfully oaked vanilla- and coconut-flavoured loganberry fruit.*	£11.80 LAI/TAN
QUINTA DA TERRUGEM ALENTEJO 2001, CAVES ALIANCA **ALENTEJO** – *A youthful sprite with attractive strawberry fruit and fine-grained tannins. Seamless and lengthy.*	£12.20 FFW/HAX MER/NYW
CARM RESERVA 2001, R MADEIRA **DOURO** – *Warm cherry and oak nose. A soft, slightly sweet palate with a spicy finish and a gentle flush of tannins.*	£12.80 HAX

PORTUGUESE RED BRONZE

COVELA COLHEITA SELECCIÓNADA 2001, QUINTA DE COVELA VINHO VERDE – *Blackberries join spicy, cigar box aromas, with generous tannins on the palate alongside plentiful fruit and well-integrated oak.*	£12.90 C&B
SOGRAPE CALLABRIGA 2000, SOGRAPE DOURO – *Perfumed, with a deep smoky nose. The palate shows excellent extraction and depth. The finish has depth and persistence.*	£14.00 BWC
QUINTA DE RORIZ RESERVA 2001, QUINTA DE RORIZ DOURO – *Coffee and dark fruit aromas lace the richly berried, firmly tannic palate. Well-structured, with carefully integrated oak.*	£14.20 G&M
QUINTA DOS CARVALHAIS TOURIGA NACIONAL 2000, SOGRAPE DOURO – *The soft chocolate-covered summer fruit palate is ripe and accessible, with a smattering of flowers and cut grass scents.*	£14.80 SGL
DOURO RESERVA TINTO 2001, QUINTA DE LA ROSA DOURO – *Baked earth and spice on the nose and thick damson fruit on the palate. Concentrated and long.*	£15.30 CCS/RWM FLY
CARM PREMIUM 2000, R MADEIRA DOURO – *Rich, very ripe fruit is displayed in this wine, as is tight acidity and a seductively warm finish.*	£15.80 HAX
QUINTA DO PORTAL TOURIGA NACIONAL 2001, QUINTA DO PORTAL DOURO – *Bramble fruits rise from a bouquet decorated with moist bark notes. Sophisticated, multidimensional, nutty, and long.*	£16.00 GRT
CARTUXA RESERVA TINTO 1999, FUNDACÃO EUGENIO DE ALMEIDA ALENTEJO – *Chocolate and spice elements. Original, balanced, and fresh, with dark berry fruit and a fine-boned structure.*	£16.50 HAX/JFE
DOURO RESERVE RED 2000, QUINTA DO VALLADO DOURO – *Supple and inviting. Studded with strawberries, dried dates, and cardamom. Deep, earthy, and complex.*	£18.00 NYW
CORTES DE CIMA ARAGONEZ 2002, HANS KRISTIAN JORGENSEN ALENTEJO – *Sweet raspberry fruit on the palate. Intriguing baked nose and a finish to be proud of.*	£19.50 ADN

PORTUGUESE RED BRONZE

CORTES DE CIMA RESERVA 2001, HANS KRISTIAN JORGENSEN ALENTEJO – *An attractive plum and cherry nose, with a touch of savoury character. Sweet fruit balanced by good acidity.*	**£19.50** ADN
QUINTA DOS CARVALHAIS RESERVA 2000, SOGRAPE DOURO – *Juicy, lively, and minerally, with attractive forest fruit flavours and a spicy, balanced quality.*	**£23.40** SGL

GOLD MEDALS HAVE SCORED the equivalent of at least 18.5/20 (or 95/100) and are exceptional. Silver has scored over 17/20 (or 90/100), bronze over 15.5/20 (or 85/100), and seals of approval over 14/20 (or 80/100).
- ☆ particularly good value
- ★ truly great value
- ▲ 50CL bottle
- ■ 37.5CL bottle
- ● 10CL bottle

FOR STOCKIST CODES turn to page 355. For regularly updated information about stockists and the International Wine Challenge, visit wineint.com. For a full glossary of wine terms and a complete free wine course, visit robertjoseph-onwine.com

REST OF THE WORLD

Having found a pigeon hole for every other wine producing country, this is the heading we are left with for Lebanon, Mexico, and England. And it would be an easy section to skip over on your way to a more familiar part of the Old World or a more exciting corner of the New World. But that would be to turn your back on some genuinely interesting wines such as the gold and silver medal winners from Lebanon and the gold medal winning English sparkling wine that earned higher marks than many a Champagne. Definitely wines to serve "blind" to your most pretentious guests.

SILVER
REST OF THE WORLD WHITE

☆ **BLANC DE L'OBSERVATOIRE 2003, CHÂTEAU KSARA** LEBANON – *Fragrant and deep, this massive wine has a generous swathe of tobacco, mandarin, and lemon flavours and aromas.*	£7.20 FFW/CVE

BRONZE
REST OF THE WORLD WHITE

SURREY GOLD 2003, DENBIES WINE ESTATE ENGLAND – *Lime flowers on the nose, and a palate of soft grapes, peaches, and melons. Fresh acidity.*	£5.50 WTS/DBS JSM
CURIOUS GRAPE FLINT DRY 2001, ENGLISH WINES GROUP ENGLAND – *Grassy notes decorate the charming notes. The palate has plenty of juicy greengage fruit flavour.*	£6.10 BNK/UNS WES/WTS WRW
CURIOUS GRAPE BACCHUS 2003, ENGLISH WINES GROUP ENGLAND – *A soft nose of white flowers and fruit, with honeyed notes. The palate has crisp, green apple acidity.*	£6.70 BNK/WSO TOS/WES MWW

GOLD
REST OF THE WORLD RED

CUVÉE DU TROISIÈME MILLÉNAIRE 2002, CHÂTEAU KSARA Lebanon – Full of eucalyptus, blackberry, damson, and tar, balanced by a firm grippy tannic structure. Sophisticated and satisfying.	**£18.50** FFW/NYW CVE

BRONZE
REST OF THE WORLD RED

LA CETTO NEBBIOLO RESERVA PRIVADA 1999, LA CETTO Mexico – Ripe and vibrant, with a clean, nutty, coal-scented nose and touches of pepper. Chunky and plummy.	**£8.50** JFE/AWS
YEW TREE PINOT NOIR 2002, DENBIES WINE ESTATE England – With a youthful, lively demeanour on the nose and palate, tart strawberry fruit, integrated tannins, and fresh acidity.	**£14.00** DBS

SEAL OF APPROVAL
REST OF THE WORLD RED

☆ **EL MECEDOR CABERNET MALBEC 2002, LES GRANDS CHAIS DE FRANCE** Mexico – Vibrant ripe redcurrants, hints of straw, and whiffs of smoke.	**£4.00** SPR

GOLD
REST OF THE WORLD SPARKLING

☆ **CHAPEL DOWN PINOT RESERVE 1999, ENGLISH WINES GROUP** England – Rich, with leesy, yeasty complexity, and waxy, honeyed texture. Tropical fruit style, good intensity, and a serious finish.	**£14.20** WES

BRONZE
REST OF THE WORLD SPARKLING

☆ **CO-OP ENGLISH SPARKLING BRUT NV, ENGLISH WINES** ENGLAND – *An unusual and long sparkling blend, with floral and yeast notes, apple fruit, and foamy mousse.*	£7.00 CWS
BREAKY BOTTOM CUVÉE RÉMY ALEXANDRE 1999, PETER HALL ENGLAND – *A restrained grapey nose with a touch of biscuit that runs through the palate. Solid weight, good length.*	£14.50 BBV /HRY EWC/BUT
QUALITY SPARKLING WINE BRUT 2000, PAINSHILL PARK TRUST ENGLAND – *Fresh acidity balances the soft fruit and creamy mousse. Fine and harmonious with nice lees character. Decent length.*	£16.00 PAI
PREMIER CUVÉE CHARDONNAY 1995, NYETIMBER VINEYARD ENGLAND – *Full and forward with a candied fruit style and honeysuckle flavours and floral sweetness. Very bright and refreshing.*	£20.40 BNK/HAX BBR/NYW OWC

BRONZE
REST OF THE WORLD SWEET

ASTLEY VINEYARDS LATE HARVEST 2002, ASTLEY VINEYARDS ENGLAND – *Star bright. Lemon curd scents and flavours. Creamy fruit, fresh acidity, and very good length.*	■£7.70 HPW/AST

SOUTH AFRICA

In the 1990s, South Africa frequently did quite poorly in competitions such as this. The years of isolation had done nothing to help wine producers in the Cape to keep up with developments elsewhere around the world. Nowadays, however, as the following results show, this country is a very impressive performer. Notice in particular how well the South Africans have done with the Sauvignon Blanc grape (producing versions to worry New Zealand and the Loire in France) and Syrah. There are great Chenin Blancs and Chardonnays, too, and unusually good examples of the often tricky Pinotage.

GOLD
SOUTH AFRICAN WHITE

☆ **THANDI CHARDONNAY 2003, VINFRUCO** WESTERN CAPE – *The relatively high alcohol gives good weight and depth and a solid background for the rich, peachy tropical fruit.*	£7.00 TOS
☆ **CROCODILE'S LAIR CHARDONNAY 2001, BOUCHARD FINLAYSON** WALKER BAY – *Leesy characteristics impart weight and texture. Good depth, richness, and complexity.*	£10.40 CCS/NYW WTS/FLY OWC
MEINERT CHENIN BLANC 2002, KEN FORRESTER WINES STELLENBOSCH – *Fabulously complex, delicately smoky and warm, with well-integrated oak that only serves to ramp up the intensity.*	£18.70 WPR/WTS

SILVER
SOUTH AFRICAN WHITE

☆ **GLENWOOD SEMILLON SAUVIGNON BLANC 2003, GLENWOOD** PAARL – *Peaches and tangerines scent the nose. The zingy palate drips with lime cordial and lemons. Full yet refreshing.*	£6.50 ROG

SOUTH AFRICAN WHITE SILVER

☆ **RAATS CHENIN BLANC 2002, RAATS FAMILLY WINES** STELLENBOSCH – *Packed with lemons, limes, grapefruit, tropical peaches, melons, and bananas. Very good intensity and depth.*	£7.00 ODD
☆ **THE MAVERICK CHENIN BLANC 2003, BELLINGHAM** COASTAL – *Delicate white spring blossom nose. The palate is clear and creamy, with a savoury tinge and seductive mango fruit.*	£7.00 TOS/WTS MWW
☆ **CEDERBERG CHENIN BLANC 2003, CEDERBERG PRIVATE CELLARS** CEDERBERG – *Very good mineral definition. Aromatic, slightly animal nose. Exuberant palate of intense yellow fruit flavours.*	£7.40 HAX
BOSCHENDAL SAUVIGNON BLANC 2003, BOSCHENDAL FRANSCHOEK VALLEY – *Minerals, passion flowers, and cape gooseberry on the nose; the vibrant palate has a summery, tropical quality.*	£7.70 CEB/TAU
BRAMPTON VIOGNIER 2003, RUSTENBERG COASTAL – *Powerful, with woody notes. Fresh and approachable, with a touch of peach sweetness on the aromatic finish.*	£8.20 VIT/CCS
BUITENVERWACHTING SAUVIGNON BLANC 2003, BUITENVERWACHTING CONSTANTIA – *As focused and tight-knit as any Sauvignon Blanc you're likely to find, with an outstanding texture and superb aromatic definition.*	£8.30 CEB/ODD JSM
ZEVENWACHT TIN MINE WHITE 2003, ZEVENWACHT ESTATE COASTAL – *Delicate freshly shelled green pea aromas. Mouthwatering lime flavours with just a touch of honeyed oak.*	£8.50 AUS
MULDERBOSCH SAUVIGNON BLANC 2003, MULDERBOSCH VINEYARDS STELLENBOSCH – *Bright colour. Powerful aromas of fresh gooseberries, lemons, grass and sweet flowers. Light-bodied, pear-flavoured, and racy.*	£9.80 WIDELY AVAILABLE
LONGRIDGE CHARDONNAY 2001, WINECORP STELLENBOSCH – *The nose is ripe with butter and grapefruit notes. The rich and concentrated palate is balanced by dancing acidity.*	£10.00 PLB
LONGRIDGE CHARDONNAY 2002, WINECORP STELLENBOSCH – *Deep greenish gold hue. Complex sweet cinnamon, tangerine, and pear aromas. Toasty, peachy, and spicy, with admirable complexity.*	£10.00 PLB

SOUTH AFRICAN WHITE SILVER / BRONZE

STELLENBOSCH CHARDONNAY 2002, RUSTENBERG **Stellenbosch** – *Sweetly ripe, with brioche, clove, and resin nuances. Big and tropical, with pineapple flavours, and good oak integration.*	£10.10 ESL/JNW FLA/CCS NYW/SHB
CROCODILE'S LAIR CHARDONNAY 2000, BOUCHARD FINLAYSON **Walker Bay** – *Medium-high acidity rends the richly oaked palate. Fine citrus, ripe mango and guava, and hints of lanolin on the nose.*	£10.60 WTS/FLY OWC
SAUVIGNON BLANC RESERVE 2003, VERGELEGEN **Stellenbosch** – *Big, smoky, grassy nose. Cleansing acidity races through the palate of lime and lemon fruit. The finish is firm and steely.*	£11.90 NYW/JSM
HAMILTON RUSSELL CHARDONNAY 2003, HAMILTON RUSSELL VINEYARDS **Overberg** – *Butter, clove, almonds and popcorn; ripe citrus, spices, and bright acidity. Creamy texture.*	£14.50 WIDELY AVAILABLE
FIVE SOLDIERS CHARDONNAY 2001, RUSTENBERG **Stellenbosch** – *Notes of smoke, panettone, and caramel. Bold and beautiful, with plenty of ripe lemon and mangosteen flavours.*	£17.60 HAX/JNW VGN/CCS NYW/OWC

BRONZE
SOUTH AFRICAN WHITE

☆ **ASDA SOUTH AFRICAN CHARDONNAY 2003, WINECORP** **Western Cape** – *Pear drops, pineapples, and sweet spices lace the nose and palate. Pronounced, open, and approachable.*	£3.20 ASD
☆ **BON COURAGE COLOMBARD 2003, BON COURAGE ESTATE** **Breede River Valley** – *The nose is a pungent array of grass, wildflowers, and herbs. The palate is fleshy, with comely pear flavours.*	£5.00 AUS
☆ **CAPE PROMISE CHARDONNAY 2002, STELLENBOSCH VINEYARDS** **Stellenbosch** – *Bright lemon gold. The subtly fragrant nose has buttery overtones. Balanced and soft, with good use of oak.*	£5.00 SAF
☆ **CAPE SOLEIL SAUVIGNON BLANC 2003, AFRICAN TERROIR** **Western Cape** – *Faintly pink straw hue. Dynamic, complex, and rich, with compelling red fruit notes. Quirky and unusual.*	£5.00 JSM

SOUTH AFRICAN WHITE BRONZE

☆ **DIEMERSDAL SAUVIGNON BLANC 2003, DIEMERSDAL** Durbanville – *Elegant and subtly complex, with ripe kiwi and gooseberry fool flavours. Long, pure, viscous, and fine.*	£5.00 IWS
☆ **HILL & DALE SAUVIGNON BLANC 2003, HILL & DALE** Stellenbosch – *Complex asparagus and floral notes assail the nose. Sweetly ripe yet bursting with fresh acidity. Persistent creamy finish.*	£5.00 MRN
☆ **ROBERTSON SAUVIGNON BLANC 2003, EXCELSIOR ESTATE** Robertson – *Understated. Excellent minerality and complexity, with a superb oily mouthfeel and green tropical flavours.*	£5.00 WTS/JSM
ASDA SOUTH AFRICAN RESERVE SAUVIGNON BLANC 2003, WINECORP Western Cape – *A toasty top note adds richness. Racy lemon zest acidity scores the nutty asparagus-infused flavours.*	£5.50 ASD
BON COURAGE SAUVIGNON BLANC 2003, BON COURAGE ESTATE Breede River Valley – *Tropical guava, passion, and pear fruit saturates the nose and palate of this long, balanced, inviting wine.*	£6.00 LAI/JFE
FLEUR DU CAP CHENIN BLANC 2002, FLEUR DU CAP Coastal – *Fleshed with sweetly ripe tropical fruit. Excellent depth of flavour; rich apple fruit and lashings of spice.*	£6.00 DIT
MONT ROCHELLE CHARDONNAY 2001, MONT ROCHELLE Paarl – *Ripe, nutty, and buttery, with honeydew melon flavours. Weighty lime juice and vanilla mid-palate.*	£6.00 IWS
SOMERFIELD LIMITED RELEASE CHARDONNAY 2002, WINECORP Western Cape – *Sweetly ripe apples and satsumas entwine on the rather rich, balanced, and long palate.*	£6.00 SMF
ZONNEBLOEM CHARDONNAY 2003, ZONNEBLOEM Western Cape – *Grapefruit and lemon flavours are scored with mineral notes. Fresh, with a finely textured mouthfeel.*	£6.00 ODD
CAPE PROMISE RESERVE CHARDONNAY 2002, STELLENBOSCH VINEYARDS Stellenbosch – *Burnished old gold colour. Rich, toasty, spiced, and ripe, with honeyed notes overlaying melon and apricot flavours.*	£6.50 WAV

SOUTH AFRICAN WHITE BRONZE

BRADGATE CHENIN BLANC SAUVIGNON BLANC 2003, JORDAN ESTATE STELLENBOSCH – *Fresh, zippy, and aromatic, with lime fruit and bean aromas. Ripeness is evident on the finish. Very agreeable.*	£6.70 GHL
ANURA CHENIN BLANC 2003, ANURA PAARL – *Soft straw yellow hue. Its fresh citrus aromas and flavours are enriched by a spicy, gingery quality.*	£7.00 IWS
CO-OP CAPE SEAL BAY CHARDONNAY RESERVE 2001, VINFRUCO WESTERN CAPE – *Round and integrated, this superripe mouthful of citrus flavour has plenty of buttery elements.*	£7.00 CWS
MOOIPLAAS SAUVIGNON BLANC 2003, VINFRUCO WESTERN CAPE – *Gooseberries and grass on the nose. Crisp acidity cuts through the lemon meringue pie flavoured palate.*	£7.00 UNS
TUKULU CHENIN BLANC 2003, DISTELL GROENEKLOOF – *Crisp and somewhat austere, with a dry, high-acid, grippy palate. Tangerines and spices. Long finish.*	£7.00 ODD
GROOT CONSTANTIA SÉMILLON SAUVIGNON BLANC 2003, GROOT CONSTANTIA CONSTANTIA – *Aromas and flavours of green apples, gooseberries, and pears. Fine texture and refreshing grapefruit rind acidity.*	£7.10 FFW/CVE
CHARDONNAY PRESTIGE CUVÉE 2003, BON COURAGE ESTATE BREEDE RIVER VALLEY – *Polished, complex, and long, this fleshy wine has creamy vanilla and ripe lemon fruit.*	£7.50 WWT/SMV TSS
VERGELEGEN CHARDONNAY 2003, VERGELEGEN STELLENBOSCH – *Mineral, toasty, and dark, its spicy depths rich and focused. Balanced and long. A good food wine.*	£7.60 BNK/FLA NYW/JSM
VERGELEGEN SAUVIGNON BLANC 2003, VERGELEGEN STELLENBOSCH – *More integration is likely on the nose and palate of this medium-bodied, clean wine with its classic green characteristics.*	£8.00 WIDELY AVAILABLE
BEAUMONT CHARDONNAY 2002, BEAUMONT WINES OVERBERG – *Focused and cool, with tightly-wound complexity and a good mouthfeel. Long, restrained, and elegant.*	£8.50 FTH

308 SOUTH AFRICAN WHITE BRONZE

GROOTE POST SAUVIGNON BLANC 2003, GROOTE POST SWARTLAND – *Asparagus and grass scents. The palate delivers an attack of sweetly ripe tropical fruit with hints of undergrowth.*	**£8.50** JAV/BCF WSO
KLEIN CONSTANTIA SAUVIGNON BLANC 2003, KLEIN CONSTANTIA CONSTANTIA – *Scented with citrus fruit and freshly cut grass. Notes of sweet oak and vegetation. Crisp, clean, and ripe.*	**£8.50** TAN/FEN OWC WRW
JORDAN BLANC FUMÉ 2003, JORDAN ESTATE STELLENBOSCH – *Attractive, with balanced, integrated wood, grassy green berries, and herbs. Long and intense.*	**£8.60** FLY
FROSTLINE RIESLING 2003, JACK & KNOX WINECRAFT WESTERN CAPE – *Apples and minerals score the nose, which is subdued but should develop. Young and forceful; stylish.*	**£9.00** VIT/ODD
MONT ROCHELLE CHARDONNAY 2003, MONT ROCHELLE PAARL – *Yellow stone-fruit scents and flavours predominate in this restrained, austere wine. Elegant grapefruit elements.*	**£9.00** IWS
PRIVATE BIN CHARDONNAY 2002, NEDERBURG PAARL – *Pronounced vanilla aromas. A big burly zesty lemon and toasty oak number with a fresh crunchy finish.*	**£9.00** HBJ
WARWICK ESTATE CHARDONNAY 2003, WARWICK ESTATE STELLENBOSCH – *The subdued, smoky nose has a delicious green tinge, whilst the palate has melon fruit and vanilla pod flavours.*	**£9.00** FLY
FAIRVIEW VIOGNIER 2003, THE WINES OF CHARLES BACK COASTAL – *Succulent varietal apricot flavours. Exuberant, balanced, aromatic, and fresh, with a satisfyingly spicy finish.*	**£9.40** BEN/TAU SOM/NYW LIB/FLY
PRIVATE COLLECTION CHARDONNAY 2002, SAXENBURG STELLENBOSCH – *Deep, pronounced, and buttery, with richly ripe sweet melon fruit further rounded by vanilla-scented oak.*	**£9.50** NRW/MOR
STELLENBOSCH CHARDONNAY 2002, NEIL ELLIS WINES STELLENBOSCH – *Fragrant, complex, and fruit-driven, with a palate of spiced oak, minerals, and weighty citrus.*	**£9.70** HAX/TOS

SOUTH AFRICAN WHITE BRONZE

BOSCHENDAL CHARDONNAY RESERVE 2003, BOSCHENDAL PAARL – *Intensely fresh, with sultry summery ripe yellow fruit flavours and touches of vanilla and butter.*	£9.80 SHJ/TO WON
DELHEIM CHARDONNAY SUR LIE 2003, DELHEIM WINES STELLENBOSCH – *Round, with notes of melon and peach on the nose and a rich citrus palate. Balanced. Integrated sweet oak.*	£10.00 JKN
FAIRVIEW OOM PAGEL SEMILLON 2002, THE WINES OF CHARLES BACK PAARL – *Light straw-gold. The palate is very ripe with lemon meringue pie flavours and a creamy finish.*	£10.00 LIB
FROSTLINE CHARDONNAY 2003, JACK & KNOX WINECRAFT WESTERN CAPE – *Green gooseberry notes mingle with creamy lemons on the nose. Tropical, oily, and concentrated.*	£10.00 VIT
PRIVATE CELLAR CHARDONNAY 2003, RIJKS TULBAGH – *Lemon zest, hawthorn, and honeydew melon busts from this achingly fresh, bright, lightly oaked wine.*	£10.50 CHN
GOUVERNEURS CHARDONNAY RESERVE 2002, GROOT CONSTANTIA CONSTANTIA – *Pure and lavishly fruited, this is a concentrated, elegant, tight wine with nutty complexity and good weight.*	£11.10 FFW/VIT CVE
CHARDONNAY VIGNERONS RESERVE 2003, GLENWOOD PAARL – *The peach and melon fruit is cut with a seam of stony minerality. Croissant aromas.*	£11.90 ROG
GLEN CARLOU CHARDONNAY RESERVE 2002, GLEN CARLOU PAARL – *High toast, hazelnuts and cream. The mouthfeel is seductively silky with a lemon twist and a puff of talc.*	£12.50 GHL/WRW ODD
KUMALA JOURNEY'S END CHARDONNAY 2002, WESTERN WINES STELLENBOSCH – *Integrated and restrained, with attractive leesy, buttery notes on the nose. Soft butterscotch texture.*	£15.00 WTS
KUMALA JOURNEY'S END CHARDONNAY 2003, WESTERN WINES STELLENBOSCH – *Restrained agrumes compote aromas. Medium-bodied, the grapefruit flavours are generously dusted with cinnamon powder.*	£16.00 UNS

SOUTH AFRICAN WHITE BRONZE / SEAL

PRESTIGE WHITE 2002, VERGELEGEN STELLENBOSCH – *White fleshed fruit, orange blossom honey, jasmine, and a dab of butter grace this delicious, complex wine.*	£21.00 NYW

SEAL OF APPROVAL
SOUTH AFRICAN WHITE

☆ **SEA OF SERENITY DRY MUSCAT 2002, LGB** WORCESTER – *Lifted aromas of honey, ripe grapes, Seville oranges, and grass.*	£3.00 IWS
☆ **ASDA SOUTH AFRICAN SAUVIGNON BLANC 2003, WINECORP** WESTERN CAPE – *Grassy and ripe. Intense yet balanced, with ripe gooseberry flavours.*	£3.30 ASD
☆ **KATHENBERG CHENIN BLANC 2003, WINECORP** WESTERN CAPE – *Ripe tropical pineapple, peach, and white guava flavours. Floral scents.*	£3.70 WRT
☆ **CO-OP BARREL FERMENTED SÉMILLON 2002, FRANSCHHOEK VINEYARDS** PAARL – *Rich and toasty, with powerful waxy lemon fruit flavours. Balanced.*	£4.00 CWS
☆ **LONG MOUNTAIN CHENIN BLANC 2003, LONG MOUNTAIN** WESTERN CAPE – *Floral notes of rose and jasmine. Light, fruit-driven, and approachable.*	£4.00 SAF/BGN EUR/NTD
☆ **NIEL JOUBERT CHENIN BLANC 2003, NIEL JOUBERT** PAARL – *Sliced apple, pineapple, and pink-guava aromas and flavours.*	£4.00 SHB
☆ **SAINSBURY'S SOUTH AFRICAN CHARDONNAY NV, DE WETSHOF ESTATE** ROBERTSON – *Unadulterated white and yellow fruit palate. Balanced and fresh.*	£4.00 JSM

TROPHY
SOUTH AFRICAN RED

☆ **STELLENZICHT SYRAH 2001, STELLENZICHT** **STELLENBOSCH** – *Huge, with piquant spice and a full body. The fruit unwinds gradually on the lingering finish.*	£10.20 HBJ

GOLD
SOUTH AFRICAN RED

☆ **NIEL JOUBERT SHIRAZ 2002, NIEL JOUBERT** **PAARL** – *A mass of black fruit on the nose. Layers of fruit, leather, sweet cedar oak, and a peppery maturity.*	£7.70 ESL/HOU
☆ **SÉNGA SHIRAZ 2002, MAN VINTNERS** **PAARL** – *Rich, ripe, and earthy with evolved gamey, smoky notes and primary blackberry and white pepper fruit running through the palate.*	£8.00 SWS
☆ **BEYERSKLOOF PINOTAGE RESERVE 2002, BEYERSKLOOF** **STELLENBOSCH** – *Clean and tight with attractive juicy blueberry and blackberry fruit. A soft tannic structure and taut acidity scaffolds the fruit.*	£9.00 JSM/WEP
SPIER PRIVATE COLLECTION PINOTAGE 2001, WINECORP **STELLENBOSCH** – *Sophisticated winemaking and fine grapes. Blueberries, peppers, and spice. Rich, weighty chocolate sweetness on the finish.*	£13.00 PLB
SPIER PRIVATE COLLECTION PINOTAGE 2002, WINECORP **STELLENBOSCH** – *Rich and intense, with lifted red fruits, oak, and spice. Lots of smoky, warm dark fruits and cinnamon oak.*	£13.00 PLB

SILVER
SOUTH AFRICAN RED

☆ **RAILROAD RED 2003, GRAHAM BECK** **PAARL** – *This beauty has the capacity to gain complexity in coming years. Eucalyptus, smoky, ripe blackcurrants, and Marmite. Savoury; medium-bodied.*	£5.00 TOS/JSM

SOUTH AFRICAN RED SILVER

☆ **LEOPARD'S LEAP CABERNET MERLOT 2003**, **LEOPARD'S LEAP** WESTERN CAPE – *With smoky currants and spicy oak, this plum jam flavoured wine has the structure to age five years or more.*	£6.00 TOS
☆ **CAPE PROMISE RESERVE PINOTAGE 2001**, **STELLENBOSCH VINEYARDS** STELLENBOSCH – *Hot soft tarmac on a summer's day laces the nose of this powerful Pinotage. The palate has savoury strawberry flavours.*	£6.50 WAV
☆ **BOSCHENDAL CABERNET SAUVIGNON 2001**, **BOSCHENDAL** PAARL – *The nose sports sweet Victoria plums, mint, cassis, vanilla, and hints of smoke. Firm tannins and medium-long finish.*	£7.50 RNS
BORDEAUX BLEND 2003, DIEMERSFONTEIN ESTATE PAARL – *Cherry purple, with a tarry blackcurrant nose and vibrant cassis flavour. Spices and smoke, firm tannins, and a savoury finish.*	£8.00 THI
FAIRVIEW CYRIL BACK SHIRAZ 2001, THE WINES OF CHARLES BACK PAARL – *Super-dense and achingly pretty, with a staggering spectrum of violets, clover, smoke, leather, farmyard, and dark chocolate.*	£8.00 SOM
PROSPECT HILL CABERNET 2002, ROBERTSON WINERY ROBERTSON – *The bright black fruits on nose and palate have herbal aromatics and toasty oak notes. Incredible length.*	£8.00 ABY/JSM
SILVER TREE SHIRAZ 2002, KWV STELLENBOSCH – *Dark purple. Spices and blackberries, ripe fruit, and powerful oak. Fresh acidity and admirable balance.*	£8.00 M&S
WOLFKLOOF SHIRAZ 2002, ROBERTSON WINERY ROBERTSON – *Bags of blackberries, mulberries and currants. This starts out quietly but grows into a bold, well-built wine with a long finish.*	£8.00 ABY/JSM
HORSE MOUNTAIN PINOTAGE 2003, HORSE MOUNTAIN WINES PAARL – *The nose is subdued; the palate is rife with Morello cherries, red earth, and toast. Chunky yet well-constructed. Savoury.*	£8.50 NYW/FLY
KEN FORRESTER GRENACHE SYRAH 2002, KEN FORRESTER STELLENBOSCH – *The palate is soft and well-balanced, with gentle spice to warm the pure, ripe fruit, and coffee tinges.*	£8.80 WPR

SOUTH AFRICAN RED SILVER 313

FAIRVIEW AGOSTINELLI 2003, THE WINES OF CHARLES BACK COASTAL – *Black cherries on the nose continue with a peppery edge onto the palate, adorning a silky, well-balanced structure.*	£9.00 LIB
LA MOTTE MILLENNIUM 1999, LA MOTTE COASTAL – *A big, balanced wine with complexity and length. Sweet, ripe berry, and mocha nose; plum, cassis, and oak palate.*	£9.00 RSS
MOOIPLAAS CABERNET SAUVIGNON 2000, VINFRUCO STELLENBOSCH – *A nose of ripe blackcurrants shows hints of development with nutmeg and mint and plenty of rich blackberries.*	£9.00 UNS
MOOIPLAAS SHIRAZ 2000, VINFRUCO STELLENBOSCH – *Deep rich fruit is cut by white pepper powder and mouthwatering green bell pepper notes on the nose.*	£9.00 UNS
BRAHMS PINOTAGE 2003, DOMAINE BRAHMS PAARL – *Bright young aromatics of raspberry fruit, caramel, and cherries; tar and milk chocolate. Very dry.*	£10.00 VGN
DELHEIM GRAND RESERVE 2001, DELHEIM WINES STELLENBOSCH – *Red stone fruit compote on the nose paves the way for a full-bodied, structured palate laden with cherry fruit.*	£10.00 SOM
GOLDEN TRIANGLE PINOTAGE 2001, STELLENZICHT STELLENBOSCH – *Smoky bacon, tar, coal, and pepper notes clinging to ripe raspberry fruit. Rich, warm and long, with robust tannins.*	£10.00 HBJ
KLEIN CONSTANTIA MARLBROOK 2000, KLEIN CONSTANTIA CONSTANTIA – *Plenty of cassis and spice. Firm tannins support soft fruit. An elegant smoky finish. Ageworthy.*	£10.00 FEN/WPR NYW/WR W
SYRAH RESERVE 2001, BOSCHENDAL PAARL – *Deep, complex and tightly-knit, the alluring blackberry fruit laced with elegant cedar bark and tar aromas.*	£10.50 WON /TOS SHJ
BILTON CABERNET SAUVIGNON 2002, BILTON WINES STELLENBOSCH – *Deep garnet, with ripe blackcurrants and smoke on the nose and a full rich palate.*	£11.00 ABG

CEDERBERG CABERNET SAUVIGNON 2002, CEDERBERG PRIVATE CELLAR W*estern* C*ape* – *David Niewoudt's Cabernets are justly famed. The nose has intense smoky bacon aromas and masses of toasted oak.*	£11.00 H&H
BEAUMONT ARIANE 2002, BEAUMONT WINES O*verberg* – *With bell pepper, blackcurrants, and chocolate, this wine displays intense purity and a little floral influence on the long finish.*	£12.00 INS
CEDERBERG SHIRAZ 2002, CEDERBERG PRIVATE CELLAR C*ederberg* – *Plummy, spicy fruit mingles with vanilla and wood on the nose, while a robust, rich palate offers fine flavours, hints of pepper, and a welcome dash of spice.*	£12.00 HAX
PRIVATE COLLECTION SHIRAZ 2000, SAXENBURG S*tellenbosch* – *A textured beauty, with intense plums, tar, flowers, and tobacco arrayed on the nose and palate.*	£12.00 NRW/NYW MOR
RAKA BIOGRAPHY SYRAH 2002, RAKA W*estern* C*ape* – *Mocha, tanned animal hide, and creamy mint intermingle. An intoxicating whiff of burnt sugar. Complex.*	£12.00 IWS
GLEN CARLOU SHIRAZ 2002, GLEN CARLOU P*aarl* – *Medicinal notes, rustic damsons, white pepper, prunes, nutmeg, and cloves, this wine displays classic varietal definition.*	£12.60 NYW
SPIER PRIVATE COLLECTION MERLOT 2001, WINECORP S*tellenbosch* – *A nose of plums with a hint of earthy maturity and an intense, round, ripe palate supported by generous tannins.*	£13.00 PLB
VERGELEGEN CABERNET SAUVIGNON RESERVE 2001, VERGELEGEN S*tellenbosch* – *Spices, cream, toasty oak, rich fruit, and distinctive tannins. Deserves a few more years in cellar.*	£14.00 JSM
GRAHAM BECK THE RIDGE SYRAH 2001, GRAHAM BECK R*obertson* – *A nose of brambles suffused with rich spice. Packed with fine, bright fruit, with savoury tinges and a warm finish.*	£14.70 NYW/FLY JSM
FAIRVIEW BEACON BLOCK SHIRAZ 2002, THE WINES OF CHARLES BACK P*aarl* – *Grown on shale, the mineral content may enhance the delicious tarry tones etched into the vivacious plum fruit.*	£15.40 BEN/TAU CCS/NYW LIB/FLY

SOUTH AFRICAN RED SILVER / BRONZE **315**

STEYTLER PINOTAGE 2001, KAAPZICHT ESTATE **STELLENBOSCH** – *Warm ripe black fruit with a firm oak backbone. Sructured, firm tannins, plenty of fruit, and a long finish.*	£15.40 HAX/VIT CCS/NYW
CORNERSTONE CABERNET SAUVIGNON 2000, GRAHAM BECK WINES **COASTAL** – *A chunky red, its formidable alcohol and grippy tannins more than matched by deep fruit and toasty oak.*	£17.00 FLY
HAMILTON RUSSELL PINOT NOIR 2002, HAMILTON RUSSELL VINEYARDS **OVERBERG** – *Bright ruby. Chocolate-covered strawberry nose. The palate is round yet structured, with woody tannins and a gently creamy quality.*	£20.30 WIDELY AVAILABLE

BRONZE
SOUTH AFRICAN RED

☆ **ORIGIN MERLOT 2003, VIN-X-PORT** **BREEDE RIVER VALLEY** – *This is why Merlot has a sound future in South Africa: attractive plum and strawberry flavours with firm tannins.*	£5.00 THS
☆ **SOMERFIELD LIMITED RELEASE PINOTAGE 2002, BEYERSKLOOF** **COASTAL REGION** – *Warm berry and spice palate of rich fruit and soft tannins. Good mouthfeel; clean finish.*	£5.00 SMF
KEN FORRESTER PETIT PINOTAGE 2003, KEN FORRESTER WINES **STELLENBOSCH** – *Muscular and meaty. Strawberry jam, briar, and vanilla aromas. Richly fruited, and dusted with plenty of black pepper.*	£5.50 WPR/TOS
LEOPARD'S LEAP PINOTAGE SHIRAZ 2003, LEOPARD'S LEAP **WESTERN CAPE** – *Cream, coconut, and blackberry fruit flavours; dry, robustly tannic, and ruby red.*	£5.50 JSM
SIMONSVLEI CABERNET SAUVIGNON MERLOT 2003, SIMONSVLEI INTERNATIONAL **PAARL** – *Smoky, slightly tarry nose. Quite deep rich fruit and good acidity, prominent but smooth tannins, and a savoury finish.*	£5.50 PTN
MHV ROURKE'S DRIFT SOUTH AFRICAN CABERNET SAUVIGNON 2003, ORIGIN WINES **WESTERN CAPE** – *With masses of blackcurrant fruit, good density, spice and oak, good concentration, and a smoky, medium finish.*	£5.60 MHV

SOUTH AFRICAN RED BRONZE

BON COURAGE CABERNET SAUVIGNON 2002, BON COURAGE ESTATE ROBERTSON – *Deep ruby-black colour. Bold ripe dusky fruits, creamy oak, and perfumed cedar. Squeaky clean acidity. Smoke notes.*	£5.90 JFE
BOLAND KELDER MERLOT 2001, BOLAND KELDER PAARL – *From a winery once more turning heads, with a rich bouquet and a fine streak of acidity.*	£6.00 FLY
BOLAND SHIRAZ 2000, BOLAND KELDER PAARL – *Expressive nose showing clear blackberry character. The palate is rich and harmonious with supple tannins.*	£6.00 FLY
BOLAND SHIRAZ 2001, BOLAND KELDER PAARL – *Blackberry scented with a leather and spice palate that combines rich fruit and supple tannin.*	£6.00 FLY
KUMALA ORGANIC PINOTAGE SHIRAZ 2003, WESTERN WINES WESTERN CAPE – *Bananas, cream, and bright strawberry fruit. Full, with a touch of sweetness and a long finish.*	£6.00 JSM
BEYERSKLOOF PINOTAGE 2003, BEYERSKLOOF STELLENBOSCH – *Modern. Red cherries and banana scents. Dripping acidity lifts the fruit, wrapped in ripe silky tannins.*	£6.10 SOM/JSM MWW
NIEL JOUBERT CABERNET SAUVIGNON 2001, NIEL JOUBERT PAARL – *The nose offers some complexity, while the palate is rich with a smoky edge and fierce tannins.*	£6.40 ESL
CAPE PROMISE RESERVE CABERNET 2002, STELLENBOSCH VINEYARDS STELLENBOSCH – *Crunchy black fruits, spices, and herbs. Fresh acidity, marked tannins and a touch of cedar.*	£6.50 SAF
RED WOLF 2003, WOLVENDRIFT ROBERTSON – *Gentle aromas of lifted currant fruits with dashes of smoke and spice lead to ripe vanilla and savoury plum jam.*	£6.60 ROG
KUMALA PINOTAGE RESERVE 2003, WESTERN WINES WESTERN CAPE – *Whiffs of ice-cream and syrup, redcurrants, and rosemary. Seductively mouthcoating.*	£6.80 UNS/WTS JSM

SOUTH AFRICAN RED BRONZE 317

FIVE HEIRS CABERNET FRANC 2001, CWP WINE BRANDS STELLENBOSCH – *There is an interplay of burning leaves, creosote, and strawberries on this rustic charmer. Long chalky finish.*	£7.00 ABY
GOATS DO ROAM IN VILLAGES 2002, THE WINES OF CHARLES BACK COASTAL – *Youthful, with undergrowth notes and lush, mouthwatering strawberry, blackberry, and currant fruit flavours.*	£7.00 SMF/TOS
PLAISIR DE MERLE SHIRAZ 2002, PLAISIR DE MERLE PAARL – *Deep coaldust, blackberry, and campfire aromas scent the nose. The palate is full, intense, and evolved.*	£7.10 HBJ
BOSCHENDAL LANOY 2000, BOSCHENDAL PAARL – *Ripe, with sweet plum and blackcurrants, a medium body and an elegant finish. Drink over the short term.*	£7.20 FEN/EVI TOS/WRW
PORCUPINE RIDGE SYRAH 2002, BOEKENHOUTSKLOOF COASTAL – *Big, tarry and firm, yet still soft and enticing, with no hard edges. Ripe and round.*	£7.30 VIT/SMF WTS
RIETVALLEI CABERNET SAUVIGNON 2002, RIETVALLEI ESTATE ROBERTSON – *A complex nose of smoky, meaty cassis, and mint with a spicy vanilla finish. Furry corduroy tannins. Fresh.*	£7.50 RWA
THE WOLFTRAP 2002, BOEKENHOUTSKLOOF WESTERN CAPE – *Gamey and spicy, with a full smoky nose and a dense palate. Chunky and ripe. Creamy oak.*	£7.70 VIT/SMF ODD
MISCHA EVENTIDE SHIRAZ 2001, MISCHA WELLINGTON – *A nose of black and red fruit tinged with coffee. Sweet fruit, soft tannins, and a fine savoury finish.*	£8.00 CCS
GRAHAM BECK SHIRAZ 2002, GRAHAM BECK WINES COASTAL – *Glowing ruby red. A pretty nose with touches of crème brûlée, and an integrated palate of toast and fruit.*	£8.70 RNS/FLY JSM
CATHEDRAL CELLAR CABERNET SAUVIGNON 2000, KWV INTERNATIONAL WESTERN CAPE – *Young and frisky, with cigarbox aromas. The fruit is more than a match for the high tannins; agreeable and accessible.*	£8.80 G&M

SOUTH AFRICAN RED BRONZE

FAIRVIEW SMV 2002, THE WINES OF CHARLES BACK **COASTAL** – *Strawberry red. Medium-bodied, round palate of ripe berries. Approachable and enjoyable.*	£8.80 WIDELY AVAILABLE
PINOTAGE BARRIQUE 2002, LAMMERSHOEK **SWARTLAND** – *Young, with intense, invigorating fruit and fine balance. High tannins brace the rich smoked fruit.*	£8.80 ROG
POST HOUSE CABERNET SAUVIGNON 2001, POST HOUSE **STELLENBOSCH** – *A rich, deep nose and an elegant palate, which is soft and fine. Plenty of integrated tannins on the finish.*	£8.80 ROG
BEYERSKLOOF SYNERGY 2001, BEYERSKLOOF **STELLENBOSCH** – *From the king of Pinotage, Beyers Truter. Classic South Africa. Firm, dry, rich, and spicy.*	£9.00 TOS
FORT SIMON MERLOT 2000, FORT SIMON ESTATE **STELLENBOSCH** – *A good wine from a hot vintage. Deep, balanced, savoury, and mature.*	£9.00 D&D
FORT SIMON SHIRAZ 2001, FORT SIMON ESTATE **STELLENBOSCH** – *Tar and blueberry characteristics. The palate shows good fruit purity and subtle use of oak.*	£9.00 D&D
SIYANBONGA PINOTAGE 2002, SIYABONGA **WESTERN CAPE** – *A robust, masculine wine, with high toast, tar and earthy ripe hedgerow fruit. Formidable.*	£9.00 ODD
CATHEDRAL CELLAR PINOTAGE 2001, KWV INTERNATIONAL **WESTERN CAPE** – *The nose is soft and jammy. The palate shows strawberries and spice, soft tannins, and good balance.*	£9.30 G&M
KAAPZICHT SHIRAZ 2001, KAAPZICHT ESTATE **STELLENBOSCH** – *Restrained aromas of hedgerow fruits. The palate is mature and lifted, with sweet ripe flavours and astringent tannins.*	£9.30 HAX/TAN VIT/CCS NYW
MISCHA ESTATE CABERNET SAUVIGNON 1999, MISCHA **PAARL** – *Deep garnet. The maiden vintage from this family run estate has light raspberries alongside notes of tobacco.*	£9.70 ESL/CCS

SOUTH AFRICAN RED BRONZE 319

BOWE JOUBERT CABERNET SAUVIGNON 2001, BOWE JOUBERT PAARL – *The nose offers stewed fruits and toasty oak, while the palate has plenty of tannins and a longish finish.*	£10.00
	IWS
DIEU DONNÉ CABERNET SAUVIGNON RESERVE 1999, DIEU DONNÉ VINEYARDS WESTERN CAPE – *The sweet elegant nose has a cedary twang, while the purple fruit palate holds its own. Balanced and long.*	£10.00
	PAT
GOLDEN TRIANGLE MERLOT 1998, STELLENZICHT STELLENBOSCH – *A big wine with a dried fig nose and a fully mature palate. Enjoy now.*	£10.00
	HBJ
KAAPZICHT CABERNET SAUVIGNON 2001, KAAPZICHT ESTATE STELLENBOSCH – *An extremely hot vintage has imparted plenty of ripeness and alcohol, all drawn together by lavish cassis and wood.*	£10.00
	VIT/CCS
SHIRAZ ESTATE 2001, ALTO STELLENBOSCH – *Textured, rich, robust, and mouthfilling, this is a deeply coloured, full-bodied Shiraz.*	£10.00
	HBJ
CLOOF PINOTAGE 2002, CLOOF WINES SWARTLAND – *A full-bodied, intense array of herbs and savoury ripe red fruit. Chewy oak. Crimson colour.*	£10.10
	TAU/NYW BWC
JORDAN CABERNET SAUVIGNON 2001, JORDAN ESTATE STELLENBOSCH – *Youthful, with a nose of spices and smoky oak, good complexity, and soft-berry fruit melting into ripe tannins.*	£10.10
	GHL/JFE NYW/FLY WRW
LORD NEETHLING CABERNET SAUVIGNON 1998, NEETHLINGSHOF STELLENBOSCH – *Leather aromas alongside cedar, tobacco and cassis. The palate is firm, dry, and elegant, with slightly astringent tannins.*	£10.20
	HBJ
LORD NEETHLING PINOTAGE 2000, NEETHLINGSHOF STELLENBOSCH – *Soft, restrained crimson strawberry fruit and toast elements. Open-textured, with woody pine cone hints.*	£10.20
	HBJ
CAPE THREE LADIES 2001, WARWICK ESTATE STELLENBOSCH – *Warm red stewed fruits on the nose, leathery notes, and plenty of juicy plums. Long finish.*	£10.70
	GHL/FLY JSM

LAMMERSHOEK SHIRAZ CARIGNAN "LA ROULETTE" 2002, LAMMERSHOEK Swartland – *Hawthorn, blackberries, apples, and cloves. The palate has fine fruit concentration, fresh acidity, and a solid structure.*	£10.80 ROG
INKARA CABERNET SAUVIGNON 2002, BON COURAGE ESTATE Robertson – *A cascade of cedar and crunchy cassis spiked with herbal notes. The palate has good depth and a smoky edge.*	£11.00 AUS
INKARA SHIRAZ 2002, BON COURAGE ESTATE Breede River Valley – *Bold and rich, with a dusty nose, farmyard hints, and a supple, juicy style.*	£11.00 AUS
WARWICK TRILOGY 2001, WARWICK WINE ESTATE Stellenbosch – *The nose is restrained, while the palate is well-rounded, with dried berry and leather elements.*	£12.30 GHL/FLY
VERGELEGEN SHIRAZ RESERVE 2001, VERGELEGEN Stellenbosch – *Fresh straw, mint, and raspberry scents emanate from the bouquet. Plums and peppery spice lace the complex, delicious palate.*	£12.50 GHL/FLA NYW WRW
VEENWOUDEN THORNHILL SHIRAZ 2001, VEENWOUDEN Paarl – *Chunky wine with thick leather and damson aromas on the nose which follow through on the palate. Decent concentration.*	£12.60 SOM/CCS
STARK CABERNET SAUVIGNON 2001, STARK-CONDÉ WINES Coastal – *Pronounced toast, cassis fruit, a touch of spice, and good length. Young, with development potential.*	£12.90 SOM/SWS
DANFORD'S CABERNET SAUVIGNON 2001, KLEIN CONSTANTIA Coastal – *A Cabernet-Syrah blend, its dark cherry fruit pillow cosseted by silky yet firm tobacco leaf tannins.*	£13.00 LAI
FAIRVIEW JAAKALSFONTEIN SHIRAZ 2002, THE WINES OF CHARLES BACK Swartland – *Intense raspberry flavours, spicy peppers, and smoke. Crisp acidity and cedary oak.*	£13.00 LIB
LONGRIDGE CABERNET SAUVIGNON 2001, WINECORP Stellenbosch – *The tannins dominate this big, generous wine, with its espresso and charcoal skeleton supporting black plum fruit.*	£13.00 PLB

SOUTH AFRICAN RED BRONZE 321

LONGRIDGE CABERNET SAUVIGNON 2002, WINECORP **STELLENBOSCH** – *Pronounced bell pepper aromas mingle with black fruits, smoke and meat on the nose. Big, rich, and round. Long minty finish.*	£13.00 PLB
LONGRIDGE PINOTAGE 2001, WINECORP **STELLENBOSCH** – *Fruit-driven, with plum and cherry aromas and sweet blackberries on the palate. Soft tannins and a harmonious finish.*	£13.00 PLB
LONGRIDGE PINOTAGE 2002, WINECORP **STELLENBOSCH** – *Cherry aromas line the nose and harmonious palate. Oak tannins are well-integrated into the juicy fruit.*	£13.00 PLB
MERLOT RESERVE 2000, VERGELEGEN STELLENBOSCH – *Deep reddish brown. A nose of ripe bramble fruit, and a full-bodied palate with prominent tannins.*	£13.00 GHL
BWC SHIRAZ 2002, BAREFOOT WINE COMPANY **STELLENBOSCH** – *Opaque. Blackberries on the nose, and a rich, firm, dense, concentrated palate. Long peppery finish.*	£13.50 HDS/HGT GGR
GOUVERNEURS MERLOT 2001, GROOT CONSTANTIA **CONSTANTIA** – *Charry oak, abundant plum fruit, a touch of stalkiness, and firm tannins. Fine long finish.*	£13.50 FFW/WPR CVE
VERGELEGEN CABERNET SAUVIGNON RESERVE 2000, VERGELEGEN STELLENBOSCH – *A highly aproachable wine with mocha notes blackberries and spice. The palate has good fruit and grip.*	£13.50 BNK/RNS
JOOSTENBERG 2002, JOOSTENBERG WINES PAARL – *The earthy cassis nose has herbal notes. Rich cassis fruit with overtones of leather and cedar. Crisp balancing acidity.*	£14.00 ELV/SSU
RAATS CABERNET FRANC 2001, RAATS FAMILY WINES **STELLENBOSCH** – *A nose of blueberries and sage. Brisk tannins, saturated black fruit flavours, and a very crisp, sustained finish.*	£14.00 ODD
CREDO SHIRAZ 2002, VINFRUCO STELLENBOSCH – *Deep, with an almost port-like quality. Aromas and flavours of allspice and raspberries; taut tannins.*	£15.00 WTS

322 SOUTH AFRICAN RED BRONZE

EIKENDAL CLASSIQUE 2000, EIKENDAL VINEYARDS **STELLENBOSCH** – *A medium-bodied example with nutty, earthy notes on the nose and dominant tannins on the palate.*	£15.00 VNO
GRANDE RESERVE 2000, BOSCHENDAL **PAARL** – *Richly oaked, the flagship red from this estate is balanced and ageing well. Fleshy, full-bodied, and powerful.*	£15.00 SHJ/TOS WON
KUMALA JOURNEY'S END CABERNET SAUVIGNON 2003, WESTERN WINES **STELLENBOSCH** – *Bright garnet in the glass. Ripe and light, an easygoing wine with good structure and a juicy finish.*	£15.00 WST
MORESON MAGIA 2000, MORESON **COASTAL** – *With a cassis-laden nose, the palate sports somewhat bitter purple fruits, fine-grained tannins, and a long finish.*	£15.00 TAU
JORDAN COBBLERS HILL 2001, JORDAN ESTATE **STELLENBOSCH** – *Black cassis and green leaves on the nose. Ripe, crisp, and long, with dill, earth, and ripe red fruit.*	£15.10 GHL/NYW FLY/WRW
FAIRVIEW SOLITUDE SHIRAZ 2002, THE WINES OF CHARLES BACK **PAARL** – *A pungent tar and violet nose leads to a rich berry palate showing ripe tannins and decent complexity.*	£15.90 BEN/CCS NYW/LIB FLY
VEENWOUDEN CLASSIC 2001, VEENWOUDEN **PAARL** – *Menthol and cherries on the nose leads to a medium-bodied palate, where the tannins take pole position ahead of fruit.*	£16.70 TAN/VIT SOM/CCS NYW
STEYTLER VISION 2001, KAAPZICHT ESTATE **STELLENBOSCH** – *A big beast, its brown tinges revealing its relative age. Rich, ripe fruit leads to a big chewy finish.*	£17.10 HAX/CCS NYW
SPICE ROUTE FLAGSHIP MERLOT 2001, THE WINES OF CHARLES BACK **SWARTLAND** – *Deep, with a big powerful palate of juicy, chewy fruit. Ripe tannins and a grippy finish.*	£18.00 ENO
SPICE ROUTE FLAGSHIP SYRAH 2001, THE WINES OF CHARLES BACK **SWARTLAND** – *Masses of black fruit, raspberries, and nutmeg. The palate has tobacco leaves and soft round tannins.*	£18.00 ENO

S. AFRICAN RED BRONZE / SEAL **/ SPARK.** SEAL **/ SW.** GOLD / SILVER

VERGELEGEN PRESTIGE RED 2001, VERGELEGEN **STELLENBOSCH** – Showing its age, with toasty depth, a palate of ripe purple fruit and balanced use of oak.	£27.10 WPR/NYW

SEAL OF APPROVAL
SOUTH AFRICAN RED

☆ **ASDA SOUTH AFRICAN PINOTAGE 2003, WINECORP** **WESTERN CAPE** – Coaldust and clove scents. Ripe redcurrants with herbal tannins.	£3.20 ASD
☆ **DUMISANI PINOTAGE SHIRAZ 2002, WINECORP** **WESTERN CAPE** – Boysenberries, saddle-leather, smoky bacon, and pepper.	£3.70 ASD

SEAL OF APPROVAL
SOUTH AFRICAN SPARKLING

☆ **KUMALA CHARDONNAY BRUT NV, WESTERN WINES** **WESTERN CAPE** – Clear, vibrant Granny Smith apple and ruby grapefruit flavour profile.	£6.50 UNS

GOLD
SOUTH AFRICAN SWEET

☆ **NOBLE LATE HARVEST CHENIN BLANC 2003, JOOSTENBERG WINES** **PAARL** – What a beauty! Intense flowers and honey on the nose. The palate is packed with Seville orange marmalade. Bracing acidity.	£10.00 ELV/SSU BEC

SILVER
SOUTH AFRICAN SWEET

☆ **NOBLE LATE HARVEST 2002, SLANGHOEK** **WORCESTER** – The Afrikaans name for Muscat is Hanepoot, and it's easy to see why. Honey and orange flavours galore.	£10.00 VER

SEAL OF APPROVAL
SOUTH AFRICAN SWEET

☆ **CO-OP SWEET SURRENDER 2003, BERGSIS ESTATE** — ■£5.00 — CWS
BREEDE RIVER VALLEY – *Luscious flavours of lychee, tangerines, pear juice, and honey.*

GOLD MEDALS HAVE SCORED the equivalent of at least 18.5/20 (or 95/100) and are exceptional. Silver has scored over 17/20 (or 90/100), bronze over 15.5/20 (or 85/100), and seals of approval over 14/20 (or 80/100).
☆ particularly good value
★ truly great value
▲ 50CL bottle
■ 37.5CL bottle
● 10CL bottle

FOR STOCKIST CODES turn to page 355. For regularly updated information about stockists and the International Wine Challenge, visit wineint.com. For a full glossary of wine terms and a complete free wine course, visit robertjoseph-onwine.com

SPAIN

The days when Spain was associated, in most people's minds, with inexpensive red Rioja, nutty, oaky white wine, and sherry are long over. Today, this is one of the most go-ahead winemaking countries in Europe – thanks largely to the efforts of ambitious new producers in previously unsung regions such as Ribera del Duero, Priorat, and Navarra, and of established, traditional names such as Miguel Torres. Anyone looking for wines "the way they used to make them" will not be disappointed, but nor will those seeking more modern fare with the flavours of "international grapes" (Chardonnay, Cabernet Sauvignon etc.) and French rather than American oak.

BRONZE
CATALONIA WHITE

CHARDONNAY SELECCIÓN 2003, RENÉ BARBIER CATALONIA – *Perfectly ripe green-gold Ogen melon flavours. Lashings of buttery oak melt into the sweet fruit.*	£5.50 ESL
TERRASOLA CHARDONNAY 2002, JEAN LEON CATALONIA – *A nose of honey and hazelnuts. Integrated and restrained, with minerals, lanolin, and soft earthy notes.*	£8.10 RAV/VIT
MAS IGNEUS FA 104 2001, MAS IGNEUS CATALONIA – *Apples, limes, spices, and nuts on an aromatic nose. This wine displays good development and some complexity.*	£8.30 VRT
JEAN LEON CHARDONNAY 2002, JEAN LEON CATALONIA – *Vanilla ice cream, peach, and pear fruit assaults the nose. The palate is sweetly ripe, light-bodied, and round.*	£11.40 RAV/VIT

GOLD
CATALONIA RED

MAS LA PLANA CABERNET SAUVIGNON 1998, MIGUEL TORRES CATALONIA – *Rich and ripe, with intense black fruits and a distinctly Iberian spiritiness. Firmly structured and hugely long.*	**£20.50** GHL/JFE NYW/JSM
PRIOR TERRAE 1999, VITICULTEURS DEL PRIORAT CATALONIA – *Big, modern, and muscular, with spicy truffle notes, tar, leather, and sweet wood overtones.*	**£150.00** CHH

SILVER
CATALONIA RED

GOTIM BRU 2002, CASTELL DEL REMEI CATALONIA – *Cherries and raspberries line this generous, concentrated, lively, and youthful wine. Excellent colour and very good balance.*	**£7.70** EDC/MOV NYW/INS OWC/MOR
COSTERS DEL GRAVET 2000, CAPÇANES CATALONIA – *One of Spain's most innovative cooperatives, Capçanes has produced a full-bodied, intensely flavoured blueberry wine. Fresh buoyant acidity.*	**£10.70** JNW/WTS
ALBET I NOYA SYRAH COLLECCIO 2000, ALBET I NOYA CATALONIA – *Rich fruit and animal aromas. This organic offering has an open and flavoursome palate with herbs and spices.*	**£12.00** VRT

BRONZE
CATALONIA RED

ASH TREE ESTATE SHIRAZ MONASTRELL 2003, FREIXENET CATALONIA – *A dash of smoke adds to the peppery red fruit on the nose. Juicy fruit on a medium-bodied framework.*	**£5.50** BNK/UNS TOS
RAMÓN ROQUETA TEMPRANILLO 2003, BODEGAS ROQUETA CATALONIA – *Intensely coloured, with aromas of French lavender. The blueberry and mulberry fruit is restrained and ruby red.*	**£5.60** LAI

CATALONIA RED BRONZE 327

RAIMAT ABADIA 2000, RAIMAT CATALONIA – Mature leathery aromas lead to an elegant palate showing raisined berry notes and sweet oak spice.	£6.70 VGN/FEN NYW
RAIMAT TEMPRANILLO 2001, RAIMAT CATALONIA – Cigars and cinnamon grace this medium-bodied, complex wine. Plenty of evolved red-berry fruit and leathery elements.	£7.00 FEN
CLOS DELS CODOLS 2001, ADEGAS GALEGAS CATALONIA – Light red-berry fruits on the palate balance with a touch of minerals and a streak of good acidity.	£7.90 FFW/RNS NRW/MER
CLOS MONTBLANC MERLOT PREMIUM 2001, BODEGAS CONCAVINS CATALONIA – Roses and cherries on the nose. A pleasing palate of good intensity and acidity. Notes of spice and leather.	£8.00 HWL/ALE
CLOS MONTBLANC SYRAH 2002, BODEGAS CONCAVINS CATALONIA – With an intense palate of fresh raspberries, fine oak, and a tangy acidity, this wine had a refreshing complexity and good length.	£8.00 HWL
LA PLANELLA 2002, CELLERS JOAN D'ANGUERA CATALONIA – A very attractive concentrated nose of raspberries and cream. Easygoing, balanced, fresh, and long.	£9.00 L&S
MASIA LES COMES 2000, BODEGAS CONCAVINS CATALONIA – A Bordeaux blend from this revitalised former cooperative. Classic Cabernet aromas; engaging soft spices.	£9.00 RIH/ROD
CABERNET SAUVIGNON LARGA MACERACIÓN CRIANZA SELECCIÓN 1999, RENÉ BARBIER CATALONIA – Notes of cedar and mint and a palate ripe with integrated tannins and light oak spice.	£10.00 FXT
CAN FEIXES NEGRE SELECCIÓ 2001, HUGUET DE CAN FEIXES CATALONIA – Delightful ruby colour, with pleasing acidity, beguiling cherry fruit, and fine-grained tannins.	£10.50 CCS
GRAN CORONAS 2000, MIGUEL TORRES CATALONIA – Tempranillo unites with Cabernet Sauvignon in structured, sophisticated union. Ripe spicy fruit shines on this dry, smooth wine.	£10.70 RAV/G&M

JEAN LEÓN CABERNET SAUVIGNON 1998, JEAN LEÓN CATALONIA – Cassis-driven, with lifted minty notes. The palate is supple and juicy with good depth and persistence.	£11.90 RAV
CLOS MASET CABERNET SAUVIGNON SELECCIÓN ESPECIAL 2000, MASIA VALLFORMOSA CATALONIA – Rich black damson fruit melds with red cedar bark and loam on the nose and palate.	£17.00 FTH
JEAN LEÓN CABERNET SAUVIGNON GRAN RESERVA 1996, JEAN LEÓN CATALONIA – The nose shows developed fig and coffee notes. The palate has finesse with ripe tannins allied to vanilla oak.	£20.00 VIT
MAS IGNEUS PRIORATO FA 112 2000, MAS IGNEUS CATALONIA – Liquorice, leather, and cherries. Drinking now, the medium-bodied palate sports poached plums and a splash of pepper.	£20.00 VRT
CASTELL DEL REMEI 1780 2000, CASTELL DEL REMEI CATALONIA – A sumptuous palate follows a mature nose. Creamy, rich black fruit and a backbone of charred oak.	£21.60 EDC/NYW OWC/MOR

SILVER
CATALONIA SPARKLING

☆ **CUVÉE DS 1999, FREIXENET** CATALONIA – Apples and a little autolysis in an off-dry style. It is lively with good weight and a persistent mousse.	£13.00 SPA

BRONZE
CATALONIA SPARKLING

☆ **ASDA CAVA BRUT NV, CODORNÍU** CATALONIA – Light floral lime notes on the nose. The palate is round, soft, and fresh, with spiced apples and savoury notes.	£3.80 ASD
☆ **SOMERFIELD CAVA BRUT CASTELL DE VILARNAU NV, GONZÀLEZ-BYASS** CATALONIA – Leesy, appley aromas of sweetly ripe fruit. The citrus palate is juicy, developed, distinctive, and long.	£5.00 SMF

CATALONIA SPARKLING BRONZE / SEAL

☆ **ASDA SPECIAL VINTAGE CAVA 2001, CORDONÍU** **CATALONIA** – *Attractively fresh with an appley yeasty weight. Just dry, with soft mousse, spice nuances, and good length.*	£5.90 ASD

SEAL OF APPROVAL
CATALONIA SPARKLING

☆ **CAVA SOLER BRUT NV, CAVES SOLER JOVE** **CATALONIA** – *Hedgerow flowers, hints of loam, and ripe pears burst from nose and palate.*	£4.00 BSS
☆ **CO-OP CAVA BRUT NV, SEGURA VIUDAS** **CATALONIA** – *Produced by a cava master. Fresh, aromatic, white-fleshed sparkler.*	£5.00 CWS
☆ **SOMERFIELD MEDIUM DRY CAVA CASTELL DE VILARNAU NV, GONZÀLEZ-BYASS** **CATALONIA** – *A hint of sweetness lifts the palate of this frothy, fresh, appley cava.*	£5.00 SMF
☆ **MHV CAVA NV, COVIDES** **CATALONIA** – *Wildflowers, pears, chalk, and subtlest white spice are all in evidence.*	£5.20 BNK/MHV
☆ **PINK PINK FIZZ NV, PERE VENTURA** **CATALONIA** – *Native Catalan variety Trepat gives this ruby-hued beauty its summer fruit flavour.*	£5.50 IWS
☆ **CODORNÍU CLASICO RESERVA NV, CODORNÍU** **CATALONIA** – *Elegant, refined and fresh, with fine mousse and starfruit and Bramley apple flavours.*	£7.00 UNS
☆ **CASTELLBLANCH BRUT ZERO NV, CAVAS CASTELLBLANCH** **CATALONIA** – *Bone-dry and very stylish. Dried-apple fruit flavours and tar nuances.*	£7.10 RAV/GHL
☆ **CODORNÍU RESERVA NV, CODORNÍU** **CATALONIA** – *Traditional varieties are selected for this smoky, white-fleshed beauty from Penedés.*	£7.50 TAU/TOS

BRONZE
RIOJA + NORTH-CENTRAL WHITE

OTAZU CHARDONNAY 2002, OTAZU **Navarra** – *Apricots and custard scents assail the nose. Clear, pure, refreshing ripe peach-flesh flavours the linear palate.*	£7.20 SOM/LIB
CHARDONNAY 234 2003, ENATE **Aragón** – *Pale yellow, with pretty vanilla and lemon scents. The creamy palate has generous helpings of sweet peach fruit.*	£9.10 FFW/CVE
MATURANA BLANCO 2002, VIÑA IJALBA **Rioja** – *Lemony and pale, with a generous palate of bright citrus, nuts, honey, and hawthorn blossom.*	£10.00 VRT

SEAL OF APPROVAL
RIOJA + NORTH-CENTRAL WHITE

☆ CAMPO NUEVO BLANCO 2003, AGRAMONT **Navarra** – *Scents of straw and flavours of crab apple and pear fruit.*	£4.00 PLB

TROPHY
RIOJA + NORTH-CENTRAL RED

CAMPILLO RESERVA ESPECIAL 1995, BODEGA CAMPILLO **Rioja** – *Perfumed with elegant cooked fruit flavours and leathery maturing notes. Concentrated palate and powerful, grippy tannic structure.*	£28.00 CTR

GOLD
RIOJA + NORTH-CENTRAL RED

☆ MARQUÉS DE VITORIA RESERVA 1998, BODEGAS FAUSTINO MARQUÉS DE VITORIA **Rioja** – *Supple, with sweet oak and a generously fruited palate. The massive tannins will soften under the full fruit.*	£9.00 PLB

RIOJA + N-C RED GOLD / SILVER

☆ **CASTILLO LABASTIDA RESERVA 1997, UNION DE COSECHEROS DE LABASTIDA** Rioja – *Farmyard, gamey hints mingle with rosehip and cherry fruit. Creamy texture and restrained vanilla oak.*	£11.00 LAI
PAGOS DE TAHOLA GRAN RESERVA 1994, BODEGAS LARCHAGO Rioja – *A classic mature Rioja with a vanilla oak, cigar leaf, sweet spice, and baked cherry palate. Ripe and round.*	£13.00 LAI
RESERVA SELECCIÓN DE LA FAMILIA 1999, BODEGAS LUIS CAÑAS Rioja – *Youthful and bold, this has mocha, chocolate, and vanilla notes well supported by black-cherry and cassis fruit.*	£13.00 CCS/MOV JSM
AMAREN RESERVA 1999, BODEGAS LUIS CAÑAS Rioja – *Complex cedar wood and cigar tobacco and an array of red- and black-berry fruits. Sweet, earthy, bold tannins.*	£27.50 CCS
ALLENDE CALVARIO 2001, FINCA ALLENDE Rioja – *Solid, deep fruit and balancing oak; a powerful, smooth intensity; a fine grippy tannic structure for shape and backbone.*	£36.20 HAX/CCS FLY

SILVER
RIOJA + NORTH-CENTRAL RED

★ **BARÓN DE BARBÓN 2003, BODEGAS MURIEL** Rioja – *Ash, coconut and tar bouquet. The tight black fruit is lifted and smoothed out by a hint of vanilla.*	£6.40 LAI
☆ **CO-OP RIOJA CUVÉE NATHALIE 2002, BODEGAS MURIEL** Rioja – *There is a mature quality to this peppery, toasty wine with its blackcurrant fruit, ripe tannins, and smoky scents.*	£7.00 CWS
LUIS CAÑAS CRIANZA 2001, BODEGAS LUIS CAÑAS Rioja – *Redcurrants, cranberries, and cherries. Silky smooth, this is a robust, tobacco-scented, vanilla-tinged, fresh yet evolved Tempranillo.*	£7.90 LAI/CCS MOV/JSM
MARQUÉS DE GRIÑÓN RESERVE RIOJA 1999, BODEGAS BERBERANA Rioja – *Caramel, liquorice, smoke, and black-cherries; ripe raspberries and hints of roast game.*	£9.00 TOS

PALACIO DE LA VEGA CABERNET SAUVIGNON RESERVA 2000, LARIOS PERNOD RICARD Navarra – *Superb wine from Navarran pioneers. Hints of cigar; sleek and medium-bodied; plush fruit and ripe tannins. Sophisticated.*	**£9.00** BGN/ODD
COTO DE IMAZ RESERVA 1999, EL COTO DE RIOJA Rioja – *The delicacy of the floral-infused strawberry fruit belies the power and earthiness of the structured, toasty palate.*	**£9.10** WIDELY AVAILABLE
PRIMICIA RESERVA 1999, BODEGAS PRIMICIA Rioja – *Cracked pepper and spice nose. Soft oak notes and strawberry and plum fruit flavours line the textured palate.*	**£11.00** LAI
TINTO RESERVA 2000, BODEGAS TOBIA Rioja – *Glamorous red-cherry fruit flavours glide effortlessly over the palate, eased by lashings of creamy vanilla oak.*	**£11.60** HAX/RAY
FINCA MONASTERIO 2001, BODEGAS BARON DE LEY Rioja – *Creamy, textured, and weighty, its ripe red-cherry flesh complimented by elegant mineral and roast nuances.*	**£12.30** SOM
CAMPO VIEJO GRAN RESERVA 1997, BODEGAS JUAN ALCORTA Rioja – *Fine, clean, and approachable, its nose and palate an interplay of red- and black-berry fruits, coaldust, and bell pepper.*	**£12.50** ODD/JSM
LA VICALANDA DE VIÑA POMAL RESERVA RIOJA 1999, BODEGAS BILBAINAS Rioja – *Mouthwatering cherry, mulberry, and blueberry fruit. Still youthful, yet displaying good integration and balance.*	**£13.00** LVN /NYW WIM/DBY HDY
JULIAN MADRID 1999, BODEGAS PRIMICIA Rioja – *Soft redcurrant fruit laced with vanilla oak. Cinnamon and nutmeg spice up the long, sweetly ripe finish.*	**£14.30** LAI
MARTÍNEZ BUJANDA GRAN RESERVA 1995, FAMILIA MARTÍNEZ BUJANDA Rioja – *Cherries and violets and warm vanilla oak. Leathery evolution hints; bright acids lend a vibrancy that belies its age.*	**£15.00** JNW/LAI VIT
FINCA VALPIEDRA 1999, FAMILIA MARTÍNEZ BUJANDA Rioja – *Raisins, game, and prunes flesh out the nose. Elegant, medium-bodied red fruit of the best quality fills the palate.*	**£16.50** LAI/VIT BWC

RIOJA + N-C RED SILVER / BRONZE

GRAN ALBINA 1998, BODEGAS RIOJANAS RIOJA – *Leather and game intermingles with delicate violet, cinnamon spice, and hedgerow fruit scents and flavours.*	**£16.80** FFW/TAU MER
MARQUÉS DE RISCAL GRAN RESERVA 1996, MARQUÉS DE RISCAL RIOJA – *Flavours of kirsch, game, dates, raisins, undergrowth, and strawberries; aristocratic clove, chalkdust, and vanilla aromas.*	**£19.10** ESL/HOU FEN/JFE MWW
YGAY GRAN RESERVA ESPECIAL 1995, BODEGAS MARQUÉS DE MURRIETA RIOJA – *A mass of rich red fruits with nuts and hints of violets. Generous leathery, meaty notes. Beautiful integration.*	**£24.10** HAX/JNW TAU/GHL EVI
GUELBENZU LAUTUS 1999, BODEGAS GUELBENZU NAVARRA – *Lashings of oak and rich brambly black and red fruit flavours coalesce into a cohesive, complex whole.*	**£25.80** EDC/OWC MOR
VIÑA DEL OLIVO 2001, VIÑEDOS DEL CONTINO RIOJA – *The palate is smooth and complex, with a rich array of damson jam, tropical clove, and cinnamon bark.*	**£44.00** FLY
ALLENDE AURUS 2000, FINCA ALLENDE RIOJA – *Its cherry fruit is mellifluous and mouthcoating. Its oak is intense yet integrated into the fruit's fabric.*	**£57.40** HAX/CCS NYW/FLY

BRONZE
RIOJA + NORTH-CENTRAL RED

☆ **VIÑA FUERTE 2003, SAN GREGORIO** ARAGÓN – *A fruity nose of cherry spice and a raspberry-fuelled palate with ripe tannins. Good honest red.*	**£4.30** IWS/WTS
☆ **CO-OP RIOJA TINTO VIÑA GALA NV, BODEGAS MURIEL** RIOJA – *Crimson red. A burst of red- and black-forest fruits, toasty oak, and deep woody tannins.*	**£4.50** CWS
☆ **BERBERANA D'AVALOS TEMPRANILLO 2002, BODEGAS LAGUNILLA** RIOJA – *Mature, with plenty of classy wood and big plum fruit flavours. The palate is lined with grainy tannins.*	**£5.00** UWO

334 RIOJA + N-C RED BRONZE

☆ **LA MARCA MADRID 2003, BODEGAS CASTEJÓN** **MADRID** – *Bursting with spiced strawberry fruit scents and flavours. The youthful palate has roundness, balance, vigour, and power.*	£5.00 GYW
☆ **PRECIOSO RIOJA NV, VIÑEDOS DE ALDEANUEVA** **RIOJA** – *Peppery redcurrant and cranberry fruit flavours; fresh coffee, cherry syrup, and leather aromas.*	£5.00 PLB
PRIMI 2003, BODEGAS LUIS GURPEGUI MUGA **RIOJA** – *The nose has enticing vanilla and strawberry perfume. Sweet and supple with good oak and fruit harmony.*	£5.40 BNK/SMF FLY/BWL
BORSAO 2002, BODEGAS BORSAO **ARAGÓN** – *Youthful ruby-purple, with lively raspberry fruit and a simply charming quality. Supple tannins.*	£5.60 FLY/AVB
AGRAMONT RESERVA 1999, AGRAMONT **NAVARRA** – *Some evolution is apparent on the nose, with spice, leather, and chocolate. The palate is leafy and dry.*	£6.00 PLB
PALACIO DE SADA GARNACHA 2003, CO-OP DE SADA **NAVARRA** – *This sleek-bodied red offers a subtle style of wine, with restrained raspberry fruit, light tannins, and good balance.*	£6.00 VGN
OCHOA GRACIANO GARNACHA 2002, BODEGAS OCHOA **NAVARRA** – *The nose is spiked with blueberries and vanilla. The ripe fuit is underpinned by supple tannins.*	£6.50 BNK/UNS FEN
VENDIMIA SELECCIÓNADA MADURADO 150 DIAS 2002, FAMILIA MARTÍNEZ BUJANDA **RIOJA** – *Clear ruby red colour. Modern and fruit-driven, with crunchy cranberry fruit and brisk yet integrated tannins.*	£6.80 LAI
TORRELONGARES RESERVA 1998, COVINCA CO-OP **ARAGÓN** – *Ripe strawberries line the light, elegant palate with vibrant fruit. A balanced, crisp finish.*	£6.90 FFW/CVE
VIÑA ALCORTA CRIANZA 2001, BODEGAS JUAN ALCORTA **RIOJA** – *Spicy cinnamon and vanilla nose. The berry-laden palate is luxuriant, soft, and harmonious.*	£7.00 WAV

RIOJA + N-C RED BRONZE

VINA CAÑA RIOJA RESERVA 1999, GONZÀLEZ-BYASS R**IOJA** – *The nose is warm with notes of vanilla and Dundee cake. The palate is rich, supple, and balanced. Nice lick of sweet oak on the finish.*	£7.00 SMF
EL COTO CRIANZA 2001, EL COTO DE RIOJA R**IOJA** – *Berry-driven, with toast, and fruitcake aromas. The palate is supple with juicy fruit and ripe tannins.*	£7.20 WIDELY AVAILABLE
RIOJA BAGORDI CRIANZA 2001, BODEGAS BAGORDI R**IOJA** – *The nose has hints of toffee. Chewy tannins underscore ripe blackberries and coffee beans in the mouth.*	£7.30 VER
NAVAJAS TINTO CRIANZA 2001, BODEGAS NAVAJAS R**IOJA** – *Spicy vanilla and berry nose and a supple palate of juicy fruit, toasty oak, and integrated tannins.*	£7.70 WIDELY AVAILABLE
MARAIN DE VEGA SINDOA 2001, NEKEAS N**AVARRA** – *Deep ruby, with a nose of toasty, spicy red fruit and well-structured rustic prune and cinnamon flavours.*	£8.00 HBJ
VALSERRANO CRIANZA 2001, BODEGAS DE LA MARQUESA R**IOJA** – *Pencil shavings, ripe Victoria plums and a host of cigar leaf aromatics. Very dry.*	£8.00 AVB
ENATE CABERNET MERLOT 2002, ENATE A**RAGÓN** – *A graceful wine bursting with ripe fruit, balanced acidity, and a persistent finish. Kudos, Somontano innovators!*	£8.10 FFW/GHL CVE
TINTO CRIANZA 2001, BODEGAS TOBIA R**IOJA** – *Spearmint and gum tree hints grace tree bark-infused, ripe, glowing wild strawberry flavours.*	£8.40 HAX/RAY
CAMPO DORADO RIOJA RESERVA 1998, BODEGAS OLARRA R**IOJA** – *Soft, fruity berry and vanilla aromas. The palate is clean and harmonious, its lush fruit overlaid by sweet oak.*	£8.70 MHV
TINTO ERA COSTANA RESERVA 1999, BODEGAS ONDARRE R**IOJA** – *Lush vanilla and toast aromas. Sweet raspberry fruit on the palate. Balanced, with supple tannins.*	£9.00 JSM

VIÑA IJALBA GRACIANO 2001, VIÑA IJALBA Rioja – *Very deep colour. Lots of black pepper, roast coffee beans, nuts, and ripe raspberry fruit.*	£9.00 VRT
PRIMICIA CRIANZA 2001, BODEGAS PRIMICIA Rioja – *Wave after wave of coconut oak, sweetly ripe blackberries, cherry fruit, and dried herbs.*	£9.30 LAI
PAGO REAL LANCIEGO LANZAGA 2001, TELMO RODRIGUEZ Rioja – *Soft and harmonious with berry and spice notes on the nose and a lick of sweet oak on the palate.*	£10.00 M&S
RIOJA EXCELSUS 2001, VIÑA HERMINIA Rioja – *A berry and vanilla nose. The palate is ripe and supple with sweet fruit and well-rounded tannins.*	£10.00 MHE
MARTÍNEZ BUJANDA RESERVA 1999, FAMILIA MARTÍNEZ BUJANDA Rioja – *Light leafy perfume, and the palate beckons with wild strawberry fruit. Savoury marmite notes.*	£10.30 JNW/LAI VIT
GUIA REAL GRAN RESERVA 1994, BODEGAS CARLOS SERRES Rioja – *The gentle berry and spice nose leads to a silky palate of integrated oak tannins and dried fruit.*	£12.50 VGN/MER
VALLOBERA RESERVA 1998, BODEGA SAN PEDRO Rioja – *Star-bright ruby red. Flavours of cherries and vanilla are accented by discernible hints of game.*	£12.80 GRT
PALACIO DE LA VEGA CONDE DE LA VEGA 2000, LARIOS PERNOD RICARD Navarra – *With brambly berries and bell pepper notes, this has youthful fruit, crisp acidity, and fine tannins.*	£13.00 WST
ALLENDE RIOJA 2000, FINCA ALLENDE Rioja – *Youthful, with scope for further development. Finely knit tannins and a flush acidity lift the black fruit.*	£13.10 CCS/NYW FLY
GUELBENZU EVO 2002, BODEGAS GUELBENZU Navarra – *Youthful velvety red stone fruit fleshes out the palate. Green peppers, herbes de Provence, cloves, and whiffs of smoke.*	£13.20 EDC/TAN NYW/BOO OWC/MOR

RIOJA + N-C RED BRONZE 337

MONTECILLO GRAN RESERVA 1995, BODEGAS MONTECILLO Rioja – *Splendidly at its peak; mature, meaty, and farmy. Evolved and integrated; soft, round, and fine. Firmly bolstered with oak.*	£13.50 HBJ
DIONISIO RUIZ TINTO 2002, VIÑA IJALBA Rioja – *Soft, approachable cherry fruit with excellent integration, a smooth texture, and smoky oak.*	£14.00 VRT
MARQUÉS DE MURRIETA GRAN RESERVA 1996, MARQUÉS DE MURRIETA Rioja – *Haunting notes of cinnamon and coal. Aged, with strawberry flavours and hints of orange rind.*	£15.00 TOS
FINCA VALPIEDRA RESERVA 1998, FAMILIA MARTÍNEZ BUJANDA Rioja – *Big sweet oak laces the nose. Raspberry fruit pervades a palate with tight-knit tannins and straightforward appeal.*	£15.30 JNW/LAI VIT
COTO REAL RESERVA 1998, EL COTO DE RIOJA Rioja – *The nose offers sweet raspberry and spice aromas. The lush fruit palate shows balance and fine tannic structure.*	£15.40 NRW/FLY
RIOJA RESERVA 1999, BODEGAS YSIOS Rioja – *Spicy, peppery nose. Pepper also adds lift to the palate of soft loganberry fruit. Integrated tannic structure.*	£15.50 HAX
VIÑA ARDANZA RIOJA RESERVA 1998, LA RIOJA ALTA Rioja – *The plum orange colour and sweet integrated oak tell of the maturity evident on the suave strawberry palate.*	£15.90 BEN/BNK ESL/HOU SHB/JSM
MUGA SELECCIÓN ESPECIAL 1998, BODEGAS MUGA Rioja – *Redcurrant flavours are sprinkled with dark cracked black pepper notes and smoky roast meat nuances.*	£16.30 VIT/SOM GHL/WRW
VENDIMIA SELECCIÓNADA 1999, BODEGAS YSIOS Rioja – *A combination of nutmeg, leather, strawberries, and honey, a mature garnet colour and seductive cigar box scents.*	£17.00 HAX
VIÑA LANCIANO EDICIÓN LIMITADA RESERVA 1996, BODEGAS LAN Rioja – *Spice and vanilla intensity on the nose and a rich fruitcake palate. Tannins are ripe and integrated.*	£18.00 SOM

RIOJA + N-C RED BRONZE / SEAL

MIGUEL MERINO RESERVA 1998, BODEGAS MIGUEL MERINO Rioja – Handsome brick red colour. Tar, coconut, rubber, and cranberries cavort on the long, textured, charmingly rustic palate.	£19.00 FLY
CUNE IMPERIAL RESERVA 1998, CUNE Rioja – Elegant wine with complex raisin and allspice. Refined palate, its sweet fruit allied to velvety tannins.	£24.50 OWC
BARON DE CHIREL RIOJA RESERVA 1999, MARQUÉS DE RISCAL Rioja – Mahogany hue. Excellent fruit/wood balance, with solid red-cherry flavours and gamey undertones.	£30.00 GHC/MW W
DALMAU RESERVA TINTO 1999, BODEGAS MARQUÉS DE MURRIETA Rioja – The nose boasts spice, cedar, and toast; the palate is fruit-rich, with fine tannins and admirable persistence.	£39.00 HAX

SEAL OF APPROVAL
RIOJA + NORTH-CENTRAL RED

☆ **GRAN LOPEZ 2003, SANTO CRISTO** Aragón – Peppery crimson fruit, fresh acidity, and good balance.	£3.80 IWS/WTS
☆ **CAMPO NUEVO TINTO 2003, AGRAMONT** Navarra – Toasty, mouthfilling, and balanced, with strawberries and crunchy cranberries.	£4.00 PLB
☆ **FOUR WINDS TINTO 2002, BODEGAS MARCO REAL** Navarra – Silky and fresh, with red-plum flavours, and medicinal notes.	£4.00 OHI
☆ **PIEDEMONTE MERLOT TEMPRANILLO 2003, BODEGAS PIEDEMONTE** Navarra – Deep purplish-red, with dark-damson and red-cherry flavours.	£4.00 IWS

SILVER
RIOJA + NORTH-CENTRAL ROSÉ

ENATE ROSADO 2003, ENATE Aragón – *Mounds of intense redcurrant fruit dripping with fresh zingy acidity. Crisp and full-bodied. Smooth texture.*	£8.80 FFW/GHL CCS/CVE JSM

BRONZE
RIOJA + NORTH-CENTRAL ROSÉ

GARNACHA ROSADO 2003, BODEGAS OCHOA Navarra – *A full nose and palate of strawberry fruit. Herbal notes. Clean, fresh, and approachable.*	£6.00 BNK/UNS FEN/FLY

GOLD
RIBERA DEL DUERO + WEST WHITE

☆ VERDEJO ERMITA VERACRUZ 2003, BODEGAS VERACRUZ Castilla y León – *This Rueda Verdejo is stunning. It has a floral spicy nose with apples and nuts. Long and intense.*	£7.90 CCS/NYW JSM/ALL

SILVER
RIBERA DEL DUERO + WEST WHITE

PAZO SEÑORANS 2003, PAZO DE SEÑORANS Galicia – *Attractive fresh light notes of apple and guava. The palate is infused with orange flowers and perfumed lemon fruit.*	£10.60 BEN/JNW TAN/VGN

BRONZE
RIBERA DEL DUERO + WEST WHITE

☆ CERROSOL SAUVIGNON BLANC 2003, BODEGAS CERROSOL Castilla y León – *Grasses and green fruit on the nose lead to a palate of weighty mandarin orange and honey flavours.*	£5.00 PLB

340 RIBERA + W WHITE BRONZE / **RED** GOLD

PALACIO DE BORNOS VERDEJO 2003, BODEGAS DE CRIANZA DE CASTILLA LA VIEJA CASTILLA Y LEÓN – *Honeysuckle and lychees burst out of this aromatic wine. Crisp and citrussy with elegant lemon fruit.*	£5.80 / RAV/WTS
VINO BLANCO RUEDA VERDEJO 2003, MARQUÉS DE RISCAL CASTILLA Y LEÓN – *Fresh yet ripe. Chinese five-spice powder scents and a vivid green fruit palate.*	£6.00 / JSM/MWW
MANTEL BLANCO VERDEJO SAUVIGNON BLANC 2003, BODEGAS ALVAREZ Y DIEZ CASTILLA Y LEÓN – *Sappy and green, this Verdejo blend has pungent greengage flavours scored with a jolt of cleansing acidity.*	£6.50 / FLY
SAINSBURY'S CLASSIC SELECTION ALBARIÑO 2003, LA RIOJA ALTA GALICIA – *Spritzy and fresh, with pear, apple, and marzipan elements on the nose and sweetly ripe palate.*	£7.00 / JSM
AURA VENDIMIA SELECCIÓNADA 2002, BODEGAS AURA CASTILLA Y LEÓN – *Richly ripe, with grassy notes on the nose and an intense asparagus-flavoured palate.*	£8.00 / AD1/WAV
MARTÍN CODÁX BURGÁNS 2003, BODEGAS MARTÍN CODÁX GALICIA – *Clear pale lemon. Aromatic and floral, with orange blossom, elderflower, and honeysuckle characteristics.*	£8.00 / ODD
PAZO DE VILLAREI 2003, BODEGAS VILLAREI GALICIA – *Elegant rose and violet characteristics. The palate has very good concentration, fresh acidity, and citrus flavours.*	£9.00 / HAX/WRK
ADEGAS VALMIÑOR ALBARIÑO 2003, ADEGAS VALMIÑOR GALICIA – *Aromatic apricot and peach aromas. The palate is fresh with creamy depth and fine acid balance.*	£11.50 / ENO

GOLD
RIBERA DEL DUERO + WEST RED

ALION 1999, BODEGAS Y VIÑEDOS CASTILLA Y LEÓN – *Jam-packed with ripe, sweet fruit. This is big, concentrated Tempranillo with subtle oak that doesn't dominate the weighty fruit.*	£26.00 / CCS/NYW

RIBERA + W RED GOLD / SILVER

LA LEGUA CAPRICHO 1999, BODEGAS EMETERIO FERNANDEZ CASTILLA Y LEÓN – *Vanilla and mocha oak, mint, and brambly spicy fruit. Layer upon layer of complexity. Optimally ripe. Generous.*	**£35.00** DUI

SILVER
RIBERA DEL DUERO + WEST RED

☆ **TINTA DE TORO COSECHA 2003, BODEGA VIÑA BAJOZ** CASTILLA Y LEÓN – *Style, substance, and sophistication define the griotte nose and palate with its grainy tannins, depth, weight, and rapier acidity.*	**£4.90** FLY
☆ **VEGA DE CASTILLA TEMPRANILLO 2002, BODEGAS FUENTESPINA** CASTILLA Y LEÓN – *Nutmeg and cigarillo nose. The palate is a modern classic, with flavours of chorizo, damson, vanilla, and cherry.*	**£7.50** WTS
ABADIA RETUERTA SELECCIÓN ESPECIAL 2000, ABADIA RETUERTA CASTILLA Y LEÓN – *Chunky and meaty, its fruit subdued by dominant oak. Complex, earthy, succulent, firm yet supple. Some evolution.*	**£9.80** SOM
PAGO DE CARRAOVEJAS CRIANZA 2001, PAGO DE CARRAOVEJAS CASTILLA Y LEÓN – *This producer goes from strength to strength. Impressive, with a veritable wall of lush red-cherries tinged with coconut.*	**£13.00** MOR
CUVÉE EL PALOMAR 2000, ABADIA RETUERTA CASTILLA Y LEÓN – *The smooth, elegant palate has plenty of aromatic cedar bark. Grippy tannins. Black-cherry fruit.*	**£16.80** SOM
CUVÉE EL CAMPANARIO 2000, ABADIA RETUERTA CASTILLA Y LEÓN – *Strawberry fruit flavours fill the mouth. Round and textured, with a creamy edge to the full, evolved profile.*	**£24.50** VIT
PAGO DE LOS CAPELLANES RESERVA 1999, PAGO DE LOS CAPELLANES CASTILLA Y LEÓN – *Well-defined earth, red stone fruit, and coconut oak fragrance. The palate is fleshy, rich, and smooth, with brisk tannins.*	**£30.60** WIDELY AVAILABLE

BRONZE
RIBERA DEL DUERO + WEST RED

CONDE DE SIRUELA RIBERA DEL DUERO TINTO 4 MESES BARRICA 2003, FRUTOS VILLAR Castilla y León – *Medium-weight, silky forest fruit palate with a caramel nose, savoury touches and dusty tannins.*	£5.50 L&S/JSM
ALAIA 2000, ADEGAS GALEGAS Castilla y León – *Developed, with medium-bodied cherrystone and loganberry flavours. Intense, forceful tannins.*	£5.90 FFW/RNS NRW/MER
ALTOS DE TAMARON JOVEN 2002, FELIX SOLIS Castilla y León – *Cigar smoke scent wafts from the glass, whilst the mouth fills with leathery cranberry fruit flavours.*	£6.00 FEE
TINTA DE TORO CANUS VERUS 2003, COVITORO Castilla y León – *Sultry attack of ripe raisined fruit escalates towards a fresh arc of acidity and a firm finale.*	£6.00 VGN/MER
PRIMICIA 2003, ABADIA RETUERTA Castilla y León – *An edgy spiciness and cleansing acidity complements full, fresh blackcurrant fruit. The toasty oak influence is subtle yet sweetly persistent.*	£6.20 VIT/SOM
TINTA DE TORO CRIANZA 2000, BODEGA VIÑA BAJOZ Castilla y León – *Firm, nervy grape tannins line the modern juicy cherry palate. A fine accompaniment to grilled meats and cheeses.*	£7.50 UNS/FLY
MIRALMONTE CRIANZA 2000, FRUTOS VILLAR Castilla y León – *Grippy tannins complement the mature, leather-scented palate of tobacco and undergrowth.*	£8.00 L&S
RIVOLA 2002, ABADIA RETUERTA Castilla y León – *Dense wall of green coffee beans and sour cherry fruit. The creamy palate has bags of bramble fruit.*	£8.70 VIT/WOI
GRAN COLEGIATA RESERVA 1996, BODEGAS FARIÑA Castilla y León – *A nervy aggregate of cedar, plums, and pencil lead. Juicy and fresh, with resounding tannins.*	£9.00 DCT

RIBERA + W RED BRONZE / SEAL 343

GUELBENZU AZUL 2002, BODEGAS GUELBENZU Castilla y León – *From a family Bodega in Ribera del Duero. Notes of cinnamon and cherry and a seam of fine acidity.*	£9.70 EDC/TAN BOO/OWC MOR
LEGARIS RESERVA 1999, LEGARIS Castilla y León – *Deep damson and tar aromas. The palate has intense black fruit allied to supple tannins and sweet oak toast.*	£10.00 NYW/LVN WIM/LBS
RIBERAL CRIANZA 1999, FRUTOS VILLAR Castilla y León – *Ripe cranberry fruit with plenty of secondary development. Stalky rosemary wood tannins.*	£10.00 L&S
ORIGIN TEMPRANILLO 2002, BODEGAS MUNOZ Castilla y León – *The nose shows saddle leather and tarry spice. The blackberry palate is ripe with good structure.*	£11.00 WXC
VALDUBON CRIANZA 2001, BODEGAS VALDUBON Castilla y León – *Loganberries and violets perfume the nose. Savoury, with smooth tannins and a long dry finish.*	£11.00 FLY
MUSEUM REAL RESERVA 2000, EL COTO DE RIOJA Castilla y León – *Garnet red hue. Loganberry fruit dances on the nose and on the palate, which has bitter chocolate hints.*	£11.30 ESL/NRW FLY
PESQUERA CRIANZA 2001, PESQUERA Castilla y León – *Complex spice, leather, and damson depth. Supple tannins emanate from a slug of sweet oak.*	£13.10 WIDELY AVAILABLE
PAGO DE LOS CAPELLANES CRIANZA 2000, PAGO DE LOS CAPELLANES Castilla y León – *The nose has leather and violet perfume. The palate shows deep fruit married to a supple structure. Smoky oak.*	£15.90 WIDELY AVAILABLE

SEAL OF APPROVAL
RIBERA DEL DUERO + WEST RED

☆ **TAPAS TINTO NV, VINNIGALICIA** Galicia – *Cinnamon spice, hints of peppercorn, and black-cherry flesh.*	£3.50 PLB

SEAL OF APPROVAL
SOUTH + THE ISLANDS WHITE

☆ **CASTILLO DE REQUENA BLANCO 2003, ROMERAL** **VALENCIA** – Understated tones of wet earth and flowers dance over the white guava fruit.	£4.00 FFW/MER

TROPHY
SOUTH + THE ISLANDS RED

LUZON ALTOS 2002, FINCA LUZON MURCIA – Heathery, earthy plum and berry notes. Spicy complex oak adds dimension to the abundant blackberry and cherry fruit.	£.00 NOT AVAILABLE IN THE UK

GOLD
SOUTH + THE ISLANDS RED

☆ **CASA DE LA ERMITA CRIANZA 2001, CASA DE LA ERMITA** MURCIA – This is a massive wine from Jumilla with huge concentration for the Crianza classification. Basketfuls of rich chocolately fruit.	£6.70 VIT/NYW ODD

SILVER
SOUTH + THE ISLANDS RED

☆ **MARQUÉS DE ROJAS 2003, BODEGAS PIQUERAS** CASTILLA-LA MANCHA – Some complexity on the nose, where black fruit mingles with coffee and spice. Still a little young, this has good fruit, balance, and a fine length.	£5.50 AVB
DOMINIO DE VALDEPUSA SYRAH 2001, MARQUÉS DE GRIÑÓN CASTILLA-LA MANCHA – Peppery fruit, oak, and a mineral twang. The palate offers up strawberries and spice scored by refreshing acidity.	£16.00 VIT/WTS

BRONZE
SOUTH + THE ISLANDS RED

☆ **XV MONASTRELL 2002, FINCA LUZON** Murcia – *An attractive nose of summer fruits; a palate of firm tannic blackberries with hints of pepper and spice.*	£4.50 CWS
☆ **ALTOZANO TEMPRANILLO 2002, GONZALES BYASS** Castilla-La Mancha – *Smoothly textured, youthful strawberry and blackberry fruit flavours. Aromas of toast and dessicated coconut.*	£5.00 SMF
☆ **MANIFIESTO MONASTRELL 2003, NUESTRA SEÑORA DEL ROSARIO** Murcia – *Fruit-driven, clean briar, and spiced plum aromas. The palate is supple and juicy with integrated tannins.*	£5.00 IWS
☆ **MAXIMO MERLOT 2002, BODEGAS MAXIMO** Castilla-La Mancha – *A modern Merlot with a liquorice and vanilla nose. Black cherry fruit and warming alcohol.*	£5.00 SKW
☆ **OSBORNE SOLAZ 2001, GRUPO OSBORNE** Castilla-La Mancha – *Soft, earthy boysenberry fruit nose. The mouth is crammed with dry, crisp, coconut-infused cherry flavours.*	£5.00 HAE
LADERAS EL SEQUE 2002, ARTADI Valencia – *Raspberry fruit melds with wood, tomato, and warm toast on the seductive, mature nose and palate.*	£5.70 JNW/BBR
CASTILLO DE CALATRAVA RESERVA TEMPRANILLO 1998, VINICOLA DE CASTILLA Castilla-La Mancha – *Opulent. The palate has ripe strawberries checked by a firm spine of acidity. Long and concentrated.*	£6.00 JSM
ROZALEME BOBAL TEMPRANILLO 2001, ROZALEME Valencia – *Forest fruit flavours. Hints of rubber add interest to the warm resonant fruit.*	£6.40 WIDELY AVAILABLE
VIÑA ALBALI GRAN RESERVA 1997, FELIX SOLIS Castilla-La Mancha – *Ruby red, with leather, cigarillo, tar and coconut notes underscoring the mature, velvety palate.*	£7.00 UNS/JSM

346 SOUTH + THE ISLANDS RED BRONZE / SEAL

CORONILLA RESERVA 2000, BODEGAS MURVIEDRO **VALENCIA** – *Blackberries and cream and a jolt of cracked black pepper. Concentrated and attractive.*	£8.00 BUC
VIÑA ALBALI GRAN RESERVA DE FAMILIA 1993, FELIX SOLIS **CASTILLA-LA MANCHA** – *Tar and saddle-leather notes complement the mature, soft strawberry flavours. No hard edges.*	£10.00 SAF
SANFIR CRIANZA 2001, BODEGAS CASA DEL PINAR **VALENCIA** – *Subtly oaked, with a soft tannic web underpinning the ripe summer fruit and saddle-leather flavours.*	£11.00 MOR
FINCA TERRERAZO 2001, BODEGA MUSTIGUILLO **VALENCIA** – *Cream and marjoram envelops the nose. The palate is a voluptuous mulberry and vanilla affair.*	£19.10 SOM/CCS NYW/LIB FLY

SEAL OF APPROVAL
SOUTH + THE ISLANDS RED

☆ **CO-OP OAK AGED TEMPRANILLO NV, FELIX SOLIS** **CASTILLA-LA MANCHA** – *Ripe red-cherry flavours and lilting vanilla scents.*	£3.70 CWS
☆ **SANTERRA TEMPRANILLO 2002, BODEGAS MURVIEDRO** **VALENCIA** – *Kirsch and blackberry flavours dominate the textured palate.*	£4.00 BUC/JSM
☆ **TIERRA SECCA TEMPRANILLO 2003, BODEGAS CENTRO ESPAGNOLAS** **CASTILLA-LA MANCHA** – *Mouthwatering, textured flavours of squashed ripe strawberries.*	£4.00 WSO
☆ **SANTERRA BOBAL ROSÉ 2003, BODEGAS MURVIEDRO** **VALENCIA** – *Drink this pretty Bobal rosé in its raspberry-infused flush of youth.*	£4.00 BUC
☆ **VIÑA ALBALI ROSADO 2003, FELIX SOLIS** **CASTILLA-LA MANCHA** – *Smooth and sensual ripe strawberry fruit flavours and scents.*	£4.00 MRN

TROPHY
SOUTH + THE ISLANDS FORTIFIED

☆ **PEDRO XIMÉNEZ VIRGILIO 1925, MORENO** **ANDALUCIA** – *Lusciously smooth and liquorously sweet, yet still fresh. Raisins, orange blossom, candied peel, toffee, coffee, and caramel.*	**£9.50** NYW
☆ **DON NUNO DRY OLOROSO NV, EMILIO LUSTAU** **ANDALUCIA** – *Complex layers of caramel, toffee, nuts, and vanilla ice cream. Keenly balanced between the big and the elegant.*	**£10.00** WIDELY AVAILABLE

GOLD
SOUTH + THE ISLANDS FORTIFIED

☆ **WAITROSE SOLERA JEREZANA DRY OLOROSO NV, EMILIO LUSTAU** **JEREZ** – *Intense nutty fruit and a lift of rancio. Roasted nuts and dried fruit are layered on the palate.*	**£6.50** WTS
☆ **OLOROSO HIDALGO NV, BODEGAS HIDALGO LA GITANA** **JEREZ** – *There are hints of raisins, toffee, walnuts, dried peel, and Christmas cake. Deliciously sweet with a dry clean finish.*	**£7.00** TAN/WRW MWW
☆ **MOSCATEL DON SALVADOR NV, BODEGAS LOPEZ HERMANOS** **ANDALUCIA** – *Complex rancio, floral, caramel, and grape characteristics. The palate has maple syrup and soft demerara sugar flavours. Nutty elements.*	**£10.00** DUI
☆ **NOÉ NV, GONZÀLEZ-BYASS** **ANDALUCIA** – *Intensely sweet bitter chocolate, black treacle, and raisin flavours. Acid propels the liquor above mere syrup, imparting fine balance.*	**£10.80** TOS/JSM
☆ **APOSTOLES NV, GONAZLEZ-BYASS** **ANDALUCIA** – *Powerful savoury, nutty characters. On the palate it has grilled almonds, a touch of raisin, and burnt-toffee flavours.*	■**£11.30** FEN/RWM JSM
☆ **DOS CORTADOS RARE OLD DRY PALO CORTADO AGED 20 YEARS NV, BODEGAS WILLIAMS & HUMBERT** **ANDALUCIA** – *This Palo Cortado certainly knows its mind. Nutty and caramelly.*	**£12.00** HOF

SOUTH + THE ISLANDS FORTIFIED GOLD / SILVER

☆ **DRY SACK SWEET OLD OLOROSO AGED 15 YEARS, BODEGAS WILLIAMS & HUMBERT** ANDALUCIA – *Pure maple syrup, but with added nuttiness and toffee and fudge fruit and buttered hazelnuts. Rich, heady, and aromatic.*	£12.00 WTS
☆ **EMILÍN MOSCATEL SUPERIOR NV, EMILIO LUSTAU** ANDALUCIA – *Roasted and rich with nutty complexity and powerful caramel and toffee flavours. Elegant floral nose.*	£13.70 GHL/CCS NYW/FLY SHB
100 ANOS CENTURY SELECTION MOSCATEL LAS CRUCES NV, EMILIO LUSTAU ANDALUCIA – *Unctuous sweetness paints the glass. Mocha and toffee duel with orange peel and fruitcake.*	£22.80 NYW/FLY
SINGLE CASK AMONTILLADO 2000, EMILIO LUSTAU ANDALUCIA – *Wonderfully rich and nutty with flor character and tangy intense flavours. Roundness and depth of character.*	£28.30 NRW/CCS MOV/NYW FLY

SILVER
SOUTH + THE ISLANDS FORTIFIED

☆ **ASDA MANZANILLA NV, JOSE ESTEVEZ** ANDALUCIA – *Walnut and sea breezes nose. Light elegant nuttiness; tangy, fresh, and long.*	£4.30 ASD
☆ **MHV GRAN CAPATAZ AMONTILLADO NV, BODEGAS BARBADILLO** SANLUCAR – *Sweet toffee and raisin scents. Minerally, delicate, sweet, and long.*	£4.50 BNK/MHV
☆ **WAITROSE SOLERA JEREZANA DRY AMONTILLADO NV, EMILIO LUSTAU** ANDALUCIA – *Developed nut and raisined character. Dry and balanced. The finish is long, with notable aromatic complexity.*	£6.50 WTS
☆ **WAITROSE SOLERA JEREZANA RICH CREAM NV, EMILIO LUSTAU** JEREZ – *Intense, aged nose. The palate has many layers of raisined fruit, molasses, and caramel. Fresh acidity. Deep rich hue.*	£6.50 WTS
☆ **TIO PEPE NV, GONZÀLEZ-BYASS** ANDALUCIA – *Lifted briny aromas lace this lemon-yellow beauty. Nuts, racy green fruit, and a mineral tang on the sustained finish.*	£8.20 WIDELY AVAILABLE

SOUTH + THE ISLANDS FORTIFIED SILVER 349

☆ **ALMACENISTA AMONTILLADO DE JEREZ NV, EMILIO LUSTAU** ANDALUCIA – *Dry, tangy, and textured, this classic has rich seductive roast almond aromas. Deep gold colour.*	**£8.90** RAV/EVI CCS/MOV NYW/FLY
☆ **ALMACENISTA MANZANILLA PASADA NV, EMILIO LUSTAU** ANDALUCIA – *Highly coloured. Crisp and clean, with a limey freshness and a salty swathe. Marzipan richness and flor elements.*	**£9.00** WIDELY AVAILABLE
☆ **LA GUITA MANZANILLA NV, HIJOS DE RAINERA PÉREZ MARÍN** ANDALUCIA – *The acidity is admirably balanced, and plenty of caramelised citrus fruit luxuriates on the textured palate.*	**£9.00** VIT/BWC
☆ **SOLERA GRAN RESERVA AMONTILLADO DON RAFAEL NV, EMILIO LUSTAU** ANDALUCIA – *Amber coloured with a rich nutty nose. The palate is dry and complex with yeast and raisined notes.*	**£9.00** LUS
☆ **SOLERA RESERVA FINO BALBAINA NV, EMILIO LUSTAU** ANDALUCIA – *Dried apples scent the nose. Light-bodied, elegant, and fresh, with excellent fruit concentration and chalky tannins.*	**£9.00** LUS
☆ **SOLERA RESERVA PALO CORTADO PENINSULA NV, EMILIO LUSTAU** ANDALUCIA – *Good concentration. Tangy and soft, with a handful of roast salted mixed nuts.*	**£9.00** LAI
☆ **ALMACENISTA OLOROSO ANGEL ZAMORANO NV, EMILIO LUSTAU** ANDALUCIA – *Caramel, baked apples, toasted almonds, raisins, brine, toffee, and dates cascade onto the long, elegant palate.*	**£9.20** BEN/ESL MOV/NYW FLY
☆ **ALMACENISTA FINO DEL PUERTO DE LA CUESTA NV, EMILIO LUSTAU** ANDALUCIA – *Extremely intense flor characteristics. This sherry is very dry, and has a winking bright pale straw gold hue.*	**£10.00** MOV/NYW
JEREZ CORTADO HIDALGO NV, BODEGAS HIDALGO LA GITANA JEREZ – *The dry palate has nutty notes and heaps of yeasty appeal. Very persistent, with excellent complexity.*	**£11.00** TAN
MATUSALEM NV, GONZÀLEZ-BYASS JEREZ – *Very long. Demerara sugar notes dance on the nose and on the medium sweet, mature palate.*	**£11.80** FEN/OWC JSM

350 SOUTH + THE ISLANDS FORTIFIED SILVER

DON GUIDO RARE OLD SWEET PEDRO XIMÉNEZ AGED 20 YEARS NV, WILLIAMS & HUMBERT ANDALUCIA – *Figs and dates, walnuts and almonds, candied oranges and lemon zest elements all vie for attention.*	£12.00 HOF
EAST INDIA NV, EMILIO LUSTAU ANDALUCIA – *Aged, with a nose of rancio, raisins, and dates. Bittersweet chocolate, figs, smoke, and toasted almonds.*	£12.50 WIDELY AVAILABLE
SAN EMILIO PEDRO XIMÉNEZ NV, EMILIO LUSTAU ANDALUCIA – *Intense with caramel and burnt orange aromas on the nose. The palate is sweet and creamy with raisined depth.*	£12.90 WIDELY AVAILABLE
JALIFA RARE OLD DRY AMONTILLADO AGED 30 YEARS NV, BODEGAS WILLIAMS & HUMBERT ANDALUCIA – *Intense aromas of chalk, cloves, and crushed white peppercorns. Big yet balanced, with excellent viscosity.*	£13.00 HOF
ROYAL CORREGIDOR RICH OLD OLOROSO NV, SANDEMAN JEREZ ANDALUCIA – *Raisin and molasses aromas. The palate is sticky and thick with rich sweetness, the finish deep and long.*	▲£13.00 RWM
CUCO OLOROSO SECO NV, BODEGAS BARBADILLO ANDALUCIA – *Espresso, crème caramel, and hazelnut nose. Lavishly fruited, with rich date and juicy prune flavours.*	£14.00 SOM/G&M
VOS 20 YEAR OLD AMONTILLADO NV, EMILIO LUSTAU ANDALUCIA – *Earth, spices, toffee, and rancio on the nose, and a palate which is clean, long, and balanced.*	£16.80 EVI/CCS NYW/FLY
ALMACENISTA OLOROSO DEL PUERTO 1/110 OBREGON NV, EMILIO LUSTAU ANDALUCIA – *Chocolate, amber, and green hues. This is light, caramelly sherry with spiced date and soft raisin flavours.*	£17.00 LUS
LA CILLA PEDRO XIMÉNEZ NV, BODEGAS BARBADILLO ANDALUCIA – *Intense and nutty with tar and molasses aromas. The palate is sweet and very concentrated.*	£17.00 G&M
EMPERATRIZ EUGENIA OLOROSO NV, EMILIO LUSTAU ANDALUCIA – *The nose is wonderfully nutty. The palate has excellent depth and harmony. The finish is long.*	£17.80 MOV/FLY

SOUTH + THE ISLANDS FORTIFIED SILVER / BRONZE

AMBROSIA MOSCATEL NV, SANCHEZ ROMATE HERMANOS ANDALUCIA – *This wine, the colour of teak, bears aromas of cooked fruit and medicine. Slight toffee and smoke characteristics.*	£18.00 HAX
ANTIQUE PALO CORTADO NV, FERNANDO DE CASTILLA JEREZ – *Attractive spicebox and slivered almond nuances. The finish is intense and very long, with warm tree bark scents.*	£19.20 FFW/V&C MER/NYW
SINGLE CASK PX MURILLO NV, EMILIO LUSTAU ANDALUCIA – *A liquid treacle palate and a pronounced burnt sugar and Cointreau nose. Depth, balance, and concentration.*	£25.60 NRW/CCS FLY
SINGLE CASK DRY OLOROSO NV, EMILIO LUSTAU ANDALUCIA – *Cinders and toffee, spices and walnuts rise from the nose. Dry, nutty, round, fresh, and very long.*	£29.40 CCS/FLY
PEDRO XIMÉNEZ RESERVADA DE LA FAMILIA NV, BODEGAS LOPEZ HERMANOS ANDALUCIA – *The viscous palate is crammed with plump raisins, citrus, and flowers. Nut and caramel nuances.*	£35.00 DUI
AMONTILLADO VIEJO NV, BODEGAS HIDALGO LA GITANA ANDALUCIA – *Vibrant, ethereal, and lingering, with spice, nut, fig, and apple flavours and scents. Structured and aristocratic.*	£38.00 BBR/SVG TAN

BRONZE
SOUTH + THE ISLANDS FORTIFIED

☆ **SOMERFIELD CREAM NV, GONZÀLEZ-BYASS** JEREZ – *Olive gold colour. Burnt sugar nose and a long, fresh, caramelly palate of Dundee cake.*	£4.00 SMF
☆ **SAINSBURY'S MEDIUM SWEET OLOROSO NV, EMILIO LUSTAU** JEREZ – *The nose shows nut and raisin aromas. The palate is rich and creamy with a harmonious finish.*	£4.50 JSM
☆ **FINO HIDALGO NV, BODEGAS HIDALGO LA GITANA** JEREZ – *Citrus fruit assails the nose and palate. Almond blossom hints. Very fresh, lean, and long.*	£5.90 JNW/WRW MWW

Wine	Price / Supplier
OLOROSO ABOCADO NAPOLEON NV, BODEGAS HIDALGO LA GITANA Jerez – *A deep amber beauty with nutty scents and dried fruit flavours.*	£8.00 WOI
OLOROSO SECO NAPOLEON NV, BODEGAS HIDALGO LA GITANA Jerez – *Silky, dark, and long, with a rich palate of nuts and dates, undergrowth, and spice.*	£9.00 WOI
SOLERA GRAN RESERVA AMONTILLADO SAN BARTOLOME NV, EMILIO LUSTAU Andalucia – *Deep nutty wine with raisin and marmite aromas. The palate is refined and the finish shows great persistence.*	£9.00 LUS
ALMACENISTA AMONTILLADO DEL PUERTO NV, EMILIO LUSTAU Andalucia – *This elegant wine boasts a mouthful of dried fruit and nuts. The finish is long.*	£9.10 WIDELY AVAILABLE
ALMACENISTA OLOROSO PATA DE GALLINA NV, EMILIO LUSTAU Andalucia – *Vivid and deep, its dates, prunes, molasses, and tree bark balanced by fine acidity.*	£9.10 GHL/MOV NYW/FLY SHB
ALMACENISTA MANZANILLA OLOROSA JURADO NV, EMILIO LUSTAU Andalucia – *Nutty almond flavours. Caramel, orange rind, and lime zest characteristics. Waxy, ripe, and persistent.*	£9.20 LAI/NYW
PEDRO XIMÉNEZ NAPOLEON NV, BODEGAS HIDALGO LA GITANA Jerez – *Light colour. The nose of figs and dates is concentrated and weighty. Very approachable.*	£9.50 TAN/WOI MWW
CAPATAZ ANDRES DELUXE CREAM NV, EMILIO LUSTAU Andalucia – *Deep raisined nose. Toffee and oranges line the intense palate with layers of sweet flavours.*	£10.10 WRK/EVI CCS/MOV FLY/SHB
DON PX DULCE GRAN RESERVA 1971, BODEGAS TORO ALBALA Andalucia – *Deep tawny, with a burnt sugar and raisin nose. Round and unctuous, with plenty of depth.*	£11.50 MOV/NYW MOR
AMONTILLADO VIÑA EL ALAMO NV, BODEGAS PEDRO ROMERO Andalucia – *Light mahogany. Minerals, raisins, and rancio aromas grace the palate of mouthwatering yellow fruit.*	£12.40 RAY

SOUTH + THE ISLANDS FORTIFIED BRONZE / SEAL 353

CARDENAL CISNEROS PEDRO XIMÉNEZ NV, SANCHEZ ROMATE HERMANOS **Jerez** – *The colour of molasses, with a nose of figs and toffee, and a rich, intense, and persistent palate.*	£14.00 HAX
SAN RAFAEL OLOROSO DULCE NV, BODEGAS BARBADILLO **Andalucia** – *The nose is complex with burnt sugar and nut aromas. The palate is rich and round and lingering.*	£17.00 G&M
ANTIQUE OLOROSO NV, FERNANDO DE CASTILLA **Jerez** – *Bright amber. Toasted cashew and coffee characteristics. Soft, harmonious, and very long.*	£17.50 FFW/HAX V&C/MER
ANTIQUE PEDRO XIMÉNEZ NV, FERNANDO DE CASTILLA **Andalucia** – *Big yet balanced; forward, round at the edges and packed with dried figs and dates.*	£18.20 FFW/V&C MER/NYW
AMONTILLADO VIEJO PASTRANA NV, BODEGAS HIDALGO LA GITANA **Jerez** – *Subtle toffee, dried fruit, and green apple scents. The firm, assertive palate has loads of roast nut flavours.*	£18.30 L&S/WOI L&W/TAN
VORS 30 YEAR OLD OLOROSO NV, EMILIO LUSTAU **Andalucia** – *Dark brown with green tinges. A classic dry Oloroso with a rich nutty character.*	£20.70 EVI/CCS NYW/FLY
SINGLE CASK PALO CORTADO NV, EMILIO LUSTAU **Andalucia** – *Dry and concentrated. Balanced, with exceedingly fresh acidity and ripe white and yellow fruit.*	£29.60 CCS/NYW FLY
OLOROSO VIEJO NV, BODEGAS HIDALGO LA GITANA **Andalucia** – *Elegant tones of sea air after a summer rain, cedar bark, molasses, and raisins.*	£45.00 L&W/BBR

SEAL OF APPROVAL
SOUTH + THE ISLANDS FORTIFIED

☆ **BUDGENS AMONTILLADO NV, BODEGAS FERRIS** **Andalucia** – *Toasted nuts, dates, apricots, and apples spill from the palate.*	£4.00 BGN

☆ **SOMERFIELD AMONTILLADO NV, GONZÀLEZ-BYASS** JEREZ – *Walnuts, raisins, and a tang of brine. A graceful Amontillado.*	£4.00 SMF
☆ **CABRERA MEDIUM DRY AMONTILLADO NV, GONZÀLEZ-BYASS** ANDALUCIA – *Hazelnut and apple flavours. A tang of dried citrus tinges the nose.*	£4.50 WRK/JFE WRT
☆ **MHV GRAN CAPATAZ FINO NV, BODEGAS BARBADILLO** SANLUCAR – *Classically yeasty, dry, and nutty. Bright balancing acidity.*	£4.50 BNK/MHV
☆ **MHV GRAN CAPATAZ PALE CREAM NV, BODEGAS BARBADILLO** SANLUCAR – *Voluptuous, intense, and rich, with flavours of toffee and butterscotch.*	£4.50 BNK/MHV
☆ **SAINSBURY'S FINO NV, GONZÀLEZ-BYASS** JEREZ – *Delicate yeast and roast hazelnut scents and mouthwatering apple flavours.*	£4.50 JSM
☆ **CABRERA FULL RICH CREAM NV, GONZÀLEZ-BYASS** ANDALUCIA – *Sweet yet balanced, with rich long date and dried currant flavours.*	£4.80 WRK/WRT
☆ **CABRERA MANZANILLA NV, GONZÀLEZ-BYASS** ANDALUCIA – *Grilled nut aromas. Flavours of yeast, dates, and grapefruit.*	£4.80 WRK/WRT WRW
☆ **CABRERA PALE DRY FINO NV, GONZÀLEZ-BYASS** ANDALUCIA – *Tangy, restrained, and yeasty, with elegant white fruit flavours.*	£4.80 WRK/WRT
☆ **LUSTAU MOSCATEL DE CHIPIONA NV, EMILIO LUSTAU** ANDALUCIA – *Intense aromas and flavours of Seville orange marmalade and honey. Fresh acidity.*	£5.00 LUS

LIST OF STOCKISTS

3DW	3D Wines	01205 820745
A&N	Army & Navy	0207 834 1234
ABG	Arlington Beverage Group	020 8395 1552
ABY	Anthony Byrne Wine Agencies	01487 814 555
ACW	AC Wines	020 7639 1875
AD1	Allied Domecq Wine UK	020 8323 8196
ADE	Adel (UK) Ltd	0208 994 3960
ADN	Adnams Wine Merchants	01502 727222
AFI	Alfie Fiandaca Ltd	0208 752 1222
AHW	A.H. Wines Ltd	01935 850116
ALB	Albion Wines Ltd	01494 864 868
ALD	Aldi Stores Ltd	01827 710 871
ALE	Alexander Wines	0141 882 0039
ALI	Alivini Company Ltd	0208 880 2526
ALL	Alliance Wines	01505 506060
ALZ	Allez Vins!	01926 811969
AMP	Amps Fine Wines	01832 273 502
ANS	Australian Wine Services	020 8653 6494
ARM	Arthur Rackham Fine Wine Merchants	01483 458700
ASD	Asda Stores Ltd	0113 241 9172
ASH	Ashley Scott	01244 520655
AST	Astley Vineyards	01299 822907
ATM	Astrum Wine Cellars	020 8870 5252
AUC	The Australian Wine Club	020 8843 8450
AUS	Australian Wineries LLP	01780 755 810
AVB	Averys of Bristol	01275 811100
AWS	Albion Wine Shippers	0207 242 0873
BBL	Bat & Bottle Wine Merchants	0845 1084407
BBO	Barrels & Bottles	0114 255 6611
BBR	Berry Bros & Rudd	0870 900 4300

BBV	Breaky Bottom Vineyard	01273 476 427
BCF	Bon Couer Fine Wine	0207 622 5244
BEC	Beaconsfield Wine Cellars	01494 675545
BEL	Bentalls of Kingston	0208 546 1001
BEN	Bennetts Fine Wines	01386 840392
BES	Bestway Cash & Carry Ltd	0208 453 1234
BGN	Budgens Stores Limited	020 8422 9511
BIG	The Big Red Wine Company	01638 510803
BLP	Belpeso	07793 606 761
BMK	Benmack International Ltd	01435 866 419
BNK	Bottleneck (Broadstairs)	01843 861095
BOF	Bowland Forest Vintners	01200 448688
BON	Bonhote Foster	01440 730779
BOO	Booths of Stockport	0161 432 3309
BOR	De Bortoli Wines UK Ltd	01725 516467
BRA	G. Bravo & Son Ltd	020 7836 4693
BRF	Brown-Forman Wines International	020 7478 1300
BSS	Besos (UK) Ltd	01243 575 454
BTH	Booths Supermarkets	01772 251701
BUC	Buckingham Vintners International	01753 521336
BUT	Butler's Wine Cellar	01273 698724
BWC	Berkmann Wine Cellars	0207 609 4711
BWL	Bibendum Wine Ltd	020 7449 4120
BWN	Boutique Wine of New Zealand	01452 863708
BWS	Bigland Wine Services ltd	01229 885 411
C&B	Corney & Barrow	0207 265 2400
C&D	C&D Wines Ltd	0208 778 1711
CAO	C & O Wines	0161 976 3696
CAS	Castang Wine Shippers	01503 220359
CAV	Les Caves de Pyréne	01483 538 820
CAX	Pernod Ricard UK Ltd	020 8538 4000
CCS	Cooden Cellars	01323-649663

LIST OF STOCKISTS

CEB	Croque-en-Bouche	01684 565612
CEC	Ceci Paolo	01531 632976
CEL	The Cellar Door	01256 770397
CEP	bringmywine.com	01992 455903
CER	Cellar 28	01484 710101
CHC	Churchill Vintners Ltd	0121 356 8888
CHH	Charles Hennings	01798 872485
CHN	Charles Hawkins	01572 823030
CHS	The Champagne Shop	0870 0130105
CIB	Ciborio Limited	0208 578 4388
CLA	Classic Drinks	01744 831 400
CMB	Colombier Vins Fins	01283 552 552
CNL	Connolly's	0121 236 9269
CNT	Constellation Wines	01372 473 000
COC	Corks of Cotham	0117 973 1620
COE	Coe of Ilford (Coe Vintners)	0208 551 4966
COK	Corkscrew Wines	01228 543033
CPR	Capricorn Wines	0161 908 1360
CPW	Christopher Piper Wines Ltd	01404 814139
CRI	Chalié, Richards & Co Ltd	01403 250500
CRS	The Co-operative Society	01706 891628
CTH	Charterhouse Wine Co Ltd	020 7587 1302
CTL	Continental Wine & Food Ltd	01484 538333
CTR	Cellar Trends Ltd.	01283 217703
CTV	Carr Taylor Vineyards Ltd	01424 752501
CVE	Casevalue.com	0845 2303773
CWS	Co-operative Group (CWS Ltd)	0161 834 1212
CYT	Concha y Toro	01865 338013
D&D	D&D Wines International Ltd	01565 650952
D&F	D & F Wine Shippers Ltd	0208 838 4399
DBO	Boyar International Ltd	0207 537 3707
DBS	Denbies Wine Estate	01306 876616

DBY	D. Byrne & Co.	01200 423152
DCT	Decanter Wines Limited	01372-376127
DEC	Decorum Vintners Ltd	020 8969 6581
DIT	Distell Europe Ltd	020 8894158
DNL	Dunell's Ltd	01534 736418
DOD	Dodici Wines	01582 767991
DOU	Dourthe UK	0207 720 6611
DUI	Dulcinea Wines	01634 293141
DUL	Champagne Duval-Leroy UK Ltd	020 8982 4216
DUN	Dunkeld Wines Limited	01350 728920
DVY	Davy & Co Ltd	020 7407 9670
DWL	Darlington Wines Ltd	01536.446.106
E&J	Ernest & Julio Gallo Winery	01895 813444
EAU	Eaux de Vie	0207 724 5009
EDC	Edencroft	01270 629975
EHL	Ehrmanns Ltd	0207 418 1800
ELD	Eldridge Pope Fine Wines	01305 751306
ELV	El Vino Company Ltd	0207 353 5384
ENG	English Wines Group Plc	01580 763033
ENO	Enotria Winecellars Ltd	0208 961 4411
EOR	Ellis of Richmond Ltd	0208 744 5550
ESL	Edward Sheldon Ltd.	01608 661409
EUR	Europa Foods Ltd	0208 845 1255
EUW	Eurowines	0208 747 2107
EVI	Evington's Wine Merchants	0116 254 2702
EVW	everywine.co.uk	0800 072 0011
EWC	English Wine Centre	01323 870164
EWD	Euro World Wines	0141 649 3735
EWW	Extreme Wines Ltd	07974174616
EXC	Ex Cellar	01372 813937
F&M	Fortnum & Mason	0207 734 8040
FAV	Frogs Alley Vineyard	01473 787016

LIST OF STOCKISTS 359

FCC	The Fine Champagne Company	01923 774053
FEE	Free Run Wines Ltd	01672 540 990
FEN	Fenwick Ltd	0191 232 5100
FFW	Fintry Fine Wines	01206 382029
FLA	Flagship Wines	01727 841968
FLW	For the Love of Wine	01359 270377
FLY	Flying Corkscrew	01442 412 311
FRI	Friarwood Limited	0207 736 2628
FTH	Forth Wines Ltd	01577 866001
FUL	Fuller Smith & Turner	0208 996 2000
FWL	Fine & Rare Wines Limited	0208 960 1995
FWM	Fields Wine Merchants	0207 589 5753
FWW	FWW Wines (UK) Ltd	01737 842 160
FXT	Freixenet (DWS) Ltd	01344 758 500
G&M	Gordon & MacPhail	01343 545111
G2W	Grape-2-Wine	01531 660599
GGR	Great Grog Company Ltd	0131 662 4777
GHC	Goedhuis & Company	0207 793 7900
GHL	George Hill of Loughborough	01509 212717
GNW	Great Northern Wine Co	01765 606767
GON	Gauntleys of Nottingham	0115 911 0555
GRT	Great Western Wine Company Ltd	01225 322800
GSL	Gerrard Seel Ltd	01925 819695
GWI	The General Wine Company	01428 722201
GYW	Guy Anderson Wines	01935 817 617
H&H	H&H Bancroft	0870 444 1700
HAE	Halewood International Ltd	0151 481 5697
HAM	Hamer Wine	020 8549 9119
HAR	Harrods Wine Shop	0207 225 5662
HAX	Halifax Wine Company	01422 256333
HAY	Hayward Bros (Wines) Ltd	0207 237 0576
HBJ	Hayman, Barwell Jones Ltd	01473 232322

HBY	Hall & Bramley	0151 525 8283
HDL	Alexander Hadleigh	01489 885959
HDS	Hedley Wright Wine Merchants	01279 465 818
HDY	Hollywood & Donnelly	0289 0799 335
HGT	Harrogate Fine Wine Company	01423 522 270
HHC	Haynes Hanson & Clark	0207 259 0102
HIL	Hoche International (Produce) Ltd	01205 292140
HMA	Hatch Mansfield Agencies Ltd	01344 871 800
HOF	House of Fraser	020 7963 2000
HOH	Hallgarten Wines Ltd	01582 722538
HOT	House of Townend	01482 326891
HOU	Hoults Wine Merchants	01484 510700
HPW	Hop Pocket Wine Co.	01531 640592
HRF	Howard Ripley Select Domaine Imports	0208 360 8904
HRY	Harvey & Son Ltd	01273 480209
HTW	H T White and Company Ltd	01323 720161
HVN	Harvey Nichols	0207 235 5000
HWL	HWCG Wine Growers	01279 873500
IDO	Indigo Wines	020 7733 8391
ILW	International Wine Shippers Ltd.	0161 904 8977
INS	Inspired Wines	01299 271 743
IWS	International Wine Services	01442 206 804
J&B	Justerini & Brooks	0207 208 2507
JAR	John Armit Wines	020 7908 0600
JAV	Arkell Vintners	01793 823026
JBF	Julian Baker Fine Wines	01206 262 358
JEF	John E Fells & Sons	01442 870900
JFE	James Fearon Wines	01407 765200
JKN	Jackson Nugent Vintners	020 8947 9722
JKS	Jacksons Stores Ltd	01482 632 099
JLV	Jones le Vin	0161 926 9864
JNW	James Nicholson Wine Merchant	02844 830091

LIST OF STOCKISTS 361

JOB	Jeroboams	020 7259 6716
JSM	Sainsbury Supermarkets Ltd	0207 695 6000
KJW	Kendall Jackson Europe Ltd	0208 747 2840
L&C	Lewis & Cooper Fine Food & Wine Gifts	01609 772 880
L&S	Laymont & Shaw Ltd	01872 270 545
L&T	Lane & Tatham	01380 720123
L&W	Lay & Wheeler Ltd	01473 313 233
LAI	Laithwaites	0118 903 0903
LAY	Laytons Wine Merchant Ltd	0207 288 8888
LBS	Luvians Bottle Shop	01334 654 820
LBV	Le Bon Vin	0114 256 0090
LCC	Landmark Cash & Carry	01908 255 300
LDS	Château de Landiras	01732-461-797
LEA	Lea & Sandeman	0207 244 0522
LEW	John Lewis	020 7828 1000
LIB	Liberty Wines	0207 720 5350
LON	Londis	020 8941 0344
LUS	Emilio Lustau Almacenista Club	01225 833 330
LUV	Epoch Wines Limited	0118 934 9944
LVN	La Vigneronne	0207 589 6113
M&S	Marks & Spencer Plc	020 7268 3825
M&V	Morris & Verdin	0207 921 5300
MAC	Makro UK	0161 786 2256
MAX	Maxxium UK	01786 430500
MCD	Marne & Champagne Ltd	020 7499 0070
MCT	Matthew Clark	01275 891400
MER	Meridian Wines	0161 908 1330
MFS	Martinez Fine Wine	01943 816515
MHE	Michael Hall Wines	01932 223 398
MHU	Moët Hennessy UK Ltd	0207 235 9411
MHV	Booker Cash & Carry	01933 371363
MHW	Mill Hill Wines	0208 959 6754

MIW	Mills Whitcombe Wine Merchants	01981 550028
MKV	McKinley Vintners	0207 928 7300
MMD	Maisons Marques et Domaines	020 8812 3380
MNH	Manor House Wine Merchants	029 2040 3355
MON	Mondial Wine Ltd	020 8335 3455
MOR	Moreno Wine Importers	020 8960 7161
MOV	Moriarty Vintners	02920 229996
MRN	Morrison Supermarkets	01924 875234
MRW	M R Wines Direct	01469 532612
MUW	Must Wines	01848 200677
MWW	Majestic Wine Warehouses Ltd	01923 298200
N&P	Nickolls & Perks	01384 394518
NDJ	ND John Wine Merchants	01792 363284
NFW	Nidderdale Fine Wines	01423 711703
NIC	Nicolas UK Ltd	0208 944 7514
NRW	Noble Rot Wine Warehouses Ltd	01527 575606
NTD	Nisa Today's	01724 282 028
NYW	Noel Young Wines	01223 566 744
NZD	New Zealand Wine Distribution Company Limited	0870 240 7460
NZH	The New Zealand House of Wine	01428 648 930
OAT	Oatley Vineyard	01278 671 340
ODD	Oddbins	0208 944 4400
OHI	Oakhouse Wine Company	01584 811747
ORB	Orbital Wines Ltd	020 7802 5415
OST	Costco Wholesales Uk Ltd	01923 225611
OWC	Oxford Wine Company	01865 301144
OWL	OW Loeb & Co Ltd	0207 234 0385
OZW	Oz Wines	0845 450 1261
P&R	Peckham's	0141 445 4555
P&S	Philglas & Swiggot	0207 924 4494
PAI	Painshill Enterprises Ltd	01932 868113
PAL	Pallant of Arundel	01903 882288

LIST OF STOCKISTS 363

PAR	Partridges	0207 730 7102
PAT	Patriarche Père et Fils Ltd	0207 381 4016
PBA	Paul Boutinot Agencies Ltd	0161 908 1370
PEF	Southcorp Wines Europe Ltd	0208 917 4600
PFC	Percy Fox & Co	01279.756200
PGR	Patrick Grubb Selections	01869 340229
PLB	PLB Wines	01342 318282
POL	Pol Roger Ltd	01432 262800
PON	Peter Osborne & Co	01491 612311
POR	Portland Wine Company (Manchester)	0161 928 0357
PPW	Portugalia Wines	020 8997 4400
PTN	Thomas Panton Wine Merchants Ltd	01666 503088
PWW	Peter Watts Wines	01376 561130
RAV	Ravensbourne Wine	020 8692 9655
RAY	Robert Anthony Wines	01274 547 794
REY	Raymond Reynolds Ltd	01663 742 230
RFM	Ricardo Francisco Martos	07903922388
RIH	Richards & Richard Fine Wines	0161 762 0022
RMO	Robert Mondavi	01491 826475
RNS	Rex Norris	01444 454756
ROD	Rodney Densem Wines Ltd	01270 212200
ROE	Roexport ltd	020 8994 6690
ROG	Roger Harris Wines	01603 880171
RS2	Richardson & Sons	01946 65334
RSN	Richard Speirs Wines	01483 537605
RSS	Raisin Social Ltd	0208 686 8500
RSW	RS Wines	0117 963 1780
RVA	Randalls (Jersey)	01534 887788
RVE	Ridgeview Wine Estate	01444 258039
RWA	Richmond Wine Agencies	01892 668552
RWM	Roberson Wine Merchants	0207 371 2121
SAF	Safeway Stores Plc	020 8848 8744

SBS	Sainsbury Brothers	01225 460 981
SCK	Seckford Wines Ltd.	01206 231 254
SEL	Selfridges Ltd	020 7318 3730
SGL	Stevens Garnier Ltd	01865 263300
SHB	Shaws of Beaumaris	01248 810328
SHJ	SH Jones & Company	01295 251179
SHR	Sharpham Partnership Ltd	01803 732203
SKW	Stokes Fine Wines Ltd	0208 944 5979
SMC	Sommeliers Choice Ltd	020 8689 9643
SMF	Somerfield Stores Ltd	0117 935 9359
SMV	Saint Martin's Vintners	01273 777 744
SOH	Soho Wine Supply	020 7636 8490
SOM	Sommelier Wine Co	01481 721677
SPA	Spain Direct	0870 0101787
SPR	Spar (UK) Ltd	0208 426 3700
SSU	Stone, Vine & Sun	0845 061 4604
SVG	Savage Selection	01451 860896
SWG	SWIG	08000 272 272
SWS	Stratford's Wine Agencies	01628 810606
TAN	Tanners Wines Ltd	01743 234500
TAU	Taurus Wines Ltd	01483 548484
TDC	The Drinks Company Ltd	01483 527527
THI	Thierry's Wine Services	01794 507100
THO	Thos Peatling Fine Wines	01284 755948
THR	Throwley Vineyard	01795 890276
THS	Thresher	01707 387 200
TOS	Tesco Stores Ltd	01992 632222
TRO	Trout Wines	01264 781472
TSS	Tate-Smith Ltd	01653 693 196
TWM	The Wineman Ltd	01635 203 050
UBL	United Brands Ltd.	0207 495 8868
UNS	Unwins Wine Group	01322 272711

LIST OF STOCKISTS 365

UWM	United Wine Merchants	028 9075 5755
UWO	United Wineries UK Office	020 7393 2829
V&C	Valvona & Crolla	0131 556 6066
VDO	Val D'Orbieu Wines Ltd	0207 736 3350
VDV	Vin du Van Wine Merchants	01233 758 727
VER	Vinceremos Wines	0113 244 0002
VGN	Virgin Wines Online Ltd	0870 164 9593
VIM	Vinimpo (UK) Ltd	01932.827150
VIN	Vinum	0208 847 4699
VIT	Veritas Wines	01223 212500
VKY	Vicki's of Chobham	01276 858 374
VLW	Villeneuve Wines	01721 722500
VNF	Vinfruco Wines	01628 763561
VNO	Vinoceros (UK) Ltd	01209 314 711
VRT	Vintage Roots	0118 976 1999
W2D	Wine 2 Dine	0121 358 2144
WAV	Waverley Group	01738 472 000
WAW	Waterloo Wine Co	0207 403 7967
WBN	Wine Barn Ltd	01962 774102
WBR	Wadebridge Wines	01208 812692
WEP	Welshpool Wine Company	01938 553243
WES	Wessex Wines	01308 427177
WFB	Beringer Blass Wine Estates Ltd	0208 843 8411
WIE	Wine Importers Edinburgh	0131 556 3601
WIM	Wimbledon Wine Cellars	020 8540 9979
WNS	Winos	0161 652 9396
WOI	Wines of Interest	01473 215752
WON	Weavers of Nottingham	0115 958 0922
WOW	Wines of Westhorpe	01709 584 863
WPR	Wine Press	01228 515646
WRC	Wine Rack - First Quench	01707 387200
WRK	Wine Raks	01224 311460

WRT	Winerite Ltd	0113 283 7649
WRW	The Wright Wine Company	01756 700886
WSG	Siegel Wine Agencies Ltd	01256 701101
WSO	The Wine Society Ltd	01438 741177
WST	Western Wines Ltd	01952 235 700
WTL	Whittalls Wines Ltd	01922 636161
WTS	Waitrose	0800 188 884
WWT	Whitebridge Wines	01785 817 229
WXC	Winery Exchange	01722 417 409
WZD	Winez Ltd	020 7841 6500
YNG	Young & Co Plc	020 8875 7000
YOB	Cockburn & Campbell	0208 875 7007
YOD	Yodeska Ltd	01604 675500

WINE INTERNATIONAL MAGAZINE
IS NOT ONLY HOME TO THE ANNUAL
INTERNATIONAL WINE CHALLENGE, IT
IS ALSO THE BEST PLACE TO FIND
AUTHORITATIVE RECOMMENDATIONS
AND UP-TO-THE-MINUTE INFORMATION
ON WINE, FOOD, AND TRAVEL
ALL YEAR ROUND.

AWARD-WINNING CONTRIBUTORS
INCLUDE MAX ALLEN, TIM ATKIN,
CLIVE COATES, ROBERT JOSEPH,
CATHARINE LOWE, CHARLES METCALFE,
MARGARET RAND, ANTHONY ROSE,
AND SIMON WOODS.

FOR A SPECIAL SUBSCRIPTION OFFER, GO TO
WWW.WINEINT.COM/BUYERSGUIDE

ACKNOWLEDGEMENTS

The production of a guide like this within the few months that separate the *International Wine Challenge* tastings and publication in time for Christmas is inevitably a team effort. I would like to give special thanks to a number of people with out whom this book would not exist.

First. there is the team led by Birgitta Beavis and Mike Florence who so brilliantly handled the frightening logstics of running the *International Wine Challenge*. Next there are the 400 top tasters headed by my co-chairmen Charles Metcalfe and Derek Smedley MW who not only decided the awards, but also penned the thousands of tasting notes from which the descriptions in this book were culled. Then there were the scribes – Richard Ross, Xenia Irwin MW, Julie Shepherd, and Mary Willmann who did that culling, and Hilary Lumsden at Mitchell Beazley who turned it all into a book. Finally, there was the crucial input of my colleagues at *Wine International* – Catharine Lowe, Tina Gellie, Sam Caporn, Anne Smith, Richard Davies, and Colin Bailey-Wood.

WINE ONLINE

robertjoseph-onwine.com. If this Guide has whetted your appetite for more information on wine, you will find plenty on offer at robertjoseph-onwine.com, includng a free interactive wine school where you can develop your vinous skills, links to, and recommendations of, wine producers, merchants, restaurants, and bars; and an online forum where you can exchange opinions with likeminded wine drinkers.

wineint.com. For more information about the International Wine Challenge, regular news, feature, competitions, events and recommendations, visit wineint.com, *Wine International* magazine's dedicated website.